The Economics of Transp

In modern society, transport plays a vital part in linking people to their work, leisure and social activities, as well as bringing goods and services within an accessible distance of the home and ensuring continued economic well-being. Despite this pivotal role, transport is also characterised by negative issues, such as traffic congestion and the detrimental impact it has on the natural environment. All of these positive and negative aspects arise as a consequence of the economics of transport.

This book provides a clear and concise explanation of the key underlying economic principles to allow the reader to come to a better understanding of the critical factors that structure and guide transport markets. This is done through an examination of the interaction between the behaviour of individual users and providers of transport services and transport authorities' actions through the implementation of transport policy. The book also considers on-going reforms in the organisation of all aspects of transport provision. These reforms seek to move transport delivery away from a model of high state intervention towards one that is far more market focused in its approach, thereby significantly increasing individuals' responsibilities for their own transport actions.

The Economics of Transport covers topics such as:

- The demand and supply of transport services
- Market structures and the underlying economic characteristics of transport markets
- The economics of transport and the environment
- Transport subsidies and regulation
- Transport forecasting and appraisal.

With a selection of case studies and exercises, this book will be of use to higher-level students. It will also be of interest to professionals in the transport planning, transport modelling and transport economics fields.

Jonathan Cowie is a lecturer in transport economics in the School of Engineering and the Built Environment at Napier University in Edinburgh.

The Economics of Transport

A theoretical and applied perspective

Jonathan Cowie

With contributions from Stephen Ison, Tom Rye and Geoff Riddington

Routledge
Taylor & Francis Group

LONDON AND NEW YORK

First published 2010
by Routledge
2 Park Square, Milton Park, Abingdon, Oxon OX14 4RN

Simultaneously published in the USA and Canada
by Routledge
270 Madison Ave, New York, NY 10016

Routledge is an imprint of the Taylor & Francis Group, an informa business

Typeset in Perpetua and Bell Gothic by
RefineCatch Ltd, Bungay, Suffolk
Printed and bound in Great Britain by
TJ International Ltd, Padstow, Cornwall

British Library Cataloguing in Publication Data
A catalogue record for this book is available from the British Library

Library of Congress Cataloging in Publication Data
Cowie, Jonathan.
    The economics of transport : a theoretical and applied perspective /
Jonathan Cowie ; with contributions from Steve Ison, Tom Rye and
Geoff Riddington.
        p. cm.
    Includes bibliographical references and index.
    1. Transportation.   2. Economics.   I. Ison, Steve.   II. Title.
    HE151.C875 2009
    388'.049 – dc22   2009002268

ISBN13: 978–0–415–41979–6 (hbk)
ISBN13: 978–0–415–41980–2 (pbk)
ISBN13: 978–0–203–87410–3 (ebk)

Contents

Figures and Tables

FIGURES

TABLES

Preface

The aim of this book is to outline and illustrate the main economic principles in theory and practice applicable to the transport industries and thereby enable the reader to come to a better understanding of the issues facing transport activities today. The book does not seek to tell the reader everything they need to know about 'transport economics' through producing endless sets of statistics on related transport 'economic' issues, as such an exercise in information transfer is one that would be of little, if any, longer-term value. On the contrary, the book seeks to communicate an understanding, through theory and practice, of the main underlying economic principles that are currently affecting transport activities. In so doing, it aims to establish an understanding of the subject and through that provide a transferable skill, or more exactly, a toolkit from which to analyse, examine and understand any major transport issue or activity. How it seeks to achieve this is by outlining the underlying theoretical concepts and then reinforcing these with practical examples from the transport industries. It is thus founded upon a large number of case studies that cover topics that are designed to underpin the economic theory being outlined. The text is designed to be thought provoking rather than dictatorial in style, thus it seeks to get the reader thinking about transport issues rather than simply telling them about them. Some proscriptive approach however is necessary, particularly when covering the basics of economic theory, as a basic working knowledge of how 'the market' operates is required before this knowledge can then be applied to transport issues. Part of this process however also includes building upon many of the ideas that are outlined. As a consequence, the exercises at the end of each chapter are not simple add-ons or afterthoughts; whilst in some cases these are merely building on the ideas outlined in the chapter, in many other cases these are designed to take the issues further and examine the topic under discussion in more detail. Within economics there are many instances where further understanding only comes through working through a specific exercise and thus seeing what is actually happening rather than simply reading about it.

The text is written on the assumption of no prior knowledge of economics, hence all concepts are considered from first principles. How this is done is by taking a conceptual overview, rather than a highly quantitative or technical approach. That said, the text does not seek to avoid or ignore the major issues, hence no compromises have been made on the underlying principles that are outlined. As a consequence, the text is not only aimed at the 'beginner' to the economics discipline, but also those that have studied the subject before should find this useful as the text is very much an outline and application of economic principles and practices. Much of the text therefore is given over to applying the knowledge and understanding gained in terms of what it means in real transport contexts. The author is also very much of the view that a good well-founded understanding of the economic principles underlying a particular issue can go a long way to understanding that issue better. The text is aimed at both undergraduate and postgraduate students who are studying transport economics and/or appraisal as part of their course. Although mainly a textbook, it is hoped that those within the transport profession who have an interest in, or that are seeking to gain further knowledge in, the economics of transport will also find it useful. Indeed anyone with an interest in transport who seeks to come to a better understanding of the major issues facing the provision of transport services and facilities today should find this book insightful.

The book is very loosely divided into 3 parts. Chapters 1 and 2 are introductory, Chapters 3 through to 8 are concerned with the workings of the market in terms of the behaviour of transport consumers and suppliers, costs in transport operations, competition in transport markets and market failures that lead to imperfect competition and overprovision of certain transport services. The part ends with a look at the pricing of transport services. Chapters 9 through to 14 examine specific issues within the economics of transport, thus transport and the environment is examined in Chapter 9, the critical issues of the regulation and subsidy of transport operations are considered in Chapters 10 and 11, the often overlooked economics of freight transport in Chapter 12, forecasting transport demand in Chapter 13 and finally, but by no means lastly, methods in transport appraisal are outlined in Chapter 14. The last brief chapter attempts to pull all of these issues together to attempt to come to some overall conclusions regarding the economics of transport.

In terms of contributing authors, I would again like to repeat my thanks to Steve Ison for contributing Chapters 8 and 9, Geoff Riddington for his good work on what is a very technical subject in Chapter 13 and Tom Rye for his clear and insightful view of transport appraisal in Chapter 14. We all hope you find the book an interesting and thoughtful read.

Acknowledgements

I would firstly like to express my thanks to Steve Ison for his input into this book. Steve is Professor of Transport Policy at Loughborough University and has taught introductory and intermediate microeconomics and transport economics courses for over 20 years. Prior to joining Loughborough, Steve was lecturer, senior lecturer and principal lecturer in economics at Anglia Ruskin University. As well as contributing two chapters, Steve was also very courteous in reading and commenting on my own material – any errors which may remain however are entirely my own. In order to bring forward the completion date and thus avoid the book becoming a never ending task, I was also fortunate to be able to call upon the expertise of two esteemed colleagues in the transport discipline, each of whom kindly contributed a chapter. I would firstly like to thank Tom Rye, who is Professor of Transport Policy and Mobility Management at Napier University in Edinburgh. As Tom's title clearly suggests, his expertise is mainly in policy and mobility management; however, in this context it is his knowledge and familiarity with the principles and practices in transport appraisal that was called upon. Tom has not only written and developed courses at undergraduate and postgraduate level in transport appraisal, but through his knowledge transfer and research activities has been actively involved in the development and analysis of transport appraisal techniques in Scotland and the European Union. Secondly I would like to thank Geoff Riddington, who is Visiting Reader in Transport Economics at Glasgow Caledonian University. Geoff is an econometrician whose particular expertise lies in forecasting and choice modelling, and he has extensively applied this knowledge in the area of transport economics and published many articles in the subject area. I would also like to thank Rob Langham at Routledge for his comments on some early drafts and his encouragement and support throughout what has been for me a major undertaking, and Elisabet Sinkie for her invaluable assistance with the preparation of the final proofs of the text. Finally, I would like to express my thanks to all of my family for their support and words of encouragement throughout this undertaking; sadly, my mum never saw this come to its final fruition, and her loss is acutely felt.

Chapter 1

Introduction to the economics of transport

Learning Outcomes:

In the course of this chapter, you will learn about:

- The economic problem and its relevance to transport issues
- The factors of production that make up the production of all transport services
- The production possibility frontier and its illustration of the three concepts of scarcity, choice and opportunity cost
- The three market systems of the free market, the command economy and the mixed market
- The combination of agents that make-up transport markets
- The relevance of economic systems to the organisation and provision of public transport systems through a case study of the Glasgow conurbation.

INTRODUCTION

Most individuals, whatever their walk of life, have a basic need to travel from one location to another. Modern life as such is structured around accessing goods and services that lie outside of the immediate vicinity of the home. Transport services are thus required to gain access to employment, education, leisure activities, personal care/health services as well as access to retail outlets for household goods such as food, clothing, electrical goods, books, CDs and so on. The development of the world wide web, whilst shifting some of these activities to home-based pursuits, has not, as yet, succeeded in turning the majority of individuals into computer geeks that need to get out more! Transport therefore still has a key role to play in modern society. This importance is further reflected in the link between transport levels and economic growth. In the past this link has been very strong, as both passenger and freight transport play a vital role in the function of the economy, with strong growth normally associated with innovative transport solutions.

It is thus no great surprise that transport issues continue to feature strongly in the newspapers and television news. Issues such as congestion and the role of road pricing, the impact of traffic on the environment, the organisation of public transport services, the rise of low-cost airlines, the capacity of the rail network, or indeed 'problems on the railways' and so on, are constantly made reference to. All of these areas are subjects which the study of economics can help to shed considerable light on.

Transport is an area that has experienced major changes in recent years. For example, governments worldwide have become increasingly aware of the need to introduce effective ways of containing the use of the private car, both as a means of tackling congestion and as a result of the negative environmental impacts its use entails. Transport in general and the movement of passengers and freight bring with it considerable negative impacts in terms of air pollution, noise and visual intrusion. There has also been regulatory change and a reduction in state ownership of transport companies in all areas of transport, from the rail and bus industries, to freight companies, and in the aviation sector. This has tended to be on the grounds of increasing competition and improving efficiency. A book in transport economics seeks to shed light on these issues and outline why such reforms have been deemed to be necessary, as well as considering the overall economic problem of moving people and goods from one location to another.

The basic tools of the transport economist are drawn from what is known as microeconomic theory. This deals with questions such as what determines the demand for a particular journey or the demand for a particular mode of transport? What may happen to the level of congestion if a road pricing system is introduced? How can an airline operator charge passengers different prices for the same flight? What influences the level of competition within the bus sector? Questions of this nature tend to deal with individual units within the economy or certain sectors of the economy, such as the transport sector, rather than the economy as a whole. These are the types of questions transport economists are interested in and with the use of microeconomic theory this book aims to aid this understanding. Macroeconomics on the other hand is the field of study that concerns the whole economy, hence would examine issues such as the level of inflation, the level of unemployment or the size of the balance of payments. Outside of transport's impact on economic growth, however, transport economists are less interested in these areas. Although clearly important, the main thrust of the book is to examine key microeconomic issues and only consider macroeconomic matters where this helps to give a wider overall perspective.

The book does not draw on one type of transport such as road, rail or air but uses examples from all modes. This is because most if not all of the economic principles covered are common to all modes. The approach taken is to reveal how microeconomic theory can be used to analyse the transport sector and come to a better understanding of the issues therein. As such, the knowledge learned should be transferable and used to analyse and understand other transport issues, not only those presented in this text. This is an important aspect of economic analysis and brings in the idea of the economic 'toolkit' of analysis, or even an 'economic' way of thinking. The text does not purport to outline 'the answer' or to even give an answer to all transport related topics, but rather should enable the reader to come to a better understanding of the underlying issues and principles concerning transport matters today. This first chapter will outline the nature of economics in terms of the economic problem and its relevance to the study of transport.

THE STUDY OF ECONOMICS AND ITS RELEVANCE TO TRANSPORT

What exactly is 'economics' all about and what has it got to do with transport? Most imagine economics is to do with money and all things financial. This can lead to some confusion, as it tends to paint a very grey picture as to the central issues with which the subject is concerned. What is required therefore is a clear definition to which various issues and topics can then be subsequently pinned. Economics is one of the social sciences, hence concerns the study of people and their actions. Therefore, whilst psychology studies how people structure their thoughts and motivations, sociology how people interact with each other (or don't!), and anthropology the study of societies and how they function, economics is concerned with how societies cater for their material wants and needs. It is therefore about the production, distribution and use of society's goods and services (to the maximum benefit of all). A rather trite example in a transport context therefore would be that it concerns who gets a Rolls Royce and who ends up with a 15-year-old mountain bike as their main mode of transport? Whilst trite, that definition does fairly clearly point to not only some critical transport issues but also the basic economic problem – there are not enough Rolls Royces to go around, hence some have to go without, the question being who will that be? This 'scarcity' of luxury motor cars can be applied to more general cases such as all private vehicles or all seats on a train during the rush hour, the difference being that some are more 'scarce' than others. As a result of this scarcity, 'choices' need to be made and each choice will come at a cost, known as the 'opportunity cost'. The basic economic problem, and hence all economic issues, can therefore be related to these ideas of scarcity, choice and opportunity cost. Note at this stage no mention or reference has been made to money matters.

SCARCITY, CHOICE AND OPPORTUNITY COST

Scarcity is a concept that is normally associated with Third World countries, where a lack of rainwater and the subsequent failure of agricultural produce cause famine and drought. Scarcity however applies not only to Third World economies but all economies, whether Third World, developing or advanced. In simple terms individuals cannot have everything that they want because there is a finite limit on the resources that can be used to satisfy these 'wants'. Any resource is therefore scarce, perhaps not at the margin as with the Rolls Royce example above or at the level of a basic necessity, but they are nevertheless scarce.

If individuals cannot have all that they want, then choices need to be made, and put simply every choice involves a cost. This will always be the next best alternative that could have had been selected when that choice was made. This is known as the opportunity cost of that decision. Thus if a particular society does not have sufficient resources to build both a new stretch of motorway and a new airport, it must make a choice between the two. If it chooses to build the motorway then the opportunity cost of the motorway is the airport that was not built. Opportunity cost therefore can be formally defined as the next best alternative forgone and is consequently not assessed using financial criteria.

These three concepts of scarcity, choice and opportunity cost can all be illustrated on what is known as a production possibility frontier.

The assumption of the production possibility frontier is that only two products can be produced, thus in Figure 1.1 the choice is between either transport services or all other goods and services. Whilst these may be very general categories, they do nevertheless show the underlying principles. As resources are finite there is a maximum level or combination that can be produced which is shown by the actual production possibility frontier (PPF). Thus if all resources are put

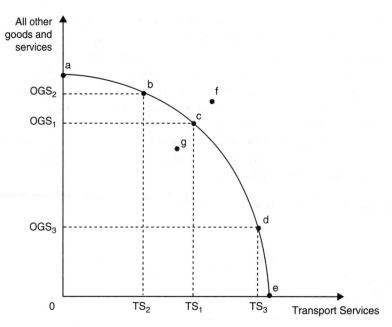

Figure 1.1 *The production possibility frontier*

into the production of all other goods and services, point a on the PPF would be achieved, whilst putting all resources into the production of transport services would result in an output level at point e. Where some combination of the two is produced, this is shown by all the intermediate points between a and e, with b, c and d highlighted for illustrative purposes. Also shown are points f and g. As point f lies outside of the PPF it is thus unattainable with the level of today's technology, but may become attainable at some point in the future through advances in technology. Such advances would cause the whole frontier to shift outwards. Point g on the other hand lies inside the frontier, hence is attainable, but would represent a position of inefficiency as society is not utilising the maximum potential of its finite resources.

If therefore these two commodities can only be produced in finite quantities, this leads into the first 'decision' to be made: namely what combination of the two to produce? If the choice was to produce at point c on the production possibility frontier, this would result in the production of TS_1 transport services and OGS_1 of other goods and services. Say however that some 'decision' was made to increase the level of other goods and services up to OGS_2, then this increase would have to be at the expense of transport services. This is because all resources are being employed in the production of these two commodities; thus in order to increase one, the resources required to do so have to be found through reduced production of the other. This is akin to an airline company that may want to increase its frequency on a particular route with immediate effect, but in order to do so it will have to find the necessary aircraft from its other routes until in a position to increase the total fleet size.

Figure 1.1 therefore also illustrates the opportunity cost of such decisions. As a result of increasing production of other goods and services from OGS_1 to OGS_2, the production of transport services has fallen from TS_1 to TS_2. This reduction represents the opportunity cost. Note further if the level of other goods and services was to be increased again, say up to the maximum at point a, then an even larger quantity of transport services would have to be given up. The opportunity cost in terms of transport services is therefore becoming greater as the production of other goods and services increases. This is because at first the resources used in the production of other goods and services will be the most suitable; however, as production steps up it will have to increasingly use less suitable resources, i.e. those more suitable for the production of transport services. Hence ever larger quantities of transport services will have to be sacrificed. This again is akin to our airline example, where the airline will firstly use those aircraft from other routes that are the most suited to the purpose; however, further increases in frequency would have to be served by less suitable aircraft.

As any economy (country) cannot provide its citizens with all that they want, i.e. there is scarcity, a choice has to be made with regard to three basic questions –

- what to produce?
- how to produce it?
- and for whom to produce it?

The first we have already seen as it concerns the question of where on the production possibility frontier should production take place. How that output should be produced concerns the 'best' use or combination of resources to ensure that there is no inefficiency (as indicated by point g on Figure 1.1). Hence an example from the energy industries would concern what is the 'best' way to generate electricity – through coal-fired power stations, by nuclear fusion, through hydro systems, wind power, solar power or finally by burning natural gas? In some ways the answer to that question will be dependent upon the resources available, hence in a country with large coal reserves the normal practice would be through the first method. The last question concerns who gets the rewards arising out of the commodities produced, or more exactly how are the benefits of wealth creation to be shared out amongst the members of society. This is our key question above as to who gets the Rolls Royce and who gets the 15-year-old mountain bike. These three questions arise as a result of the basic economic problem – scarcity – hence, you can't always get what you want. The mechanism used to address these three critical issues of what, how and for whom to produce is what would be referred to as 'the economy'. This has led to the development of different economic systems or types of economies to answer these questions, and these can generally be classified as command, free market or mixed market.

Command, free and mixed market economies

A command economy is where the state, i.e. the government, directly addresses the three questions posed above. That is, the government decides what to produce, how it will be produced and who will receive the resultant output. In the past this has normally been centred on a system of plans, in which five-year plans are subdivided into one-year plans, then area plans of production, then by town, by company, by individual plant and so on down. The government also decides how the *factors of production* are employed. Factors of production are the resources that are used in the production process. All production processes can be broken down into three factors of production or basic inputs – land and raw materials, labour and capital. Land/raw materials and labour are fairly self explanatory as regards production resources, capital on the other hand is any equipment that is used in the production process. Thus a basic ship's voyage is produced by a labour element (the ship's crew), a capital element (the ship itself) and land/raw materials (the fuel used to power the ship and the natural environment in which it operates, e.g. the open sea or coastal waters). Under a command economy system, the state organises the factors of production to resolve the first two questions of what and how to produce, and distributes the resultant production on the basis of equity, i.e. if you work hard you reap the rewards. Note that in theory under such a system there is no need for any form of money, as goods and services are distributed on the basis of decisions by government or some other delegated central body. Such a system was in the past associated with the former communist countries in Eastern Europe; however, historically they have not solely been associated with the political left, as demonstrated by the German economy under the extreme right wing National Socialists from 1933 to 1945.

Today the relevance of studying such systems may appear to have completely disappeared with the collapse of the European communist states and their associated command economies in the late 1980s and early 1990s. Nevertheless, it gives the important theoretical perspective of the role of government in the running of the economy: it is key and central to the whole operation.

At the other end of the spectrum is the free market economy. In its most extreme form, a completely free market economy has no government input into the decisions of what, how and for whom to produce. Government's only function is to provide law and order. Economic decisions are left purely to the market in the form of private buyers and sellers, with the price mechanism and the profit motive playing central roles in the operation of the whole economic system. The price mechanism transmits signals from the market to the various interested parties, with the underlying philosophy being that trade is never a zero sum game, as both parties (usually) benefit in any exchange. Added to this is the idea of consumer sovereignty, i.e. the consumer is king. In simple terms, if consumers want more of something they will go out and buy it, and this will cause the price of that commodity to rise. Thus through the price mechanism a signal is sent to producers that consumers want more of that particular product and driven by the profit motive they will produce more of it. Hence in Figure 1.1, where to produce on the production possibility curve is decided by consumers. If for example consumers express a desire for more transport services, then through their market actions, by for example showing a willingness to pay a higher price for them, producers will shift resources out of the production of other goods and services and into the production of transport services. Another far less esoteric view of this example is that some firms producing other goods and services will go bust due to a lack of consumer demand for their products, and all of these resources will then be released and reemployed in firms producing transport services, i.e. a commodity for which there is strong consumer demand and consequently one in which a good profit can be made.

In a free market economy therefore the issue of what to produce is resolved by consumers through the ideas of consumer sovereignty, the price mechanism and the profit motive. How these should be produced is addressed by producers combining the factors of production in the lowest cost combination in order to obtain the maximum profit. This again is based upon the price mechanism and is driven by the profit motive. Every factor of production has a 'price'; hence if for example the price of labour is relatively 'cheap', then a large amount of labour will be used in the production process. Should however the price of labour increase, then producers may consider replacing or substituting labour with capital. By such processes questions regarding the 'best' combination of factors of production to use in the production process are thus resolved.

This only leaves the question of 'for whom?' In a free market economy, again this is based (in theory!) on equity. If you work hard, you will gain the rewards. Unlike in the command system, however, where it is the state that decides the merit of your claim, in a free market economy it is through the price mechanism. If a particular individual possesses highly sought after skills that are in very short supply, such as those of a transport economist(!), then in theory that individual will command a relatively high price in the market place, i.e. high wages. The subsequent accumulation of higher wages will enable that individual to obtain more of the (scarce) resources of the economic system than the average person. In simple terms, they will be able to afford to buy more goods and services and these will generally be of a higher quality. Through the price mechanism therefore, in this case relating to labour markets, the free market systems resolves the question of for whom to produce.

The last of the economic systems examined is the mixed market economy. If you have understood the previous two examples then the mixed market economy is the most straightforward of the three. As the name clearly indicates, it is a market based system, i.e. one primarily (but not entirely) based upon the price mechanism, and one that uses a mix of public decisions of the state and the private decisions of the market to determine the outcome to the questions of what, how and for whom to produce. A simple way to consider the mixed market system is to think of the free market economy, but rather than simply having two agents in the market place, private buyers and sellers, there is a third, the state. Through its function as a provider and purchaser of goods and services and also its function as a governing body, the state will heavily influence the workings of the economy and thus all decisions are not market based. The state for example may decide to provide some goods and services for a zero user charge, such as health, education and many social services. This can be for a variety of reasons, from simple political gain, to reasons of equity or some may even be provided on the basis of economic welfare. For example, there are some economic goods that could almost be termed 'common goods'. These are what would be technically known as public goods. Probably the best example of a public good is a lighthouse. Once a lighthouse has been constructed and is in operation, then it is very difficult, if not impossible, to charge for its use. Hence if one of the major shipping lines was to construct a network of lighthouses, every other shipping line would be able to use them for free. This is known as the free rider problem. Under a free market system, the first shipping line would be driven out of business due to its higher costs of operation because of the added expense of running the lighthouses: what would happen to the lighthouses then? As a result, no lighthouses would be constructed even though their value is beyond doubt. In other instances the free rider problem arises where the cost of implementing the charge is higher than any fee that could be imposed for the use of the service. The net result in both instances is that despite considerable benefits, such goods and services would not be provided by the market as those involved simply could not charge for their use. Under a free market system, therefore, there would be no public goods such as lighthouses; however, in a mixed market system the intervention by the state to provide such goods overcomes these problems.

In practice all economies fall into this last category, with the only difference being the level of state involvement. Hong Kong and the US are generally viewed as nearer the free market end of the spectrum, whilst the social economies of many European countries such as France, Denmark and Sweden are generally viewed as having a relatively high level of state involvement. Note however that 'a relatively high level' is nowhere near the level of a pure command economic system and is also a term that over time has come to mean significantly less government intervention in absolute terms. This is no more clearly exemplified than within transport markets, where the last thirty years in Britain has seen the transfer out of the public sector into the private sector of a large number of transport service providers, most notably the National Freight Corporation (road haulage), the National Bus Company and Scottish Bus Group, British Airways, British Airport Authorities, British Rail and Associated British Ports. This process is best summarised by the title of Dennis Swann's excellent 1988 book *The Retreat of the State* (Swann, 1988). Many other examples exist throughout Europe and other parts of the world of this general retreat of the state and specifically in the provision of transport services, where many bus companies and freight orientated railways have been similarly privatised.

Figure 1.2 attempts to contextualise the above discussion and further illustrate its relevance to transport markets. What it shows is a simplified version of transport markets in most of today's developed and developing countries. 'Transport markets' lie at the centre, around which revolve a combination of government agencies and private individuals. It is through the interactions of these parties in the form of their market actions that result in the production of all transport services, whether private, public or freight. Government intervention in transport markets comes in a number of different forms which can be broadly split between direct provision, where the state effectively does it itself, or through control by legal measures the actions of private agents (buyers and sellers) in the market. In many instances financial measures, both persuasive and punitive, will also be used to 'steer' these agents towards a particular outcome. Much debate in transport economics surrounds the reform of the provision of transport services and infrastructure

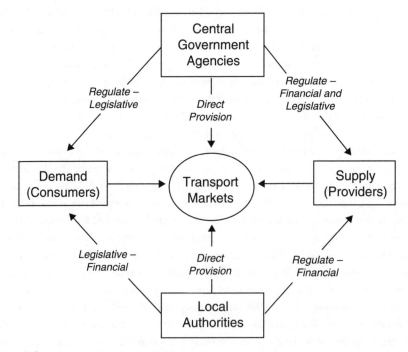

Figure 1.2   The mixed transport market

through a switch in the balance between direct provision by the state and the implementation of state policy/actions through the direction of others. This in a nutshell is the public v private debate. Much debate and reform also surrounds the question of the extent to which the state should continue to 'do it (all) itself' or the degree to which it should make individuals far more responsible for their own transport related activities. Both of these aspects are considered throughout the book.

Whilst applying to most of today's developed and developing countries, the level of control and intervention between the two tiers of government illustrated in Figure 1.2 will vary from country to country. The level of action at the national and local levels will depend upon the political constitution of the country concerned. Some hold far more political power at the 'state' or regional level, whilst in others this power is heavily centralised. The figure very much reflects the British model, where most transport policy is set and generally implemented at the national level; this is particularly true of air, rail and shipping services. Locally based public transport, however, such as the bus, light rail and local ferries, are generally implemented at the local level, and clear divisions of responsibility exist in the provision of private transport facilities between national and local governments. Other forms of this general overview exist, however, such as the 'regionalisation' of many rail services in countries such as Germany and Sweden and to a lesser extent in Britain, where some rail services are specified and financed at the local level, hence creating a clear division of responsibilities for rail services in much the same way as there are clear divisions within Britain between 'national' and 'local' roads.

In many respects Figure 1.2 illustrates exactly what this book is about. Chapter 2 sets the context of the importance of transport to economic welfare and society in general, Chapters 3 through to 8 explain the workings of the market and their relevance to transport provision, Chapter 9 sets transport markets in the wider context of the natural and built environments, Chapters 10 and 11 concern the actions of government agencies in the workings of transport markets. Chapter 12 then specifically examines the economics of freight and the wider global economic environment, and finally Chapters 13 and 14 examine some of the technical aspects of forecasting future transport demands and appraisal methods for future transport projects.

To return however to the issue of economic systems, a practical example may help to reinforce and expand on a number of the ideas outlined in the above text. The example used is the provision of public transport services in Glasgow, as the various modes operated provide an interesting mix in terms of command (or planned) v free market economics.

Case study 1.1 Private and public sector roles in the provision of public transport in and around the Glasgow conurbation.

Glasgow makes an interesting case study of different economic systems in the provision of its public transport services. It is nevertheless very typical of the type of model of public transport delivery that can be found in all of the major cities in Britain outside of London, and all aspects of provision can be found in every major city including London across the globe. In Glasgow there are basically three main forms of public transport: the bus, the train and the iconic Glasgow underground. Whilst all three operate through the price mechanism, i.e. a fare is charged for their use, the provision of each mode operates along very different economic principles. Bus services tend to operate along the lines of the free market system, where privately owned and operated companies decide which bus services they will operate.[1] This is usually based upon providing a network of services that they believe will make them a profitable return, i.e. services that consumers are willing to pay for. Thus if there should be a reduction in the number of users of a particular bus service, the revenue (amount taken through the fare box) associated with that bus route will fall. If say this trend was to continue, then the point would be reached where the revenue gained from the service would fail to cover the cost of its operation and the service would be withdrawn.

In simple terms, through the market system 'consumers' have effectively decided that they no longer want that bus service and the operator, now making losses, consequently withdraws the service. This may lead to a 'downsizing' of the company, or more radically where this was the only service operated, the liquidation of the firm, i.e. it goes bust. The 'resources', i.e. land, labour and capital, that were employed in the provision of the service are then 'freed' to be engaged in producing something more profitable, i.e. something that consumers have decreed they want through showing their willingness to pay for it. That's the theory at least but one that does not always work out in practice, as it can often leave resources unemployed, i.e. inefficiencies in the system.

With regard to rail services, Glasgow has the largest suburban rail network in the UK outside of London and is thus a crucial element in the transport system of the city. The provision of services however is quite different in nature to that of the provision of bus services. Transport governance in Scotland, however, particularly with regard to the railways, is a complicated issue but one that should not distract from the key points in this case study. It is a government body, Transport Scotland, that decide what services to provide based not on the profit motive, but rather on the basis of the public interest. Thus Transport Scotland determines the pattern of rail services to be provided and sets the fares to be charged. It then however contracts a private sector operator – First Scotrail – to provide the services to the specified pattern and fare structure. This contract is on a fixed price basis, where First are awarded a fixed financial sum and expected to operate the service on that amount. Any revenue or cost reductions First can achieve above/below that will contribute to the company's overall profits. Thus if say patronage on a particular route was to fall, the decision as to whether to continue operating that service would lie with Transport Scotland and not with the private operator. The latter would have to continue to operate the service until the contract was up for renewal. At that time, Transport Scotland would then have to decide whether to spend the extra funds to retain the service in the face of falling passenger revenue. This decision would be taken on the grounds of what could be done with the funds if the service was to be withdrawn, i.e. the opportunity cost of the service. Therefore, unlike in the case of buses, the service would not be automatically terminated as it is not provided on the basis of the profit motive.

The 'model' of provision of services on the Glasgow underground is different again. In this case the public body, the Strathclyde Passenger Transport (SPT), act as both operator and principal funder of the system. Hence the SPT owns all the rolling stock and operates the service. SPT sets the fare and service patterns, and as with rail services these are provided on the basis of the public interest, hence passenger revenues fail to cover the cost of operation. The economics of the whole venture however still need to add up, thus the difference between costs and revenues are made up by subsidy (which amounted to £7.2m in 2006/07). This has been reduced over the last few years through increases in fares in real terms, i.e. above the rate of inflation, in order to lessen the financial burden of the underground on SPT's funds.

This case very effectively illustrates the operation of all three different types of market systems in the provision of transport services – buses are planned and operated by private sector companies in pursuit of profits, i.e. largely along free market principles, rail services are provided along mixed market principles through the combination of a private sector operating company and a public sector planning body, and the underground along planned or command economy principles, with the services planned, owned and operated by the public sector. In some ways, these differences in the mode of delivery are related to the economic characteristics of each mode of transport, which results in the outcome that one mode of delivery does not fit all. These are facets to be explored later in the text. It is also worth highlighting that the distinction between the different 'types' of economic approaches/systems in the delivery of public transport services was based on a division between three different functions, that of ownership of the actual transport assets, i.e. buses, trains and related infrastructure, the planning of the services and finally the operation of the services. This division of responsibilities is also another facet of transport services that will be further developed in the course of the text, but it is one that has particular significance with the reform of public transport services.

One final point of reflection on this case study, and one repeatedly seen in later chapters, is that there has been a considerable shift away from direct public sector involvement in the provision of public transport services throughout the world, towards one that involves far more private sector involvement. If we were to travel back to 1980, which we can do through Youtube,[2] then we would find that Glasgow bus services were owned and operated by the SPT and rail services in the city provided by the nationalised British Rail in conjunction with the SPT. Since that period only the Glasgow underground remains in public ownership and operation, but it is now one of the few examples of such a model of provision remaining in Great Britain.

CHAPTER SUMMARY AND REFLECTION

In this chapter we have considered the economic problem and identified that this is primarily concerned with scarcity, as individuals can't always get what they want. This leads to choices being made, hence, to follow the analogy, individuals should get what they need. How society's economic problems are resolved is through a market based system, specifically a 'mixed' market based system, and in transport markets the 'mix' is probably larger than in most others. Transport services are therefore provided on the basis of the interactions between private agents in the market and central and local government agencies 'guiding' their behaviour either through direct command or through the imposition of financial penalties or incentives. Importantly, however, the market lies at the centre of this activity. The following chapter takes these ideas further to examine the basic workings of the market for transport services. You should not forget however that it is mainly through the market mechanism that society resolves the basic economic questions outlined in this introductory chapter, they should never be considered as separate issues.

CHAPTER EXERCISES

As an introduction, this chapter only has one exercise in identifying transport economic issues.

Exercise 1.1 Transport economic problems?

Listed below are nine major transport related issues facing society today. Your task is to identify which ones are related to 'the economics of transport', in other words those you believe to be economic issues, as opposed to being related to other dimensions such as political or social factors. Although you should always try to come to a clear answer for each issue, what you may find is that for some the division is not always entirely clear or in other cases there may be several different factors present. Where you find this to be the case you should consider those other factors and thus where the economics of the issue 'fit' in the wider picture.

1 Politicians and business managers in general in Britain are often said to suffer from a disease known as 'short-termism'. This is where only the short term is considered with no or little thought given to the longer term. There are numerous examples of this disease in British transport policy, the prime example probably being the privatisation of the railways.
2 The negative impact on the natural environment of all transport related activities.
3 Increasing levels of traffic congestion in towns and cities.
4 The high levels of subsidy required to sustain public transport industries.
5 The increasing amounts of land that are being given over to support transport activities.
6 The role of transport in 'unifying' the European Union.
7 The subsidisation of public transport services in rural and socially deprived areas.
8 The role of education in changing travel behaviour to reduce local and unnecessary journeys.
9 The impact of an ageing population and the changing transport needs that this presents.

Transport and economic development

INTRODUCTION

Transport has played a vital role in economic development and in the evolution of society to the point where we are at today. Stretching far back when people lived in caves, modes of transport simply did not exist. Consequently, all basic wants and needs, in this case those required for a basic existence, had to be found within walking distance. Whilst shelter was provided by the cave, food had to be hunted which also provided some form of protection from the natural environment from the fur of the animal hunted. In today's terms, we would describe such a life style as self-sufficient, where there is no division of labour and all basic needs are provided solely by the individual. Importantly in our context, we would say there was no separation of production from consumption. In other words, where things were 'produced', such as meat for consumption, was the same location where they were consumed, and hence did not require to be transported over any great distance.

Within such an existence, one important factor missing was the trade of goods and services. Importantly, however, trade could not take place without transport. In turn, as transport systems became more efficient and sophisticated, the more trade became a viable possibility and subsequently did take place. Whilst this may seem like a rather brief history of civilisation as we know it, this is, in fact, a continually evolving process and one that is still on-going today, fostered and overseen by the World Trade Organisation (WTO). The WTO was founded on 1 January 1995 as the successor to the General Agreement on Tariffs and Trade (GATT). In simple terms the WTO is an international organisation that oversees trade agreements between its members. Since the creation of the original GATT in 1947, this has seen a progressive reduction in the institutional barriers to trade (e.g. import taxes, import quotas etc) and has been largely responsible for what we now refer to as the global economy.

Whilst such a brief overview of the role of transport in the development of society has a clear focus on freight transport and the movement of goods (and completely ignores the importance of money markets and foreign exchanges), these ideas should not be solely limited to the transport of cargo. It can also be expanded to the movement of people and the role that increased mobility has played in economic development. This is clearly the case in the provision of services, which in most cases are provided by an individual. Hence it is very difficult to get a haircut without the movement of people – either the consumer moving to the barber's, or the barber coming to the individual. It is not only in the direct provision of services however that the movement of people plays an important role, but also in the bringing together of individuals into a group where their individual specialities can be allowed to be developed and enhanced to the maximum. Thus synergies can be created where the whole is greater than the sum of the individual parts. With regard to the movement of people into such groupings, this of course relates to the employment of labour in private companies/public bodies. Through the provision of efficient transport services individuals are able to access work opportunities where their skills will be valued the highest and hence be of most benefit to society.

All of these issues will be further explored and developed in this chapter. The purpose of the chapter however is not to examine the economics of transport but rather to bring out the importance of transport in the development of society today and hopefully in turn to then illustrate why getting it 'right', i.e. the transport problem, is important.

THE LINK BETWEEN TRANSPORT LEVELS AND ECONOMIC WEALTH

The link between transport levels and economic wealth has never been in question, the two are highly correlated. This is best illustrated by a simple figure, which is given opposite.

Figure 2.1 shows the level of freight transport as measured by tonne kilometres and the level of GDP, in real terms, i.e. adjusted for inflation. GDP is an important measure of 'National Income' and in very simple terms is the aggregation of everyone's income. Both these variables are shown as an index, hence Figure 2.1 tracks the changes that have occurred in both variables since 1953. What this clearly shows is the closeness of the relationship between the two. What it also shows however is the dramatic increase in tonne kilometres over the period, hence in 2004 freight transport levels had almost trebled since 1953. Whilst that may be simply stating the obvious from the figure, it does raise the question as to why such a dramatic increase has occurred. One answer is population growth, but at around 20 per cent over the whole period that on its own does not account for such a large increase in freight transport levels. The real driving force behind the increase has been society's continued evolution and movement away from a subsistence-based economy towards one with an ever increasing demand for more material goods and services. These

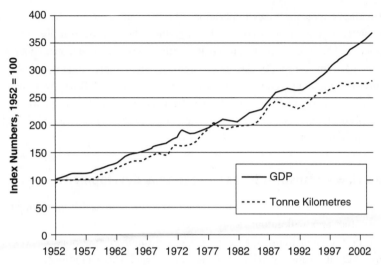

Figure 2.1 *Freight transport and real Gross Domestic Product, Great Britain, 1953 to 2004*

Source: Compiled from DfT (2007) and Eurostat Figures

can only be provided through trade, either international or domestic, both of which then generate a demand for transport.

It is not only simply increased trade however that accounts for this increase, but also the movement towards a consumer society. As a consequence, rather than just simply more goods and services being demanded, it is the fact that such goods and services are being demanded at a faster rate. In simple terms, people consume goods and services quicker than they used to (hence more waste), therefore there is a need to produce more. This in turn requires more people to be employed, hence incomes rise, hence people spend more, hence increased demand for freight transport services and so on. This 'virtuous circle' is a simple form of what is known in economics as the multiplier effect, where a pound, Euro or dollar is spent more than once. Hence what I spend on having the plumbing in my house fixed, is in turn my plumber's income, which he then goes out and spends on other goods and services that in turn is the recipient's income and so on. Note however that at each stage some of the money will slip out of the system. For example, not all that I pay my plumber will end up in my plumber's pocket, some will be taxed. Or indeed he may not spend it all, but save some of it to spend on future consumption. Nevertheless, this is a simple explanation for the rise in both variables, and the closeness of association between the two.

Whilst this association has long been recognised (and clearly shown in Figure 2.1), there remains real question marks over the direction of causation. Clearly one would imagine that a higher level of GDP causes a higher level of freight transport. Or put another way, as incomes rise (GDP), more goods are demanded and these need to be transported from the point of production to the point of consumption. This view fits very much with the classic notion of the derived nature of transport demand. However, it is not quite as simple as that. Advances in freight transport will result in reduced transport costs and this in turn will lead to more goods being produced (and transported) as the final price in the market will now be lower and more competitive, i.e. profitable. In this case, therefore, it is advances in freight transport that lead to increases in GDP.

This difference has important policy implications. As an example, would the economic problems affecting a particular region be overcome by upgrading the transport access infrastructure or would such actions have little impact? If it is believed that increases in GDP cause increases in trade (and hence the need for transport), then in simple terms such improvements would be a waste of public resources, as the improved infrastructure would be little used. If however one believes that transport causes increases in GDP, then clearly the answer would be yes. This has led to two different schools of thought on the issue, the supply led and the demand led models of economic development and transport.

Supply led view – transport leads to economic development

To adopt a supply led model is to suggest that the causal relationship is that improving the transport infrastructure of an area will automatically stimulate economic activity and stimulate economic development. Increasing or improving the quality of the supply of transport services or transport infrastructure will automatically bring about such a change. This would occur for a number of reasons:

- Widening of markets, increased production and multiplier effects
  It is the provision of high quality transport facilities that leads to the widening of markets, hence rather than being restricted to selling in local markets that are easily accessible, the range of potential markets will be expanded. This is important because the potential that these newly accessible markets offer will only be exploited if a profit can be earned. If this is not the case, there is no point in doing it. This will therefore directly increase wealth in the area and almost certainly lead to an increase in the production of that particular good or service. In order that more be produced, more resources will be required, in particular labour, and this labour will have to be sought from either other industries or from those not currently employed. Either way, this leads to a general increase in incomes as employees will only change jobs where it is worth their while to do so, and in most cases such changes of job will be motivated by higher incomes. This will also lead to multiplier effects, as those increased incomes will in the main be spent on local services, hence the idea of 'recycling' increased income back into the local economy. The basic argument is that markets that were too costly to service in the past now become more cost effective to serve as the transport gap that did exist between producers and consumers is narrowed. The improvement of transport provisions therefore is the spark that sets the whole process off.
- Indirect effects on employment in construction and operation
  Whilst termed 'indirect' effects in many ways these are the direct effects of upgrading transport links or services. Many such projects will consist of major infrastructure improvements, such as the building of bridges, the construction of new roads and railway lines or the installation of light rapid transit systems. These projects will directly create an increase in the demand for local labour both in the construction of such systems as well as their operation once in place. This again will lead to an increase in local incomes with all the associated multiplier effects.

As regards examples of supply led transport improvements, the most obvious is the role of the railways during the Industrial Revolution in Britain. It is said that the rapid construction of the railways throughout Britain in the mid 1800s literally 'powered' the Industrial Revolution, i.e. the movement from an agricultural to a manufacturing based economy, across the whole country. The railways enabled production to be linked to markets, hence led to the separation of consumption from production and thus helped to stimulate economic development. An often overlooked facet is that mass production cannot exist without mass consumption, and the railways enabled or even caused that mass consumption to become a reality. The second far from righteous example of supply led development is the exploitation of the Brazilian rainforest. The pursuit of better lines of communication to the more remote parts of Brazil led to the provision of better transport infrastructure. This in turn led to vastly improved access to the resource of timber, and in turn this led to mass exploitation. This is almost the spider's web argument, where areas that had been remote and distant in the past become more accessible as transport links are improved. This in turn leads to the improvement of further links into ever more remote areas in the pursuit of the exploitation of timber reserves.

Demand led models – economic development drives demand for transport

Contrasting with the supply led view is the alternative idea that transport provision is invariably a response to a basic demand, hence the casual relationship is that economic development leads to a demand for better transport facilities. Without a basic demand for an area's goods and services, then irrespective of the quality of the transport infrastructure this will never stimulate that demand and hence the subsequent economic development that would follow. As highlighted above, this is the classic view of transport as a derived demand. To take an extreme example, there is little point in upgrading the A9 to a four lane dual carriageway north of Inverness to John O'Groats as basically there is insufficient demand between the two locations to justify such a large capital expenditure. It may stimulate some form of economic development; however, this will be relatively minor in relation to the expenditure incurred. What is lacking is the basic demand for transport to and from John O'Groats. Even the unlikely discovery of a large unexploited diamond reserve on the outskirts of the village is unlikely to stimulate such a demand as the current infrastructure would be more than adequate to cope with the increased transport involved.

The basic demand required arises from one of two sources, revealed and latent demand.

- Revealed demand

  Revealed demand is expressed in the journeys that are actually made or the goods that are transported using the existing infrastructure. If this increases, it may be found that the existing infrastructure requires upgrading in order to cope with the current level of demand, e.g. the packed London Underground or the heavily congested M25 circular motorway around London. This higher demand therefore directly impacts on the improvement in the infrastructure.

- Latent demand

  There is also however what is known as a latent demand. In technical terms, latent demand is that segment of the demand curve to the right of the equilibrium point. This will be examined in Chapter 3; however, in this context latent demand exists where there is a demand but one that cannot be satisfied due to inadequacies in the existing infrastructure. In

17

other words, individuals may wish to travel to a particular location, hence the basic demand, but the cost in terms of the time that it would take to actually get there more than offsets any benefit gained from undertaking the journey. As a consequence, the journey is not made. If however the current provision is improved, then the cost of the travelling would fall and hence some of those who had not previously travelled will now make the journey.

Under this view of the relationship between transport and economic development, transport's role in the process is seen as one of a facilitator. Improving transport links is a necessary but not sufficient condition for development. Transport is the means by which demand for goods and services is satisfied but that demand must already exist, as improvements in transport will not on their own create such a demand. Hence simply improving a road into an area where there is no demand for the area's goods and services will not stimulate economic development in that region, the demand for the region's produce or services must already be present, and will be shown by existing links being under strain and hence clearly inhibiting economic growth.

What can be taken from this albeit brief review of the relationship between economic development and transport is that whilst the two are closely associated there is no clear answer as to the direction of causation between the two variables. You will no doubt be aware of examples of significant improvements to infrastructure facilities that are considerably under utilised whilst at the same time you will also be aware of other infrastructure links that are under severe pressure. The first example would be a clear case where a supply led view was mistakenly taken, whilst the second is an example of a demand led syndrome. As to which of the two schools of thought is the 'correct' one, the simple answer is that there is no one correct view that would fit all situations. Both views are consistent, as there exist some situations in which the supply led factor is more apparent, whilst in other instances the demand led view is more pertinent. In terms of policy initiatives, the important aspect is in understanding the basic drivers underpinning the local economy and the role that transport plays in supporting these drivers. Under a supply led view, improving transport services and/or upgrading the infrastructure is a necessary and sufficient condition for improved transport to lead to economic development. Under a demand led view, however, it is a necessary but not sufficient condition, i.e. the only condition required. There has to also be a basic derived demand for transport services in order for transport developments to then facilitate economic development.

The role of passenger transport in economic development

Whilst the role of freight transport in economic development is clear and founded upon the principle that trade is never a zero sum game, what may not be so evident is the role played by passenger transport. As before, the relationship between passenger transport and economic growth can be shown graphically.

Figure 2.2 clearly shows the very close association that exists between passenger transport and the level of GDP, revealing very similar overall trends to that shown above between GDP and freight transport. Interestingly in this case, the association clearly broke down in the mid to late 1980s, a period in UK economic history which has now become known as 'the Lawson Boom'. This was a period of unsustainable economic growth overseen by the then Chancellor of the Exchequer, Nigel Lawson, and cited as an economic miracle at the time. As the figure illustrates,

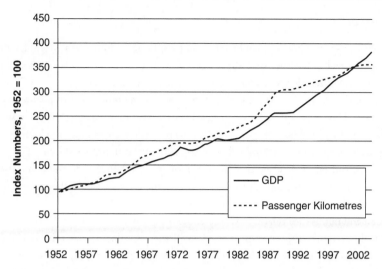

Figure 2.2   *Gross Domestic Product and passenger kilometres travelled, Great Britain, 1953 to 2004*

Source: Compiled from DfT (2007) and Eurostat Statistics

however, this ended in recession in the early 1990s. The Lawson Boom as such appears to have effectively halted the closeness of the association between economic progress and passenger transport for some 15 years before it appeared to have resumed in the late 1990s; however, the latest years appear to show a slower growth in passenger travel than GDP.

Looking at Figure 2.2, does this mean therefore that by simply travelling around people become better off? In some ways the answer to that question is actually yes, but due to the derived nature of demand it is obviously dependent upon what they do once they get to where they are going. The question thus again arises as regards the direction of causation, does increased GDP lead to increased passenger travel or is it the other way around? As before, this can be best characterised as demand led and supply led effects.

Supply-led effects

Under a supply-led effect the simple act of upgrading existing transport links will increase passenger travel and thereby increase GDP. It could be argued therefore that with regard to passenger travel there will be no supply-led impacts, all effects will be demand led. In simple terms, if people don't have a motivation (i.e. a need) to travel to a particular location, then building a new road won't make any difference. Over the last few years, however, Britain and many other countries have seen a considerable rise in the commuter belt zone. These are areas that lie around the main economic centres from which people commute. In some ways this is a supply-led effect, as the upgrade of links between the centre and the commuter belt has caused people to move out to those areas. An example of this is shown later in the chapter in Case study 2.2.

Demand-led effects

Unlike freight transport where demand effects can be split down into revealed and latent demand, with passenger travel a third demand effect is present, which can be best described as a derived demand effect. Revealed demand will be shown where the existing transport infrastructure is under pressure, hence clearly displaying a high demand for the movement of people between two given locations. This most often arises in heavily used commuter routes where roads become severely congested and public transport services overcrowded. Economic development therefore may be suppressed due to the lack of sufficient capacity in the transport system. This would be a clear case of the old business adage that 'time is money', and hence time stuck in a traffic jam is time not spent earning an economic return. Improving the transport links therefore removes such constraints and economic development can flourish.

Latent demand in this case relates to where individuals may travel to a particular area but do not do so due to limitations in the transport services. If these limitations are removed, then as with freight, individuals may then make the journey but will only do so if it increases their net benefit, which then indirectly leads to economic progress. A rather simple example would be where an individual may not commute between Bristol and London due to the journey time involved, and also would not re-locate due to social ties and the higher cost of living, particularly housing, in and around the London area. If however a high-speed railway line was to be constructed between the two locations, then with considerably reduced journey times more individuals are likely to make the daily commute from Bristol to London.

As regards derived demand effects, increased wealth generally creates a demand for more leisure activities, or ever more sophisticated leisure activities. Thus as incomes rise, individual's may take two foreign holidays rather than one, and/or have more weekends away from home, thus higher incomes lead directly to increased passenger traffic. A second derived demand factor exists where higher incomes tend to produce a modal switch away from public transport towards private transport, hence increasing the number of multiple-car households. As travel is now 'easier', this will directly increase the level of passenger transport.

Case study 2.1 Transport impacts on economic development

This case study attempts to underpin most of the main ideas outlined in the previous sections by looking at research into the impact of transport improvements on economic development. Whilst so far we have examined the potential impacts that transport can have on economic development, we have not considered the size that such effects are likely to be. By examining these factors, this should also help to tease out further some of the issues in the relationship between transport improvements and economic development.

We begin the case with the considerable amount of research surrounding the American experience of the relationship between highway development and economic growth. Purvis (1985) highlights that this originated from the mass of literature that appeared following the downturn in American productivity and economic growth levels from 1973 onwards. This sparked a considerable amount of research to investigate why this economic downturn had occurred. This brought to the fore issues such as increasing labour inefficiencies, wages effects and energy price increases as all potentially being responsible for the downturn. None of this literature however mentioned public capital expenditure, and in particular public spending on transport infrastructure, thus largely overlooking this as a potential cause. Gillen (1997) in a review of the literature highlights the work of David Aschauer as changing this whole perspective. Aschauer (1989) examined the relationship between public investment and economic growth over time in order to calculate the elasticity of aggregated output with respect to infrastructure spending, i.e. the extent to which the former changed with respect to changes in the latter. He found that the decline in relative expenditure on public highway infrastructure accounted for around 60 per cent of the decrease in private sector productivity, hence suggesting that transport impacts were considerable. Further studies during this period produced similarly large estimates, with most elasticities falling in the range between 0.3 and 0.6. Munnell (1992) for example, estimated that a $1 increase in the public capital stock raised output in the economy by $0.60.

Simply taking the results of this early research would indicate that transport investment has a major impact on economic development. Subsequent literature however has viewed these figures as overoptimistic in the extreme and suggested that what was identified was an association between the two variables rather than a causal relationship, i.e. both variables were dependent upon an unidentified third factor. This has become commonly known as the 'Aschauer Effect' (Ezcurra *et al.*, 2005). Harmatuck (1997) for example agrees that highway infrastructure capital does have an effect on aggregate output and productivity, but suggests that the size of such estimates from previous research are highly questionable. Reworking Aschauer's findings to correct for a statistical property known as non stationarity, Harmatuck produced an elasticity estimate of 0.03 for non-military public expenditure on output, considerably smaller than the original work. This lower figure is confirmed by Gillen's (1997) review, as he highlights that most of the subsequent research reviewed suggests that although public capital expenditure does have a positive effect on output, it tends to be small in comparison to private capital and labour effects.

Whilst such studies indicate the potential impact that transport investment can have on production, they tell us nothing of the processes involved, i.e. how one transmits into the other. In order to come to a better understanding of the relationship between highway infrastructure investment and increases in productivity, the Federal Highway Administration (FHWA) (cited in Gillen, 1997) examined the impact of transport improvements on the performance of 226 manufacturing firms over a seventeen year period from 1969 to 1986. They found that the three principal reductions in production costs as a result of highway improvements arose from savings on inventories, the attainment of scale economies due to the widening of markets and finally a reduction in regional warehousing requirements as a result of more direct deliveries being made. Their research also showed that such savings had reduced over time, suggesting a diminishing return on aggregate investment in highways. This in many ways makes sense, as initial investments in highways are made in the most critical areas.

Harmatuck (1997) also highlights that the return on public highway expenditure will decline over time simply due to the fact that emphasis will switch away from new investment to the maintenance of existing highways – what Americans term the 4Rs of resurfacing, restoration, rehabilitation and reconstruction. Furthermore, research by the Congressional Budget Office[1] in 1991 (CBO, 1991) highlighted that 4R programmes had a higher rate of return than new investment. This is for the simple reason that new roads cannot be built simply for the sake of building new roads and increased economic activity expected to follow. More acutely, this is the difference between supply and demand led developments, where there comes a point in time when the balance switches between these two effects and the benefits arising out of maintaining existing highways more than outweighs the benefits of new investment.

Similar research has been carried out in a European context, although this has tended to focus on the impact of all transport infrastructure and not just roads, hence has included rail, airport and sea port infrastructure. As an example, Ezcurra *et al.* (2005) used a panel data set to examine the impact of all public infrastructure stock on private sector production costs for Spanish regions over the period 1964 to 1991. In two separate specifications of the function, the authors' firstly examined the impact of public capital stock (which included all public capital in terms of transport, education, urban and health care infrastructure) and secondly the impact of a far more narrowly defined variable that isolated the effect of transport infrastructure stock on production costs. Their estimations also allowed their results to be broken down by the industrial sectors of agriculture, manufacturing and service. What they found was that transport infrastructure effects relating to agriculture were insignificant. This is partly to be expected due to the large spatial dimension in this sector and hence limited demand for the use of transport infrastructure. For the period 1964 to 1976, therefore, cost elasticities were −0.004 in manufacturing and −0.029 in services, and in the period 1977 to 1991 the respective figures were −0.01 and −0.043. Thus, for example, between 1964 and 1976 a 10 per cent rise in the value of the transport infrastructure capital stock would produce an average of a 0.04 per cent fall in the production costs of manufactures and a 0.29 per cent fall in the production costs of services. In many ways the larger impact that transport infrastructure stock had on services makes sense, as service industries tend to have a higher labour element. Improvements in transport infrastructure therefore are likely to have a larger impact in that sector as a result of the more efficient movement of people.

Rodríguez-Pose and Fratesi (2004) examined the impact of transport infrastructure as part of a far broader remit when they examined the impact of European Structural Funds in under-developed European Union regions (known as Objective 1 areas). What they found was that despite a very high proportion of development funds being spent on transport infrastructure, the returns on these investments in terms of economic development were virtually zero. They found a larger return on development funds spent on education and human capital. In simplistic terms, this may be an indication of supply led effects, which would explain why the investment in transport infrastructure has little impact due to a lack of demand. Under such conditions, however, spend on human capital in the form of training and education is likely to have a far larger effect on economic growth. Another factor to take into account is that many of these regions had an agricultural-based economy, in which we have already seen that the impact of transport developments on this sector can be limited.

As a more direct measure of the impact of transport facilities on local production, Prud'homme and Lee (1999) examined the extent to which time savings in the transport network would result in productivity increases. In a study of 22 French cities they found that an increase in city-wide travel speed of 10 per cent would result in a 2.9 per cent increase in productivity due to an increase in the efficiency of labour markets, suggesting that the efficiency of transport networks have a very large impact on local economic production.

More recent research has focused on the idea of transport's impact on economies of density.

Whilst there may be economies of scale, i.e. advantages in production to larger-sized firms, brought about by the widening of markets, there may also be certain advantages to having firms of a similar nature located close to each other, i.e. economies of density. Rice and Venables (2004) highlight that differences in productivity levels across the UK can in part be put down to differences in industrial concentration. Thus improving the transport links into these industrial centres could increase productivity due to what are known as economies of density. The author's figures suggest that a 10 per cent reduction in average driving times would increase UK productivity by 1.12 per cent. This is based primarily on an elasticity of production with relation to density of 0.05, i.e. the extent to which production increases with economic concentration. This is broadly confirmed by Rosenthal and Strange (2004) in a review of the literature on city size/density and production, where they find a range of between 0.04 and 0.11. Finally, Graham (2005), in research undertaken for the DfT, used a disaggregated approach by industrial sector and geographical region to produce a national average of 0.04, which ranged from a high of 0.193 for Transport, Storage and Communication in the East Midlands, to a low of 0.001 for Public Administration, Media and Other in both the North East and in Yorkshire and Humberside. Two industries produced zero agglomeration economies, those being Primary Industries and Electricity, Gas and Water. This is perhaps no great surprise, as in the former case many of these industries, e.g. agriculture, tend by their very nature to be low density industries in which economies of density are likely to have little impact or in the case of the power and public utilities industries these are fairly evenly spread across the country due to local consumption, hence again little economies of density.

To briefly summarise this case, the size of the impact of transport infrastructure improvements on economic development can vary considerably depending upon the level of industrial concentration, the economic conditions facing the area and the industrial sector being examined. Impacts tend to be at their highest for service industries where there is a high level of industrial concentration. The size of such impacts need to be weighed up when transport developments or improvements are being considered to ensure that the scheme that will be implemented is the one that will most benefit the economy. This is a topic to which we will return when we consider transport appraisal.

Decoupling freight and passenger traffic from GDP

As seen earlier, there is a very close association between both freight and passenger traffic and GDP; in simple terms, in the past increases in economic wealth have been associated with increased transport in all forms. This has now become a major problem, however, as the adverse effects of transport are better known and understood, particularly the negative impact on the environment. Such trends of ever increasing economic wealth and levels of increased transport cannot be continued into the future for a variety of reasons. These not only include negative environmental impacts but also concerns surrounding the use of land. Ultimately there is only so much land that can be used in the production of transport services, as it has a clear finite limit and thus is a scarce commodity. This is particularly true in heavily populated areas, such as in major conurbations or through particular corridors. In a nutshell, such trends are unsustainable as there will come a point when if unchecked there will be no more land available to provide for increased transport services.

This may therefore suppress economic growth as this would be clear evidence of a demand-led effect, however one for which there was no clear solution due to the shortage of suitable land. This in part is widely recognised as the folly of a policy stance known as 'predict and provide' (Banister, 2002), where under such a paradigm government's role is to simply forecast future transport trends and then ensure that the capacity is available to support such levels. The limitations of such a policy approach are now well known and understood. Not only economic factors are present however but also other quality of life issues. For example, can sitting in a traffic jam for 2 hours every day be taken as a sign of progress, or what about living in a highly polluted environment, does this equate with better living? Whilst GDP may be a reasonable indicator of the level of general social progress, it is certainly not without its limitations. The main one being that it assumes that people who are wealthier are automatically better off. Such an assumption however clearly does not hold, as other factors of a non-monetary nature are also present, such as the state of health, the 'quality' and availability of leisure time and so on. More time spent in a traffic jam may well result in less time spent with family and/or friends, and hence difficult to describe as 'progress'.

One of the major issues facing policy makers therefore is what is known as the 'decoupling' of GDP from transport, so that GDP can continue to grow without being associated with the same growth in transport levels that it has been in the past. Based on the albeit simplistic evidence presented in this chapter, it would appear that some progress has been made with decoupling freight transport from GDP, with freight levels flattening off since around the late 1990s whilst GDP has continued to increase. As this chapter has also shown, however, the 'decoupling' issue is equally applicable to passenger transport. Whilst the Lawson boom of the late 1980s did have a long-term effect on the relationship, we still have rising levels of economic wealth and rising levels of passenger travel. In some cases this may be less crucial, particularly if the transport undertaken is of the derived nature outlined above, i.e. higher GDP leads to higher levels of leisure travel; however, the increase in passenger transport continues to be far more than could be accounted for by such impacts.

Much of this text is taken up with flushing these issues out to hopefully come to a better understanding of the causes of the problem and the viability of the potential solutions. It will also however consider the other side of the coin, i.e. the constraints that may impact upon the 'simple' solutions.

TRANSPORT AND THE LOCAL ECONOMY

Up to this point we have only considered the relationship between transport activities and the level of economic development at the macro level, i.e. from a national or overall perspective. In this short section we consider the impact and necessity of transport activities to the welfare and basic operation of the local economy.

Presented in Figure 2.3 is a very simplified version of what is known as the circular flow of (national) income which we can use as a simple representation of any local economy, or indeed any economy at any level.

Figure 2.3 is the traditional representation of the circular flow of income which shows the basic economic relationships that exist in the economy. Households provide factors of production in the

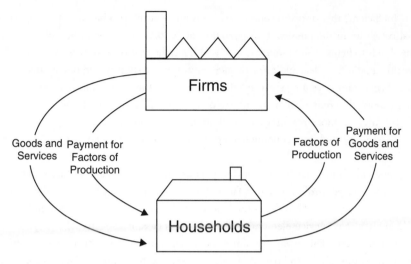

Figure 2.3 *Simplified version of the local economy*

form of labour, capital and raw materials to firms, who then use these resources to produce goods and services that they then sell back to households. Note therefore that in this rather simplified world all firms are owned by households (a not unrealistic assumption). Households receive payment for providing these factors of production in the form of wages for labour, dividends for capital, interest for finance, rent for property and so on. In simple terms, as more money circulates around the system, this represents a higher level of economic activity and thus a greater level of economic prosperity; in effect the whole system is becoming larger. The diagram therefore also shows how the level of Gross Domestic Product, or national income, can be calculated – either by adding up all household income, all household expenditure or finally by the total value of output of firms. Essentially, in this rather simplified world, all three should equal the same. In reality, however, this is exactly how it is measured, and hence this may help to further explain why GDP has followed such a close path with levels of freight and passenger transport.

In very simplistic terms, any external injection into the local economy in Figure 2.3 will have a greater impact the less of that injection that leaks out of the system. Any intelligent reader however will see where the leakages are likely to occur, as they are essentially the main economic flows that are missing from the figure. Hence, not all money from households goes to firms, some is saved, some is taxed, and some is spent on imports. Likewise, not all firms' income comes from households, as some comes from banks in the form of loans, some from other firms for the purchase of goods used in their production processes, i.e. capital goods, and some from foreign customers in the form of exports.

What is perhaps not so obvious however is the import role and impact that transport services have on the actual linkages that are shown on the diagram, particularly at the level of the local economy. The transport system, or more precisely an efficient transport system, allows these flows to take place far more easily and leads to more of the actual 'value', or wealth creation, to be transferred from one part of the economy to another. As a consequence the benefits of trade can be maximised and the local economy enhanced. If on the other hand the physical transportation process is inefficient, then more resources are consumed in the production of transport services and are also tied up in the physical transportation of goods from firms to households and labour from households to firms. Less resources, or less of the right type of resources, remain to devote to actual wealth creation. A clear indicator of such a transport system would be one that was heavily congested, hence more resources are needed to produce the extra transport services that are required to move different elements, either goods or people, around the whole system. More significantly, however, more resources are tied up in transit and thus are engaged in unproductive activities. As a result, the local economy will not be as efficient as it could be with better transport links.

This again is the almost classic view of transport as a derived demand, in that wealth is created in firms and the transport role is one of a facilitator that is a necessary but not sufficient condition for economic development. Thus the latter follows the former (i.e. is purely demand led). Indeed this would apply to any service element in that whole process, irrespective if it is transport, legal services, insurance etc. This is an oversimplistic view; however, as with respect to an efficient transport system, this allows any particular good or service to attain its highest economic value, i.e. be positioned where it is valued the highest, thus transport is in effect directly adding to wealth creation. Thus a rare first edition copy of J.R. Hartley's *Fly Fishing* can be auctioned worldwide through eBay in the knowledge that the book can be quickly and efficiently transported to the winner of the auction at a cost that is not prohibitive to the buyer. It will therefore obtain a far higher value than if it was simply advertised locally. Whilst not a particularly good example (as it relates to a second-hand good, hence wealth transfer and not creation), it does clearly illustrate the basic principles that also apply in the case of newly produced goods or services.

To return directly to Figure 2.3, how households and firms are physically linked is a vital element in the whole process. More specifically, at the level of the local economy an efficient transport system allows:

- The easier movement of labour from households to firms
- The easier movement of goods and services from firms to firms
- The easier movement of goods and services from firms to households
- The easier switch of labour from one firm to another and the easier switch of goods and services from firms to households.

Whilst most of these points are fairly clear and have been covered above, the last one is perhaps less obvious. Whilst the first three aspects relate mainly to the current state of the local economy, things seldom remain static for very long. Hence the last point listed above relates to the medium and longer terms. Using labour rather than goods as an example, the easier it is for labour to move from one firm to another, the more efficient will be the local economy and the greater the level of local economic development. This is because it will assist the transfer of labour from one firm to another and increase the odds that the person employed in any vacancy will be the most highly qualified person for that particular post.

An alternative way of thinking about the role of transport in the local economy is the extent to which the multiplier effect is allowed to function at the local level from any external injection. The better the physical links within the local economy, then the easier it is for the benefit from any external injection to spread out and have a full impact and thus less is lost in the transfer. In simple terms, at the level of the local economy an efficient transport system allows a greater physical separation of production and consumption, without which we would all still be living in caves!

One may rightly argue that this is an oversimplification that overstates the importance of transport in the operation of the local economy as it completely ignores the issue of location, and particularly locality decisions. Many theorists such as Weber (1909) and Hotelling (1929) would both suggest that firms of a similar nature will tend to be located near to each other for a variety of reasons. In the case of Weber, these are based primarily on the location of raw materials (which for our purposes we can extend to skilled labour) and the location of the market. Inevitably, therefore, firms in the same industrial sector are likely to come to similar decisions regarding the ideal location. Thus, for example, we end up with Silicon Glen in California or even the Golden Triangle of Motor Racing in South East England (where most of the current F1 teams are based), or in past days the agglomeration of shipbuilders on the Clyde or car manufacturers/accessory firms in the West Midlands. Such location decisions by and large overcome some of the problems associated with transport deficiencies. Indeed, these have been used as an argument for improved transport links in order to create such industrial 'clusters' (as was shown in Case study 2.1). Clearly however there is a balance somewhere between the two, which at some point tips one way or another. For example, without significant improvements in transport services we would still have shipbuilders on the Clyde and a large motor industry centred upon Birmingham. Furthermore, the decision of Guinness to close its London brewery at Park Royal in 2005 and ship all its beer directly to the British market from Dublin, is a classic example where the improvement in transport services has over-ridden original location decisions. Whilst this closing discussion on location does perhaps go slightly further than just the local economy, clearly the trade-off between location and transport issues is no more acutely felt than at the local level.

Case study 2.2 The local economy, transport and the Edinburgh housing market

The case study concerns the problems surrounding the Edinburgh housing market. Whilst initially this may seem to have little to do with transport and/or economic development, the link should become clear as the case evolves, particularly the relationship between transport facilities and the local economy. Listed below in Table 2.1 are the top twenty (of thirty-two) average house prices in Scotland between April and June 2008.

As can be seen from the table, on average the city of Edinburgh has the highest house prices in Scotland. Of the 20 local authority areas shown, however, it has experienced one of the lower rates of increase over the preceding year, at 5.9 per cent. Despite the onset of falling house prices in the British housing market due to the credit squeeze, house prices in Edinburgh appear to be holding up better than most areas in Scotland. Nevertheless, this is partly as a consequence of the housing market problems in Edinburgh and the general 'overheating' of the market. If house prices are higher in Edinburgh than elsewhere in the country then fewer people can afford to live there. Local employers therefore may struggle to fill vacancies, not only at the lower end of the labour market but also in the middle and higher income categories as those best qualified are put off by higher housing costs. This will have two possible direct impacts upon the local labour market. Firstly, it may result in wages rising in order to attract the 'right' people.

Table 2.1 *Average house prices by local authority area, top 20, Apr to Jun 2008*

Rank	County	Aver price	Quarter	Annual
1	Edinburgh, City Of	221209	6.3%	5.9%
2	East Renfrewshire	215805	7.1%	6.2%
3	East Dunbartonshire	198352	10.2%	8.9%
4	Aberdeenshire	197353	5.4%	12.0%
5	East Lothian	192747	3.8%	0.1%
6	Perth And Kinross	178701	5.3%	10.8%
7	Stirling	178249	−8.5%	2.5%
8	Aberdeen City	173730	1.7%	4.7%
9	Midlothian	170889	4.2%	1.3%
10	Scottish Borders	162988	−2.3%	1.0%
11	Highland	160130	2.4%	9.4%
12	South Ayrshire	147439	−4.8%	−4.0%
13	West Lothian	145729	5.3%	3.1%
14	Argyll And Bute	145364	1.0%	−1.9%
15	Angus	144787	5.8%	2.3%
16	Dumfries And Galloway	142971	3.3%	7.1%
17	Fife	142197	4.0%	9.0%
18	Moray	141411	2.6%	5.7%
19	Glasgow City	139371	1.1%	−1.5%
20	South Lanarkshire	135801	0.5%	3.9%

Source: Edited from BBC (2008)

Higher wages are required to offset higher house prices or the increased travel costs and inconvenience factors (mainly time) encountered in order to work in the Edinburgh area. The second possible effect is that lesser qualified, but 'available', individuals will be employed. Either way, the local economy in the longer term may suffer through higher costs in the production of goods or services. This will either be as a direct consequence of paying higher wages or indirectly through inefficiencies caused by the employment of underqualified individuals in posts to which their abilities and skills are not best matched. Clearly this is an over-simplification of the issue, as for example there also exists the rented sector of the housing market as well as the 'development' of less prosperous but 'emerging' areas within Edinburgh itself; nevertheless it does bring the issues into clearer focus.

If Edinburgh cannot always draw on the local labour market, therefore, firms within the city will have to look further afield to attract the 'right' kind of people at the 'right' kind of wages. Part of the problem however is Edinburgh's physical location, as to the immediate north of the city lies the Forth estuary and to the south the Pentland Hills with the largely rural Borders area beyond that. The nearest crossing point on the Forth estuary lies six miles to the west of Edinburgh. This consists of a road crossing that opened in 1964 that is now managed by the Forth Estuary Transport Authority (FETA), and a rail crossing, the Forth Bridge, now maintained and operated by Network Rail.

This severely restricts access to the North, with long delays experienced on the road bridge around peak period times, which begin at around 7am in the morning and last long into the early evening. Nevertheless, Dunfermline to the north of Edinburgh continues to be an attractive commuter zone for the city. As can be seen in Table 2.1, house prices in Fife, the county in which Dunfermline lies, are considerably less than in Edinburgh. Not shown by the table however is the quality of the housing stock, hence not only is the average price lower in Dunfermline, but almost certainly the average size of property will be considerably larger, particularly with large areas of new build over the last twenty years or so.

Given these constraints, it is also perhaps not surprising that East Lothian, which lies to the east of Edinburgh, also has relatively high house prices, lying fifth in terms of Scottish counties. Surprisingly, however, West Lothian, to the other side of Edinburgh, has not. Part of this difference in house price increases will be due to the different nature of the two areas. West Lothian traditionally had a high reliance on the mining industry whilst East Lothian tends to be far more rural. The difference in the average housing price therefore will also be due to major differences in the housing stock in the two areas, with the latter tending to have a far higher percentage of larger properties. Nevertheless, some of this difference may also be put down to the transport links between the two counties and Edinburgh. The east side tends to be less congested on the approach roads. The west side of the city on the other hand has far more population, with commuters coming from as far as the west of Glasgow, and hence links to the west tend to come under far more pressure.

Given the above factors, it is perhaps not surprising that Edinburgh was the third city in the UK to seriously consider introducing a congestion charge within the city boundaries. This was put to a public referendum in October 2005 but was unsurprisingly rejected by an overwhelming majority (almost 80 per cent), hence such plans have been abolished and other options considered.

To summarise, this case has outlined the overheating housing market in Edinburgh, heavy congestion in the city centre, and increased pressure on transport links to the north and west of the city. What is outlined below are the main transport initiatives currently being undertaken to help overcome these problems:

1   A second Forth road crossing. After much debate and discussion the approval for a second road crossing across the Forth was given in February 2007. Serious doubts currently exist concerning the available capacity of the existing bridge in the future, due to the condition of the suspension cables, which have been found to be suffering from corrosion. At the time of writing, it is not yet known whether the cables can be repaired or not. Nevertheless, given the long lead time for such projects (the second crossing is not expected to open until 2016/17), approval has been given. In terms of our under-standing of the relationship between economic development and transport, this would be clearly seen as a demand led scheme. Current capacity is under severe strain, and hence it could be argued that economic activity is being limited by the capacity of the bridge.

2   Re-opening of the Waverley Railway Line to the south of Edinburgh. The Waverley line ran south from Edinburgh and was a late casualty of the Beeching era of rail closures, closing in early 1969. The line originally extended through the Borders and continued on to Carlisle. Ever since its demise, however, it has been broadly recognised as a rail closure too far. Approval for the re-opening of the line as far as Tweedbank, 60 miles south of Edinburgh, was given in June 2006. One of the major driving forces behind

this initiative has been to improve links between Edinburgh and the Borders and to bring the Borders area into a viable commuting distance of Edinburgh. Road links in the area tend to be limited, with few if any dual carriageways and only low grade 'A' roads. The promoters of the project claim there will be £130m investment in new housing stock associated with the project (Waverley Rail Partnership, 2007). They also predict that the project will result in 1,800 new homes in the Borders and Midlothian as well as greatly enhancing the already proposed 2,200 new houses in Shawfair just to the south of Edinburgh. The Waverley line re-opening can be clearly viewed as a supply-led development, as this may lead to some population shift to the Borders and 'enable' some of the wealth being generated in Edinburgh to be spread to the Borders area. Indeed the project's promoters estimate that £285m will be injected into the Borders economy over thirty years and within 5 years 550 sustainable jobs created in the area.

3 LRT. The third project highlighted in this case study is the construction of a light rapid transit system in Edinburgh under the title of 'Trams for Edinburgh'. Like most cities in the UK the tram system was decommissioned in the 1950s, 1956 in the case of Edinburgh. The new LRT system is to run from the Airport on the west side of Edinburgh, through the city centre and down to Leith on the north east of the city. After much controversy over the real necessity of the scheme, the project was finally approved in March 2006 with construction beginning in late 2007 and an expected opening in 2011. The scheme's promoters, Transport Initiatives Edinburgh (tie), cite the forecasted increase of 30,000 new jobs in the city by 2015 as one of the main reasons for construction of the LRT, as well as the linking with several park and ride sites to the city centre (tie, 2007). Unlike the first two projects highlighted in this case, this last one is not concerned with connecting Edinburgh to its environs and improving accessibility between the two, but rather is a city-located scheme. The link between the two however should be clear, as if more individuals are to be 'pulled' in from outlying areas then they need to travel reasonably freely around the city. This last transport initiative can be primarily viewed as a demand led initiative, as whilst bus services are on the whole heavily used, with some exceptions they are not under pressure, whilst the transport infrastructure, namely the roads, are. It does however also have some strong aspects of supply led characteristics, as improving links into the city will result in increases in travel around the city.

Whilst the case highlights the problems facing Edinburgh and how transport links and projects can in part assist to overcome some of these issues, Edinburgh is far from unique. Other parts of the UK and continental Europe have the same kind of problems with transport developments being used to assist in overcoming many of these issues.

TRANSPORT AND SOCIETY

Whilst the author may be biased in their view of the importance of the study of economics, particularly the essential part it plays in understanding 'the world' as we know it today (!), we finish this chapter with a brief look at transport's role in the development of society. Whilst one may argue that the economy is the system by which society provides for its material needs and wants, society as such is more than just an economic system but operates at a higher level and includes governance issues, social interactions and individual motivations. Therefore, it is important to look at transport's role in the development of society as a whole.

Outlined below is a psychological theory that dates from 1943 known as Maslow's Hierarchy of Needs. This was named after the American psychologist Abraham Maslow, and was a fairly early attempt at explaining human motivational behaviour, in much the same vein as the equally controversial Sigmund Freud and his notion of the id.

Whilst not our main concern, the main thrust of the theory is that an individual is motivated by a series of needs which are in the form of a hierarchy. Thus an individual's prime motivational drivers move to the next level as each prior group of needs are satisfied. Hence the first group of needs are the basic essentials of life, thus in order to survive an individual needs to meet their hunger and thirst needs. These are primarily physiological rather than psychological needs, i.e. a must. Once these are met, then the individual may wish to secure such requirements into the future, hence this brings in to play issues of security and protection. Once these are secured and thus the individual is living in a reasonably 'safe and plentiful' environment, then they may want a bit more out of life, and thus move on to psychological needs or even sociological needs – the company of others, the love of others and a sense of belonging. This may then change from a simple membership role to a leading role, hence bringing in issues of self esteem, recognition and status. The very top of the hierarchy is 'self-actualisation', which is said to be about how people think about themselves; some debate however surrounds what is actually meant by the term 'self-actualisation'. A simple view would be the individual's achievement of their full potential.

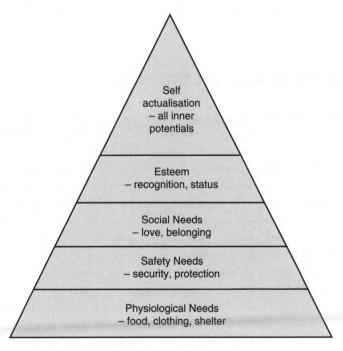

Figure 2.4   Maslow's Hierarchy of Needs

Whilst heavily criticised as unrealistic and far too simplistic at the individual level, Maslow's hierarchy of needs tends to have more credence at a societal level, and what may motivate societies, and consequently, societal development. Hence basic societies are primarily concerned with providing the essential requirements of food, water and shelter, with some even struggling to do this. Assuming these needs are met, however, then some sense of protection and society stability may be sought, and then once that is achieved the society may develop along a route which gives it a wider sphere of influence, hence allowing it to begin to influence factors beyond its borders. In the days of nations, this would be evidenced by higher levels of global influence through bodies such as the United Nations, the aforementioned World Trade Organisation and the G8, or even in more basic terms through sheer military might. This may then progress into a leading role in such bodies and then ultimately what is known as 'hegemony', or simply THE lead role. Britain for example is said to have had global hegemony from around the Industrial Revolution in the 18th century until World War II, after which it has been surpassed in terms of global influence by America.

Transport's role in societal development should now be clearer. In simple terms, the higher up the hierarchy then on the whole the higher the demand for transport, as generally these needs will require to be sought from further afield. Furthermore, increased and more sophisticated transport systems make meeting the needs of the lower levels of the hierarchy far easier. Hence for example transport allows specialisation and therefore individuals can concentrate and develop skills in a particular area (for the greater good), and all within the society need not be concerned with providing the basics of life. It also means that less time needs to be devoted to providing for such essentials and more time given over to nurturing and maintaining social relationships. Through such a course, the society as such is far more likely to achieve its full potential. Transport therefore not only has a vital role to play in economic development but also in the more general progress and development of society and to a certain extent will help to shape the degree to which it can reach its full potential.

CHAPTER SUMMARY AND REFLECTION

This chapter has examined the link between transport and economic development. Whilst not a direct topic of the book, it is important to realise that all transport services, whether passenger or freight, do not operate in a vacuum and hence transport 'problems' are not problems for their own sake but rather need to be viewed from an economic or social context. Thus we first examined the relationship between transport and economic development and found that economic development has been closely associated with increases in both passenger and freight transport. This highlighted that one of the major issues facing transport policy makers and planners today is what is known as the 'decoupling' of economic growth from transport, as for a number of reasons highlighted in the text such increases in transport are simply unsustainable. Overcoming this problem however is dependent upon understanding the basic relationship between the two; thus does transport act as a supply-led determinant (i.e. leads to economic development), or is transport a demand-led factor (i.e. needs a basic demand)? Finally in the chapter we briefly examined the role of transport as part of a more general societal development, and saw that generally higher levels of society development could be associated with the provision of more transport and importantly more efficient forms of transport. In other words, transport is important.

CHAPTER EXERCISES

Exercise 2.1 Supply and demand led transport initiatives

a) Listed below are nine major transport projects from the very old to the very new and even those that are currently still at the planning stage. Whilst it is difficult to clearly define such projects as either demand led or supply led, some will display more characteristics of the former whilst others will be more akin to the latter. In this exercise you are asked to simply divide these into these two categories and to consider the reasons why you came to that particular view. Note that in many cases you do not need to know the specifics regarding the particular transport project to come to an educated guess.

- CrossRail – this project is to build two new railway connections under central London. CrossRail 1, approved in 2007, will run east–west and is due to open in 2017. It will complement Thameslink services, which commenced north–south rail services through the re-opened Snow Hill tunnel in 1989.
- The Channel Tunnel that was opened in 1995 and links Britain to France
- The opening of the M6 Toll motorway around Birmingham in December 2003, thus effectively providing a Birmingham by-pass and considerably reducing through journey times.
- The Great Belt Link, opened in 1995 between the island of Zeeland and (in effect) the rest of Denmark, and providing a road and rail link.
- The Skye Bridge – this linked mainland Scotland to the island of Skye and was opened in 1995, originally with a highly controversial toll (i.e. only slightly cheaper than the former ferry fare) that was eventually abolished at the end of 2004.
- The Golden Gate Bridge across the opening of San Francisco Bay, completed in 1937, which provided the first fixed link northwards out of San Francisco.
- The opening of phase one of the high-speed train line (the TGV Est) from Paris to the west of Nancy in June 2007. The line is also served by Germany's Inter City Express (ICE) high-speed trains. Phase two, which will take the line all the way to Strasbourg near the German border, will not be completed until around 2014. TGV Est is sometimes referred to TGV EstEuropéen.
- The construction of a container terminal at the port of Mundra on the Gujarat coast in North West India. This will be the port's first container terminal.
- The Jubilee line extension, opened in 1999, which connected the London Underground system to then developing Docklands area in London.

b) From the examples listed, what overall conclusions can you draw regarding supply led and demand led transport initiatives, particularly the balance between the two?

c) In the case of the Skye Bridge, did the imposition of a high toll make a difference as to which effect was stronger?

Exercise 2.2 Transport and your local economy

a) Think of your own local business environment, and the main transport initiatives or projects that have been undertaken over the last 50 years. As a side note, you do not need to be over 50 to do this exercise(!),simply consider all projects undertaken in what could be considered to be the modern era. These should not be too difficult to identify. Think of the extent to which these are demand or supply led initiatives, firstly at the (rough) time of construction and secondly in the present day. As an example, the Forth Road Bridge cited in the above case study, would have been mainly supply led at the time of construction in 1964 in order to create a more direct link from Edinburgh to the north. Now, however, the bridge would undoubtedly be demand led due to the resulting increased commuter belt zone that its construction created in the longer term.

b) Probably a valid criticism of transport planning is that too much onus is given to the potential impact of grand schemes and not enough attention paid to smaller initiatives. In this part of the exercise, therefore, you should consider the role played by individual transport modes, both in terms of public/private and passenger/freight, to the functioning of your own local economy/ wider society. You should consider the role played by each mode and the 'function(s)' that it fulfils with regard to economic activity and society interaction. How do you see these roles or functions changing over the next 20 years?

c) Re-visit part (b), except in this case draw comparisons with another area or city that is familiar to you. Do you come to any different conclusions regarding the functions of particular modes of transport? If so, why so, if not, why not?

Chapter 3

The market for transport services

Learning Outcomes:

In the course of this chapter, you will learn:

- The law of demand and the main factors that impact upon the general demand for transport services as well as individual transport modes
- The theory of supply and the main factors that impact upon the supply of transport services
- The market and economic principles that underpin the provision of transport services and ensure that such services are provided to those that are willing and able to pay the market price
- The important role of the price mechanism in balancing the needs of the users and providers of transport services
- That even where transport markets are closely controlled and regulated by public authorities, underlying economic principles still apply.

INTRODUCTION

We have already seen that within modern society, all individuals need to use transport services in order to access a range of work and leisure activities that lie out with the immediate vicinity of the home. This chapter will take a closer look at the main factors that impact upon the demand and supply of these services. It will consider the economic principles that affect both sides of the market; the demand side in the case of consumers and the supply side in the case of suppliers. The chapter seeks to put across the basic ideas of the workings of the market, and hence assumes a completely free market in the provision of transport services. In the analysis of transport markets, such an understanding is not only important in its own right, but is also required as a basis for understanding government policy, as much of this policy is enacted through intervention in transport markets. Furthermore, many of the problems associated with the provision of transport services and facilities are because the market as such does not work, and hence we need to consider first how it 'should' work before going on to consider in subsequent chapters why that is not always the case and the possible solutions that may be available.

We begin first however with a simple definition of a 'market' in order to clarify what is meant by this key concept. In simple terms, a market is a meeting place for buying and selling. A simple illustration is the traditional market place in towns which normally consists of a large number of self-assembled stalls selling a variety of goods. Car boot sales would be a further illustration or eBay where online buyers bid for various goods. This last example illustrates that a market does not have to be a physical location. In a transport context a market is where the consumers of transport services are brought together with the provider of such services. In some cases, therefore, this market is quite rigidly defined, although it is difficult to consider a bus as an actual market-place! In other instances, however, the 'marketplace' is less well defined, as it may not be an actual physical location and the market as such can be made up of a high number of inter-related activities that contribute towards the final transport service. This can involve a large number of different bodies, both public and private, all of which contribute different aspects to the activity. Private motoring would be a good example of such an activity, where generally the infrastructure, i.e. the roads and related equipment, are supplied by government bodies, the vehicles, fuel and related equipment by private companies for profit, and finally the skills required to use such facilities by the actual consumers themselves.

In the analysis of transport or indeed all markets, the assumption of *ceteris paribus* is made, which is the original Latin phrase meaning 'all else remains equal'. Thus for example when examining the effect of a change in the price of petrol on private car usage, it is assumed that this is the only change impacting upon the demand for private car usage at that time. Thus other factors, such as the knock-on effect this will have upon public transport markets, are ignored. This allows focus to be given to the issue being considered, otherwise there is a danger that the whole thing could become a mess of interconnected loops and kickbacks in which the original issue becomes completely lost. Thus in the following text, whilst not specified, the underlying assumption is of *ceteris paribus*.

THE LAW OF DEMAND

The demand for a good is the 'number of units per unit of time that consumers purchase at any given price'. Notice therefore that demand relates to actual purchases, and not wants or 'demands' as such. Demand is a result of consumers expressing their own preferences between goods at the relative prices that they face, taking into account all money that they have available to them. The term 'demand' may be used in different contexts to describe an individual's preferences, the preferences of a particular market segment or the whole market.

In examining the demand for transport services, we start with the very basic assumption that the decision as to whether to travel or not is based solely upon the price of that journey. Common sense would therefore clearly suggest that as the price of transport services rises, the quantity demanded will fall. In simple terms, less people will travel. For a better understanding as to why this may be the case, however, we need to supplement common sense with something that can be rationalised. The basic argument lies in the idea of the opportunity cost of any (economic) decision. As the price of transport rises, individuals will then have to weigh up the benefits of continuing to travel against all other goods and services they purchase or could purchase. This is because the increased price or fare will mean they have less of their income remaining to spend on those other goods and services. Economic rationality would state that as all individuals have a limited income, they will seek to maximise the benefit obtained from that income. This is termed utility (satisfaction) maximisation. Should the price of any (including transport) of the goods and services that an individual consumes change, this would cause them to re-evaluate the basket of goods and services that they currently purchase to determine if there would be another 'mix' that would better meet their wants and needs. Consumers are therefore said to seek to maximise their utility. Following that logic, therefore, if the price of a particular mode of transport was to rise we would expect demand to fall as individuals switch to alternative modes or do something else with their income that gives them greater satisfaction.

Using the assumption of consumer utility maximisation, the basic price/quantity relationship can be graphed for transport services. This is known as the Demand Curve, which is shown in both a theoretical and a simplified form in Figure 3.1.

Price is graphed on the vertical axis and quantity demanded on the horizontal, thus the demand curve for transport services slopes downwards from left to right. Note however on the diagram on the left (the theoretical shape) that as price falls increasingly larger quantities are purchased. This is because at very high prices, small price reductions will have little impact on the quantity demanded as most still cannot afford to buy it. As the price falls, however, the good or service is becoming increasingly accessible to more potential consumers, hence at the bottom end price changes have far larger impacts on the quantity demand. On the right is drawn a simplified version of the demand curve, where the demand 'curve' is shown as a simple straight line. Except in special cases, this is the representation that will be used in the rest of this text; however, always remember that the demand curve is in fact curved or non-linear!

The demand curve gives the basic price/quantity demanded relationship; however, the assumption that quantity demanded is only dependent upon the price is far too restrictive for any meaningful analysis of transport markets. Relaxation of that underlying assumption allows other determinants of demand to be introduced into the analysis. Importantly, however, all factors

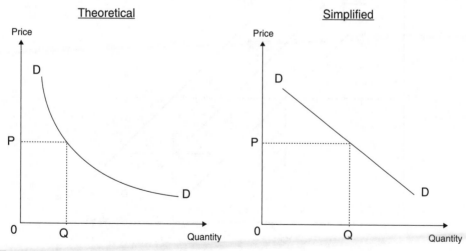

Figure 3.1 Basic relationship between the price and the quantity demanded for transport services (theoretical and simplified)

identified impact upon the basic price/quantity relationship, i.e. the demand curve. We first examine the effect of changing incomes.

Income

If everything else remained equal, a general increase in incomes would enable more people to afford the use of transport services and hence increase demand. A decrease in incomes on the other hand would be expected to have the opposite effect. Such changes would be shown by a shift of the demand curve, to the right in the case of an increase in income and to the left in the case of a decrease. Both of these cases are shown in Figure 3.2.

In Figure 3.2 before any changes in income occur, the market demand curve is shown by the line labelled D. Hence at price P the quantity demanded is given by Q. If incomes rise, more transport services would be demanded at each and every price. This would be shown by a shift in the demand curve to the right and labelled D_{inc}. Hence at price P, demand increases to Q_{inc}. If on the other hand incomes were to fall, this would be illustrated by a shift in the demand curve to the left and labelled D_{dec}. Thus at price P, demand would fall to Q_{dec}.

Whilst increases in income will cause an overall increase in the demand for transport services, rising incomes may not be expected to have a uniform impact across all transport modes. Indeed the demand for some may actually be expected to fall. Whereas the demand for private transport, rail services, freight services and air services for example may all be expected to rise with an increase in income, the demand for bus services may be expected to fall. This is because some individuals, with an increased income, will 'trade up' to a perceived better quality of transport –

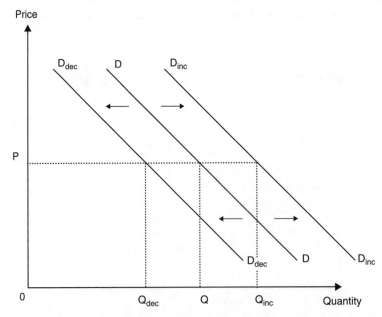

Figure 3.2 *Change in the conditions of demand for transport services shown by a shift in the demand curve*

some for example will buy a car and hence no longer need or use public transport. This example allows a distinction to be drawn between what are referred to as 'normal' and 'inferior' goods. A normal good is where demand increases with increases in income, whilst an inferior good is one that falls with increases in income. All of the following analysis, except where otherwise stated, concerns normal goods.

In practice, changes in income have had a major impact on the demand for transport services, and the full extent of this is illustrated later in Case study 3.1.

The price of other goods and services

There are two categories of other goods and services that may impact upon the basic price/ quantity relationship: substitute and complementary goods. Substitute goods can either be inter modal, e.g. the bus verses the train, the car verses the bus and so on, or intra modal, such as the red bus versus the blue bus, the no frills 'low cost' airline versus the traditional airline. Substitute transport services therefore are those that can be used to fulfil the same basic transport need. In some cases different services may fit that basic need almost as well, such as in the previous example of the red bus versus the blue bus service. In other cases, however, although the same basic need is met the competing service may not do the purpose as well, such as in the case of the no frills versus the traditional airline. Thus the closeness of the substitute goods will determine the actual size of the impact on the market. To take as an example the demand for bus services, a rise in the price of rail travel will cause the demand curve for bus services to shift to the right, i.e. an increase in demand. This is because rail travel now represents less value for money, and as consumers seek to maximise utility, some will switch to alternative modes such as the bus. Not all will switch, however, because in those areas where rail travel provides the only viable means of transport there will be little alternative but to pay the increased rail fare. Overall, however, demand for bus services will increase. A decrease in the price of rail services on the other hand will cause some consumers to switch from the bus to the train, hence the demand curve would shift to the left (a decrease in demand). Note again that only those that have that alternative available to them, i.e. where the train is a close substitute, can make such a switch. Note also that although in this example the price of rail has decreased, the fare may still be more expensive than the bus. Despite this higher fare, some may switch because they would feel that rail is a higher quality service and now the decrease in the price differential between the two is of such a level that it is worthwhile to 'trade up'.

Complementary goods on the other hand are goods or services that are consumed at the same time. The price of petrol, for example, may be expected to impact upon the use of the car, as fuel costs are one of the major determinants of private motoring. If for example the price of petrol was to increase, this would cause a shift of the demand curve for private motoring to the left. This is because some consumers will be more conservative with their car usage whilst others may take their car off the road or sell it and use public transport. It is not always clear however what actually constitutes a complementary good. For example, before rail freight transport can be used a company would need to install a railway siding to its premises; hence rail freight and railway sidings are actually complementary goods. Furthermore, there may be a large number of separate markets that are complementary to each other. Thus whilst the price of petrol may well impact on the use of the car, it is not the only good or service required to (legally) use the car. Thus the price of car insurance, vehicle excise duty, vehicle servicing and so on will all impact on the level of private motoring. The point to stress with complementary goods is the idea of the overall cost of consumption, and that a change in the price of any component will impact upon all other components that are consumed when undertaking a certain activity, in this case, private motoring.

Fashions or trends

At first it may seem odd to include an item such as fashions or trends as a determinant of the demand for transport services – when was transport ever fashionable or trendy? For every good and service, however, not just those associated with the fashion related or image conscious industries, fashions or trends may turn in favour or against the item over time. A move towards the good or service will cause an increase in demand and shift the demand curve to the right, whilst a move away will have the opposite effect. Cigarettes provide a very good example, with old movies from the 40s and 50s highlighting that smoking was once highly fashionable, whilst today to smoke is to almost be a social outcast. Transport is no different, and over time this determinant has had a massive impact upon transport markets. Over the last thirty or so years, for example, there has been a big swing towards more fuel-efficient vehicles and less environmental harmful fuels, e.g. unleaded petrol.

Unlike the first three determinants of demand already outlined, however, it is difficult to make generalisations about fashions and trends. In simple terms, each case needs to be treated on its own merits. A rise in environmental awareness, for example, may cause a decrease in demand for transport services or a switch to less environmentally harmful modes of transport, e.g. from private to public transport. More directly, the recent trend away from bike geek to bike chic has resulted in increased use of the bike, particularly those of a vintage nature, as a mode of transport.

Fashions and trends can also be manipulated through various measures, with the most commonly used being advertising. Through advertising consumer awareness of the good or service can be raised and the positive attributes associated with consumption reinforced. The whole point of advertising is to change or reinforce consumer demand. Other measures exist, however, such as more directly raising awareness by education or through research. It is knowledge of the harmful effects of smoking for example that have brought about the aforementioned radical change in smoking habits. As mentioned, however, each case needs to be treated on its own, as similar knowledge of the harmful effects of vehicle emissions, whilst having had some impact, has not produced the same radical change in consumer behaviour.

Expectations of future price rises

With the only possible exception of hangovers, how people behave today will be affected by their expectations of what will happen tomorrow. The demand for transport services is no different. Hence how the price of transport services will change in the future will affect what is purchased today. For example, an individual may delay purchasing a motor vehicle if the situation regarding the future price of oil is unknown. On the other hand, a daily commuter may purchase a one-year season ticket if fares are expected to rise in the foreseeable future. Thus individuals may pull forward purchases where prices are expected to rise in the future, thereby increasing demand, whilst they will delay purchases where prices are expected to fall in the future, hence decreasing demand.

Other factors specifically relating to the demand for transport

The five basic factors outlined above, the price of the good, income, the price of other goods and services, fashions or trends and future price expectations will impact upon the demand for any good and service. This applies to everything from a lowly tin of beans through to a luxury yacht moored at Monte Carlo. There exists however a further three factors that need to be considered when examining the demand for transport services.

Demand for transport is a derived demand

Modern life, as already outlined, is structured around accessing goods and services that are outside of the home and require some form of transport in order to be obtained. It follows therefore that an individual's demand for transport is instigated through their demand for something else. Hence the need to work in order to earn an income generates a demand for transport. Demand for transport is therefore said to be a derived demand. Few individuals demand transport services purely for their own merit. Even those with flashy cars only have a flashy car for some other purpose, i.e. to impress others! There are always exceptions to the rule, however, such as 'Mad Hamish' who spent his time happily travelling around the 9 miles of the Cathcart Circle line on the south side of Glasgow. Fortunately, such exceptions tend to be very rare.

Demand for transport is time specific

In simple terms, when transport services are demanded they are demanded NOW. Unlike say a chocolate bar that can be purchased and consumed later, on the whole the demand for transport is required at an exact, or near exact, time. Another way of putting this is that the demand for transport has a very short expiry date, and due to the derived nature of demand, once that expiry date has passed then the need to make that particular journey will almost certainly no longer exist. Even where the ticket is purchased in advance, the actual journey that is purchased is made at a fairly specific time period in the future. Demand for transport is therefore time specific.

Demand for transport follows peaks and troughs

Hard to believe, but the demand for most goods and services follows some kind of cyclical pattern, whether that be throughout the year, throughout the month, week or day. For example, the demand for the aforementioned chocolate bar will be higher in the winter than in the summer and will also vary at certain points over the day. With transport services, however, this particular issue is a major factor and especially acute. Most if not all will be familiar with the terms 'the morning rush hour' and 'the evening rush hour', and it is this very factor that these relate to. Basically a substantially higher number of people need to travel (because demand is derived and time specific) to and from work between certain hours of the day. This has a significant impact upon the way in which transport services are provided and indeed the whole 'economics' of transport operations.

In order to underpin some of these ideas, we end the examination of the determinants of demand with a practical look at the effect of income on the demand for transport services in Case study 3.1.

Case study 3.1 Determinants of the demand for transport services – a practically based discussion on the effect of income on demand

As outlined above, income is a major determinant of the demand for transport services. This is almost exclusively due to the derived nature of demand. It could be strongly argued that the demand for transport is derived from a combination of the pursuit of income earning opportunities – namely financial profit and/or employment – and in the subsequent spending on essentials and leisure pursuits of that hard earned income. As already seen in Chapter 2, there is a close relationship between the demand for both passenger and freight transport and national income as represented by Gross Domestic Product (GDP). Again as we saw, as economic activity increases this increased trade creates a demand for the transport of goods and services from one location to another, thus creating increased demand for freight transport. Passenger travel however also increases for a number of reasons. Firstly, increased trade creates a need for more individuals to travel in the course of business. Secondly, higher incomes affect labour markets and will almost certainly result in increased commuting as individuals travel further in order to access higher paid jobs. Finally, higher incomes require more spending and this in turn requires more transport. The relationship between GDP and passenger transport has already been outlined in Chapter 2; however, here we examine this relationship in more depth in order to identify some of the wider impacts on transport demand of increasing incomes.

Figure 3.3 below shows two trends, one for GDP since 1980 and one for total passenger kilometres (measured in billions) since 1980. GDP is measured in terms of constant prices (i.e. adjusted for changes in inflation) and both variables are specified as index numbers (with

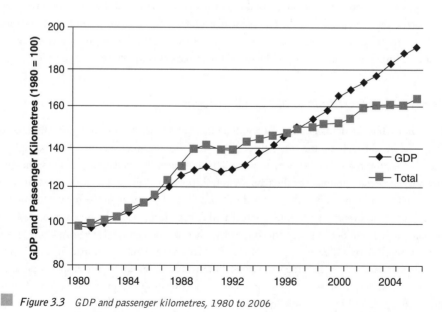

Figure 3.3 GDP and passenger kilometres, 1980 to 2006

Source: Compiled from DfT Statistics (DfT 2007)

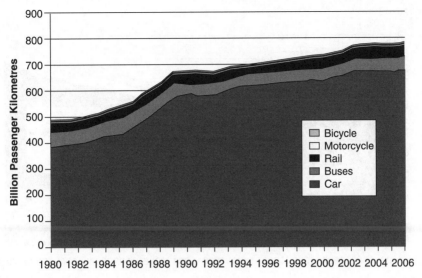

Figure 3.4 *Passenger kilometres modal split, 1980 to 2006*

Source: Compiled from DfT Statistics (DfT 2007)

1980 = 100) to show the overall trends over the last twenty-five years. The figure shows a very clear association between the two, and also highlights the impact of the previously mentioned Lawson Boom of the mid to late 1980s. What is interesting is that until that period changes in national income were matched almost exactly by the same percentage changes in billion passenger kilometres. Since the early 1990s, however, whilst the two are still closely related, increases in GDP have been matched with smaller increases in passenger kilometres. For example, over the whole twenty-six-year period GDP rose on average by 2.4 per cent per year and passenger kilometres by an average of 1.8 per cent per year. Since 1992, however, a 1 per cent change in GDP has been associated with a 0.4 per cent change in passenger kilometres. Whilst this does not suggest the two are now completely de-coupled, it does suggest that the effects of increases in income are now far less direct, and this may well be the result of considerably improved communications over the period. It does nevertheless underline that transport services clearly constitute a normal economic good, although it should be noted that in this case the relationship between income and transport demand is (still) particularly strong.

Figure 3.4 above breaks down the total passenger kilometre figures into five different modes of transport – car, bus, rail, motorcycle and bicycle. What this clearly shows is that most, if not all, of this growth in passenger kilometres has been due to a significant increase in car usage. Rising incomes therefore would appear to have had little impact upon all other modes of transport apart from the car. This can be examined further by breaking down the modal split for non-car-based modes of transport, as is done in Figure 3.5.

This shows a clearer picture for non-car-based modes of transport and indicates that since 1980 use of the bus has decreased, use of the train has increased and the other two modes have shown reasonably (low) constant values over the period. This would confirm the bus as an inferior good and that with rising incomes many individuals have, over time, 'switched' from the

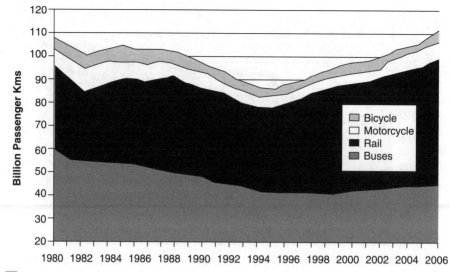

Figure 3.5   *Modal splits, non car modes of transport, 1980–2006*

Source: Compiled from DfT Statistics (DfT 2007)

bus to the car and the train. Bus usage however appears to have bottomed out from around 1998 onwards, which almost exclusively relates to increased use in London counteracting continued decline elsewhere in the country. For 2006, however, there was also a small overall increase in bus usage in other parts of the country as well.

Whilst rising incomes therefore have changed the conditions of demand away from the bus, some other determinant, particularly in the case of London, has in more recent years produced a shift back towards this mode of transport. This particular period has seen the introduction of many bus priority measures on most of the main corridors in all major UK cities and increased investment from bus operators. With this increase in the quality of the service provided, the travelling experience of bus users has significantly improved and resulted in attitudes that are more favourable towards bus use. At the same time usage of the car, particularly at certain times during the day, has become far more problematic. Therefore tastes or 'fashions' in bus usage have improved, whilst the general cost of the car, i.e. one that includes the time element, has increased.

What this example shows is the impact of the determinants of demand on market conditions and that in many cases these operate over a protracted period of time, underlining that nothing remains constant over time. Incomes may have increased allowing more individuals access to private transport, but this has brought its own problems in the form of increased traffic conges-tion. This in turn has impacted back upon transport markets and particularly the determinants of demand for other transport modes.

The determinants outlined in this section are the main factors that affect the demand for transport services. This however is only half of the market; that relating to the consumers of such services. The other half relates to the providers of these services, whose market actions are explained by the theory of supply.

THE THEORY OF SUPPLY

As most individuals have a basic need to travel from one location to another, in a market based economy this presents an opportunity for other individuals to profit from that basic need. Trade is never a zero sum game, hence both parties should benefit otherwise the trade would never take place. In this example the first individual benefits by getting to where they want to go, whilst the second benefits from a financial reward for transporting that person to that location. Where a basic need exists, therefore, there will always be individuals willing to provide a good or service to meet that need at a given price. Central to any such trade is the price mechanism, as this allows the exchange to take place. Consequently when examining the theory of supply we begin with the same basic assumption that, in this case, the level of transport services provided to the market is only dependent upon the price of the service. As before, this raises the question of the relationship between price and the quantity supplied.

Again common sense would suggest that as the price rises the quantity supplied to the market will increase. The basic rationale as to why this would be the case once more revolves around the idea of opportunity cost. As the price of any mode of transport rises, producers weigh up the benefits of supplying to that particular market against all other markets they could operate in. This is akin to the idea of the venture capitalist seeking the maximum return for their capital and who is not particularly bothered where those funds are actually invested. Consistent with such a view, the underlying assumption used to explain producers' behaviour is that they seek to maximise profits. If prices are (relatively) low within a given market, few (if any) producers will be able to make a profit in that market as revenues may not cover costs. As the price rises, however, this represents better profit opportunities for producers and the quantity supplied would increase. This is because at higher prices the profits to be made in a given industry are higher than the next best alternative, i.e. the opportunity cost. Again if the price was to change then this may cause producers to re-evaluate their position, voluntarily or otherwise. As an example, price cuts may force certain operators out of business.

Assuming that producers seek to maximise profits, therefore, the basic price/quantity relationship can be outlined. This is known as the Supply Curve and is shown in Figure 3.6, again as theoretical and simplified versions.

Figure 3.6 shows that the supply curve for transport services slopes upwards from left to right, hence more is supplied at higher prices. On the theoretical diagram, while the supply curve slopes upwards, ever higher prices will produce smaller changes in the quantity supplied. This is due to the scarcity of resources available to produce a given good or service, in which it becomes physically much harder to find the resources required to produce ever increasing quantities. This can only be done therefore if a considerably higher price is gained from production of the good or service. In fact, there is a finite maximum value at which point the supply curve becomes vertical. This would occur at the unlikely point where all resources are used in the production of a single

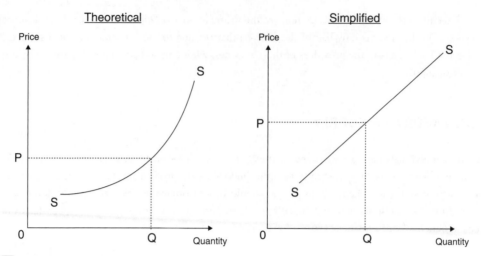

Figure 3.6 *Basic relationship between the price and the quantity supplied for transport services (theoretical and simplified)*

good or service, hence in simple terms as all resources are already employed in the production process none remain to produce any increases.

This basic supply curve is shown on the right in a simplified form in which the curve is drawn as a straight line, and again this is the representation that will be used in the rest of the text. As above however you should remember that like the demand curve, the supply curve is curved!

Having established the basic relationship between price and the quantity supplied, other factors can now be introduced into the analysis to give a more complete picture of the conditions of supply. Again all factors identified will impact upon the basic price/quantity relationship, i.e. the supply curve, and a change in any of these factors will constitute a change in the conditions of supply.

The cost of production

Cost is a large determinant of the supply of transport services. Production costs are one half of the profit equation (profit = revenue − cost), and hence a change in the cost of transport operations will impact upon profits and thus the supply of services to the market. In simple terms, an increase in costs will reduce the level supplied. As all operators are assumed to be profit maximisers, an increase in costs reduces profits and hence some, but not all, operators will leave the market to seek better profit opportunities elsewhere. Others will be driven out of business as revenues fail to cover costs. Conversely, a reduction in costs will bring about an increase in supply. Existing suppliers/operators will supply more to the market (as all else being equal this will increase profits) and new entrants will enter the market as profit opportunities are now higher than before.

A change in costs therefore will impact upon the basic price/quantity supplied relationship. An increase in costs is shown by a shift in the supply curve to the left, whilst a reduction in costs is shown by a shift in the supply curve to the right. Both situations are outlined in Figure 3.7.

In Figure 3.7, prior to any change in costs, the market supply curve is shown by the line labelled

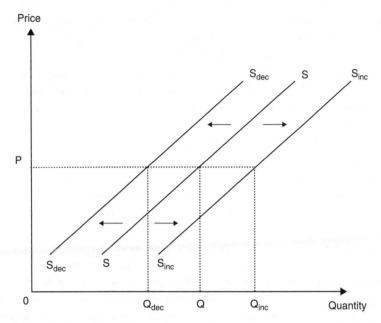

Figure 3.7 *Change in the conditions of supply for transport services shown by a shift in the supply curve*

S. At price P, the quantity supplied is given by Q. If costs increase, less transport services would be supplied at each and every price. This would be illustrated by a shift in the supply curve to the left to S_{dec}. Thus at price P, the quantity supplied would fall to Q_{dec}. Conversely, if costs were to fall this would be shown by a shift in the supply curve to the right. At price P, supply would increase to Q_{inc}. A practical illustration of the effect costs have had on the provision (supply) of transport services is given later in the chapter in Case study 3.2, which examines the consequences of changing costs on the supply of British bus services.

Government policy

As already seen in Chapter 1, governments intervene in transport markets to 'guide' the market to meeting its policy objectives. Government policy as such, particularly in public transport markets, has a very large impact on the supply of transport services. For instance, without state intervention the provision of rail services throughout Europe would be considerably diminished – the Scottish rail network for example would probably only consist of a single 60 kilometre line between Glasgow and Edinburgh rather than the 4,000 kilometres of lines that currently exist. For the whole of Britain, the notorious Beeching in his report of 1965 (BRB, 1965) identified only 11,250 kilometres of railway for 'development' in order to make the railways profitable by 1980. Switzerland is probably an even more extreme case, where outside of the main intercity routes all of the branch lines and the multiplicity of locally owned and controlled railways are very large loss makers.

At the most basic level government policy can be implemented through one of three general policy tools. Firstly by direct provision, where the state takes on the full responsibility for providing transport services through public ownership of the means of production. A second approach is where services may be provided by private sector companies however the state 'steers' the market to its desired objectives through the imposition of taxes and the provision of state subsidies. The third and final general policy tool is through regulatory/legislative measures, where the state directly commands or prevents by law certain actions in order to achieve policy aims. All three forms of measures can impact directly upon the supply of transport services. Thus for example a 'change' to direct provision, i.e. nationalisation, may result in an increase in supply, as transport services are no longer provided for profit but rather in the public interest. With regard to taxes and subsidies, the effects of these policy tools on supply are very similar to the impact of the costs of production, and are often listed as a sub-category of costs. An increase in a tax on a good or service will decrease supply, as the cost of providing such services would rise. For example an increase in fuel duty would decrease the supply of road haulage as this will directly increase the overall cost of haulage operations. The payment or increase in a subsidy on the other hand would result in an increase in the supply of that good or service. This is because subsidies to operators have the effect of off-setting production costs. Thus the payment of a subsidy to rail freight operators would result in the increase in the supply of rail freight services. The effects on supply of regulatory or legislative actions on the other hand are very difficult to generalise, as some may limit market supply whilst others increase it. A night ban on lorries for example would reduce the supply of road haulage, whilst an increase in legal maximum vehicle weights would increase it. This whole issue of the impact and implementation of government policy on both the supply and demand sides of transport markets is a key area, and hence is developed further in Chapters 10 and 11.

The price of other goods and services that can be produced using the same factors of production

Given that producers are assumed to profit maximise, then if the price of any good or service that could be produced using the same factors of production was to rise, producers are likely to switch production to that particular market. This would cause a reduction in the level of supply at each and every price for the current good or service. Within transport markets opportunities for such changes are limited – a bus and a bus driver can only produce bus services. There may however be some movement between different transport market segments. For example, a rise in the price of scheduled air fares may cause a decrease in the supply of chartered services. This is because the resources required to meet the higher volume of demand for scheduled services are virtually the same and, in the short run at least, have to be found from somewhere else.

The price of goods in joint supply

In simple English this means the price of goods that are produced at the same time and best illustrated by an example from aviation. The last twenty years or so have seen a massive increase in the level of air freight services. The reason for this is due to the increase in passenger travel, as most air freight, around 60 per cent, goes via the cargo hold of passenger aircraft. Hence rising passenger demand has been met by large increases in the supply of passenger planes, and with that increase has come more cargo holds within which freight can be carried. Consequently, the increase in the available supply of passenger aircraft has automatically resulted in the increase of air freight capacity as these two products are goods in joint supply.

Goods in joint supply also relates to the production of by-products that are created as a result of production of the primary product. As firms are profit-maximisers they will attempt to sell any such by-product for which there exists a market. All by-products should not be considered as pure waste, as those that can be sold should be thought of in more lateral terms as goods in joints supply. A good example is bus shelters. An increase in the production of bus shelters would result in the by-product of more advertising space that can be sold to potential advertisers. This is why the maintenance costs of bus shelters in many major cities are paid for by the advertising space sold.

Natural shocks

Natural shocks simply relate to natural events and disasters such as the weather, flood, drought, pests etc, or abnormal circumstances arising from war, fire, political events etc. The oil crisis in the mid-1970s, for example, when the price of oil quadrupled in the space of six months, was originally sparked off by the Yom Kippur Israeli–Egyptian war that affected world supplies of crude oil. As regards the effect of natural shocks on supply, each case should be considered on its own merits. An outbreak of war, for example, will lead to an increase in the supply of armaments, whilst a drought will considerably reduce the supply of agricultural produce.

Aims of the producer

Highly relevant to the supply of transport services to the market are the aims of the producer. Although the underlying assumption is that profit maximisation drives producers' market actions, this may be considered to be a long-term aim that may be pursued in the short term in a number of different ways. A switch in the emphasis of the aims of producers may result in a change in the level of supply to the market. If for example a bus operator decided that in order to maximise profits in the long run it needed to expand its market share in the present, this would almost certainly lead to an increase in supply at each and every price. This is because the operator would have to attempt to enter new markets at a competitive level. Such behaviour would be consistent with the aim of sales maximisation where lower profitability levels are accepted in the present in order to expand market share in the future. There are other situations where the aim of sales maximisation is entirely consistent with the aim of profit maximisation. Passenger railway companies, for example, are said to sales maximise (Cowie, 2002), because the cost of carrying an extra passenger on a train is extremely small. Consequently, any revenue gained comes at a very small additional cost. Thus the aim of the train operator is to attempt to fill the available capacity with revenue-paying customers, and hence if priced correctly this should result in full trains and maximised profits.

After government policy, the cost of production has probably been the next largest determinant on the level of supply of transport services. This is practically illustrated in Case study 3.2, which looks at the cost of bus operations in Britain and the impact that this has had on the supply of bus services.

Case study 3.2 The British bus industry – a practical illustration of the impact of costs on the supply of services to the market

Table 3.1 and Figure 3.8 illustrate the cost per vehicle kilometre in constant 2005/06 prices as calculated by the Department for Transport (2007). They also show the level of vehicle kilometres operated on staged bus services for each year. These are both shown as three point moving averages to smooth out any yearly 'blips'.

Table 3.1 Annual bus vehicle kilometres and the cost per bus kilometre, 1995/96 to 2005/06

Year	Vehicle km (millions)	Cost per km (pence)
1995–96	2639	117
1996–97	2632	113
1997–98	2633	111
1998–99	2647	110
1999–00	2655	112
2000–01	2648	115
2001–02	2631	119
2002–03	2610	122
2003–04	2597	124
2004–05	2581	128
2005–06	2606	131

Source: Adapted from Department for Transport (2007)

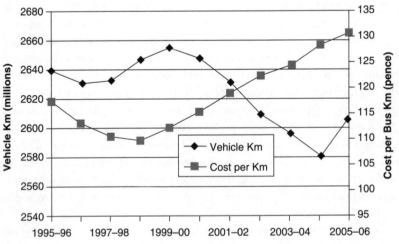

Figure 3.8 Annual bus vehicle kilometres and the cost per bus kilometre, 1995/96 to 2005/06

Source: Adapted from Department for Transport (2007)

Figure 3.8 opposite shows that as costs have increased, vehicle kilometres supplied to the market have fallen. Outside of the first three years shown, these two variables have moved in opposite directions. We could therefore state that over the period 1995 to 1999 the supply curve for bus services continually moved to the right (an increase in supply) as costs in the industry were falling. This reduction in costs 'allowed' more services to be provided at the prevailing market prices. From 2000 onwards, however, costs in the industry have risen significantly. This would be consistent with a shift in the supply curve to the left, which would suggest that supply at prevailing market prices would decrease. This is exactly what the vehicle kilometre trend shows, with an increase to 1999 and then a decrease between 2000 and 2005.

The more observant will notice that the scales on the above graph paint an overly pessimistic picture with regard to the decrease in the level of vehicle kilometres supplied to the market. Whilst costs rose by over 14 per cent in the last five years, bus kilometres, despite what the graph may suggest, only fell by just over 1.5 per cent. At this point however all that is important is that there is a clear relationship between the two and that costs impact upon supply to the market. The size of that impact however is a different issue and will be examined in subsequent chapters. Note also that this only examines one dynamic in the market, the effect of changing costs on supply. Other factors were present in the bus market over this period of time, most notably decreasing demand, which not only will have had a direct impact upon the level of supply but also on the quality of that supply. The quality of bus services in 2005/06 was much improved from that of 1995/6, where in some towns and cities services were basic to say the least. In order to attract new bus users and keep the ones that they have, bus companies have been increasingly required to provide a higher quality product (Cowie, 2008), thus impacting both on costs and the quantity supplied.

THE MARKET FOR TRANSPORT SERVICES

So far we have examined the demand and supply of transport services as two distinctly different concepts. They are however simply the two different sides of the transport market, that of buyers (demand) and sellers (supply). These two concepts can be brought together in order to determine the market for transport services. As both the demand and supply curves use the same labelled axes, price and quantity, they can simply be drawn on the same graph. This is shown in Figure 3.9.

As before, demand is shown by the line labelled D and supply by the line labelled S. These two lines intersect and this intersection produces a market price of P_e with the quantity traded shown by Q_e. This is known as the equilibrium price and quantity, i.e. the point at which the market is in balance. It is worthwhile however to consider why P_e is the market clearing price. As it stands, this is simply the case because that is how these lines have been drawn. Consider the example shown in Figure 3.10.

This is the same diagram of the market as before, except in order to help focus thoughts a second price, P_{XS}, has been added. This price is above the market clearing price of P_e, and would result in an imbalance in the quantity supplied, shown by Q_S, and the quantity demanded, shown by Q_D. Such a situation would be known as excess supply, as the quantity supplied exceeds the

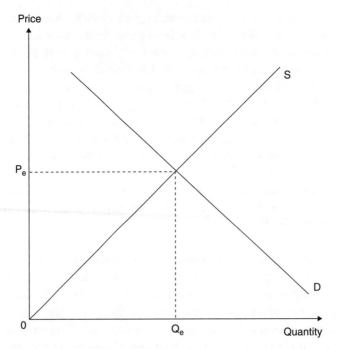

Figure 3.9 *The relationship between supply and demand for transport services*

quantity demanded. As not all that is being produced is being consumed, there would either be a high degree of wastage or stocks of finished goods would pile up. If, for example, this related to the market for bus services, this would result in a high level of capacity for which the operator was not receiving a financial return, i.e. a large number of empty seats on each bus journey. In some cases this would result in losses, either to the entire bus company or on particular routes or services. Several possibilities are likely to result – some bus operators would be driven out of business, hence reducing the quantity supplied, whilst those that remain are likely to withdraw unprofitable services, hence again reducing the quantity supplied. Over time, therefore, the level of excess supply would be reduced. Alternatively (or additionally), suppliers may reduce the price in an attempt to fill the spare capacity, and thus at least generate some revenue from what were empty seats. Quantity demanded would therefore increase. These processes would continue until the market was in balance, which only takes place at price P_e. At that price the market is said to be in equilibrium (balance). Consider the scenario in Figure 3.11.

In this case the second price that has been added to the graph, P_{XD}, is set below the market clearing price and would result in the quantity demanded, Q_D, far exceeding the quantity supplied, Q_S. This would be known as excess demand, shown by $Q_D - Q_S$. In this case there exists a consumer demand that is not being met by producers. Again using bus services as an example, this would be most vividly illustrated by over-crowding on buses and long queues at bus stops. In order to meet this excess demand, some suppliers will increase the quantity being supplied. This however can only be done if the price increases. These 'extra' services (at least in the short term)

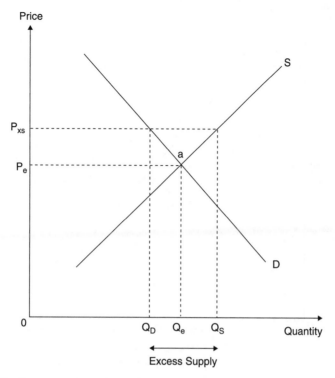

Figure 3.10   Excess supply in the market

will have to be provided by buses that are currently operating on other routes or in other market segments. As operators are profit maximisers, quantity supplied can only be increased if a higher level of return can be earned from switching buses to this route/sector. In this case there is an unmet demand at the prevailing market price, hence prices can be increased, i.e. the market will bear it. The increase in price however will reduce the quantity demanded, as being utility maximisers some consumers may decide that the use of the bus no longer represent the best value of their (limited) incomes. Some therefore may either not travel at all or use some other form of transport. Either way, quantity demanded falls. As illustrated before, this process will continue until all excess demand disappears. This only takes place at the market clearing price P_e.

This illustration clarifies the basic workings of the market and the importance of the price mechanism in equating the needs of consumers (demand) with the requirements of producers (supply). It also illustrates the important concepts of excess supply and excess demand and why there is an in-built tendency for the market to be in equilibrium.

The workings of the market

All of the ideas introduced in this chapter can be brought together to analyse the impact upon the market price and quantity if there should be a change in any of the determinants of supply or

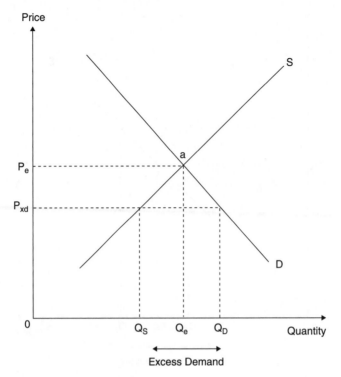

Figure 3.11 *Excess demand in the market*

demand. Continuing with the use of the market for bus services as the example, the impact of a change in the price of a substitute service can be used to illustrate the effect of a demand side factor on the market price and quantity traded. It should be stressed however that the principles outlined apply in the case of any of the determinants of demand introduced earlier. To return to the example, if rail fares were to rise, then the effect on the demand side of the bus market would be illustrated by a shift in the demand curve to the right. This is shown in Figure 3.12, which is a simple expansion of the basic market illustrated in Figure 3.9.

Figure 3.12 shows the market for bus services in equilibrium at point a (demand = supply) with price P_e and quantity traded Q_e. Following an increase in rail fares, some rail consumers will change to a substitute service, in this case the bus. This change in the conditions of demand for bus services is illustrated by a shift of the demand curve to the right from D to D_1. At the existing equilibrium price of P_e, therefore, there is now excess demand, as shown by Q_{xd} minus Q_e. This situation has already been examined under Figure 3.8 and would result in the excess demand being eradicated through an increase in the price/fare by suppliers. This would cause a reduction in the quantity demanded, as shown by a movement along the new demand curve D_1 from point c towards point b. The increased price however will also cause an increase in the quantity supplied, and hence a movement along the existing supply curve S from point a towards point b. This process continues until the market is back in equilibrium at point b with a new market price of P_1 with the associated quantity traded of Q_1. The net outcome therefore of the increase in rail fares on the

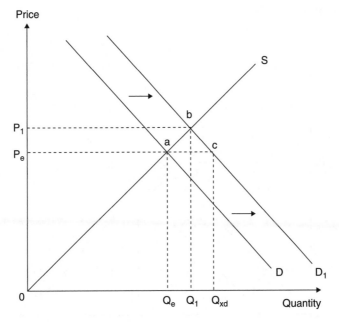

Figure 3.12 *Effect of an increase in the price of rail services on the market for bus services*

market for bus services was to increase the price from P_e to P_1 and an increase in the quantity traded from Q_e to Q_1.

To illustrate the effect of a supply side factor, the effect of an increase in the level of subsidy paid to bus operators is used. Such an increase would be represented by a shift of the supply curve to the right, i.e. more would be supplied at all prices. This is shown in Figure 3.13, which again has been developed from Figure 3.9.

Prior to the increase in subsidy, the market is in equilibrium at point a with a market price P_e and quantity traded Q_e. The increase in subsidy is shown by a shift in the supply curve to the right (this is akin to a reduction in costs), hence at price P_e there is now excess supply of Q_{xs} minus Q_e. This is the same situation as illustrated in Figure 3.10 above and would result in suppliers decreasing the price in order to fill the available capacity. The quantity supplied therefore would move along the new supply curve S_1 from point c towards point b. As the price falls, the quantity demanded would increase, as shown by a movement along the existing demand curve D from point a towards point b. As before, the net outcome would be that the market would end up back in equilibrium at point b with a new price P_1 and quantity Q_1.

The effects of the various determinants of supply and demand on the market price and quantity traded could endlessly be illustrated. In reality, there are constantly forces at work in the market that impact upon demand and supply. In saying this, the basic market principles outlined above hold true. Thus further examples of changes in demand and supply are left to the exercises at the end of this chapter. Meanwhile, these ideas are developed further in Case study 3.3, which examines the market for urban road space.

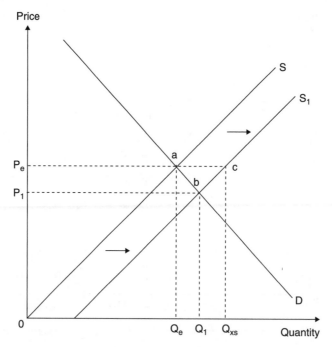

Figure 3.13 *Effect of an increase in the level of subsidy paid to bus operators on the market price and quantity traded of bus services.*

Case study 3.3 The market for urban road space – a practical illustration of the working of the market in transport services in the case of London car and bus usage

The analysis of the market for urban road space provides an interesting illustration of the working of the market with regard to transport services, as it underlines how the market actually works (or often doesn't!). The following case is outlined in theory before the practical aspects are considered. London provides the backdrop, as this allows the impact on the market of a number of the determinants of demand and supply to be examined, with the main focus on the introduction of a congestion charge.

In Figure 3.14, the top diagram shows the market for private motoring, i.e. private car usage. The demand and supply curves follow normal principles and before imposition of a congestion charge the market is in equilibrium at point a, hence there is no excess demand or supply. The diagram below represents the market for road space (which could be viewed as a complementary good for private motoring, i.e. one that is consumed at the same time). The first point to note is the vertical supply curve in the market for road space. This is because this example concerns (London) urban road space; hence no matter what the price the supply of available road space simply cannot be expanded (at least certainly not in the short term). The second point to note is that although prior to the imposition of a congestion charge the price to the user

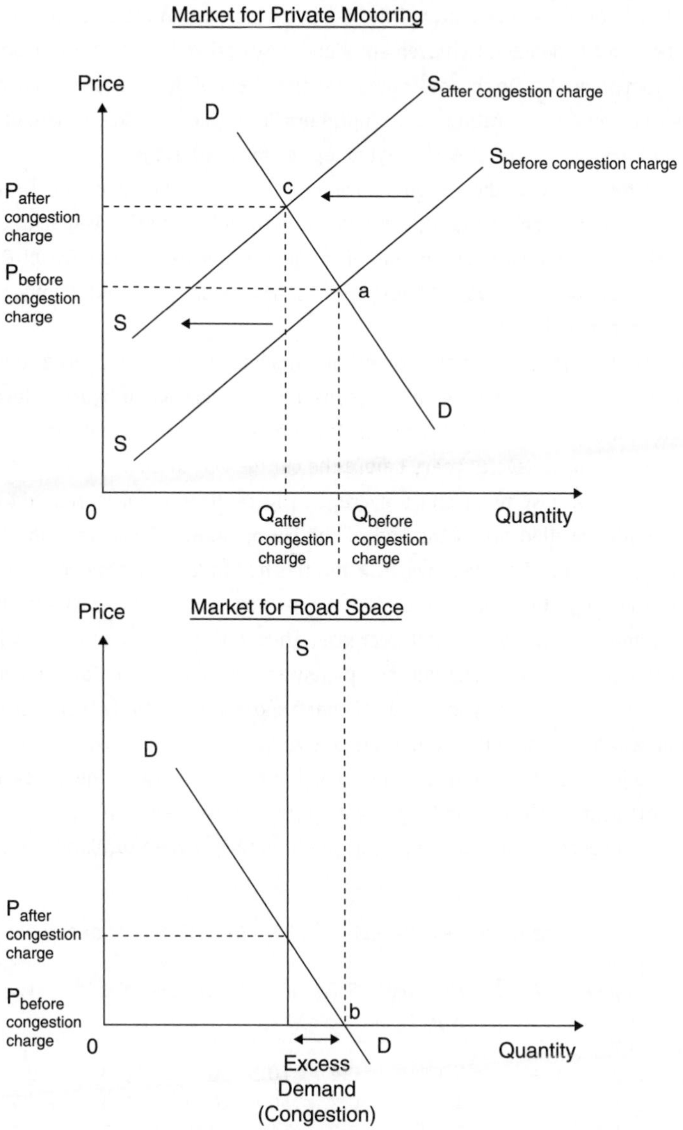

Market for Private Motoring

Price

D

$S_{\text{after congestion charge}}$

$S_{\text{before congestion charge}}$

$P_{\text{after congestion charge}}$

c

$P_{\text{before congestion charge}}$

S

a

S

D

0

$Q_{\text{after congestion charge}}$ $Q_{\text{before congestion charge}}$ Quantity

Price

Market for Road Space

S

D

$P_{\text{after congestion charge}}$

$P_{\text{before congestion charge}}$

0

b

D

Quantity

Excess
Demand
(Congestion)

Figure 3.14 *Market for private motoring and the market for road space*

(at the point of use) is zero, market principles still operate and the market equilibrium is at point b. The associated 'price' is actually paid through general taxation and not directly by the user. The same principles for example operate in the UK's National Health Service, which users indirectly fund through the payment of taxes. Returning to this example, because the price to the user is zero there is excess demand. As a consequence, the road network is operating at above its optimum capacity and this results in congestion.

By imposing a congestion charge, this has the effect of increasing the cost of motoring. Cost is a major determinant of supply, hence the supply curve in the market for private motoring shifts to the left (a decrease in supply). This causes an increase in the price of motoring and a decrease in the quantity demand (a movement along the existing demand curve, from a to c) and a new equilibrium point at c. On the lower diagram, the effect of this reduction in demand is that now the road network is operating at its optimum level (i.e. no excess demand, hence no congestion) and the user is now directly paying a price for road usage.

That is what the theory predicts should have happened after the imposition of a congestion charge, but is there any evidence that this is what actually did happen? Given below in Table 3.2 are travel statistics for the Greater London area taken from the London Travel Report 2007 (TfL, 2007). For the period 1993 to 2006, these show the daily average number of journeys broken down by the modal split.

The figures are for Greater London rather than simply the congestion charge zone, hence to a certain extent the impact of the scheme is dissolved in the aggregated figures. Nevertheless, in many ways the statistics highlight London's traffic problems and show that the issue of conges- tion was having an impact several years before the charge was implemented (in 2003). Whilst the car has by far the largest modal share, average daily journeys by car increased to 1999 after which they virtually levelled off to the end of the period shown. Thus while in 1993 the car accounted for 46 per cent of all journeys, by 2006 this had fallen to just under 40 per cent. The main effect of the congestion charge therefore appears to have been to restrain growth in car usage, with limited evidence of a small decrease. Thus whilst the lower part of Figure 3.14 predicts that the congestion charge will completely remove congestion, an element of it still exists. Thus a charge considerably in excess of that imposed (£5 initially then increased to £8) would be required to eradicate it. From Table 3.2 what there is more evidence of is a market effect (increased journey times) that was having an impact on the use of the car even before the charge was implemented. The demand for private transport was being affected by the quality of that transport and hence some users (albeit in small numbers) were turning to other modes of

Table 3.2   *Average daily journeys by mode, 1993–2006, Greater London area*

Year	Rail	Under-ground	DLR	Bus (incl tram)	Taxi	Car	Motor-cycle	Bicycle	Walk	All Modes
1993	1.4	2.0	–	3.1	0.2	10.5	0.2	0.3	5.2	22.9
1994	1.4	2.1	–	3.1	0.2	10.6	0.2	0.3	5.2	23.1
1995	1.5	2.1	–	3.3	0.2	10.6	0.2	0.3	5.2	23.4
1996	1.5	2.1	–	3.4	0.2	10.7	0.2	0.3	5.3	23.7
1997	1.6	2.2	0.1	3.5	0.2	10.8	0.2	0.3	5.3	24.2
1998	1.7	2.4	0.1	3.5	0.2	10.8	0.2	0.3	5.3	24.5
1999	1.8	2.5	0.1	3.5	0.2	11.1	0.2	0.3	5.4	25.1
2000	1.8	2.6	0.1	3.7	0.2	11.0	0.2	0.3	5.5	25.4
2001	1.8	2.6	0.1	3.9	0.2	11.0	0.2	0.3	5.5	25.6
2002	1.9	2.6	0.1	4.2	0.2	11.1	0.2	0.3	5.5	26.1
2003	1.9	2.6	0.1	4.6	0.2	11.0	0.2	0.3	5.5	26.4
2004	1.9	2.7	0.1	5.0	0.2	11.0	0.2	0.4	5.6	27.1
2005	2.0	2.6	0.1	5.0	0.2	10.9	0.2	0.4	5.6	27.0
2006	2.1	2.7	0.2	5.2	0.2	10.9	0.2	0.5	5.6	27.6

Source: TfL (2007)

transport. In particular, bus usage increased by 68 per cent over the period, the train by 45 per cent and the underground by 36 per cent. The London bus market in particular makes an interesting study.

Bus fares and service levels within London are set by the transport authority, Transport for London, and not by the free market. Nevertheless, the sector still follows market principles. Consider Figure 3.15, which attempts to explain this concept.

Figure 3.15 may at first seem rather complicated. However, if we begin with the market supply without subsidy and the market demand before congestion charging, then the equilibrium price where the market would clear is at point a with a price of $P_{free\ market}$. The regulated price set by the transport authority, however, is set below the market clearing price at $P_{regulated}$. Despite the price being set by the authority, however, market forces still operate, and without any further measures there would be excess demand, shown by the difference between Q_{Supply} and Q_{Demand}. As outlined in the main text, this would be exemplified by long queues and over-crowding on buses. In order to overcome this problem, the transport authority pays a subsidy to operators. This shifts the supply curve to the right from $S_{without\ subsidy}$ to $S_{with\ subsidy}$ (as it effectively reduces the costs to operators), hence bringing the market back into equilibrium at point b with a price $P_{regulated}$ and quantity Q_{Demand}.

With the imposition of a congestion charge, this would cause an increase in the price of private transport, a substitute service to the bus. Some car users would therefore switch to alter-native modes, and in the London case this appears to have in the main been the bus. This would cause a shift in the demand curve to the right for bus services (an increase in demand). Under normal free market principles, this would put upward pressure on the price, and the market

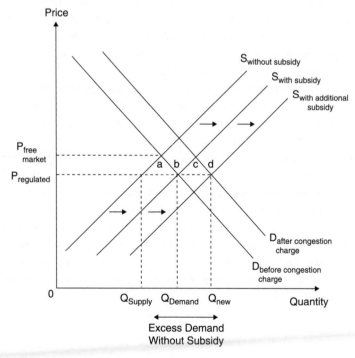

Figure 3.15 *The market for London bus services*

would reach a new equilibrium at point c. Under a regulated market, however, the same market forces would apply; however, in this case the price cannot increase in order to clear the market. The authority would have to either set a higher regulated price or alternatively increase the level of subsidy paid to operators to allow them to provide more services at the current regulated price. This would therefore shift the supply curve further to the right to $S_{with\ additional\ subsidy}$. The result would be a new equilibrium point d with a price $P_{regulated}$ and quantity Q_{new}. This produces an apparent contradiction of paying more subsidy with increasing passenger numbers; however, this is exactly what has happened in the London case. Furthermore, the authority has been forced to increase the price of Outer London journeys by some 35 per cent.

Despite being a regulated market, the London example provides an interesting case as to how the market operates. It underlines that even where fare and quantity levels are set by an authority, market principles still apply and the economics of the whole system need to operate in order to provide an efficient solution. The London congestion charging scheme will be considered further in Chapter 8, and the public transport market in Chapter 10.

CHAPTER SUMMARY AND REFLECTION

In this chapter the two sides of the market, demand and supply, have been introduced and examined. The general principles relating to all goods and services were introduced along with more specific determinants that affect transport markets. Demand and supply were then combined in order to examine how the market operates in practice. Principally this is through the price mechanism, with price rises caused by excess demand (too many consumers chasing too few goods), and price decreases caused by excess supply (too many producers chasing too few consumers!). Through market price signals, the actions of consumers, in terms of the quantity demanded, and producers, in terms of the quantity supplied, are balanced and the market will always tend towards market equilibrium. Whilst such principles apply to the operation of a pure free market, i.e. one without any government intervention, the illustration of the market for urban road space showed that market principles still apply even where heavy government intervention exists.

As a final point, and particularly for those new to economic analysis, hopefully in the course of this chapter you have not felt too overwhelmed with diagrams. Counting all graphs separately, some sixteen diagrams have been used in order to illustrate the various concepts in this chapter, a large number. In practice, however, when various effects on the market are considered we would never contemplate using as many as that, but only one or two at a time. It is important however to stress the use of diagrams in economic analysis. This should provide a framework for analysing situations and structure thinking around a given situation to give focus to the issue at hand. These basic tools of analysis will be used in subsequent chapters to further examine the major economic issues affecting transport markets.

CHAPTER EXERCISES

Exercise 3.1 Increasing the use of the railways

Almost without exception European governments have as one of their main transport policy objectives an increase in the use of passenger rail travel. The simple question is, using your new-found knowledge of economics, how can these governments assist the market to achieve this aim? If we assume from Figure 3.16 that the government wished to see the quantity used of rail services increase from the current position of Q_e to the level indicated by Q_x, for environmental and social reasons.

Then you should use this diagram as a basis to outline the various options available and consider both direct government intervention in this market as well as intervention in other transport markets that will bring about such a change. Further assume however that the aim would be to increase the level of rail travel without causing a major modal shift from other public transport markets. You should illustrate each of your scenarios with a relevant diagram. You should also consider all of the implications of your decisions, particularly with regard to the political logic of some of the options. (HINT – there are three basic possible scenarios, although you may come up with more!)

Of the scenarios that you have devised, which do you consider would be the most effective?

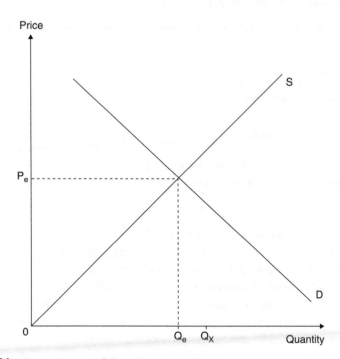

Figure 3.16   Increasing use of the railways

Exercise 3.2 Demand and supply exercises

You should now consider each of the following scenarios on the price and quantity traded for the market highlighted. This is a series of straightforward exercises in which you should identify what side of the market, demand or supply, is being affected, which particular determinant has changed and you should explain your reasoning at arriving at your answer.

- A general rise in incomes on the market for bus services
- A rise in the demand for passenger air travel on the market for air cargo
- An increase in fuel duty on the market for road haulage services
- A fall in the costs of production of bus services on the market for rail services
- The publication of a government report on the detrimental effects of environmental change on the market for private motoring
- A weekend ban on lorry movements on the market for rail freight
- The abolition of what had been strict government controls on the entry of new airline operators on the airline market
- The announcement of increased grants available for the installation of rail freight facilities (infrastructure) on the actual market for rail freight services
- A change in the short run aim of a bus operator that has a cost advantage away from profit maximisation to sale maximisation in order to eradicate the competition currently in the market.

Exercise 3.3 Demand and supply curves

The equation for a demand curve for the daily demand of a particular bus service is given by:

$$D = 20 - 15P$$

And the supply curve by the equation:

$$S = 10P$$

Where P is the price and both supply and demand are specified in thousands. Starting at a maximum price of £1.50 and reducing to zero in steps of 10p, sketch out the demand and supply curves for this bus service.

a) What is the equilibrium price and quantity?
b) If a rise in the price of rail fares is estimated to add a daily demand of ten thousand passengers at all prices, specify the equation of the new demand curve and find the new equilibrium price and quantity by adding the new demand curve to your sketch.
c) From the original market demand curve, however, a rise in incomes is predicted to reduce daily demand by five thousand passengers at all prices. Again, specify the equation of the new demand curve and find the new equilibrium price and quantity.

Transport demand elasticity

INTRODUCTION

As a general rule, when the price of any good or service rises the quantity demanded will fall. Whilst useful as an analytical tool and as a method of improving our understanding of transport markets, in most cases, particularly those of a practical nature, we will want to know more than that. What is important is not the fact that demand will fall (as that is given by the basic law of demand) but rather by how much the quantity demanded will fall, and thus how price sensitive are consumers in the market? For example, how sensitive are people to purchasing train tickets if the fare was to rise by 2 per cent, 5 per cent or even 20 per cent?

The answer lies in the concept of price elasticity of demand, as this indicates the responsiveness of passengers or potential passengers to changes in the prices on offer. As such, it has a huge impact on transport policy and decision making. Given that all transport markets, particularly those relating to public transport services, are regulated to a greater or lesser extent in most countries, setting the 'right' fare is essential to achieving policy aims and objectives. With fare and/or capacity levels set by the transport authority rather than the market, an understanding of elasticity of demand, even at a basic level, is essential to achieving policy objectives. García-Ferrer *et al.* (2006) for example highlight that transport services need to be priced at an appropriate level to determine best operating practice, and for this to happen it is essential to have a knowledge of how users will respond to changes in price and service characteristics. Furthermore, Goodwin (1992) notes that the price mechanism can be used as an important tool of policy to either raise revenue through the imposition of a tax or by affecting demand through the payment of a subsidy to reduce price. The effectiveness of such a policy tool however is to a very large extent determined by the degree to which consumers are responsive to changes in the price of transport services. For example, paying a subsidy to a transport service where consumers are not price sensitive will only result in lowering the price and have little effect on the numbers using the service.

In a more general sense, such an understanding of transport behaviour is important for any analyst of transport markets. Although most of the focus of demand elasticity tends to be on changes in the price, the idea of elasticity involves the responsiveness of the consumer to changes in any of the determinants of demand, not only the price. Hence the effect of changes in income are measured by income elasticity, cross price elasticity measures the effect of the change in the price of one mode on the demand for another, service elasticity the effect of improvements in the quality of service on demand and so on. A general definition therefore of elasticity of transport demand would be the responsiveness of demand for a transport mode to a change in one of its determinants.

This chapter, under the title of transport demand elasticity, will further focus on the factors behind the demand for transport services by individual consumers before the following chapter provides further focus on supply in the form of the costs of providing transport services. Here the main types of elasticity will be outlined and some simplified elasticities calculated. The chapter also provides a practical perspective to the topic by giving an overview of some of the estimations that have been made of transport elasticities, and this will also help to reinforce many of the ideas presented in the chapter.

PRICE ELASTICITY OF DEMAND FOR TRANSPORT SERVICES

Price elasticity of demand for transport services, as discussed previously, is the consumers' demand responsiveness to changes in the price. This applies to all areas of transport, hence would refer to the operator's price in the case of public transport, the supplier's price in the case of freight carriage and the total price in the case of an individual's private transport. Price elasticity is often referred to as 'own' price elasticity to draw a clear distinction from 'cross' price elasticity, which is the cross-over effect of price changes and will be examined later. In the face of price changes, the law of demand states that consumers (in total) will react by either consuming more in the case of price cuts or less in the case of price increases. As stated above, however, what is of more value is the extent to which consumers react to price changes, i.e. price elasticity.

Price elasticity is therefore the formal mechanism in economics by which price sensitivity is assessed and analysed. This is measured on a quantitative basis, i.e. a number is derived in order to assess the level of price elasticity, which is given by the formula:

$$\text{Price Elasticity of Demand} = \frac{\text{Percentage Change in Quantity Demand}}{\text{Percentage Change in Price}}$$

Or this equation may be expressed in its shorthand form of:

$$\text{PED} = \frac{\%\Delta D}{\%\Delta P}$$

Where: PED = price elasticity of demand
% = percentage
Δ = change (represented by the Greek letter 'delta')
D = quantity demanded
P = price

Price elasticity therefore is an assessment of the relative changes in the quantity demanded to relative changes in price, and as such provides an indicator of the price sensitivity of consumers. To give a hypothetical example, say an operator was to increase its fares by 4 per cent but the quantity demanded was to fall by only 1 per cent, then price elasticity would be −0.25, as calculated by:

$$PED = \frac{\%\Delta D}{\%\Delta P} = \frac{-1\%}{+4\%} = -0.25$$

Notice that the sign of PED is negative. Certainly within transport services this will almost always be the case. This, again, is the basic law of demand. A rise in price (a positive figure) will cause a fall in the quantity demanded (a negative figure). Likewise, a fall in price will cause a rise in the quantity demanded. Thus when working out price elasticity of demand, either a negative figure is divided by a positive one or a positive figure divided by a negative one. Either way this produces a negative value. This of course applies to the definition of a 'normal' good, where a rise in the price will cause a fall in the quantity demanded. Contrast this with what is known as a 'Giffen' good, which exists where an increase in the price of a good or service actually brings about an increase in the quantity demanded, not a decrease. This may apply for example to goods such as cheap jewellery, where a price increase may lead to a perception of higher quality, and hence quantity demanded increases. In such cases, the price elasticity of demand would be positive. Giffen goods however tend to be very rare, although we will see an example of one later.

In the above equation, however, what does the PED figure mean? If say we obtained a value of −2.0, what does that actually signify? Before answering that question, the first important observation to make is that 'higher' elasticity values will always refer to higher *negative* values. Consider the following quote taken from the Southend–London Route Study (Competition Commission, 2004, p. E4):

> 'For most categories of rail traffic, estimated elasticities on the basis of existing studies, particularly in the short run, are likely to be smaller than −1: i.e. an increase in price would lead to a less than proportionate decrease in number of passengers, hence revenue and profits would increase. Rail demand as a whole could therefore be regarded as a separate market. However, for leisure travel on certain routes, elasticities are likely to be larger than −1: i.e. a price increase would lead to a more than proportionate reduction in (the) number of passengers, reducing revenues.'

What it actually means in the first sentence however is that elasticities on the basis of existing studies are likely to produce smaller *negative* values than −1. The same applies later in the quote where it refers to 'larger than −1', hence −1.5 would be 'larger' than negative one. Hence note that 'larger' values will always refer to larger negative values.

65

To return to the original question, what does the PED value mean? Price elasticity is a formal measure of the rate of change of the quantity demanded in comparison to the rate of change of the price. Where the price elasticity is greater than negative one, as highlighted in the above quote, this means that the proportionate change in demand is greater than the proportionate change in price. For example, if PED was −2, then the percentage change in demand would be twice the percentage change in price. This would be known as *elastic* demand. Where PED is less than negative one, then the proportionate change in quantity demanded is less than the proportionate change in price, and this would be known as *inelastic* demand. To use our price sensitivity terminology, in the case of elastic demand this would indicate that consumers are relativity price sensitive, whilst inelastic demand that consumers in the market have a relatively low level of price sensitivity. Another way to think about this is that the formula for PED is simply a formal method for comparing changes in demand to changes in price. The value can then be measured against a common scale in order to determine the extent of the price sensitivity of consumers: values greater than negative one indicate they will react strongly to changes in price and values less than negative one that they will not, although note from above that 'large' or 'greater' relates to larger negative values.

If negative one is the important dividing line, what therefore are the upper and lower limits of this 'scale'? Taken to its ultimate conclusion, the most extreme case of elastic demand would exist where any change in the price, either up or down, results in the quantity demanded falling to zero. This would be known as perfectly price elastic demand, as illustrated in Figure 4.1.

Whilst in this context this is purely a theoretical concept, perfectly price elastic demand does have practical implications that will be examined later in the text (this may for example be the demand curve facing an individual firm, i.e. it can only sell at one price, rather than the market demand curve). Importantly in this context, it gives an upper limit for the range of possible price elasticity values. If, for example, the price P_{pe} in Figure 4.1 was £4, at which the quantity demanded is infinite (i.e. the firm can sell as much as it can produce), and then the firm for an

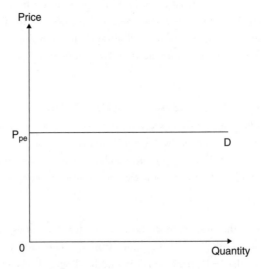

Figure 4.1 *Perfectly price elastic demand*

unknown reason was to increase its price to £5, demand for its product would fall to zero. Price elasticity of demand in this example would therefore be given by:

$$PED = \frac{\%\Delta D}{\%\Delta P} = \frac{-\infty\%}{25\%} = -\infty$$

This therefore gives the upper limit on our common 'scale' of negative infinity (as given by the symbol ∞). The other extreme would be where a change in price would produce absolutely no change in the quantity demanded, i.e. consumer behaviour is completely unaffected by changes in the price. They will purchase exactly the same quantity of the good whether the price rises or decreases. This extreme case is known as perfectly price inelastic, and is shown in Figure 4.2.

Where demand is perfectly inelastic, then no matter the price consumers will purchase exactly the same quantity of the good or service, i.e. the demand curve is vertical. As this is an extreme case, again this has few practical applications although certain habit-forming goods will tend to be highly inelastic as consumers will generally purchase the same quantities irrespective of the price. Using our previous example of increasing the price from £4 to £5, then the value in this example of PED would be given by:

$$PED = \frac{\%\Delta D}{\%\Delta P} = \frac{0\%}{25\%} = 0$$

Zero is therefore the lower boundary of price elasticities values on our common scale. Note however that these upper and lower boundaries only relate to own price elasticity of demand and not the other types of elasticity outlined later. To complete the set, a final example would be where a relative change in price is exactly matched by the same relative change in the quantity demanded. This is known as unitary price elastic demand and is shown in Figure 4.3.

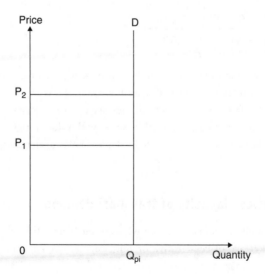

Figure 4.2 Perfectly price inelastic demand

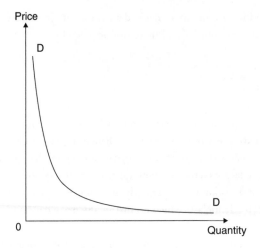

Figure 4.3 *Unitary price elastic demand*

In this diagram the simplified method of drawing demand curves as straight lines has been relaxed, as in simple terms unitary demand cannot be shown on a straight line. This is because the level of price elasticity will vary along different points on any straight line; however, in this case it is the same across the whole curve.

Using again the example of a price increase of £4 to £5, then rather than demand falling to zero (perfectly elastic), or remaining unchanged (perfectly inelastic), demand falls in direct proportion to the change in price. Thus if the quantity demanded was say 100 units at £4, then the increase to £5 would produce a reduction in the quantity demanded of 20 per cent, i.e. the same proportionate change, hence demand would fall to 80 units. Just to confirm, price elasticity of demand under such a scenario would be given by:

$$PED = \frac{\%\Delta D}{\%\Delta P} = \frac{(80 - 100)/100}{(5 - 4)/5} = \frac{-20\%}{20\%} = -1$$

To quickly summarise the main issues surrounding price elasticity of demand, this measures the relative level of consumer price sensitivity. If consumers are relatively price sensitive, then market demand will be relatively elastic; if consumers are not price sensitive, then market demand will be relatively inelastic. It is measured on a quantitative scale, with values ranging from zero to negative infinity which allows elasticity values to be divided into inelastic demand, unitary demand and elastic demand.

Determinants of price elasticity of transport demand

If that is what price elasticity of demand is, then what are the factors that affect the extent to which consumers in the market are price sensitive or not, i.e. the determinants of price elasticity of transport demand? In summary these can be grouped under three headings; however, some confusion can arise between determinants of price elasticity and the actual determinants of demand itself, such as the price, income, the price of substitutes and complementary goods and so on. The important distinction is that the determinants of demand are the factors that determine the quantity of goods or services that consumers will purchase at a given price (and as such represent the conditions of demand). The determinants of price elasticity of demand on the other hand are those factors that determine the extent to which the quantity demanded will change in reaction to changes in the price. These are therefore the factors that determine the extent to which consumers in the market are price sensitive.

The three basic determinants of price elasticity of demand for transport services are:

- The number and closeness of alternative modes of travel (substitutes)
- The proportion (and timing) of disposable income purchased on the mode of travel
- The time dimension.

The number and closeness of alternative modes of travel (substitutes)

The higher the number of alternative modes available and the closer they are in meeting the same basic travel need, the higher will be the price elasticity for a particular transport service. If I use the Blue Bus Company's service to travel to work, and Blue Bus should increase its price, then I am far more likely to switch to an alternative mode if that alternative is readily available. If the Red Bus Company's service left from the same stop one minute later and took the same journey time, then for this particular trip that would be an almost perfect substitute for Blue's service as I could easily make the switch to Red Bus. If however Blue's service was the only one available to me, then the only alternatives I would have would be to either pay the higher fare or not make the journey, i.e. quit my job! This, for example, is one reason why the price of petrol in particular localities varies very little from petrol station to petrol station; there exists a high number of available substitutes (Esso, BP, Shell, Jet, Morrisons, Sainsbury etc etc) and it is an identical product that is being sold. Hence there is a very high level of substitutability, and if one company was to increase its price then consumers can easily switch to one of the other providers.

Proportion of disposable income spent on the mode of travel

We have seen income already as a determinant of demand, i.e. the quantity purchased. The proportion of income spent, however, is also a determinant of price elasticity of demand. It refers however to the proportion of disposable income as opposed to net income, i.e. income after tax has been paid. In simple terms, the higher the proportion of disposable income spent on the mode of travel, then the higher the price elasticity of demand. If consumers are about to part with a large part of their income on any good or service, then they are likely to shop around first to ensure they are getting the best deal. No one however would shop around before purchasing a chocolate bar because it is simply not worth it – the amount saved is likely to be marginal and certainly less than the cost involved (i.e. time) of ensuring that the lowest priced chocolate bar has been purchased. Generally speaking, within transport services the proportion of income spent in most (but not all) instances will be relatively small, although these will add up to significant amounts. That does raise the question of just what proportion of income is spent on transport activities. This is shown in Figure 4.4, which outlines the relative percentages of consumer household expenditure on various goods and services for the UK in 2007.

69

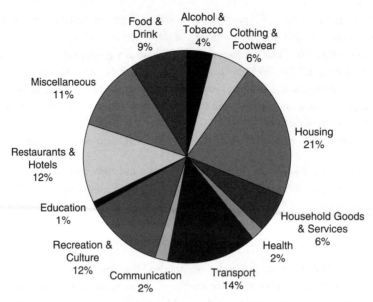

Figure 4.4   *Shares of household final consumption expenditure, 2007*

Source: Drawn from ONS Statistics (ONS, 2008)

This gives the percentage breakdown of consumer expenditure by type of good or service purchased. It is therefore expenditure net of taxes and savings, i.e. all monies actually spent. Thus for example expenditure on Education and Health services are very low, only accounting for 3 per cent of the total, because for most households these are provided by the state and funded out of general taxation. The first point to note is the relatively high level of expenditure on transport. What is perhaps most surprising is that more is proportionately spent on transport than on food, recreation and clothing. In fact, only housing has a higher percentage of disposable income spent on it. It should be remembered however that this is for the 'average' household and there will be considerable variations in household structure. Large-family groups for example may be expected to spend a lower proportion on transport in relation to other goods and services (particularly food!), whilst single-occupier households would spend a relatively higher percentage on transport. It should also be noted that this takes no account of the actual income bracket of the 'household'. Other statistics from the Department for Transport (DfT, 2005) strongly suggest that lower-income groups spend a higher proportion of their income on transport services. This is for the simple reason that in a market-based economy most households need to earn an income, and thus transport costs as such are an unavoidable expense of earning that income (i.e. a derived demand), irrespective of the level of income ultimately earned. Putting these two issues together regarding household structure and income levels, there is no such thing as 'the average' household, as no household type could be described as 'typical'. Figure 4.4 however does give a very general idea as to the proportion of income that is spent on transport.

Relatively speaking, therefore, in a developed economy a large proportion of income is spent on transport. Most of this however will relate to expenditure on private vehicles. Using figures from the DfT (2007), the 'average' household owns 1.11 cars (note the point above about the 'average' household!). Cars new and old tend to be a major drain on household finances. We may expect therefore that taken on its own, demand for private motoring should be fairly elastic; however, from the limited evidence presented later in Case study 4.1, that is very much not the case. If we consider housing, interest rates have a major impact on the housing market, for the fact that a high proportion of household income is spent on housing, thus house buyers are very price elastic. Why therefore is this not the case for the second largest item, transport? The simple fact is that it is the other determinants of elasticity that are over-riding this effect. Hence it is not so much the number, but very much the 'closeness' of substitutes to the car that are generally perceived to be few in number. Not only that, however, what this stresses are the first two sentences of this book – 'Most individuals, whatever their walk of life, have a basic need to travel from one location to another. Modern life as such is structured around accessing goods and services that lie outside of the immediate vicinity of the home.' Transport is therefore essential, and in the main that trans-port comes in the form of a car, because the car is viewed as the most convenient way of doing it and is thus seen as a necessity of modern life.

A second point is that it is not the actual expenditure that is important, but rather the perception of that expenditure that matters as ultimately it is perceptions that affect behaviour. Unlike housing where a large proportion of income is spent in a single large amount, i.e. the monthly rent or mortgage payment, transport expenditure in many cases is far more scattered and, outside of car purchase, tends to be in relatively small amounts. Thus whilst spending a pound each way on the bus journey to work is a very small proportion of income, over the course of a month or a year this adds up to a fairly significant total. Thus the actual proportion of income spent on transport is likely to have less of an impact on the elasticity of demand than say for housing, as the perception of that expenditure will be to considerably underestimate it – ask any individual their monthly rent or mortgage payment and they will give you a very accurate figure, ask them how much they spend a month on transport and they will almost certainly understate the total.

Time

The final determinant of price elasticity is the time factor. In many instances in the short term individuals are tied in to using a certain company's products or services; however, time may bring about a change in behaviour. To use our Blue Bus Company example from above, while this was the only service in the short term I would have little choice but to use their service, hence price elasticity of demand would be relatively inelastic. In the longer term, however, I may decide to purchase a car or alternatively another bus company, such as Red Bus, may decide to start up a competing service. In this case demand would be more elastic. Time therefore is an important dimension in determining price elasticity of demand as elasticity can vary between the short and long run. Over a longer period of time, habits can change, thus there will almost always be a difference between long- and short-run elasticities, with the former almost certainly more elastic.

Also closely related to the time dimension is the essential nature of the journey to be under-taken. An essential journey, such as where commuters have to travel into the centre of a city each day for work or business purposes, will have relatively inelastic demand, as there is little choice but to make the journey at that point in time. With non-essential journeys on the other hand, such as a family day-out to the countryside, there is a far higher degree of flexibility with regard to when the journey can actually be made, and hence this would be more price elastic. The extent to which a particular journey can be deemed to be essential or not is therefore related to time as essential journeys have a very narrow time frame within which they need to be undertaken, and hence this also affects the price elasticity of demand.

Case study 4.1 Practical estimations and reviews of own price elasticity of demand for transport services

We have outlined the theory behind price elasticity of demand; however, there has been much research carried out into the actual values of transport elasticities. This can however be a particularly confusing area of study, as most studies provide different answers that in many cases are in complete contradiction of one another. In simple terms, therefore, there is no definite answer to general questions such as 'What is the price elasticity of rail services?', as it depends upon the particular characteristics affecting a particular rail market. Pucher and Kurth (1995) highlight that demand elasticities will vary between different locations, different modes, times of the day and so on. In simple terms, consumers in different situations will respond in different ways to changes in the price of any of the other determinants of demand. There is therefore no general value attributable to all situations in all locations, although there is a common consensus that public transport demand is relatively inelastic (Pucher and Kurth, 1995). Nevertheless, an overview of some of the estimations that have been derived for price elasticities in transport is useful to examine the practical issues involved and to reinforce the theory outlined above.

The starting point when considering any research into (own) price elasticity of demand for transport services is Professor Goodwin's review and assessment of around 180 elasticity studies for car and bus travel throughout Europe (Goodwin, 1992). For urban bus travel, the review calculated an average value of price elasticity of −0.41, but indicated a wide variation between short- and long-term impacts. These are reported fully in Table 4.1.

Table 4.1 *Urban bus price elasticities broken out by time period*

Time period	Average elasticity
Around 6 months	−0.21
0 to 6 months	−0.28
0 to 12 months	−0.37
Over 4 years	−0.55
5 to 30 years	−0.65

Source: Goodwin (1992)

From Goodwin's review, a very clear trend emerges with regard to price elasticity and time – over time demand becomes more elastic. Whilst this is consistent with the theory outlined earlier, the range of values found, from −0.21 in the very short term to −0.65 in the very long term, do underline the importance of the time dimension as a determinant of the price elasticity of demand for transport services. What, however, do these values mean? As a basic illustration, consider the price elasticity of demand equation given below:[1]

$$PED = \frac{\% \Delta D}{\% \Delta P},$$

then for the period zero to 6 months:

$$PED = \frac{\% \Delta D}{\% \Delta P} = -0.28$$

Thus a 10 per cent increase in price will produce a 2.8 per cent decrease in demand, i.e. demand in the short term is highly inelastic. Over time, however, elasticity increases. Thus over the following six months, demand would fall by another 0.9 per cent, and over the next three years after that by a further 1.8 per cent. Thus over that whole 4-year period, demand would have fallen by 5.5 per cent. Goodwin's review also indicated that over time elasticity values for transport have been increasing, hence consumers of transport services have been becoming more price sensitive over time.

Goodwin's research may be considered to be slightly dated now, particularly given the time period reviewed. Examination of more recent studies into the subject however confirms that elasticity figures have increased slightly over the intervening period. These are best summarised in TRL (2004), a summary of which has since been published in Transport Policy under Paulley *et al.* (2006), who conducted an extensive review and study of public transport elasticities. Their research team concluded that with regard to bus fare elasticity, broadly speaking average values of −0.4 in the short run, −0.55 in the medium term and −1.00 in the long run could be considered to be the norm, slightly higher than Goodwin's 1992 values.

As both the TRL and Goodwin reviews are overviews that derived average elasticities from the literature reviewed, what they do not communicate is the high degree of variability between most elasticity studies and that each finding only applies to that particular situation. This can be illustrated by García-Ferrara *et al.'s* (2006) study of public transport in the Madrid Metropolitan Area. The authors calculated price elasticities using monthly data over the time period January 1987 to December 2000. They compared two of the four basic modes available, namely the Metro and the Municipal Bus Company services, by ticket type – single and ten trip tickets for bus and metro and a regular travel card covering all modes for adults and juniors. The actual elasticity values found are given in Table 4.2.

Table 4.2 *Elasticity values, Garcia-Ferrara* et al. *(2006)*

Ticket type	Single	10 Ticket	Travel card
Bus	−1.06	−0.52	
Metro	−1.03	−2.17	
Adult			−0.01
Junior			0.56

From Table 4.2, in simple terms single fares were found to be generally unitary elastic, the 10 ticket metro ticket highly elastic whilst the 10 ticket bus fare was relatively inelastic. Finally the adult travel card was almost perfectly inelastic, and interestingly the junior travel card with a value of +0.56 off the end of our scale! What the last value means is that as the price increased for the junior travel card, demand increased. This is a classic case of a Giffen good highlighted earlier in the chapter; in this case the increase in price probably raised awareness of the junior travel card and hence led to more people buying it. Table 4.2 illustrates the very high degree of variation in the elasticity values derived, and suggests that the relatively high values found for the single and 10 journey tickets were primarily due to the travel card option. This indeed was the case, as the backdrop was one of a transport authority that had actively pursued a policy of encouraging travellers, through the price mechanism, to use the travel card in preference to single and multiple tickets. By 2001, for example, 60 per cent of trips were made using the travel card. What this shows is that elasticities can vary considerably between different settings, policy contexts and different ticket types. In this example the −1.06 value for the single bus fare could never be generalised to other contexts as this value is only relevant in this particular context.

As demand for transport is a derived demand, elasticity has also been found to vary depending upon the purpose of the journey. The normal division is made between business, commuting and leisure trips. Research into rail fare elasticities for example (ATOC, 2002) found values of −0.2 for business, −0.3 for commuting and −1.0 for leisure, which underlines the greater flexibility involved in the last purpose mentioned. Other studies, such as White (1981) and Grimshaw (1984), have examined the impact of the distance travelled on the price elasticity of demand. Not surprisingly, for bus journeys elasticities have generally been found to increase the longer the journey under consideration. White (1981) for example found that a price elasticity value of −0.4 for medium-length trips doubled to −0.8 for longer-length journeys. This however is not simply a function of distance, but rather reflects the magnitude of say a 10 per cent rise on a £1 fare compared with that of a 10 per cent rise on a £20 fare, i.e. the key determinant is the proportion of disposable income spent on the transport. Furthermore, longer journeys are made less frequently, thus people are more likely to shop around prior to purchase than for shorter distances. They also tend to involve leisure rather than business travel. Note also that since most of that research was published (in the mid 1980s), price elasticity for longer distances has probably become even more elastic, as the rise of the internet has made it easier for individuals to compare prices and the relative merits of different alternatives.

However, as before, the issue is not as straightforward as it may at first appear. Preston (1998), for example, in an examination of the effect of distance on price sensitivity for rail services, found that whilst the pattern was not particularly clear, overall it appeared that elasticity decreased with distance, hence became more inelastic. This effect for rail services has also been found by other research in this area. This led Paulley et al. (2006) in their review to cite the 'tapering' effect of rail fares as the main reason behind this effect, where the unit cost per kilometre travelled falls the further the distance travelled. As a full explanation however this is not entirely convincing, with a possible further reason being that over longer distances the number of real viable alternatives to rail (e.g. bus and car) may be far fewer. As a consequence, individuals are less price sensitive to changes in the price of long-distance rail journeys.

Finally, whilst earlier we saw that over time elasticities would be expected to increase over the longer term, the one good that appears to buck this trend is the elasticity of petrol, with some studies finding a larger short run than long run effect. For example, research by Barns (2002) into the effect of price changes on demand for petrol derived elasticity values of

−0.195 for the short run and −0.065 for the long run. Some other studies have produced similar results, with Puller and Greening (1999) finding a stronger initial reaction to petrol increases in the quarter of the price rise, but in subsequent quarters behaviour in terms of vehicle miles travelled returning to where it was before. This suggests that after the initial price increase, there is a general drift back towards the original position. Khazzoom (1991) (cited in Barns, 2002) argues that initially a price rise will reduce short-run demand, but why travel behaviour returns to the original position in the long run is due to consumers switching to vehicles that are more fuel efficient. Note also in Barns' study with such low elasticity values that an increase in the tax on petrol in order to attempt to limit car use would have very little impact.

As said at the very beginning of this case study, research into this area can be confusing and contradictory. A basic understanding of the issues involved however is vital to understanding the effect of using the price mechanism to influence travel behaviour. To summarise and finish, values of around −0.4 and −0.8 can be taken as 'ball park' figures for short- and long-run public transport own price elasticities; however, these can vary considerably under different contexts.

Price elasticity, total revenue and demand curves

Before going on to look at cross price elasticity, it is worthwhile to first consider further the significance of price elasticity in the analysis of transport markets. The preceding section has shown it to be a mechanism for assessing the extent to which consumers will react to changes in the price or other demand determinants of transport services. Does price elasticity of demand however have any further practical implications? The answer is yes, but first requires a simple lesson in algebra before examining it.

Put in simple terms, a company's total revenue from selling a good or service can be found by multiplying the quantity sold by the price of each unit sold. If for example 100 units are sold at £5 each, then total revenue would simply be £500. In a more generic form, this could be written as $P * Q$, where P is the price (£5) and Q is the quantity sold (100 units). This can be illustrated using demand curves, as is done in Figure 4.5.

Basically, the area of the rectangle outlined by points 0, P_a, a and Q_a shown in light grey in Figure 4.5 is the total revenue received from selling at price P_a. Using the example of a £5 selling price from above, then the area would be given by the length (100 units) times the breadth (5 pounds) and would represent the total revenue, £500. If the price was to increase to P_b, then we could show the gain and loss in revenue such a price change would bring about. If the firm was to increase price, it would sell less units (basic law of demand), but would receive more per unit sold, hence the overall impact this would have upon total revenue would not be known. This is illustrated further in Figure 4.6.

Beginning at price P_a (examined above), the company sells quantity Q_a, and the rectangle outlined by the area 0, P_a, a, Q_a represents the total revenue to the firm. This is just what was shown in Figure 4.5. Using the same logic, however, if the firm was to sell at price P_b, it would sell quantity Q_b and the total revenue would be given by the rectangle outlined by 0, P_b, b, Q_b. What you should be able to see is that there is a common area shared by these two different scenarios. That is the cross-hatched area above and labelled unimaginatively as the 'Common Area'. In effect, that proportion of revenue will accrue to the firm if it applies price P_a or price P_b. If however the

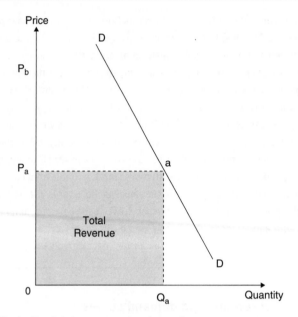

Figure 4.5 *Illustrating total revenue using demand curves*

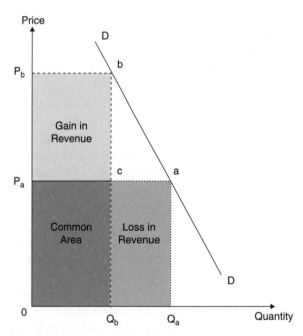

Figure 4.6 *Illustrating changes in total revenue using demand curves*

firm was to increase its price from P_a to P_b, then it would not receive the revenue in the area labelled 'Loss in Revenue' as it would be selling less units overall. This 'loss' however would be offset by a gain in the revenue received for each unit sold, labelled 'Gain in Revenue' in Figure 4.6. The key issue to be examined is the balance between the gain per unit sold and the loss from selling less units. You should be able to see that in this example the area of the gain is greater than the area of the loss. Hence increasing price from P_a to P_b will lead to an increase in total revenue. This is because demand is relatively inelastic. If however this example had concerned a cut in the price from P_b down to P_a, then total revenue would actually have decreased.

At this stage, the effect on profitability is unknown, because the supply side of the market (specifically the effect on costs) has not yet been examined. For example, if in the previous example the price had been cut from P_b to P_a, then this would have decreased total revenue. However, the potential effect on unit costs from increasing supply from Q_b to Q_a is unknown, thus nothing can be said about profitability. If unit costs were for example to reduce significantly, then such a price cut may reduce total revenue but actually increase total profit.

To further illustrate, consider the graph shown in Figure 4.7 where demand is relatively elastic.

In this example, a rise in price from P_a to P_b will reduce demand from Q_a to Q_b, with the loss in revenue given by the area Q_b, c, a, Q_a and the gain shown by the area outlined by P_a, P_b, b, c. In this case, therefore, the increase in price has led to a decrease in total revenue. Note again that if the price change had been the other way around, then total revenue would have increased.

Whilst only affecting total revenue and not profit, this does nevertheless have important implications in many transport markets. Reconsider the quote from the Competition Commission regarding the Southend–London rail route on page 65, as it specifically states that if demand is

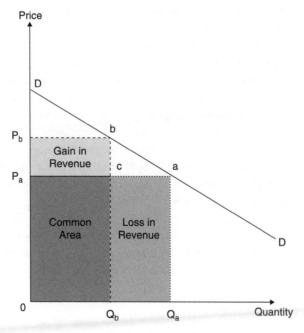

Figure 4.7   *The effect on revenue of price changes of a relatively elastic good*

inelastic, i.e. less than negative one, then increasing the price will increase both revenue *and* profits. In this example why this is the case is that the level of output will not change, as train-operating companies are contracted under the terms of the franchise to run at specific frequencies. Thus if the level of output will not change, it follows that the level of costs will not change either. Therefore in this instance, increasing revenues equates to increasing profits. This is not an unusual occurrence in many public transport markets, where certainly within the short run a network of services is operated regardless of small changes in demand, and thus any change in revenue directly impacts on profits. This idea is considered further in Exercise 4.2 at the end of the chapter.

A final thought on price elasticity of demand

As shown in Case study 4.1, the demand for urban bus travel is relatively price inelastic, with Goodwin (1992) calculating an average value of around −0.4. This indicates that a 1 per cent increase in fares will lead to a 0.4 per cent decrease in demand. In terms of total revenue, therefore, a fare increase would increase the total revenue take, as the revenue lost from the reduction in passengers (0.4 per cent) will be more than offset by the additional revenue gained from the fare increase (1 per cent). If this is the case, therefore, why don't operators simply keep increasing the fare? Given our knowledge of theory to date, plus if it is assumed that bus companies operate essentially the same network and services, costs would remain unchanged whilst revenue would increase, thus the increase in revenue would be all profit. Such actions would be consistent with the underlying assumption of profit maximisation.

The insight into research on price elasticity of demand for transport services however has already partially answered this question by drawing a distinction between short-run and long-run elasticities. Whilst in the short run such an action by operators would increase profits, in the longer run some passengers would find alternative modes, hence revenue would fall. That said, Goodwin's (1992) value for long-run elasticity was −0.65, i.e. still price inelastic. On its own this would still suggest that operators should increase the price, as in the long run this would increase revenue and given the assumption of an identical network of services, increase profits. This issue can be resolved by examining the other determinants of price elasticity of demand, and firstly the proportion of income spent on the good or service. As prices increase, so also does the proportion of income spent on travel, and hence elasticity would increase, even in the short run. A second determinant that would be likely to change with such action would be the number and closeness of substitutes. As prices increase, this would present an opportunity for new operators to enter the market and hence compete away the higher profits now being achieved, which in the longer term would almost certainly be more detrimental to the existing operator. The market itself therefore would regulate against such action. The point to stress is that although demand for a certain good or service may be inelastic (hence suggesting a price rise), there are other factors (the determinants of price elasticity of demand) that also need to be considered in any such evaluation. These will determine the extent to which 'the market' regulates against such action.

CROSS PRICE ELASTICITY

Most of the concepts examined under own price elasticity of demand also apply to the other types of elasticity of demand. Rather than the sensitivity of consumers to changes in price, however, it is the sensitivity of consumer demand in relation to a change in one of the other determinants of demand, whether that be income, price of other goods, advertising and so on. Two of these are formally examined here, but these ideas apply to any of the determinants of demand.

The first to be examined is known as cross price elasticity of demand. This is a measure of the effect of a change in the fares or rates of one mode of transport or transport operator on the demand for the services of another mode/transport operator. Again this is assessed quantitatively, and formally calculated as:

$$\text{Cross price elasticity} = \frac{\text{Percentage change in quantity demanded of service A}}{\text{Percentage change in price of service B}}$$

Or using a shortened formula:

$$\text{CPED} \quad = \quad \frac{\%\Delta D_A}{\%\Delta P_B}$$

Where: CPED   =   cross price elasticity of demand
               D_A =   quantity demanded of service A
               P_B =   price of service B

Examination of cross price elasticity of demand therefore involves examining two goods or services. Within the transport sector, these services could be examined at different levels. This could be the cross price elasticity between two different transport modes, such as the train versus the car. Secondly, cross price elasticity could be calculated within the same mode, such as National Express's East Coast Glasgow to London rail service versus Virgin's West Coast Glasgow to London rail service. Finally, it could be examined within a single operator if they offer a variety of fares for the same journey but different standards of service. For example a train operator could examine the quantity demanded of their standard service versus the first class fare charge. This would assess the extent to which changes in the price of one of the services offered (first class) impacts upon demand for the other (standard class), and hence gives the elasticity between different market segments.

Cross price elasticity of demand also allows a distinction to be made between substitute goods and services and complementary goods and services. If the effect of a price increase in one good has a positive effect in terms of the demand for another, then these two goods or services would be considered to be substitutes. For example, say a reduction in the subsidy paid to rail operators caused an increase in the price of rail services, then what may be expected to happen in the gas market is shown in Figure 4.8.

This is the standard demand and supply curves from Chapter 3, with the reduction in subsidy to rail operators effectively representing an increase in costs. This causes a shift in the supply curve to the left and eventually leads to an increase in the price (P_{R1} to P_{R2}). As in many locations bus

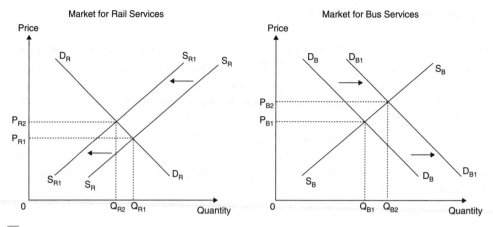

Figure 4.8 *Cross price elasticity of demand, substitutes*

services are an alternative to rail travel (i.e. a substitute), then this increase in the price of rail will cause an increase in the demand for bus services. This is shown on the right hand diagram in Figure 4.8 by a shift of the demand curve to the right from D_B to D_{B1}. You should be able to clearly see that in terms of the price of rail travel, P_{R2} is greater than P_{R1}, thus when this difference is expressed as a percentage this will produce a positive value, i.e. a price increase. Likewise, in terms of the bus market, the quantity traded of Q_{B2} is greater than Q_{B1}, thus again when expressed as a percentage will produce a positive value, i.e. a quantity increase. When these values are put into the cross price elasticity equation we obtain:

$$\text{CPED} \quad = \frac{\%\Delta D_B}{\%\Delta P_R} = \frac{^+ve}{^+ve} = {^+ve}$$

Where:

$\%\Delta D_B$ = percentage change in quantity demanded of bus services
$\%\Delta P_R$ = percentage change in the price of rail services
^+ve = a positive value

As a positive value is divided by a positive value, the net outcome would be a positive CPED figure. Thus for substitute transport services, cross price elasticity will always be positive. As the price of one service rises, demand for the alternative service also rises and vice-versa. The greater the degree of substitutability between the two services being compared, then the higher the value cross price elasticity will be. Note however that unlike own price elasticity of demand, there is no particular significance attached to the value of 1 and there are no upper or lower limits to the scale.

By the same logic, the cross price elasticity of demand will be negative for goods and services that are complements. Consider the following example of the price of cars and the market for petrol. If the cost of manufacturing motor cars was to rise, then this would cause an increase in the price of cars and a reduction in the level of quantity demanded. If there are less cars on the road, then less petrol will be required, hence there will be a decrease in demand for petrol. These are illustrated in Figure 4.9.

Again, this is illustrated by standard demand and supply curves, with the increase in the cost of manufacturing motor cars shown by a shift to the left of the supply curve and resulting in an increase in the price (P_{C1} to P_{C2}). As cars and petrol are consumed at the same time, this increase in the price of cars changes the market conditions for petrol, causing a decrease in demand, as shown on the right in the market for petrol by a shift in the demand curve to the left. As with above, you should be able to see that in terms of the price of cars, P_{C2} is greater than P_{C1}, thus when the difference is expressed as a percentage, this will be positive. This time, however, in terms of the quantity traded of petrol, Q_{P2} is less than Q_{P1}, thus when expressed as a percentage this produces a negative value. As above, when these values are put into the cross price elasticity equation, we obtain:

$$\text{CPED} = \frac{\%\Delta D_p}{\%\Delta P_C} = \frac{{}^{-}ve}{{}^{+}ve} = {}^{-}ve$$

Where:

$\%\Delta D_p$ = percentage change in quantity demand of bus services
$\%\Delta P_C$ = percentage change in the price of rail services
${}^{-}ve$ = a negative value

As a negative value is being divided by a positive, this produces a negative figure. Thus for complementary transport services, cross price elasticity will always be negative. As the price of one service rises, demand for the complementary good or service will decrease and vice-versa. Again the higher the negative value, the more the two goods are interdependent. Where the value is around zero however, this indicates that the two goods are completely independent, i.e. neither substitutes nor complements.

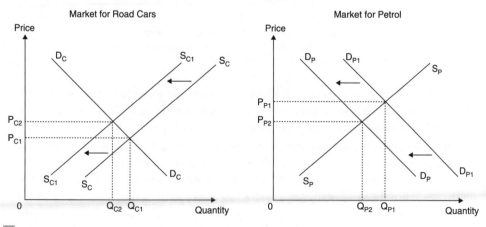

Figure 4.9   Cross price elasticity of demand, complements

To summarise, cross price elasticity of demand measures the interdependence of two modes of transport or services. Where this is positive, these are substitute services, with higher values indicating closer substitutability between the two modes being examined. Note also that this partly ties in with own price elasticity of demand, as other things being equal, if two products have a high cross price elasticity of demand then by implication own price elasticity should be highly elastic. This is because each of these services has a very close substitute available, which was the first determinant of price elasticity of demand examined. Complementary goods on the other hand will produce negative cross price elasticities, as these goods/services are consumed at the same time, thus a rise in the price of one will produce a decrease in the demand for the other.

Case study 4.2 Issues in cross price elasticity of demand

This case study takes a closer look at cross price elasticity and highlights a number of important issues surrounding the topic. It uses three research studies into cross price elasticity to illustrate these ideas, although many others exist. This should allow us to explore the topic further and as we will see, whilst the equation for cross price elasticity may appear to be fairly straightforward, working with some real life examples should help to bring certain aspects into perspective. We begin with Oum et al.'s (1990) review of around 70 studies relating to both passenger and freight transport with regard to both own and cross price elasticities. Here we are only concerned with cross price elasticity, thus a summary of the results of two of the studies examined, with the first set concerning freight presented in Table 4.3.

Table 4.3 *Cross price elasticities freight transport demand in Canada, mid range values, summary of Oum et al. (1990)*

Mode	Truck	Rail	Waterway
Truck	–	0.127	−0.100
Rail	0.020	–	0.175
Waterway	0.005	0.710	–

Source: Adapted from Oum *et al.* (1990)

Note: the change in quantity A is shown on the rows, hence for example the truck-rail figure of 0.127 is the percentage change in truck haulage as a result of a price increase in rail freight.

The first point to note is that both these figures and the ones shown later in Table 4.4 relate to Canada, and this will have implications on the interpretation of the findings, particularly the geographical aspects of the country and the sheer distances involved. This will impact directly on the values shown, because as with own price elasticity, cross price elasticities will vary from market to market. For example, in an earlier study on Canadian freight, Oum (1989) found a mid range value of +0.16 for Rail-Truck, significantly higher than that shown in Table 4.3. The difference is that the earlier study only examined the interregional market, rather than the total market, and hence the two modes are more likely to be substitutes in the longer-distance sector of the market. A further point to note purely for reference, is that the review originally devised a subjective range of upper and lower values from the studies examined, hence to simplify the mid range point is shown in Table 4.3. Returning to the table, you should note that there is no 'symmetry' in cross price elasticity values, i.e. a comparison of rail-truck is not the same as a comparison of truck-rail. The difference is that in the former it is the effect of a change in the price of truck on the demand for rail services, whilst the latter examines the effect of a change in the price of rail on the demand for trucking services. There is no reason to believe that rail users, due to an increase in the price of rail services, would react in exactly the same way by switching to truck haulage as truck haulage users would react by switching to rail as a result of an increase in the price of road haulage. The two are quite different concepts and we will see a clearer example of this below.

In Table 4.3, the highest value at +0.710 is given for the Waterway-Rail comparison. The positive value indicates that these two modes are substitute goods, and if this value is put into the CPED equation, we obtain:

$$\text{Cross elasticity} = \frac{\text{percentage change in quantity demanded of service A} - \text{waterways}}{\text{percentage change in price of service B} - \text{rail freight}}$$
$$= 0.710$$

Thus using a 10 per cent increase in the price of rail freight as an illustration, this would result in a 7.1 per cent increase in the demand of water transport, underlining the apparent high degree of substitutability between the two modes. These two modes therefore would appear to be in competition with each other, but even so it should be said that this is a very large value for a cross price elasticity. Rail-waterway on the other hand shows a very much smaller figure, at 0.175, indicating less cross over to railways as a result of increases in the price of water transport. Given the geography of Canada and the fact that 93 per cent of domestic water transport is located in only four provinces, this makes sense. Thus whilst water is a substitute for the train, the train is far less a substitute for water transport. Another key point to note, however, is that cross price values will be dependent upon relative market shares, with those modes with higher market shares having lower cross price elasticities as the relative increase in demand will be lower. This is best illustrated by an example. Say 100 million tonne kilometres go by water and this represents 20 per cent of the market, and a 10 per cent increase in the price of water transport results in 5 million tonne kilometres shifting to rail. If prior to the price increase rail carried 200 million tonne kilometres and thus 40 per cent of the market, this would give a cross price elasticity value rail-water of +0.125, as the 10 per cent increase in the price of water transport would cause a 1.25 per cent increase in the level of rail freight. If then the price of rail was to increase by 10 per cent and as a result the same shippers moved their cargo back to water, the cross price value water-rail would be far higher at +0.256, which is almost double because rail has double the market. Thus the 5 million tonne kilometres that are switching between the two modes is far less of a proportion of total rail transport than it is of total water transport. The impact of this effect on our Canadian freight example is that just under twice as much freight tonnage goes by rail than water in Canada. Thus whilst this partly accounts for the difference between the two cross price values, it still strongly suggests that water transport is more of a substitute for rail than rail is for water.

The second set of figures relates to passenger transport, and these are shown in Table 4.4.

Table 4.4 *Cross price elasticities intercity passenger transport demand in Canada, mid range values, Oum and Gillen (1983)*

Mode	Air	Bus	Rail
Air	–	−0.015	0.025
Bus	−0.085	–	−0.340
Rail	0.295	−0.675	–

Source: Adapted from Oum *et al.* (1990)

Note again that quantity A is shown on the rows.

A far clearer picture emerges with these figures. In simple terms, there is little substitutability between air and bus, and it is only in the bus and rail markets that there appears to be a two-way degree of dependence between them. Interestingly, however, the negative sign in both cases indicates they are complementary goods. As this concerns intercity services, this is a surprising result, although may indicate that bus services feed into intercity rail services, and that this effect is far stronger than the direct competition between the two on intercity routes. The table also shows that while the plane competes with the train, the train does not compete with the plane. Put another way, a change in air fares has an impact on rail travel demand, but a change in rail fares has little effect on air travel demand. This is because whilst a decrease in the air fare may cause some rail passengers to 'trade up' to air travel, a decrease in the price of rail travel will not have the same effect of causing some air travellers to 'trade down' to rail.

Turning to public transport, given below are the results of a study undertaken by Gilbert and Jalilian (1991) estimated from a monthly time series that covered the period 1972 to 1987. This study examined own and cross price elasticities for the London bus and underground, with the short run elasticity values reported in Table 4.5.

Table 4.5 *Short run own and cross price elasticities, London bus and underground ordinary tickets, Gilbert and Jalilian (1991)*

Mode	Prices		
	Bus	Underground	Rail
Bus	−0.839	0.476	0.082
Underground	0.041	−0.355	0.160

Source: Gilbert and Jalilian (1991)

This also appears to be more straightforward than our previous freight example. Reading for the bus first of all, then again taking a 10 per cent increase in the average fare as an illustration, this in the short run would be expected to produce an 8.39 per cent fall in bus usage. This contrasts quite markedly with Goodwin's −0.41 figure from above, and would suggest that the demand for London buses is far more price elastic than in other parts of the country. This value however was one of the highest estimates seen in the compilation of this case study for the elasticity of London buses, hence may be overstating the 'true' value. Nevertheless, continuing with our 10 per cent example, this would also cause a 4.76 per cent increase in underground patronage. The bus-rail cross elasticity suggests that the impact of changes in rail fares is very small on the demand for bus services. Speaking in general terms, therefore, the bus own price elasticity is very high, the underground is a substitute for the bus and the effect of rail prices on bus usage is very small. This suggests that in London the bus and railways serve two distinct markets.

Having analysed the impact of a change in the fare of the bus, the results for the underground should not be unexpected, and this is indeed the case. For the underground, own price elasticity of demand is far smaller (almost half the value of the bus), and an increase in the underground fare would cause only a very small increase in patronage of the bus. For example, using our 10 per cent example from above would only cause a 0.41 per cent increase in bus patronage. The impact of rail fares on underground usage although larger than for the bus is still relatively small. This study again underlines the non-symmetrical nature of cross price elasticities, showing that whilst the underground is a substitute for the bus, the bus is not a substitute for the underground. We could also perhaps further conclude that the proportion of trips on the underground that could be considered as 'essential' to be far higher than for the bus. This is because an increase in the price would lead to a far lower decline in patronage on the underground than the bus.

Combined with the earlier section on research into own price elasticities, there is a lot in this section to digest, and certainly a lot that can lead to confusion – even basic issues such as the direction of the comparison is not always clear. The point of the exercise however was not to bewilder or even to give 'definitive answers' to transport elasticities, as none exist that can be applied to all situations. Rather, the point is to give a realistic feel for the issues surrounding transport elasticities, how these can be used to analyse transport markets and to focus thinking on these key topics. This last example underlines particularly well the issues involved, and hopefully has illustrated the significance of own and cross price elasticity when planning any transport system.

INCOME ELASTICITY

Income elasticity of demand is a measure of the responsiveness of demand to changes in income. As real incomes are likely to increase over time, income elasticity identifies those markets that may be expected to see an increase in demand in the future and those markets that perhaps, if other things remain equal, may expect to see a decline.

Income elasticity of demand is calculated as:

$$\text{Income elasticity} = \frac{\text{Percentage change in quantity demanded}}{\text{Percentage change in income}}$$

Or using a shortened formula:

$$\text{YED} = \frac{\%\Delta D}{\%\Delta Y}$$

Where: YED = income elasticity of demand

D   = quantity demanded of the good or service

Y   = income

By this stage you should notice that when any elasticity is being measured, changes in demand are always put on the numerator and changes in the determinant being examined on the denominator. Note also that income is always represented in economics by the letter Y, as similarly price is always represented by the letter P. Hence, YED stands for the income elasticity of demand. When income elasticity is measured, it is not the total income of consumers that is used in the assessment but rather disposable income, i.e. net of income tax.

As outlined in Chapter 3, transport is defined as a normal good, in that more is demanded at higher levels of income. It should follow therefore that income elasticity of demand should be positive for transport. A re-examination of Case study 3.1 from Chapter 3 should confirm that this is indeed the case, which showed that as national income (GDP) has risen, so also has the level of transport. With regard to individual modes, however, whilst the car, the train and air travel, all of which are generally used by higher-income groups, would be considered to be normal goods, this does not apply to all modes of transport or to all situations. The bus for example may be considered as an inferior good, in that demand will fall for this form of public transport as incomes rise. Again, Case study 3.2 would appear to verify this.

Does this mean therefore that because real incomes have been rising over time (and continue to rise), the demand for bus services will eventually disappear altogether? Whilst there are many products in the past that have now vanished from the market due to this effect, this is highly unlikely for bus travel, and again a distinction needs to be drawn between the short and the longer terms. In the short term, income elasticity for bus travel is negative, and hence as real incomes increase consumers will use other forms of transport, most notably the private car. For this to continue into the longer term, however, all other things would have to remain equal. With particular reference to the bus, it is extremely unlikely that this will be the case, as issues such as pollution, land use, safety and so on become more acute. Hence in the longer term the income elasticity of demand for bus services is likely to become less negative. This effect is something again that Case study 3.2 illustrated had already taken place in the case of London, where bus patronage has been rising since the mid 1990s.

Finally, it is worth highlighting that not only can income elasticity change over time but also that there are limits on short-term income elasticity because travel is limited by the amount of time available. It has been suggested that although business and leisure travel increases with income, there comes a point when the demand curve flattens out or even begins to fall because limits are placed on the time available for travel. What this means is that incomes have little effect on travel demand as in simple terms there is simply no more time available to use on the activity.

Case study 4.3 Issues surrounding income elasticity of demand

This is the last case study into the issues surrounding demand elasticities, and should be the most straightforward. Nevertheless, there are some important considerations when examining income elasticity of transport demand which this case will attempt to bring out, again with the assistance of real life examples. The first is what is known as the 'car ownership effect' (TRL, 2004). This occurs where the income elasticity for public transport is affected both directly by the increase in income that will be generating an increased demand for travel, but also by increasing levels of car ownership. Thus for example an increase in income will cause an increase in the demand for rail travel; however, this would be smaller than expected if everything else remained equal as it will be partially offset by increasing levels of car ownership. Some studies adjust for such effects whereas others do not. A second point is that whilst it may be expected that there will be a greater overall consistency in income elasticity of demand for transport than for either own or cross price elasticities, it will nevertheless still be to a large extent dependent upon the area and hence the transport market in which people travel. In London, for example, the car ownership effect will tend to be far smaller as opportunities for actually using the car are far more constrained, hence if not taken into account income elasticities for public transport will tend to be larger. As we will see, however, this is not the case for other major conurbations in Britain.

We first examine the effect of changes in income on bus demand. Table 4.6 presents values from Dargay and Hanly (1999), who examined demand elasticities in the British bus market and broke these down into ever smaller geographical areas. Hence national refers to the total, which is then broken down into around 11 regions and finally county and PTE areas (the 6 largest English conurbations outside of London) within these regions. They also importantly broke elasticity effects into short and long run periods. The short run was defined as anything less than a year, the long run anything over that.

Table 4.6   *Bus-income elasticities*

Journeys	Short run	Long run
National Data	0.00	−0.45 to −0.80
Regional Data	0.00 to −0.29	−0.64 to −1.13
County Data	−0.30 to −0.40	−0.60 to −0.70
PTE Data	−0.70	−1.60

Source: Dargay and Hanly (1999)

These values for income elasticity of demand for bus services confirm that the bus is considered as an 'inferior' good. This is because all are negative. Hence, as income rises demand for bus services falls. Using the short run PTE value of −0.70, this means that a 10 per cent increase in real incomes will lead to a 7 per cent fall in the use of the bus in the major conurbations outside of London. Again, notice that in all cases the long run effect is significantly larger than the short run, hence following an increase in income consumers will continue to switch to alternative modes of transport over time. In this study, the relative breakdown into the different geographical areas also makes interesting reading. Changes in income have the largest impact on bus services in the PTE areas, i.e. the largest conurbations in Britain, and the lowest impact on the regions. This may be directly related to usage, where the level of car ownership tends to be far higher in more sparsely populated areas, thus whilst strange to say, those not using the bus are already not using it and thus the effect of income on bus usage will be lower.

Turning to the train, very different results may be expected and the findings presented in Table 4.7 from a study by the ATOC (2002) confirm this to be the case.

Table 4.7   *South East Britain income rail elasticities (2002)*

Area	Income elasticity
South East to London	2.07
London to South East	1.90
South East Non London	0.89
Non London	0.11

Source: ATOC (2002)

The ATOC study was based upon relatively short journeys (of less than 20 miles/32 kilo-metres), and as expected all are positive; hence an increase in income would result in an increase in the demand for rail services. The variations between the different area/routes however are quite substantial. This is obviously strongly related to the economic importance and pulling power of the British capital, London. Trips into London therefore from the surrounding districts would increase the most with changes in income. In this case, however, some symmetry between the income elasticity of trips out of London to the South East and from the South East into London may be expected (as for example commuters have to go both ways!); however, the estimates have put the former at a slightly higher value. It is nevertheless worth remember-ing the basic formula for income elasticity of demand, and hence a 5 per cent increase in incomes in the south east would lead to a 10.35 per cent increase in rail travel from the south east to London, which represents a massive impact. Outside of the south east, however, the effect of rising incomes on the demand for rail travel is far less pronounced, which may be related to a greater choice of alternative modes, particularly the car, in those areas. That said, the disparity between the south east and the rest of the country would appear to be overly stated, with the last figure appearing to be unrealistically low (TRL, 2004). Further research by TRL (2004) found this value to be +0.41 for non PTE areas, which would appear to be more realistic.

This case has examined the impact of changes on income on the demand for transport. Despite initial expectations in the introduction of a higher level of consistency in values across markets, the actual case study does not appear to have borne this out – long run bus income elasticity values ranged from −0.45 to −1.6 and rail showed an even higher variation between markets from +0.41 up to +2.07. This again reflects different market conditions, and hence the effect of an increase in income will be different across these markets. Generally speaking, in highly densely populated urban areas impacts on rail transport will tend to be strong in an upward direction, whilst in less populated areas the relatively higher car ownership levels will tend to dominate and consequently income elasticities for public transport as a whole are likely to be considerably lower.

One final thought on this case study is to return to the question posed before – with rising real incomes, will the bus vanish as a mode of transport? What current income elasticity values, even those relating to the long run, are picking up is that if real income levels increase at present rates, then the overall demand for transport will increase and this will not be by the bus. The final thought is that in many urban areas, if mobility levels do considerably rise, then the bus, whilst space efficient, will not be able to satisfactorily cope with the rise in demand, and other more efficient 'movers of the masses' will have to be introduced. This of course refers to light rail and metro systems and hence in some areas, despite the earlier proposition, the bus will indeed die out as a mode of transport.

CHAPTER SUMMARY AND REFLECTION

In this chapter we have examined the elasticity of demand of consumers. Three types of elasticity relevant to the transport sector have been outlined, namely own price, cross price and income elasticity, although the elasticity of any of the determinants of demand can be assessed using the same principles. Elasticities are measured quantitatively with the change in demand on the numerator and the change in the determinant being examined on the denominator. The main determinants of own price elasticity were examined and a practical illustration on the size of such values showed that there are no generic values for the elasticity of public transport services, as how consumers will react to price changes will vary from one situation and one market to another. Ball park values of −0.4 for the short run and −0.8 for the long run however would appear to be reasonable. Both cross price and income elasticities also showed the same level of variation from one situation to another, similarly reflecting differences between markets.

Demand elasticity will feature in subsequent chapters. We have already seen that elasticity values vary from market to market, and this is primarily due to the number and closeness of substitutes in these markets. Market structure, therefore, has a big impact on demand elasticity. This will be considered further in Chapter 6; however, the next chapter examines the supply side of the market and the issues surrounding the cost of providing the service.

CHAPTER EXERCISES

Exercise 4.1 Own price elasticity

Presented below are price and quantity figures facing a UK rail operator. The current price is £1 and estimated demand figures are given for sequential price reduction from £6 down to a free fare, and demand rises from zero up to 240. What you have to do is calculate the missing figures, and then graph out the relationship between price and quantity and quantity and revenue on something akin to the two blank charts below before answering the following questions.

Table 4.1a

Price	per cent Change	Quantity	per cent Change	PED
6	–	0	–	–
5		40	–	–
4		80		
3		120		
2		160		
1		200		
0		240		

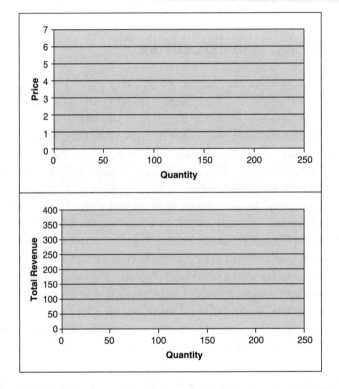

a) How does this exercise relate to the theory concerning price elasticity of demand outlined earlier in this chapter?

b) What does this tell us about the profit maximising position of the company?

c) What do you consider to be the main determinant that is affecting the elasticity values as the price falls?

Exercise 4.2 Price elasticity of demand, a practical exercise

A local bus company is facing strong competition in its 'home' market, as a consequence its demand curve is relatively elastic due to the existence and closeness of a high number of readily available substitute transport services.

Nevertheless, the workforce of the company, after years of accepting low pay deals, have put in a wage demand significantly above the rate of inflation which could potentially put £1m onto the costs of the firm. In order to counter this potentially serious situation, the management board have brought you in as a consultant to advise on its possible courses of action. After studying the situation, you outline three alternative 'strategies' that are open to the board. These are:

1   Bargain strongly with the workforce from the negotiating position that large pay increases will cost jobs.
2   Agree to the workforce's pay claim, but tie any such payment agreement with significant increases in productivity and possible redundancies.
3   As with two above, agree to the workforce's pay claim, tying in any such pay agreement with significant increases in productivity, but in this case undertake an expansionist competitive position by slightly increasing services levels and cutting prices.

When you put these options to the board, they 'like' option 1 although they don't quite understand it, option 2 they simply don't understand and are completely baffled by option three. They point out that as the firm is facing potentially a large increase in its costs, that will surely mean increased fares and a possible reduction of services, which is the exact opposite of option 3. Your counter that it is all to do with the price elasticity of demand fails to shed any further light on the matter.

Part A

i   In order to convince the board of the viability of each of your options, briefly outline the concepts of elastic and inelastic demand.
ii Outline each of the alternative options explaining how they 'work'.
iii Point out to the board what their options (and the related 'strength' of their bargaining position) would have been if demand for their services had been relatively inelastic.

Now that you have explained that, the board seem quite keen to pursue option 3. As a consequence, you advise them to commission a market survey to investigate the possible effect of changes in the fare on the company's total revenue. The results of this survey are presented below.

▨ *Table 4.2a*

Fare	Demand (million journeys per year)	Total revenue (£ms)	Old cost (£ms)	New cost (£ms)
£0.80	18.0	14.4	11.0	12.0
£1.00	12.0	12.0	11.0	12.0
£1.20	8.0	9.6	11.0	12.0

As it stands, the company currently charge a £1 flat fare on all of its routes at all times, hence the £1 fare above represents the current position in terms of fare and demand levels. With the current wage agreement, profits are therefore £1m per annum. As can be seen, however, this profit may be entirely wiped out if the workforce's pay claim is agreed without any concessions. If the company was to increase the fare to £1.20 then the survey confirms that this would actually significantly increase losses. Even at the 'breakeven' position of the £1 fare, the firm would have no funds for investment and could potentially in the longer term be driven out of business as it would have no profits from which to fund new buses when the existing stock wears out.

Part B

In order to further illustrate the principles involved to the board, you should answer the following three questions:

i Calculate the price elasticity of demand for the price decrease of £1 to 80p and for the price increase from £1 to £1.20.
ii Should the firm have brought you in earlier as a consultant, i.e. was the fare set at the right level at the beginning in order to maximise profits?
iii With regard to the 80p fare reduction option, the above information is accurate as long as the increase in demand is met by current underutilised services. As highlighted above, however, some increase in services will be required to meet this increased demand – how should the board decide whether this is a viable option or not?

Part C

i What is the major assumption that the above analysis presupposes?
ii What, if anything, have you learned from undertaking this exercise?

Exercise 4.3 Income, own and cross price elasticities

This is a totally artificial exercise; however, it is designed to try to get you to think about own price, cross price and income elasticities. Presented below are some completely hypothetical passenger figures for public transport services in a hypothetical city somewhere near you!

Transport Mode:	Rail	Bus	Underground	Total
Annual usage (millions):	38	90	23	151

For this hypothetical public transport market, the following elasticities apply:

▨ Table 4.3a

	Rail	Bus	Underground
Income elasticity of demand:	0.41	−0.50	0.32

		Price		
Own & cross price elasticities		Rail	Bus	Underground
	Rail	−0.45	−0.40	−0.30
Quantity	Bus	0.08	−0.40	0.10
	Underground	0.02	0.05	−0.20

Note: modes listed on rows relate to the quantity change in demand, those listed in columns relate to change in price

Using all of these values you should be able to answer the following questions – as a side note, if you have the necessary skills you may find a spreadsheet useful to assist with this exercise.

a) If there is a 5 per cent rise in income, what would be the new daily modal splits and the new total daily usage?

b) Using your answer for the new total daily usage from part (a), what is the overall income elasticity to travel?

c) How does your answer from part (b) compare with the results presented in Case study 3.1 in Chapter 3 and what might be the reason for any such differences? (Hint: you will need to calculate a rough elasticity from the values presented in the case study.)

d) Calculate the effect on modal splits and the new monthly usage of the impact of the following factors (each should be considered on its own) and from your answers highlight which modal fare has the largest impact on the overall demand for travel in this city.

    i a 15 per cent increase in the level of rail fares

    ii a 15 per cent increase in the level of bus fares

    iii a 15 per cent increase in the level of underground fares

e) What might be expected to happen to the cross price elasticity of the train across all other modes if the level of rail travel was to significantly increase? Why would this happen?

f) Roughly speaking, why have we got the answers that we have got for part c and what does this underline with regard to own and cross price elasticities of public transport services?

Exercise 4.4 Elasticity and the tax take – why all the good things in life are taxed!

In order to finance a considerable improvement in public transport provision, the government needs to raise significant levels of public finance. Increasing income tax is not seen as a realistic option due to the unpopularity of such taxes with the electorate. The government therefore decides to raise this finance through an expenditure (as opposed to an income) tax. What type of good (price elastic or inelastic) should the government impose this tax upon? In order to help answer this question, you should draw two illustrations in the form of the basic market graph, which illustrate the shift in the supply curve as a result of the increase in tax and then note the effect this would have on an elastic and an inelastic good. Note also that the resultant change in revenue would be the effect on the total tax take, as all additional revenue raised is tax. What does this exercise tell us about general taxation policies; are, for example, cigarettes taxed purely for health reasons or petrol taxed purely because of environmental/conservation concerns?

Transport costs

INTRODUCTION

Whilst elasticity of demand impacts upon the demand side of the market, a major factor affecting the quantity supplied is the cost of production. Transport costs however fall into a variety of different classes. There are those costs that impact on the individual user of a particular mode of transport who directly benefits from undertaking a journey. These are known as private costs and would include both the financial costs involved, such as the fare in the case of public transport, as well as non financial costs, such as the time involved in undertaking the journey. Taken together these are known as the 'generalised cost'. There are then the costs of transport that fall on non users of the transport service who do not benefit from that transport service. This includes what could almost be termed the unwanted by-products from the undertaking of transport activities, such as polluted air, the congested road, noise and visual intrusions. These are generally referred to as public costs, and as these are a significant factor in the provision of transport services these will be examined in some depth in various chapters later in the text. Finally there are production costs that fall on the operators of a transport service or in the case of private transport the financial costs incurred when undertaking the activity. In many ways these are essentially private costs, as the individual that incurs the cost (the operator/road user) is the one that benefits from the provision of that service (i.e. profit/benefit from the journey). This chapter is specifically concerned with costs that fall into this last group, particularly in the production of public transport services. Road user issues are examined later in Chapter 8 under pricing.

Public transport costs have received a large amount of attention over the years, as these services are a vital component of the economy and society and have been to a greater or lesser extent subsidised by national and local governments. In simple terms, high cost levels restrict transport authorities' options and constrain the level of public transport services that can be provided. Even where such services are not subsidised and are provided by profit-making private companies, the constraints placed on supply arising from costs still apply: you should remember from Chapter 3 that the cost of production is one of the main determinants of supply. Following that logic, if costs can be reduced more transport services can be provided, i.e. supply can be increased. In subsidised markets, of course, lower costs reduce the need for subsidy.

Attempting to reduce and maintain downward pressure on public transport costs has therefore been a main concern of government policy. This has been one of the main reasons for on-going moves by authorities to shift transport operators more towards 'the market' rather than operating as state owned and controlled public enterprises. This move has resulted in a substantial shift from publicly owned operators towards privately owned companies and the introduction of market principles, most visibly, through competition in one form or another in the supply of transport services.

The actual size of costs and authorities' attempts to keep them as low as possible however are not the only issues surrounding costs. How costs are incurred is also important. For example, in many instances there may be a large initial overhead incurred by the firm but the actual cost of providing one extra service or carrying one extra passenger may be very small. For example, the extra cost to a bus or train operator of transporting an additional passenger, if they are operating at less than full capacity, is negligible. Alternatively, there are other cases where there is a very low initial overhead but most costs are incurred as a direct result of providing the transport service. Even at a more basic level, are large companies more cost effective than small companies or does an 'optimum' size exist, i.e. not too big and not too small? There may for example be certain advantages to being a large-scale operation that leads to certain cost savings; however, in other cases the sheer size of the firm may cause certain inefficiencies to arise. All of these issues will heavily influence the structure of the transport sector and determine how transport services are provided to the market.

THE EFFICIENT PRODUCTION OF TRANSPORT SERVICES

The costs of transport operations are primarily dependent upon a combination of the production processes used and the efficiency of the management of that production process. Not only that, however, but the physical characteristics of the operating environment in which transport services are provided will also impact upon costs. The start/stop nature of urban bus operations due to high densities of population, for example, tend to make such an environment more costly to provide public transport services per vehicle kilometre than in rural areas – DfT statistics (DfT, 2007) for example show the cost per bus kilometre to be some two and a half times higher in London than for the rest of England outside of the metropolitan areas. The reason for this is the considerably longer running distances between stops and overall faster running speeds in rural areas. There is little that transport management can do however about these aspects of operation. In terms of controllable costs, therefore, it is only the production process that is under the direct control of management, and consequently is the main determinant of costs to the operator.

It may be difficult to reconcile transport operators with the idea of the traditional firm, where inputs are fed in at one end of the factory and finished goods emerge from the other. The main difference of course is that transport is a service, and thus production is concerned with producing 'service units'. In order to measure the output of the transport firm, therefore, such 'service units' need to be quantitatively defined. This first raises the question of what exactly do transport operators produce, which is not as easy a question to address as it may first seem. What needs to be considered is what are transport operators actually attempting to achieve. The answer may appear to be obvious; a public transport operator, for example, simply moves people from A to B. Output would therefore be measured in terms of the journeys undertaken, either directly by the number of journeys or by the total number of passenger kilometres to also account for differences in distances travelled. Strange as it may appear, however, in many cases moving people from one location to another is not the aim of a public transport operator. Many instances exist where operators are contracted by transport authorities to provide transport services within a given area or location, irrespective of the number of people moved. Rather than journeys, therefore, the output would be measured in terms of the number and level of services produced, and hence could be expressed in terms of vehicle kilometres. How, therefore, should the output of the transport firm be measured, by journeys or by vehicle kilometres produced?

These two different outputs can be equated by the idea that what operators attempt to do is move people from A to B, but how this is achieved is through the production of vehicle kilometres. The idea of producing vehicle kilometres is far more consistent with the traditional view of production, but this whole topic needs to be related to the aims of the producer, which you may remember is one of the determinants of supply. These can vary from profit maximisation in a completely free transport market where revenue is only related to the carriage of passengers, to sales maximisation in a tightly regulated market where the transport company is directly paid to operate the service and hence profit maximises by attempting to fill the available capacity. Passenger journeys as the output would be more consistent with the former as revenue is only connected to the carriage of passengers, whilst vehicle kilometres specified as the output would be more consistent with the latter, as the firm is paid to provide services and hence profits are maximised through filling the available capacity, i.e. sales maximise. What is important in this context is that there is some measurable output at the end of the production process, whether that be the number of journeys or the number of vehicle kilometres produced, and this will largely be dependent upon the type of market the firm is operating in.

You should already be aware of the concept of production; however, in this context it specifically relates to the process whereby economic inputs or resources in the form of the factors of production (recall from Chapter 1 that this relates to inputs in the form of land, labour and capital) are brought together by entrepreneurs (or firms) in order to produce goods and services. This basic process is outlined in Figure 5.1.

As illustrated by the figure, the production process consists of converting the inputs of Land/ Raw Materials, Labour and Capital, by way of a combination process, into the outputs of Transport Services and By-Products. Transport Services are then sold for an economic return, with the aim being that the transformation process should convert the inputs into something of a higher economic value. The revenue generated from the sale of the output therefore should be greater than the payment for the inputs. Also shown in Figure 5.1 is 'By-products'. Not all of the output of the combination process is sold for an economic return, as the process also results in the output

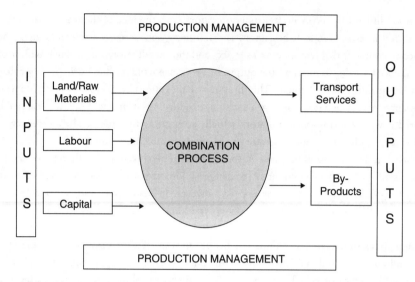

Figure 5.1 *The production process*

of other factors such as wastage or pollution. Often overlooked, this has to be included in the outputs of the production process and has important implications for transport markets.

To directly relate Figure 5.1 to transport industries, 'land' is an important factor in the production process, but of the three it is the one that is least under the control of transport operators. This is because land in many cases relates to the 'suitability' of the prevailing geographical environment to the provision of transport services. This was exemplified above by the urban/rural split, although many other examples exist. The provision of rail services, for example, will be relatively easier in areas of flat terrain (such as many parts of Belgium) rather than in mountainous regions (such as many parts of Switzerland). This is because the latter will require a far higher level of tunnels and bridging, i.e. less 'land' and more capital, in the production of services.

The other two factors of production are far more straightforward and more under the direct control of the firm. Put simply, labour relates to all staff involved in the production of transport services, whether that be operational or administrative staff, whilst capital relates to any goods that have been manufactured in order to be put into the production process. This obviously not only includes the vehicle stock, but also any other physically made equipment, e.g. terminal buildings, infrastructure, bridges, tunnels, handling equipment, depots and IT facilities.

The transformation process outlined above is known as production, and the relationship between the level of inputs and the level of the outputs achieved known as the production function. This is formally specified below:

$$Q = f(A, L, K)$$

Where:

Q = quantity of output produced
f   = 'some function of'

A = quantity of land and raw materials used in the production process
L = quantity of labour used in the production process
K = quantity of capital used in the production process

This equation simply states that the level of output is some function of land/raw materials, labour and capital, with the letters L and K always used in economics as the shorthand notation of these two inputs. Where an increase in the inputs leads to an increase in the outputs, which should virtually always be the case, then production would be said to be monotonic. Whilst appearing to be common sense, this is actually an important theoretical consideration as real life data does not always fit with what would appear to be a very basic theoretical concept. The inputs/outputs ratio is also one of the main bases for assessing whether a given operation can be described as 'efficient' or not. The idea of efficiency in the production of public transport services is an important concept, and as noted above has received considerable attention in the academic literature. 'Efficiency' however is an often over-used term and has different meanings to different people. Within the field of transport, it has been used in the past to describe issues such as reliability, punctuality, pricing, costs, subsidy levels, number of passengers carried and so on. Within economics, however, there are only three basic 'types' of efficiency although these may be seen elsewhere under slightly different terms. However, they are:

Technical efficiency – this relates to the outputs to inputs ratio, with a technically efficient operator being one that uses the minimum level of inputs to produce the maximum level of outputs. Alternatively, this may be achieved where the minimum level of inputs is used to produce a given level of output. Both measures are highly relevant in the study of transport industries, as in many transport markets the output level is set by a transport authority and hence for the operator the technical efficiency question is one of input minimisation.

Cost efficiency – sometimes referred to as productive efficiency, or even cost allocative efficiency, cost efficiency arises because there may be several different ways to produce the output, all of which would be technically efficient. For example, a high level of capital and a low level of labour could be employed, or alternatively a high level of labour and a low level of capital employed. Both production processes may be technically efficient. The issue therefore becomes which one is the 'best'. In order to answer this question, the relative prices of labour and capital are examined and the one that produces the lowest cost combination deemed to be the 'best' or more exactly the most cost efficient.

Allocative efficiency – even within the study of economics, there is much confusion over the term 'allocative efficiency', which is quite surprising given it is almost the holy grail of the economics discipline! Allocative efficiency however relates to usage. As many of the former Eastern European countries showed in the past, there is little point in producing goods and services that are technically efficient in the lowest cost combinations if no one wants them. This is a total waste of resources and hence could never be considered as efficient. Allocative efficiency is therefore said to exist where goods and services are produced cost efficiently and in the 'right' quantities. Where this exact position is found is where the price paid for the good, which can be used as in indicator of the additional benefit received from that good, equals the extra cost of producing that good. This however is an issue which will be returned to in greater depth in the following chapter.

The first two of these efficiency concepts can be illustrated graphically, which is done in Figure 5.2.[1]

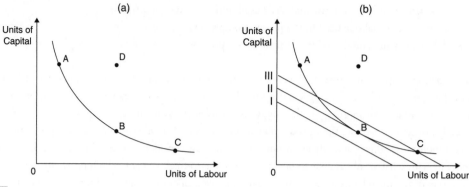

Figure 5.2 *Technical and cost efficiency*

On the left, Figure 5.2 (a) illustrates the combinations of labour and capital required to produce a single unit of output. Consequently, points nearer the origin are more efficient, as relatively speaking less of the inputs are used in the production process. Also shown are the relative positioning of four hypothetical firms, A to D. In this example there exists a large range of combinations of the two inputs that can be used; this varies from a high element of labour and a low amount of capital (firm A), to a high level of capital and low amount of labour (firm C). Whilst this may appear to have little relevance to transport services where the relative quantities of labour and capital are unlikely to vary greatly across firms in the same industry, some variation does exist and this is often the situation with regard to the carriage of people and freight across a number of different modes. These tend to employ varying levels of capital and labour in order to achieve the same purpose. In Figure 5.2 (a) firms A, B and C have the lowest possible combinations of labour and capital, thus an efficiency frontier can be drawn between these points. Consequently points above that 'frontier' would represent inefficient firms and points below simply unobtainable with the level of today's technology. You should hopefully recall that this is identical to the idea of the production possibility curve introduced in Chapter 1, only expressed in a different way: in this case the focus is on minimising inputs rather than maximising the output. The frontier is curved for theoretical reasons that surround variations in the way that one input is substituted by the other across different levels of the inputs, known as elasticities of substitution. As firms A, B and C outline the actual technical efficiency frontier, all three would be deemed to be technically efficient. This is because there is no way of assessing which is the 'best' combination of the two inputs – technical efficiency is simply concerned with the lowest combination of units used in the production process, not whether this represents the best 'mix' of the inputs to use. Firm D however lies above the frontier and thus would be said to be technically inefficient. This is because D is using a higher amount of capital than firm A and also a higher level of labour than firm B in the production process.

As regards the best combination of labour and capital to use in the production process, this can only be assessed once the prices of the individual factor inputs are introduced into the evaluation. Assuming that all firms within the industry face identical cost conditions, this is done in Figure 5.2(b). Added to the figure are budget lines, which are linear combinations of the costs of employing labour and capital and are drawn as straight lines out from the origin. These are straight because the combination of prices of the inputs are fixed, hence the cost of substituting one input for another is fixed over the various combinations of capital and labour that can be employed. The slope is determined by the relative prices of the two inputs of labour and capital.

The first 'viable' budget line on Figure 5.2(b) is line II, as this is the first that is tangential to the technical efficiency frontier. Firm B therefore has the lowest cost combination of inputs, as it lies both on the technical efficiency frontier and the lowest budget cost line. Note that in the case of the two other technically efficient points illustrated in Figure 5.2(a), firm C is on a higher budget line and hence would have a higher cost combination, and point A would lie on a higher budget line again.

These are the basic principles concerning the efficient production of transport services, but note these only concern production and not actual usage, i.e. allocative efficiency. This could be measured based on profit, as that would account for usage and whilst incredibly naive, profitable firms must be efficient as the output being produced is not only being used by consumers, but is also valued by them at a higher price than it cost to produce – hence they make a profit. It would be very difficult in practical terms however to use profit as a measure of efficiency, due to the presence of other (external) factors. Indeed these lead to the conclusion that it is virtually impossible to accurately assess the level of allocative efficiency in transport markets. As an example, the provision of a little used rural bus service may be essential to the daily functioning of a local community. However, if the level of allocative efficiency was to be assessed based on profit, then due to the relatively large number of resources (inputs) being used to move a relatively small number of people, this would always make a loss and hence be considered to be highly inefficient. Nevertheless, removal of the service on the grounds of allocative inefficiency may reduce overall welfare because a significant percentage of the benefits arising from the service do not accrue to the direct users of the service and hence would not be included in any such evaluation. In an entirely free market, however, that is exactly what would happen. This raises many issues, which we return to later in the text; however, the rest of this chapter concentrates on costs and production.

The economist's definition of time

We begin our examination of costs by firstly considering the issue of time. This needs to be examined in order to devise formal definitions for what is a relatively 'short' period of time and what is a relatively 'long' period of time. The reason for doing this is that costs may behave quite differently depending upon whether a relatively short period of time or a relatively long period of time is being considered. Time is defined in terms of the extent to which the factors of production can be varied in order to produce a different level of output.

The short run

In economics the short run is formally defined as that period of time during which at least one of the factors of production is fixed. This could in theory be any of the inputs; however, it normally relates to capital. The implication therefore is that variations in the level of output can only be achieved through variation in one or more of the other inputs, normally labour. This may be achieved through overtime working, employment of agency labour and so on.

The long run

In the long run, variations in the level of output can be achieved through variation of all of the outputs, thus the firm is not restricted to using only one of them. Capital can therefore be expanded to achieve such gains.

As regards an actual time period for the short and long runs, i.e. months, years and so on, this can vary considerably from industry to industry. In relatively labour-intensive industries, i.e. those that employ a relatively high degree of labour, such as the bus industry, the length of time in the short run can probably be measured in days or weeks. Hence a few days or a couple of weeks is roughly the length of time it would take a bus company to increase the capital stock of the firm, i.e. purchase a second-hand bus, assuming they are available. Procurements of new buses, however, will probably take considerably longer and would be measured in months. In more capital-intensive industries, i.e. those that employ a relatively high degree of capital in the production process, such as the rail industry, the short run can probably last up to a number of years. Thus for a railway company, the gap between ordering new rolling stock and it actually being introduced into service will take a minimum of roughly two years and can take anything up to five. There is therefore no fixed period of time as such with regard to the short and long runs, it will vary from industry to industry dependent upon how long it takes to vary all of the factors of production.

The very long run

The final definition of time in economics is the very long run. In simple terms the very long run is that period of time where all factors of production are variable, including the level of technology. Thus production levels that are not possible today may be possible in the very long run due to an increase in the level of technology.

COSTS AND PRODUCTION IN THE SHORT RUN

Having considered what constitutes 'efficient' production and the time dimension in production economics, the actual production process in the short run is now considered and the underlying economic concepts underpinning production theory examined. Short run production is considered first as this is the most basic form of the production function outlined earlier, as only one input is varied to produce variations in the level of output. The total output produced is known as the total product, with other important concepts in short run production being the average and marginal outputs (of the variable factor), known as the average and marginal products. The average product is simply the total product divided by the number of units of the variable factor, and hence in the case of labour would be more commonly known as labour productivity, i.e. the average amount produced by each person employed. The marginal product is the change in the total product that results from adding one more unit of the variable factor into the production process. Thus, for example, say two people are employed to drive a taxi which results in a daily mileage of 100 miles. The average product would be 50 miles. If however daily coverage was to be expanded, in the short run as one of the factors of production is fixed this could only be achieved by either increasing the number of drivers, or increasing the number of taxis, but not by increasing both. If therefore say one further driver was employed and the daily mileage rose to 120 miles, then average product would be 40 miles and the marginal product 20 miles. The theoretical relationship between total, average and marginal products is illustrated in Figure 5.3.

The main issue to consider here is the shape and relative positions of these three curves. Firstly, the total product curve – this is in the form of an 'S' shape. Hence, as more units of labour are added to the fixed amount of capital, production not only increases but increases at an increasing rate. This is up to point a in Figure 5.3, which is the point of the highest marginal product as shown in the lower diagram. Beyond point a, as more of the variable factor is added production still rises, but at a decreasing rate, reaching the highest point of average product curve at point b before eventually total product declines after point c. Thus in the short run some form of maximum output is reached. This tailing off effect after point a is known as the law of diminishing marginal returns. Peppers and Bails (1987) clarify that the marginal product of the variable factor of production will eventually decline if enough of it is combined with the fixed factor. In other words, a variable input cannot endlessly be added to a fixed factor to continually achieve ever increasing levels of output. A second point to note is that the marginal product curve cuts the average product curve at the latter's highest point. This relationship between the marginal and the average is an important concept in economics and one that will appear in many other contexts. It is however a simple mathematical relationship. In this example, while extra units of labour are increasing total output by more than the average, then this will increase the average. If however the

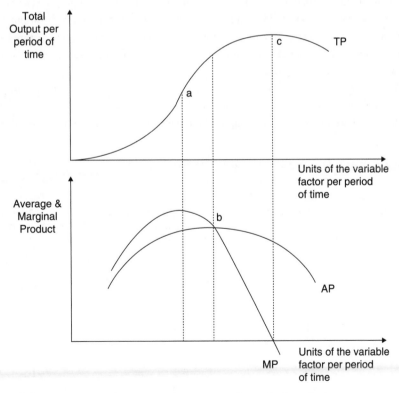

Figure 5.3   Short run production, total, average and marginal product

last person employed should add less to the total output than the average, this will pull the average down.[2]

Points b and c in Figure 5.3 can be used to break down the production process into three stages, known conveniently as Stage 1, Stage 2 and Stage 3 production. The divisions are based upon the total and marginal products. In Stage 1 production, the marginal product is always increasing, hence total product is increasing at a rising rate. This would be up to point b in Figure 5.3. In Stage 2 production, diminishing marginal returns set in. Thus although the marginal product is positive it is falling in value, and thus total product is increasing at a declining rate; in other words from point b to point c. The earlier taxi example was a case of Stage 2 production, as the last driver added reduced average product from 50 to 40 miles per employee. Finally in Stage 3 production the marginal product becomes negative and total product is decreasing, as shown by all points beyond point c in Figure 5.3.

All of these ideas are best underpinned by a practically orientated example. Table 5.1 outlines a hypothetical case of a bus operator and the short run production of bus services. It shows what happens to output levels, in this example measured in vehicle kilometres, as more units of labour (between 0 and 9) are added to a fixed capital stock, i.e. a fixed fleet size.

The first column in Table 5.1 simply gives the number of labour units employed in the production process. The second column is the resultant output from combining the variable units of labour with the fixed capital stock. The third column introduces the idea of the average product. This is simply the second column divided by the first, and as highlighted above, would usually be referred to as labour productivity, i.e. the average units produced per employee. The last column calculates the marginal product. In simple terms this is the extent to which output rises as a result of employing one extra unit of labour in the production process. These three measures therefore give the total, average and marginal products which follow the same general shape of the theoretical curves shown in Figure 5.3.

As all output variations are produced by the addition of the variable input, all changes in the level of output are ascribed to that variable input. Starting at zero, no output is produced, as the only factors of production that are employed are the fixed factors, in this case capital. However,

Table 5.1 *Variable labour and the production of bus services*

(1) Labour units	(2) Total product (thousands)	(3) Average product (thousands)	(4) Marginal product (thousands)
0	–	–	1
1	1	1.0	6
2	7	3.5	11
3	18	6.0	8
4	26	6.5	6
5	32	6.4	5
6	37	6.2	3
7	40	5.7	2
8	42	5.3	−1
9	41	4.6	

all factors are required to produce any output – buses cannot operate without drivers. Even after a single unit of labour is employed, however, still no output is produced. This is because by the time the single employee has opened up the bus station/depot, cleaned the facilities, carried out all of the administrative and maintenance tasks, there is no free time left to actually drive a bus!

When a second labour unit is employed, however, then a degree of specialisation can occur – one can look after the bus station/depot whilst the other drives a bus. As more units are employed, then more specialisation and/or the better scheduling of inputs can occur and hence the level of output increases at an increasing rate. This is shown by an increase in both the average product and the marginal product figures in Table 5.1. Output levels are therefore increasing at an increasing rate (as evidenced by the ever increasing figure of the marginal product), i.e. we are in Stage 1 production. This continues up to where five labour units are employed, at which point the marginal product reaches its highest value. With the employment of a sixth person, total output is still rising but now at a declining rate. The marginal product therefore begins to fall and diminishing marginal returns set in, which would be at point a on Figure 5.3. Although each person employed is still increasing the total output, they are not increasing the output by as much as their predecessor and Stage 2 production is entered, i.e. beyond point b on Figure 5.3. Note that this has nothing to do with individual 'productivity', i.e. the sixth person not being as hard working and/or as skilled as the fifth person employed, but rather is related to the combination of inputs employed in the production process. By the time nine labour units are employed, total output actually falls, thus Stage 3 production is entered as shown at point c on Figure 5.3. This can be for a number of reasons many of which are related to the productivity of the individual. For example, employees may now be getting in each other's way (remember, all other inputs are fixed). This may not be physically but rather figuratively, such as in the case where one employee has to wait until a colleague returns the bus to the depot before they can start using it and hence being productive.

As highlighted above, there is only so much output that can be produced by the fixed factor. In this example, buses could only be run for around 20 hours a day maximum (allowing for refuelling and maintenance). Whilst that may be the maximum level, there will also be an optimum level, i.e. a level of the variable factor (labour) that the fixed factor was 'designed' to be operated by. As this level of output is approached, productivity will increase. Once that point is exceeded however and the maximum level is approached, overall productivity will be reduced as the fixed factor is being 'overworked' whilst the variable factor in many respects is being underutilised.

Case study 5.1 Costs and production in transport operations

Although costs are not introduced until the next section, it is worthwhile at this stage to look at the actual inputs used in terms of the factors of production that are employed in the production of transport services through an examination of their respective costs. Irrespective of the mode, at the most basic level all transport operators will employ the same inputs in the production of transport services. At this crude level, these will consist of a combination of a vehicle, a driver/operative and a power source. The output would normally be measured in terms of the vehicle kilometres produced through the combination of these inputs, and the inputs would be viewed as being complementary, i.e. all three are required to produce transport services, rather than substitutable, i.e. using one rather than the other. There will nevertheless be a degree of substitutability between these basic inputs at the margins. The Docklands Light Railway in London for example uses driverless vehicles, which technically is a substitution of labour for capital.

Unfortunately with regard to the production inputs involved in transport modes, beyond this basic level is where the similarity ends. Starting at the most basic split, passenger versus freight operations, one of the major advantages of passenger services are that passengers by and large load themselves on to the vehicle, whereas freight has to be physically loaded. Freight operations, in terms of producing vehicle mileage therefore, will be less 'productive' as the level of inputs required will be higher. Little research exists in this area, however, as few operators serve both freight and passenger markets. This initially would suggest that there are little if any advantages in running both passenger and freight operations; however, railways and airlines are the two notable exceptions. In the case of railways, companies have tended to run both types of service due to economies of scope, and airlines carry large volumes of freight in the cargo hold of passenger aircraft due to goods in joint supply (both these concepts are examined further in Chapter 12). The only major direct comparative study on the topic was undertaken by Professor Chris Nash in 1985, who found that a higher labour component of around 1.45 was required for freight as opposed to passenger rail operations (Nash, 1985). Although limited, this is consistent with the view that freight operations will tend to be less productive in terms of vehicle kilometres. For airlines, however, the loading of freight onto passenger aircraft will be part of the general servicing of the aircraft whilst at the airport, and as all of this cargo is containerised the extra inputs required are likely to be relatively low.

In order to bring out the differences in factor inputs further, however, the costs of five different transport operators in five different markets are examined in Table 5.2. These have

Table 5.2 *Mode cost comparisons*

Operating Cost	Airline		Ferry Operator		Bus Company		Railway Company		Parcels	
	British Airways 2005/6		Caledonian Mac. 2005/6		First Glasgow 2005/6		Virgin West Coast Value 2005/6		Parcelforce Value 2005/6	
	Value	%	Value	%	Value	%	Value	%	Value	%
Labour Costs:	2346	30.0%	45.0	51.7%	45.4	69.2%	102.2	17.7%	5968	71.8%
Vehicle Costs:	1302	16.6%	18.0	20.7%	5.8	8.8%	171.7	29.8%	1392	16.7%
Infrastructure Costs:	0	0.0%	0.0	0.0%	0.0	0.0%	141.4	24.5%	0	0.0%
Fuel Costs:	1632	20.8%	9.5	10.9%	10.0	15.2%	15.6	2.7%	0	0.0%
Terminal Costs:	1514	19.3%	12.6	14.5%	0.0	0.0%	17.5	3.0%	530	6.4%
Other Overheads:	1034	13.2%	1.9	2.2%	4.4	6.7%	128.5	22.3%	426	5.1%
Totals:	7828	100.0%	87.0	100.0%	65.5	100.0%	576.9	100.0%	8316	100.0%
Fixed Inputs:	2816	36.0%	29.0	37.7%	5.8	8.8%	330.5	57.3%	1922	23.1%
Variable Inputs:	5012	64.0%	48.0	62.3%	59.7	91.2%	246.4	42.7%	6394	76.9%

Sources – Compiled from Company Annual Reports, 2005/6

been adapted from the original accounts by grouping costs into six common headings. It is important to stress even at this stage that the actual costs themselves are not what is important. This book for example is not entitled 'Transport Accounting' and hence this should not be viewed as an exercise in cost accounting. Rather, what is important is the balance between the different types of costs and the likely impact such a balance will have on the structure of production, the firm and the market. This exercise after all is about attempting to understand the economics of transport operations, hence the choice of title of the book!

The above examples of transport operators clearly illustrate through cost differences variations in the structure of production in the modes examined. What is important are not the actual amounts, as these reflect the different scale of operations of each company, but rather the relative levels spent on each input. This reveals a very high level of variation of input factors between modes. As staff costs are a direct measure of the relative proportion of labour used in the production of transport services, the above figures indicate that parcel and bus operations are more labour-intensive industries than the railways, ferries and airlines. In turn, railways, ferries and airlines would appear to be more capital intensive than the others shown. What is also interesting to note is the relative level of fuel costs – although only shown for four out of the five modes (due to accounting differences), these account for somewhere between around 3 and 20 per cent of all operating cost. Interestingly, fuel costs in the bus and airline companies are around the two highest relative shares of operating costs, suggesting that the level of fuel costs is independent of the labour and capital intensity of the production process within the industry. Note however that all transport modes employ a high level of capital equipment in the production of transport services, as for example few rickshaws exist as a mass mover of people in the Western world! What is being compared here therefore is the relative levels of labour used to work the capital equipment, and hence some transport modes are more highly capital intensive than others.

Listed at the bottom of Table 5.2 is a very rough division where costs have been arbitrarily split between those that relate to factor inputs that may be considered to be fixed and those considered to vary directly with production. Of the five modes shown, passenger railways appear to have the highest level of fixed inputs, at around 57 per cent, ferries and airlines have around 36 to 37 per cent of fixed costs, whilst parcels (23 per cent) and the bus company (9 per cent) appear to have by far the lowest level of fixed costs. The real significance of this division between fixed and variable is that variable inputs are only employed when transport services are actually provided, whilst fixed inputs will incur a cost even where no output is produced and hence accumulate with the simple passage of time. If a high proportion of operating costs relate to variable inputs, this means that in a service industry such as transport most costs are only incurred when in revenue earning service. In many ways this considerably simplifies the planning of operations and also in theory makes entry into a new industry/market easier, as all else being equal, start up finance requirements should be relatively smaller as revenue streams are more evenly matched with cost outgoings.

This division between fixed and variable factors and the associated costs has major implications on the structure of the market, as a high level of fixed costs coupled with a capital-intensive production process would suggest large firms, which would act against market entry and competition in the market. On the other hand, it may be expected that in more labour-intensive transport industries, such as the bus and parcel markets, competition in the market should be both achievable and sustainable. To some extent this would certainly appear to be the case with parcels, where a number of national and international couriers compete fairly intensively in the market place. In the bus industry, however, outside of a few isolated cases, there is only limited competition in the British deregulated market and the country tends to be divided into distinct bus company 'territories', hence little direct competition exists. This suggests that the structure of costs, whilst an important determinant, is not the only factor in determining market structure and that other characteristics need to be considered when examining such markets. This will be taken up in the next two chapters which examine the issues of market structure and competition in transport markets.

Costs in short run production

Before considering how costs can be classified, it is important to stress that costs in economics include profit, or to be more exact, what is known as normal or economic profit. A simplified definition of normal profit would be the opportunity cost of being in business plus some form of risk premium in recognition of the risks that the investor is taking. Hence for example say the next best alternative was for the investor to deposit the funds in the bank rather than invest in the business, and for this they received a 5 per cent annual return. Then in order to be worthwhile investing in the business, the investor would have to earn more than the 5 per cent per year earned at the bank, as that gain is virtually guaranteed. Normal profit is therefore the cost to the firm of the investor's outlay, and this is normally paid in the form of a dividend. As such, this has to be included in costs in much the same way that staff salaries are included in costs. Anything earned above the level of normal profit would be termed abnormal or supernormal profits, as these are rewards in excess of the risks of being in business.

Classifying costs

White (2008) highlights a number of possible ways of classifying costs in transport operations. Firstly, costs can be classified by input, hence all labour costs are grouped together, all vehicle costs and so on; this essentially is what was done in Case study 5.1. Secondly, costs can be classified by the associated production of various outputs, such as passenger operations and freight operations, or scheduled and chartered flights in the case of an airline. Finally, costs can be classified by the activity performed, thus a railway could group its costs under the headings of sales and marketing costs, train services costs, infrastructure costs, station costs, administration costs and so on, with each classification of costs relating to a specific activity of railway operation. All of these enable the analysis of different costs to be made. Within transport economics, however, costs are generally classified into fixed and variable. As the names suggest, a fixed cost is one that does not vary with the level of output, whilst a variable cost does. As seen in Case study 5.1 above, this division and the balance between fixed and variable costs can have considerable implications on the structure of transport markets.

Fixed costs are input costs that are sometimes classified as 'indivisibles' or unavoidable costs, as these costs must be paid even if no output is produced or service provided and cannot be divided or bought in parts, e.g. you cannot purchase half an aircraft or bus. This includes costs such as leasing charges; rents and rates that relate to offices, depots and stations; management salaries and costs and administrative expenses such as telephone line rentals. Variable costs on the other hand relate to the direct expense of providing the output, such as the wages of employees, fuel costs, power and electricity for heat and light. Many costs however fall somewhere between the two, as they partially vary in relation to output, hence technically these are semi-variable. Labour costs, specifically wages, although normally classified as a variable cost, would actually be a good example of such a semi-variable cost, as within a wage there is a basic weekly sum that can be supplemented with overtime working. Only the overtime element would be directly variable, hence wages technically are a semi-variable cost.

Depreciation

Depreciation is an important concept that it is worth spending some time on in order to clarify the issues. One of the main problems associated with this cost is that 'depreciation' is the reduction in economic value to the firm of using an asset in the production process. There will come a point in time where it will be more cost effective in the longer term to replace that asset rather than continue to patch it up through maintenance and keep it running. The more it is used, the quicker that point will be reached, hence technically depreciation as a concept is a variable cost. To return to transport accounting, however, this reduction in value is assessed in company accounts as only an approximation of the real reduction in value. There are two main methods used. Firstly, the straight line method. Under this method, the scrap value is subtracted from the purchase price and then divided by the number of expected years of usage. That then gives the value of 'depreciation' to be written off annually. The second approach is the reducing balance method, where a percentage of the value is written off each year until the scrap value is reached. Both approaches are best illustrated through the use of an example, and again a bus company is used.

Say for example a new bus costs £110,000, has a scrap value of £10,000 and has an expected useful life of ten years. The value to be written off therefore is £100,000 and over the useful life of ten years this would be done by subtracting a straight value of £10,000 a year. In ten years therefore it would be shown in the books as having a value of £10,000, i.e. its scrap value. This would be the straight line method. Alternatively, a percentage of the book value could be written off each year, in this case 21.3 per cent, and this will achieve the same effect of reducing the value to (almost) £10,000 in ten years' time. This would be the reducing balance method. The annual depreciation charge is then written off against profits, as this is the cost to the firm of using the capital equipment. Both approaches are fully illustrated in Table 5.3.

Note that under the reducing balance method higher values are written off in the earlier years, and this is said to better reflect the decreasing value of such assets in that earlier period. Irrespective of what method is used, however, neither takes into account usage. For example, as illustrated under the straight line method £10,000 is written off the value of a bus each year irrespective of the extent to which that bus is used. In this sense, therefore, it is a fixed cost, as it is one that does not vary with the level of output produced. In the longer term, however, if that bus was little used it would retain its economic value (obsolescence accepted) beyond the ten years, and hence would still be useable and thus of value to the firm after it had been written off in the books. There are many such examples of transport assets that have long been written off in the company accounts but are still in use today, such as the Severn Rail Tunnel and the Forth Bridge.

Table 5.3 *Illustration of depreciation by straight line and reducing balance methods*

Year	Straight line method			Reducing balance method		
	Value at the beginning of year	Annual depreciation charge	Value at the end of year	Value at the beginning of year	Annual depreciation charge	Value at the end of year
1	110,000	10,000	100,000	110,000	23,430	86,570
2	100,000	10,000	90,000	86,570	18,439	68,131
3	90,000	10,000	80,000	68,131	14,512	53,619
4	80,000	10,000	70,000	53,619	11,421	42,198
5	70,000	10,000	60,000	42,198	8,988	33,210
6	60,000	10,000	50,000	33,210	7,074	26,136
7	50,000	10,000	40,000	26,136	5,567	20,569
8	40,000	10,000	30,000	20,569	4,381	16,188
9	30,000	10,000	20,000	16,188	3,448	12,740
10	20,000	10,000	10,000	12,740	2,714	10,026

Short run average and marginal costs

As total, average and marginal products are plotted against labour, costs are normally plotted against the output produced by that labour. This then illustrates how costs vary over different levels of the output. These are known as the average and marginal costs curves, in this case those relating to the short run. The 'S'-shaped production function outlined earlier will in turn produce an 'S'-shaped total cost curve, therefore consistent with this the average cost curve is 'U' shaped. In simple terms, as total productivity increases (Stage 1 production), then average costs fall, whilst when total productivity decrease (Stages 2 and 3 production), average costs increase. This is shown in Figure 5.4.

This is the stylised textbook version of the short run marginal and average cost curves. As more of the variable input is added, average costs at first fall, are then minimised at the optimal output level of production at point b, and then increase beyond that optimum point. Having outlined the basic shape of these curves, what is important is why the short run average cost curve should be U shaped. As this relates to the short run, one of the inputs in the production process is fixed and hence will be subject to the law of diminishing marginal returns, which in turn will be related to utilisation of the fixed input. Say for example in the production of bus services, the number of buses is fixed. As highlighted previously, this means that there is an optimal production level, i.e. an ideal output size. Any production level that is under that point will lead to the under-utilisation of the fixed resource and consequently higher average costs. As that optimum point is approached, i.e. point b on Figure 5.4, these fixed resources are increasingly being utilised, hence average costs fall. Any point beyond the optimum however will lead to the over-utilisation of resources. Furthermore, as the level of output can only be altered by varying the level of the variable factor, in this case labour, then in order to increase labour this may involve paying over-time rates, hiring agency labour at a higher cost and so on, thus incurring a higher overall average unit cost.

In order to examine average and marginal costs further, Table 5.4 expands the previous

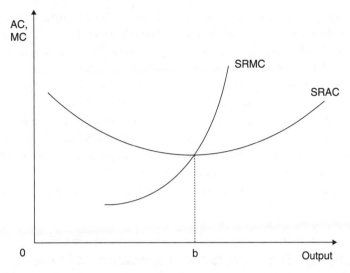

Figure 5.4 *Short run average and marginal cost curves*

Table 5.4 *Variable and fixed costs of short-run production of bus services*

Production				Costs				
Labour units	Output produced (000s)	Average product (000s)	Marginal product (000s)	Total fixed costs	Total variable costs	Total costs	Average total costs	Marginal costs
0	–	–	1	80000	–	80000	–	30.00
1	1	1.0	6	80000	30000	110000	110.00	5.00
2	7	3.5	11	80000	60000	140000	20.00	2.73
3	18	6.0	8	80000	90000	170000	9.44	3.75
4	26	6.5	6	80000	120000	200000	7.69	5.00
5	32	6.4	5	80000	150000	230000	7.19	6.00
6	37	6.2	3	80000	180000	260000	7.03	10.00
7	40	5.7	2	80000	210000	290000	7.25	15.00
8	42	5.3	–1	80000	240000	320000	7.62	–
9	41	4.6	–	80000	270000	350000	8.54	

example regarding the production of bus services in the short run by including cost data. In this case it has been assumed that fixed costs are £80,000 and the variable factor, labour, costs £30,000 per unit.

The first four columns are taken from Table 5.1, and to this have been added five new columns to include the relevant cost data. Total Fixed Costs, as outlined above, do not vary with the level of output, hence remain fixed at £80,000 irrespective of the level of output produced. These are the costs associated with the fixed factor, in this case capital. Total Variable Costs are simply the number of labour units employed times the cost of each unit, and total costs the addition of fixed and variable. Average total cost is therefore the total cost divided by total output, and marginal cost the cost of the last unit produced. When for example labour is increased from one to two units, output increases by 6,000 units and costs rise by £30,000. The marginal cost of the last unit therefore is the difference in output divided by the difference in costs and hence is £5.

Notice also that when only production is examined the highest level of labour productivity occurs at 4 units; however, the lowest average cost occurs when 6 labour units are employed. The reason for this difference is because the average cost also includes the capital cost, whilst no account is taken of capital inputs under the previous calculation as all variations in output were apportioned to the labour factor. This is one reason why productivity measures based on a single input, such as labour in this case, can be misleading.

The importance of the idea of the average cost is illustrated in the next case that looks at the operational characteristics of low-cost airlines.

Case study 5.2 The importance of average cost in the business model of low-cost airlines

It is difficult, if not impossible, to have a chapter on transport costs without having a specific look at the model of the low-cost airline. As the name of these carriers strongly suggests, this is a business model of airline operation that is heavily based on achieving low average costs in the operation of services. It should be stressed however that whilst 'low cost' is a philosophy that is central to these companies' operations, this is only one part of a complete business model that is geared towards achieving 'low cost' through not only cutting costs directly but also by a number of other measures as well.

The first acknowledged low-cost carrier was the American airline, Southwest, which began operating along low-cost principles in 1978, not long after deregulation of the US Domestic airline market. This business model however did not spread to Europe owing largely to the heavily regulated air market that had been exempt from both the initial Treaty of Rome in 1957 and the Single European Market in 1986. As a result, the European Air Market operated restricted capacity on routes and regulated prices and was largely dominated by state-owned National Airlines. In the early to mid 1990s, however, the EU passed a number of packages of air regulation reforms that opened up the market to potential new entrants. By doing so, this also presented an opportunity for the entry of low-cost operations, and this was initially taken up with considerable success by the Irish operator Ryanair. This model of operation has since been followed by a large number of other airlines, including easyJet, Flyglobespan.com and Flybe. These airlines operate on the basis of offering low priced fares based on a low average cost. Note that this is slightly different from an out and out low cost, as in this business model it is the achievement of low average cost that matters, not just 'low cost'. This obviously has implications on the operations of the airline, and in particular also puts great emphasis on aircraft utilisation. The general 'model' of the low-cost carrier can be summarised as consisting of the following main elements:

- Low staff costs
- Low aircraft turnaround times

- Route network based around secondary or regional airports rather than major hubs since they are usually less congested
- On line ticket sales only with ticketless travel
- Cabin crew perform other duties during turnarounds, such as cleaning the inside of the aircraft
- Simplified point-to-point operations rather than complex hub and spoke
- All 'extras' beyond the basic seat incur an additional charge, e.g. in flight catering or priority in boarding
- No spare aircraft capacity held in reserve to cover in the case of unforeseen break-downs or delays
- Fleet based on a single aircraft type to reduce maintenance costs.

In order to tease out these differences, the costs of three airlines are examined below in Table 5.5. These have been grouped under five common headings in order to attempt to bring out these differences. The first airline, British Airways, can be viewed as a 'traditional airline', whilst the other two, easyJet and Ryanair, operate largely along low-cost principles, the latter more so than the former.

All costs are taken from the respective 2006 Annual Reports; however, not all costs are directly comparable. Despite the existence of Standard Statements of Accounting Practice designed to ensure consistency across company accounting practices, differences will always remain. Comparison differences therefore cannot be taken as 'exact'. As an example, easyJet only include Crew Costs (cabin and flight deck) as specific staff costs in their annual reports, whilst British Airways (BA) include all staff costs, e.g. cabin and flight deck crew, administration staff, sales and marketing staff and so on. Nevertheless, the above costs do give some basis for an overall appraisal of different costs.

BA provides an interesting starting point to examine firstly the overall cost structure of airlines and secondly where any savings in operating costs could be made in what would be perceived as a traditional airline. Starting with labour costs, these account for around 30 per cent of all operating costs. Whilst this is a significant proportion, in transport operating terms this suggests a relatively capital intensive industry – as was seen earlier, for bus companies staff costs account for around 65 per cent of operating costs. Examining the other costs for BA, direct operational costs such as fuel and oil, engineering and maintenance costs, landing fees

Table 5.5 Operating costs, British Airways, easyJet and Ryanair, 2006

Airline:	British Airways		easyJet		Ryanair	
	Actual	%	Actual	%	Actual	%
Staff costs	2346.0	30%	75.2	11%	171.4	13%
Selling costs	449.0	6%	26.0	4%	13.9	1%
Aircraft costs	2446.0	31%	366.8	54%	590.1	45%
Fuel costs	1632.0	21%	165.9	25%	462.5	35%
Other costs	955.0	12%	42.2	6%	85.6	6%

Source: Adapted from the respective company accounts

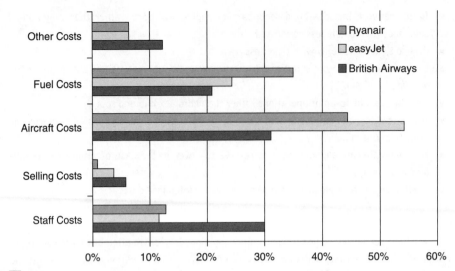

Figure 5.5 *Percentage breakdown, operating costs, British Airways, easyJet and Ryanair, 2006*

Source: Compiled from the respective company accounts

and so on account for just under 50 per cent of operating costs. It is in these two areas, staff costs and operational costs, where the biggest differences between BA and the two LCAs emerge. BA has a far higher proportion of operating costs ascribed to staff and a far lower proportion accounted for by direct operational costs than either easyJet or Ryanair. The other area of difference is in selling costs, although these on the whole are a small proportion of total operating costs.

This is where an understanding of the differences between fixed and variable costs becomes useful, as also does knowledge of how employment contracts are drawn up. Labour, for example, would virtually always be classified as a variable cost. Where employees are salaried, however, as in this case, then in the short run this is a fixed cost. A similar argument applies to depreciation and aircraft lease costs, as again in the short run capital equipment will be fixed and hence the depreciation or lease charge relatively fixed. Following this logic then, in fairly rough terms all operational costs are variable whilst all other costs, including labour and aircraft costs, are fixed. In the case of BA, therefore, around half of the costs are variable whilst for the other two airlines this is far higher at nearer 70 per cent.

Whilst the airline can do little about variable costs such as fuel and oil as these vary directly with output, these costs are zero while the aircraft is stationary. Fixed costs however are not. For example, cabin crew are still employed (being paid) after the aircraft has reached the airport gate and all passengers have disembarked, hence such costs are incurred even although the aircraft is technically not in revenue earning service. This is achieved only when the aircraft is in flight, therefore what becomes crucial in any such business model of low-cost operation is aircraft utilisation – the higher the utilisation, the more fixed costs are spread over output, the average cost reduces and the proportion of fixed to variable cost also reduces. Thus high turnaround times become the vital element in this type of operation. easyJet for example operate something like an absolute maximum of a 45 minute aircraft turnaround time and in most cases considerably less than that. Also what is important is that staff while on the ground, such as cabin crew, are actively employed to service the inside of the aircraft while it is stationary, hence they are being 'productive' during what would normally be 'dead' time. Note also that 'dead time' as such is far shorter due to fast turnaround times.

Another important aspect in reducing average cost is the lack of any slack in the whole system of operation. Spare aircraft are simply not an option, as this would constitute a fixed cost with zero output, hence any faults that develop in the fleet during the daily operation can have considerable and long-lasting (i.e. all day) knock-on effects on the whole system. Those with some experience of LCAs for example will be familiar with the announcement of 'flight delayed due to the late arrival of the incoming aircraft' which although a completely meaningless statement does highlight the lack of any slack in the whole system. Why LCAs can get away with such practices of course is due to the charging of low air fares.

The key to success in the operation of LCAs, therefore, is not 'low cost' per se but rather the attainment of a low average cost (per passenger carried). Few pilots for example work for low wages; however, the key to effectively reducing a pilot's wage is through increasing the number of hours worked (within regulatory limits of course).

In many senses, LCAs have changed the whole economics of airline operation where traditional thinking was in terms of an industry with a high proportion of capital costs and a relatively low level of variable costs. Furthermore, most variable costs were associated with take-off and landing, with respect to landing and terminal charges and most importantly fuel costs – a high proportion of the fuel consumed on a flight is during take-off and landing phases, sometimes as high as 50 per cent. All of these factors would suggest far higher unit prices on short-haul flights as the average cost of such a flight would be far higher.

All of these factors surrounding air transport economics however were known for some time, particularly the aspect of aircraft utilisation being the key to success in the airline business. Why they had not been fully exploited before is due to other factors, most notably market conditions and regulatory regimes. Facing such conditions, it made economic sense for the operator to restrict supply as this increased profits. In the LCA model, however, profits are maximised through low profit margins and high passenger volumes.

COST AND PRODUCTION IN THE LONG RUN

The first point to note about costs and production in the long run is that because all input factors are variable there is no division between fixed and variable costs. To briefly recap, whilst a firm may be planning a new production facility or entering a new market, it is operating in the long run. Once however it builds the new factory or sets up the new depot to service the new market, it is then operating in the short run (because at least one of the factors of production is fixed).

How costs behave in the long run is closely related to the behaviour of production and thus what happens when more inputs are added to the production process. There are some important differences between production and costs; however, these will be further developed later. To begin, Figure 5.6 illustrates a long run production function.

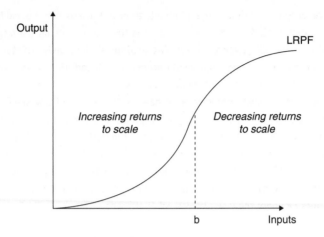

Figure 5.6 *The long run production function*

As with the short run, the long run production function is S shaped in nature. At first there are large gains when firm size increases – the relative percentage gain in output is greater than the relative percentage increase in inputs. Note also that this effect increases as firm size increases. These gains in total productivity, or increasing returns to scale, continue up to point b on Figure 5.6. Once firm size (as measured by the level of inputs) rises past point b, however, the proportionate gains from adding more inputs are not as large as before, hence the firm experiences decreasing returns to scale. This decline continues until increasing firm size has very little effect on the level of output. The main reasons for this general pattern of increasing and decreasing returns to scale that define the shape of the long run production function are outlined below.

Sources of increasing returns to scale

Specialisation of labour – larger firms allow more specialisation of the workforce to occur. If this is considered at the most basic level of a one-person sole-trader business, then the owner has to undertake all of the tasks involved in the running of the business. They therefore become a 'jack of all trades and master of none'. As firm size increases, more labour can be employed in specialised tasks and thus become more proficient at those tasks. Consequently productivity would be expected to increase. Note also that as this is the long run, there is potentially no ceiling on this effect and is probably best exemplified in Fordism large-scale production, where individuals can become 'experts' at very specific tasks.

Scheduling of inputs – this is similar to the specialisation of labour source but refers to the scheduling of all of the inputs, a factor that is particularly prevalent in the transport industries. As firm size increases, there exists greater flexibility in how the inputs can be combined and hence better utilisation of all of the inputs may be expected, i.e. higher total productivity. For example, in larger road haulage companies, there may be more flexibility in the scheduling of drivers to ensure that the vehicle stock is operated over the longest possible number of hours. This would ensure higher total productivity.

Capital inputs – this concerns a number of issues that are broadly grouped together here under the title 'capital inputs'. Firstly, some capital inputs can be very expensive to purchase. Only larger firms can afford to spend on these inputs, but they only do so on the basis that this will lead to improved efficiency (i.e. higher productivity) in the longer term. For example, increasing a railway line from single to double track increases capacity by a factor of four, hence potentially significantly increasing the productivity of rail services.

The second issue also relates to specialisation. Using the sole-trader example, then it may well be that the company vehicles consist of a single solitary van. This van will have to fulfil all of the transport requirements of the company, some of which it may be better suited to than others. As firm size increases, however, then the company fleet can be increased not only in size but also in scope, hence more suitable vehicles can be used for more suitable tasks. This should lead to higher productivity.

Thirdly, it may make more sense for larger companies to carry a larger number of spares and maintenance facilities, hence downtime of capital equipment as such should be reduced and consequently higher productivity achieved. It should be noted that even with 'just-in-time' production methods and the contracting out of maintenance and servicing facilities (as has happened with many bus companies), certain advantages with regard to this issue may still be expected. It may be anticipated for example that larger companies will have far more influence with the suppliers of such services that results in quicker response rates to service requests. Capital downtime, therefore, may be expected to be lower.

Indivisibilities – the standard example of an indivisibility is a telephone line. When setting up in business, a company will need to install and rent a phone line. With small expansions in size, there will probably be no need to install a second phone line, hence this 'input' is spread over a larger output. There will obviously come a point where a second phone line will have to be installed, but this would only be done if it was advantageous to do so, e.g. if it improved 'productivity'. Another example of an indivisibility of course is our sole trader's van. As firm size increases, the van's overall utilisation would improve.

All of these sources of increasing returns to scale should be reasonably clear, but what may cause this increase in productivity to tail-off, i.e. sources of decreasing returns to scale? This is particularly prevalent in the long run as there is no upper constraint in the form of a fixed input.

Sources of decreasing returns to scale

Loss of control – as firm size increases, there is a loss of control over the whole organisation. This loss of control decreases overall productivity. Under this heading it is worth highlighting the concept of 'X-inefficiency', originally devised by Leibenstein (1966). In simple terms, X-inefficiency relates to general management slack, and large (publicly owned) organisations are said to be particularly vulnerable to this concept. In less academic terms, in larger organisations there may be a loss of the 'sense of the individual' and more opportunities for general slack working practices, hence leading to lower productivity levels.

Geographical location – particularly prevalent in the bus industry, but true of other transport industries, when a firm initially sets up in business it will probably be on or near to the optimal location. Increasing size in the longer term means building other production facilities, such as depots, and these will not necessarily be at the best location. This can result in fairly long distances between the depot and the market served, hence a significant proportion of time is spent in driving vehicles between the two and not actually providing transport services. As a result, productivity decreases.

Administration procedures – large firms often require many more layers of middle and upper management, plus administration procedures, in order to control costs and processes within the organisation. This is commonly known as 'bureaucracy'; however, in this situation this should not be confused with 'red tape', as that is considered in the next section. More specifically, this refers to the time dimension that such 'form filling' requires and hence the opportunity cost of this form filling is the distraction of employees from the production process. When measured in terms of overall output, therefore, it requires on average a higher number of employees to produce a higher level of output.

Average and marginal costs in the long run

Having considered production in the long run, it is possible to see how costs would be expected to behave in the long run. These are graphed in Figure 5.7.

As can be seen from Figure 5.7, average costs at first fall as firm size (as measured by output) increases. This continues up to the point where average costs are minimised at the optimum level of production, known as the minimum efficiency scale (MES). After this point the trend is reversed and average costs rise as firm size increases. Along the part of the curve where the average cost is falling the firm would be said to be experiencing economies of scale. Very often these are incorrectly termed increasing returns to scale; however, returns to scale relates to production output while economies of scale relates to production costs. Along the part of the curve where average costs are rising the firm would be said to be experiencing diseconomies of scale, or again often incorrectly referred to as decreasing returns to scale.

This does once again pose the question as to why long run average costs should first fall and then rise as output (and hence firm size) increases. This is explained below.

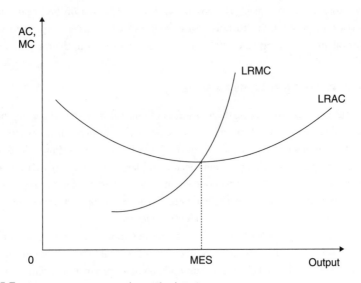

Figure 5.7   Long run average and marginal costs

Sources of economies of scale

Increasing returns to scale – as seen above, at first as firm size increases it encounters increasing returns to scale i.e. ever higher levels of productivity. This increased productivity therefore means that relatively lower levels of the inputs need to be employed to produce higher levels of output, hence the average costs per unit of output falls.

Bulk buying – larger firms can normally obtain some form of discount for buying capital equipment and supplies in larger numbers, and hence average costs would be expected to be lower for larger firms. Bus companies are a good example of this, where large group holding companies can negotiate discounts on fuel and tyres due to the sheer volume that the company will use in the course of its normal operations. Due to this volume, suppliers can afford to concede larger discounts and still return acceptable profits.

High cost inputs – these have already been examined under returns to scale, hence most are associated with improving productivity rather than directly reducing average costs. It is worth highlighting however that advertising is also sometimes cited as a high cost input, but it is debatable if this really leads to economies of scale. In the Cola market, for example, it almost certainly does. By advertising extensively, firms seek to increase the size of the market and hence allow them to increase production in order to take advantage of other economies of scale.

Financial economies – larger firms are normally better placed to secure additional finance as they can offer greater security. Interest rates therefore may be lower as there is a lower risk involved to the finance company, hence average costs are lower.

Sources of diseconomies of scale

Decreasing returns to scale – as highlighted above, there are a number of sources of technical inefficiencies that lead to reduced productivity for larger firms, thus the average output per unit of input falls. In order to produce higher levels of output, therefore, relatively higher numbers of inputs need to be employed, and this adds to costs causing diseconomies of scale.

Red tape – as noted above, larger firms often require many more layers of middle and upper management, plus administration procedures in order to control costs and processes within the organisation. This is 'red tape' and the actual cost of this added administration burden will add to costs, hence increasing the average cost per unit. Note however if we are being absolutely correct, the extra staff results in decreasing returns to scale (as proportionally less staff are directly involved in production), whilst the added costs associated with red tape such as stationery costs, the need for greater office space and more IT facilities and so on result in diseconomies of scale.

The coverage of costs in the long run is completed by examining economies of scale in railway operations and the impact that this can have upon how services are actually provided to the market.

Case study 5.3 Economies of scale and reform in railway operations

The general view of economies of scale within the rail industry is that, due to a high capital requirement in the provision of rail services, economies of scale are significant and hence company size needs to be large in order to capture all of these effects. In the past this was one of the main reasons which led to the nationalisation of railway industries across Europe (the first being Switzerland in 1901 and the last Britain in 1948), where most of the main-line railways were taken under the control of a single company so that economies of scale could be achieved. There were also a number of other important reasons for nationalisation; however, here we only concentrate on the economies of scale argument. This particular view of railway economics has become known as the traditional view (Preston, 1994), in which infrastructure and services are part of an integrated system and economies of scale in both are significant. Organisationally, therefore, services and infrastructure should be part of the same (large) company.

In recent years, however, virtually every European country has re-organised their railway systems, with many separating both organisationally and financially infrastructure from services, i.e. one company owns and operates the infrastructure whilst a different company owns and operates the rolling stock. This is known as a vertically separated railway. In Europe, Sweden was the first country to organise its rail system along these lines. All the infrastructure functions were separated out into the Swedish National Rail Administration (Banverket) whilst services remained within the Swedish State Operator (Statens Järnvägar). In contradiction to the traditional view outlined above, however, such a division is consistent with what has become known as the revisionist view of railway economics. Under this belief, the central premise is that economies of scale are only associated with the infrastructure and not with services. Therefore, scale effects will still be taken advantage of as long as infrastructure is retained as a single entity. As regards the size of operating companies, this is unimportant as there are no economies of scale associated with this activity. The advantage of such a system over the traditional railway is that different operators can operate on the network and hence some form of competition introduced into the provision of rail services.

Note that both the traditional and revisionist views are merely matters of opinion, and for a better understanding we need to examine the empirical research carried out on the topic. This would suggest that the theoretical U-shaped cost curve (and hence S-shaped production function) applies to railway operations. For example, Preston (1994) in a study of 15 Western European (integrated) railways found diseconomies of scale for larger train systems such as (West) Germany and Britain, and increasing returns for smaller rail systems such as Ireland, Switzerland and Belgium. In an updated study, Shires and Preston (1999) found that the MES (minimum efficiency scale) for integrated railways was around about the size of the Danish and Belgian rail networks. The implication, if only economies of scale are considered, is that countries with large networks such as Britain should organise their rail system into three to four integrated railways (perhaps on a regional basis) rather than as one single national operator. Such a structure would place each system close to the MES point and hence eradicate diseconomies of scale.

Within smaller railway systems, scale effects have been found to be even more substantial. Filippini and Maggio's (1992) study of the Swiss 'private' rail network revealed scale effects to be considerable, leading the authors to conclude that there were potentially substantial benefits to be gained from end-to-end and parallel mergers within the Swiss industry. Cowie (1999) also found scale effects to be significant in the Swiss industry. Switzerland is made up of a single national operator, CFF, on the main lines, and around 60 to 70 mainly publicly owned local railways on the local lines, varying in size from as small as 4 kilometres up to around 400 kilometres in length. Significant scale effects in such small systems would again be consistent with a U-shaped cost curve. This is because the gains that could be achieved in terms of lowering average cost for smaller systems by increasing output would be higher than for medium-sized operators (have a look at Figure 5.7 to confirm this).

To date, however, very little research has been carried out on the impact of separating operations from infrastructure on economies of scale. In one of the few such studies, Cowie (2002) examined the British train-operating companies and found that scale effects were significant, hence suggesting that the pure revisionist view, that there are no economies in operation, was not true. Size, therefore, with regard to how train companies are organised, is important. Scale effects however were found to be smaller than for integrated railways, with the MES point found to be around two thirds of the output level of Preston's earlier study based upon integrated railways. It nevertheless suggests that in Britain there should be around four to five train-operating companies rather than the current number of seventeen. The research also suggested by implication that there existed significant economies of scale in the provision of infrastructure.

Economies of scale have a major impact on the consideration of the best size of railway to produce rail services, as clearly if scale effects are considerable then costs can be significantly reduced by having a very large operator. Costs however are only one half of the profit equation, and hence where railways are heavy loss makers and thus heavily subsidised (as is the case in most of Europe), the attainment of economies of scale in the production of services whilst important is only one aspect amongst many other considerations when policy makers consider how 'best' to organise a rail system. For example there may be benefits in having a higher number of rail operators than the 'optimal' level due to an increase in competitive pressures, particularly for the market.

SHORT AND LONG RUN AVERAGE COSTS

We briefly end the chapter with a look at the relationship between the short and the long run average and marginal cost curves. This is shown in Figure 5.8, and is useful to further underline the relationship between all of these concepts.

In Figure 5.8, the long run average cost curve is a summation of a series of short run average cost curves. Beginning at an output level of Q_1, the firm is operating at point a on both the short run and long run average cost curves. Note that the short run average cost curve is tangential to the long run average cost curve at that level of output. Note also that at each point on the long run average cost curve there is a similar short run average cost curve which is tangential to it. If the firm was to increase production from Q_1 to Q_2 in the short run, however, i.e. where at least one of the inputs is fixed, average costs would increase to point c on the short run average cost curve. This would be considerably higher than if production was increased to Q_2 in the long run, in which case the average cost would be found at point b on the long run average cost curve. This is because in the short run the firm would encounter the law of diminishing marginal returns, and hence because one of the factors is fixed, say vehicles, the variable factor, labour, cannot be fully utilised. If however production is increased in the long run, then diminishing marginal returns will not be encountered and in this example, the firm will experience economies of scale as it approaches the

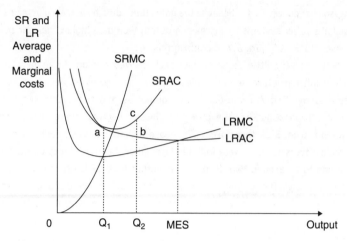

Figure 5.8 *Long and short run average and marginal cost curves*

MES point. An alternative way of viewing this is that short run costs are higher because when operating in the long run the firm effectively has a blank sheet of paper (in theory at least), and hence can plan for the lowest cost level of production. Once one of the factors is fixed, however, then it is more confined in what it can do and has to work around this constraint, which will incur a higher average (short run) cost. This relationship between costs in the short and long runs is important, particularly when examining transport markets. Very short increases in demand have to be met by a short run increase in supply, which in turn would incur higher costs. Given the peak nature of most public transport markets, the result is that firms can very seldom 'optimise' on the long run average cost curve, as supply needs to be flexible to meet these peaks in demand.

CHAPTER SUMMARY AND REFLECTION

In this chapter the focus has been on transport costs. This began with a definition of production, in which it was revealed that the definition of the short run is where at least one factor of production is fixed. We then examined the behaviour of costs both in the short and long runs, and found that both the short and long run cost curves were U shaped. In the case of the former this was due to the law of diminishing returns and the latter due to economies/diseconomies of scale. We finished the chapter by detailing the relationship between costs in the short and long run. A case study of the rail industry revealed that costs in practice would appear to follow the theoretical concepts, with studies indicating that average cost curves are U shaped in both vertically and integrated railway systems. Whilst not explicitly stated, it also highlighted the effect of costs on the structure of the industry, where for example if other things remained equal then it would be expected that more firms would operate in say the road haulage or bus markets than the passenger or freight rail markets primarily due to the differences in cost structures and the effects of economies of scale. What has also been highlighted is that costs are only one part of calculating the profit level and consequently only one factor in the planning of transport operations. Revenues, both in terms of that collected directly from the passenger and also sums paid by transport authorities in the form of transport subsidies, are also required since profit is revenue minus cost. The following chapter builds directly on the ideas outlined in this chapter and introduces revenue into the analysis in order to provide a complete insight into both sides of the transport market. Subsequent chapters will then consider the organisation of transport services and transport subsidy, both of which are heavily influenced by the structure of the costs of provision of transport services. From a public perspective, however, the financial costs, both in terms of capital and operating, need to be offset against not only the financial gains but also wider public benefits, and this topic is taken up further in Chapter 14 on transport appraisal

CHAPTER EXERCISES

Exercise 5.1 Technical, cost and allocative efficiency in bus operations

The following table gives some basic information relating to two small-scale bus operators:

	Company A	Company B
Number of buses:	3	5
Number of employees:	13	21
Average wage:	19000	16000
Vehicle kilometres run:	210000	300000
Bus cost per kilometre (including fuel costs):	0.36	0.30
Annual number of passengers carried:	370000	460000

a) Consider the following questions:

   i Which of the two companies is more technically efficient in the production of bus services (note: you will need to separately calculate labour productivity and bus productivity and compare the two figures)?
   ii Which of the two companies is more cost efficient in the production of bus services?
   iii Which of the two companies is more allocatively efficient?

b) In your answer to part a. (i) you should have found that Company A had an advantage in both productivity ratios, hence by implication is more technically efficient. However, say this had not been the case. For example, if Company B had only 16 staff rather than 21 then it would have a superior labour productivity but an inferior bus productivity, hence there would be no clear answer (you should check this), as that would be dependent upon the balance of the two inputs used in the production process. In other words, such evaluations need some way of combining these ratios to come up with a single answer. One fairly simply way of doing this would be to weight each productivity ratio by that factor inputs share of costs. This would be a basic form of what is known as a Tornqvist productivity ratio. You should now calculate this index for both Company A and Company B using B's revised labour figure of 16 staff to determine which company is more technically efficient.

Exercise 5.2 Total, average and marginal products and costs

This exercise concerns the provision of rail services, and the task is comparatively straightforward if slightly involved. Quite simply, you have to fill in all the blanks, for which you will need the following information:

Fixed Costs: 100000
Price of a variable factor: 50000

You should round all figures to two decimal places.

■ *Table 5.2a*

Labour	Output(000s)			Costs				
Units	TP	AP	MP	TFC	TVC	TC	ATC	MC
0	0							
1	50							
2	110							
3	180							
4	260							
5	350							
6	420							
7	480							
8	530							
9	570							
10	590							

TP = total product
TFC = total fixed costs
ATC = average total costs

AP = average product
TVC = total variable costs
MC = marginal cost

MP = marginal product
TC = total costs

Once you have completed this table, you should use your calculations to answer the following questions:

a) At what level of output should the firm operate at?
b) What is the most 'efficient' level of output in terms of:

    i   Technical efficiency?
    ii Cost efficiency?
    iii In terms of measuring the firm's 'efficiency', which of these two measures should be used and why?

c) What units is the level of output measured in?

Exercise 5.3 Economies of scale in railway operation

Re-examine Case study 5.3 and answer the following questions:

1   Briefly outline your understanding of the traditional and revisionist views of railway economics.
2   List what you believe to be the main sources of economies of scale in the rail industry. Once you have produced this list, indicate which arise as a result of returns to scale and which are cost savings.
3   What on the other hand do you believe are the main sources of diseconomies of scale in larger integrated railways?
4   If you were a rail industry regulator in Britain today, what other factors apart from economies of scale would you take into account when deciding on the number of operators to have in the market?

Chapter 6

Perfect competition in transport markets

Learning Outcomes:

On reading this chapter, you will learn:

- The theory of the firm
- The position of profit maximisation for the provider of transport services
- The underlying conditions required in order to ensure that competitive pressures on transport operators are maximised
- That such a level of 'maximum' competition ensures that economic efficiency is attained in the provision of transport services
- A formal definition for what constitutes 'market failure' in transport markets.

INTRODUCTION

This chapter will examine competition within transport markets by identifying the key elements that shape both the number and the structure of firms competing in the market place. The general view regarding competition in markets would be that it is a 'good' thing, and no competition, a monopoly, a 'bad' thing. On the whole that lay person's perception would be correct; however, it neither explains why it is a good thing except in very general terms nor the actual process of competition amongst transport firms that brings about such good things. More importantly, it does not highlight those situations where competition may not produce the best outcome, and this is particularly relevant where transport services are concerned.

One of the key issues in this and the subsequent chapter, if not the key issue, is to try and provide an understanding as to how competition works to produce economically efficient transport services, why that very often is not the case, and hence give a better perspective of the need for intervention in the form of government policy and involvement in transport markets. As you will see, the rationale for this form of intervention would be based on the notion of market failure.

BACKGROUND

Much of what is outlined in this chapter is drawn from what is known as the theory of the firm as applied to transport organisations and firms. The theory of the firm is a neo-classical concept that has been widely used and applied to examine industry structures and productive efficiency. It was one of the main theoretical underpinnings for Margaret Thatcher's privatisation programme in Britain during the mid to late 1980s which had, and continues to have, such a profound effect on transport industries in Britain and further afield. As such, its applications have been far and wide reaching. Much economic change concerning the organisation of transport industries over the last 30 years has as its basis a practical application of the theory of the firm. Whilst most extensively applied in Britain, further re-organisations have followed and continue to this day throughout the European Union and the rest of the world. The principal concern has revolved around introducing competition into transport markets as the theory predicts that such markets are more economically efficient.

One of the major problems with transport markets however is a general lack of competition. This leads to various problems, many of which reach far beyond 'simple' transport issues due to the derived nature of demand and the close association between transport services and economic development. Consideration of these types of 'imperfect' market structures however is left for the following chapter, as here only 'perfect' competition is considered.

As has already been seen in Chapters 3 and 4, demand can vary between highly elastic right through to highly inelastic. Unsurprisingly, price elasticity of demand, both in the market and that facing the individual firm, is heavily dependent upon the prevailing market conditions the firm encounters and thus an indicator of the level of competition within a given transport sector. This in turn is partly dependent upon how production costs vary with the level of output, i.e. the division between fixed and variable costs, as this will determine the number of firms in the market and thus the level of competition, i.e. the market structure. All of this you should already be aware of, since a basic market is made up of the forces of demand and supply that interact to produce an equilibrium price. That in turn will ultimately determine the price paid by the consumer, the level of subsidy required in order to meet transport policy objectives and finally the level of costs and profit associated with that level of supply of transport services. In this chapter we more closely examine the supply side of the basic market and specifically the impact of prevailing market conditions on the price, costs, efficiency and profits of transport companies. Taken together, all of these factors determine the balance of benefit from the provision of those services between the consumer and the provider of the service. This adds up to what is known as 'economic efficiency'. This and the next chapter thus bring together all of the concepts examined previously to develop a number of scenarios each of which represent a precise set of market conditions. In doing so, this should highlight some of the problems with transport markets and why in many, if not most, situations they cannot be left entirely to market forces.

The ideas developed in this chapter are key to understanding what follows in the rest of the text as applied specifically to transport services. This is because much of the understanding of the economics of transport is directly related to a basic understanding of market principles and why they do not always 'work' in transport situations. The structure of the chapter therefore is heavily dependent upon theoretical underpinnings; however, practical illustrations are given where relevant and the chapter ends with a case study on the road haulage industry. The topic is continued in the following chapter, where comparisons are drawn between perfect and imperfect markets in the provision of transport services.

PROFIT MAXIMISATION

Until now we have simply taken profit maximisation as a general assumption that underpins the transport firm's behaviour in the market; however, the issue has not been addressed beyond that general assumption. This issue can now be further examined by drawing together the basic concepts covered in previous chapters. Profit maximisation is said to occur at that level of output where:

Marginal Cost (MC) = Marginal Revenue (MR)

You should recall that marginal cost is defined as the 'rate of increase in costs with respect to output'. A more basic way of expressing this is that the marginal cost is the cost of the last unit produced. Hence for a bus company, the marginal cost would effectively be the cost of the last person carried. We have not however come across the idea of the marginal revenue before. This can be defined as the additional total revenue gained by selling one more unit (per time period). In our example, therefore, is this a case of identifying how much the last person on the bus paid for their journey? In some respects the answer is yes but unfortunately it is not quite as straight-forward as that. In order to sell more journeys per time period the bus company will have to charge a lower price for *all passengers*, not just a lower fare to the last person. This is simply the law of demand. Marginal revenue therefore should not be mistaken with the idea that a firm can sell a number of units at one price and then in order to sell an 'extra' unit in that time period simply cut the price. Rather, marginal revenue is the difference in total revenue per time period as a result of cutting the price in order to carry one extra passenger, and thus includes the possibility of a negative value when market demand is inelastic. Marginal revenue will therefore always be lower than average revenue as the firm must reduce the fare in order to increase patronage, even if this is only by one. An illustration of marginal revenue would look something like Figure 6.1.

In Figure 6.1 the demand curve has also been labelled as the average revenue curve (AR), because if the firm sells say 100 units at £5 each the average revenue gained for each unit is simply the price of £5. Notice also that the marginal revenue curve is twice as steep as the average revenue curve and thus at all levels of output, as explained above, marginal revenue is always less than average revenue. What the firm actually does regarding the price charged and the level of output produced will be dependent upon the elasticity of demand (as cutting the price may increase revenue) and the cost of production. It will produce where profits are maximised; however, this leads back to the key question of identifying the level of output at which that occurs. This is found where:

MC = MR

In order to understand further why this is the case, it is easiest to consider when this position does not exist. This is shown graphically in Figure 6.2.

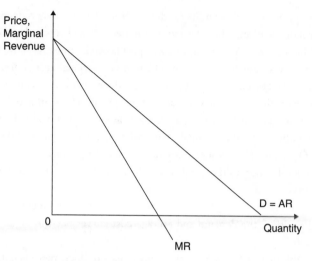

Figure 6.1 *Marginal and average revenue curves*

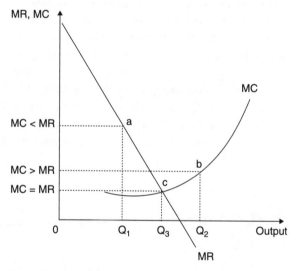

Figure 6.2 *Basic profit maximisation*

For simplification, Figure 6.2 only shows the marginal cost and marginal revenue curves. As output increases these two variables move in opposite directions, thus as output rises marginal costs rise and marginal revenue falls. This is because if the firm wants to sell more it needs to always lower its price, hence falling marginal revenue, whilst increasing output will have rising marginal costs over most of the range of output (see Chapter 5 for a reminder). Therefore, beginning at position a, for output level Q_1 marginal revenue is greater than marginal cost. The last unit produced therefore generated more revenue than it cost to produce, thus this unit made a profit. However, in order to increase total profit the firm should actually increase production as this will generate more profit from these units produced. Note that this may reduce the profit margin achieved on each individual unit, but the extra volume sold will more than offset any reduced profit margin and increase total profits. In this way profits can be maximised by increasing output. Moving to point b, however, at the level of production Q_2 marginal cost is greater than marginal revenue. In this case, the last unit sold cost more to produce than the revenue which it generated, hence making a loss on these units and reducing total profit. The firm should therefore reduce production and not produce that last unit, as this will increase total profit. It should continue to reduce production until marginal cost equals marginal revenue. In Figure 6.2 this occurs at point c and output level Q_3. Note that because marginal costs and marginal revenue move in opposite directions with the level of output there will always be a point of convergence and it is at that point where profits are maximised.

In order to determine the actual level of profits (or indeed losses) incurred by the firm at the profit maximising position, the demand and average cost curves need to be added to Figure 6.2, as shown in Figure 6.3.

Whilst to some this may at first appear as simply a mass of lines, there is nothing that has been added to Figure 6.3 that has not been introduced before either in this or previous chapters. What it shows is the basic production and market conditions facing a theoretical provider of transport services. Hence, the profit maximising position is found as above where marginal cost equals marginal revenue, i.e. where the MC and MR curves intersect. This is found at point a and gives a profit maximising output level for the provision of these services of Q. At that level of provision, the prevailing market conditions allow a fare of P to be charged, as shown by point c on the demand curve. The average cost of each passenger carried is found at point b on the average cost curve. Total revenue is therefore given by the area outlined by 0, P, c, Q and total costs by the area outlined by 0, AC, b, Q. The net difference, i.e. the area AC, P, c, b, is the profit, or to be more exact the abnormal profit, to the operator and this is the maximum profit that can be returned for the provision of these services under the prevailing production and market

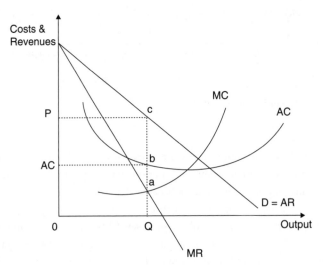

Figure 6.3 Profit maximising position for the firm

conditions. It is also useful, certainly in the context of transport operations, to consider that the profit maximising position need not necessarily produce a profit. Study the situation shown in Figure 6.4 below.

As with above, the 'profit' maximising position is found at point a where marginal cost equals marginal revenue. The associated average cost of each passenger carried is again found at point b, giving an average cost of AC. Finally, the fare that can be charged is found at point c on the demand curve, giving a fare of P. As can be clearly seen, the fare paid by each passenger is less than the cost to the operator of providing the resources for that journey, thus in this case the company is making a loss. The total amount of loss is outlined by the cross hatched area P, AC, b, c. In the long run however this is not the 'loss minimising position' as by simple logic that will always occur where zero output is produced. In the short run, as long as the firm is covering its variable costs, in most cases it will continue in operation until the capital is life expired, at which point it will close down. In this case note that where only a single price can be charged in the market the operator can never make a profit from providing this service. This is because at no point is the demand curve, i.e. what the market will bear, above the average cost curve. We will see a similar case in Chapter 8 however where the ability to charge users of the service different prices may enable the operator to make a profit. Whilst Figure 6.4 was produced essentially by manipulating how the diagram was drawn, such a situation is not purely theoretical and is one that often prevails in the provision of transport services. This is particularly the case where services are provided on equity grounds, such as those deemed to be social necessities in which the total revenue gained from the passenger will never cover the costs of providing the service. Subsidy is thus required in order to allow production of the service and bridge the gap between costs and revenue, and in this case the amount of subsidy paid would be the cross hatched area in Figure 6.4. Note however that in some ways this is a market-based solution, i.e. where the transport company produces at the 'profit' maximising level of output. Given however that the provision of such a service would have little or no market basis, the level of provision would be set at a point by the relevant authorities deemed to be consistent

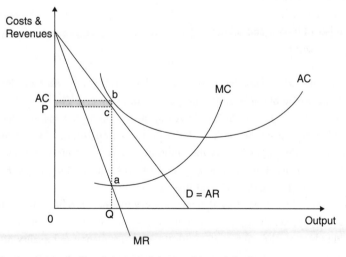

Figure 6.4 *Losses at the 'profit' maximising position of the firm*

with meeting their objectives. This may mean however that the authority would have to pay a higher level of subsidy, as would be the case for example for output levels to the right of Q in Figure 6.4. This is an important issue to which we return later in Chapters 10 and 11.

This basic framework of profit maximisation for a theoretical provider of transport services can now be used to examine the effect of competition, i.e. a change in one of the basic market and production conditions, on the fare charged, the average cost incurred and the profit attained from providing the service. These three aspects are important, as in simple terms they add up to what is known as economic efficiency, at which point the benefits arising out of the production of a given transport service are maximised and shared equitably between the operator and the consumer. We begin with a position of 'maximum' competition, more commonly known as 'perfect' competition, before looking at the other extreme in the form of a monopoly market in the following chapter.

PERFECT COMPETITION

As allocative efficiency was described in Chapter 5 as almost the holy grail of the economics discipline, perfect competition is the mechanism by which that holy grail is found. This is because perfect competition is one of the major requirements in order to achieve allocative efficiency, and we will see exactly why this is the case by examining the concept further. In simple terms, perfect competition is a highly competitive market where competition itself 'regulates' the market and ensures economic efficiency is achieved. In order for competition to be maximised, however, a number of market and production conditions must be met. The full list of these assumptions will be considered later in the chapter, as these are almost always overlooked in introductory texts but many are of particular significance to transport markets. In order to introduce the topic, however, the basic four conditions or assumptions of perfect competition are considered, namely:

- Freedom of entry and exit
- Homogeneous product
- High number of buyers and sellers
- Perfect information.

Freedom of entry and exit means that buyers and sellers are free to enter and leave the market as they see fit, there are no obstacles preventing them from doing so. The opposite of this is where barriers to entry exist and these may have a strong impact upon the market structure through limiting the number of firms in the market. Under perfect competition, however, no such barriers exist, thus new entry is always possible. Within transport markets, therefore, any operator would be at liberty to enter the market and compete on equal terms with existing firms. Freedom of exit means that they can exit the market without financial penalty.

A homogeneous product means that all firms produce identical products, thus a bus service is a bus service is a bus service, there is no difference between say a red bus service and one that is operated by a blue bus, on the same route, with the same frequency and quality of service. As all operators produce identical services, or at the very least services that are perceived to be identical, the consumer can switch from one operator's service to another's at a zero (transaction) cost. In more formal terms, all services are said to be perfectly substitutable, i.e. the demand curve for the individual firm is therefore perfectly elastic.

The third assumption of a high number of buyers and sellers is hardly one that should come as a surprise as a pre-requisite of competitive markets. What it means however is that no single operator or buyer of transport services has any degree of market power. If any operator was to leave the market then their market share would be so small that in simple terms it would have no impact on the prevailing fare charged. As a consequence, it is the market that sets the fare, not individual firms or buyers, and all buyers and sellers are 'price takers' not price setters. Contrast this with a 'pure' monopoly situation where there is only one operator, thus the firm would have a very strong market position and could exercise a high degree of control on the market through the level of output it produces. Restricting the level of output would increase the price, while increasing output would reduce the price. The OPEC countries in the mid and late 1970s for example operated very successfully as a cartel (née monopoly) to restrict the supply of oil to the world market and by so doing brought about major increases in the price of oil. Similarly, a small number of buyers in the market can impose great control over sellers – grocery retailers such as Sainsburys, Morrisons and Tescos are in a position to exert strong downward pressure on the prices charged by their suppliers. With a high number of buyers and sellers, however, this means that no single individual or organisation has any control over the market, hence all are price takers.

The last assumption is perfect information. This means that buyers, sellers, potential buyers and potential sellers know everything there is to know about the market. Hence there are no trade secrets (as this may also be a barrier to entry) and all profit and market information is common knowledge. In simple terms, therefore, consumers know the prices of all competing services and potential entrants know the level of profits being made in the industry. Perfect knowledge is thus a pre-requisite to ensure that buyers and sellers come to the right economic decisions regarding the goods they purchase and the markets served.

One may wish to question the highly restrictive nature of these four basic assumptions and ask if perfect competition exists in practice. The market which is usually given as the nearest example is that of agriculture, as this tends to operate on a global scale and thus has many suppliers (i.e. individual farmers) and consumers, and the produce is similar if not absolutely identical. The US bicycle industry has also been cited as a case in perfect competition (Townley, 2006). In both these industries however there are deviations from the perfect competition model, and thus the simple answer is that the assumptions of the model are too restrictive to exist in reality. Perfect competition is simply a 'benchmark' to be used to compare an ideal with reality to allow market failures to be identified. Whilst the term 'market failure' is commonly used in everyday (business) English as a general term for when things go 'wrong', by definition market failure occurs when one of the assumptions of perfect competition is breached and hence the market does not achieve economic efficiency. We will constantly return to this issue later as transport markets suffer from a high degree of market failure. For now, however, these assumptions can be used to examine the effect on the price, average cost and profits of perfectly competitive firms. This is shown in Figure 6.5.

One obvious difference with Figure 6.5 to previous figures in this chapter is that there are effectively two diagrams. What is not so obvious at first, however, is that the figure on the right is the effect of imposing the assumptions of perfect competition on the previous Figure 6.4, i.e. changing the market conditions facing the individual operator. On closer inspection, it should be

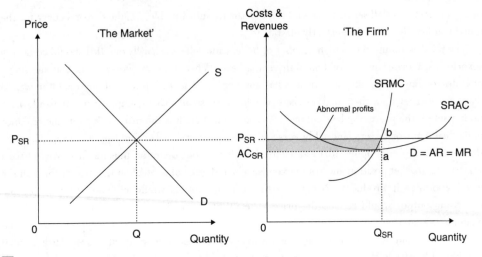

Figure 6.5 *Perfect competition, short run position (profits)*

clear that the only difference is that the demand curve facing the individual firm is perfectly elastic, i.e. horizontal at price P_{SR}, due to perfect substitutability between rival services. Thus under the conditions of perfect competition, average revenue equals marginal revenue. The rest of the figure relating to costs is identical. Turning to the figure on the left, the market sets the price at P_{SR} and due to a high number of buyers and sellers the firm is a price taker. It can therefore only sell at the market price P_{SR}. Note that if the firm was to charge a price above P_{SR}, demand for its service would drop to zero. This is because all services are the same (homogeneous), and further that all consumers know that all services are the same because of perfect information. Note also that there is little point in the operator charging a price below P_{SR}, as it can sell as much as it wants at the prevailing market price, hence any price reduction is simply cutting its own profits. This is a further reason why under this scenario marginal revenue is equal to average revenue, as the firm does not have to cut its price in order to sell more.

As normal the firm is assumed to be a profit maximiser, hence produces where marginal cost is equal to marginal revenue, highlighted by Q_{SR} for the individual firm. This however is purely a short-run position. As the firm is making abnormal profits, shown by the cross hatched area AC_{SR}, a, b, P_{SR}, then perfect information and an absence of barriers to entry ensure that new operators know of such abnormal profits and enter the market in the long run to compete these away.

This effect of new firms entering the market is shown in Figure 6.6, where as a result the supply curve has shifted to the right. The market price therefore falls to P_{LR}. The individual firm adjusts its level of output to the new profit maximising position, which is now at Q_{LR}. Note that at this point the firm is producing at the lowest point on the long-run average cost curve, hence productive efficiency is ensured, and as this is the long-run situation there is no incentive to change from this position. Note also that the firm is only making normal profits, which means it is covering all its costs including the cost of capital. In some ways, the abnormal profits that were being made in the short run have now been 'transferred' to the consumer in the form of lower prices. It is for these reasons that perfect competition is said to be the most economically efficient market structure, as

134

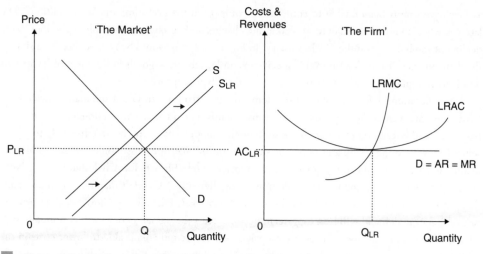

Figure 6.6 *Perfect competition, the long run position*

the first two conditions of allocative efficiency, that is technical and cost efficiency, are both achieved. We will see shortly that the third requirement, producing goods and services that will maximise consumers' benefit or utility, i.e. ones that they really want, is also met through such a market structure. One final point to note from both Figures 6.5 and 6.6 is that the level of output of the individual firm will be found by the profit maximising position on the marginal cost curve, thus the marginal cost curve is the supply curve of the individual firm. Consequently, the market supply curve is the summation of each firm's marginal cost curves.

To further underpin the ideas of perfect competition, outlined in Figure 6.7 is an example where there is a long-term shift in demand away from a good or service. There are numerous examples of goods or services that have become obsolete or whole industries that have disappeared

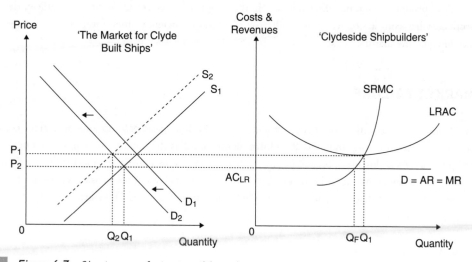

Figure 6.7 *Short run perfect competition – losses*

135

as they have simply been unable to continue to compete in the prevailing market conditions. The latter is what is known as 'structural' economic change, and an obvious example is the long-term decline of shipbuilding on the Clyde Estuary. In Figure 6.7, this would be represented by a shift in the demand curve to the left, as in this specific example, substitute goods in the form of lower cost non British shipbuilders take demand away from the Clyde shipyards.

In this situation, due to the shift in the demand curve from D_1 to D_2, at the market price P no Clydeside yard can make a profit. What subsequently occurs is a contraction in the industry (supply), in this case represented by a shift in the supply curve to the left from S_1 to S_2, as shipbuilders leave the Clyde and output is slowly reduced. This process would continue until the market is back in equilibrium and the market price re-established for Clyde-built ships. Note however the industry on the Clyde would now be smaller ($Q_2 < Q_1$). Ultimately, only those firms that produced at the lowest cost could survive in this market. Further note however that in many cases the shift in demand will be a long-term decline. Thus the demand curve will continually shift leftwards increasing downward pressure on prices. Therefore only firms able to lower costs in the long run, i.e. move to a lower average cost curve by achieving economies of scale, are ultimately able to survive in the industry. This is exactly what happened on the Clyde through a large number of mergers and acquisitions and considerable consolidation in the industry. Even this however failed to stem the long-term decline, as what was ultimately required to remain competitive was a very long-run downward shift in the average cost curve. Most shipbuilders however were unable to keep pace with this technical change and this led to the almost complete demise of shipbuilding on the Clyde.

Note also from this discussion that through the market mechanism there is what is termed consumer sovereignty. In simple terms, firms respond to the demands of consumers by producing what consumers want. Firms that fail to do so will be forced to leave the industry due to the losses being incurred. Consumer sovereignty also dictates that a longer-term shift in (consumer) demand away from a particular good or service will result in it no longer being produced. The resources that were thus employed in producing that good are now 'freed' to produce something that consumers actually want. As highlighted above, therefore, perfect competition is said to be an ideal as it does produce economic efficiency, i.e. in the long run scarce resources are used efficiently to produce what consumers want. An indicator of market efficiency, therefore, is that the price should equal the marginal cost.

MARKET FAILURE

What has been outlined in the previous section are the four basic assumptions of perfect competition that are normally outlined at an introductory level as the conditions required for perfect competition. As highlighted, breach of any of these assumptions constitutes market failure. With regard to transport markets, however, it is worth going beyond these basic assumptions and detailing the full list that are required for perfect competition to exist. These are:

Basic Assumptions:

- Many buyers and sellers
- No barriers to entry or exit

- All firms are profit maximisers
- All consumers are utility maximisers
- Perfect information
- Homogeneous product.

Further Assumptions:

- Non increasing production technologies, thus there are no economies of scale
- Non rivalry in consumption – consumption by one individual does not preclude consumption by another
- Absence of externalities, all benefits and costs are private and thus taken into account in market based decisions
- No government intervention to 'interfere' between the forces of demand and supply.

Whilst not explicitly mentioned, the basic assumptions of perfect competition also include producer profit maximisation and consumer utility maximisation, two underlying assumptions already outlined in the analysis of the demand and supply of transport services. These however are necessary conditions required to derive the market demand curve and the output level of the individual firm. Both however require perfect information, as without it neither the firm nor the consumer will be in a position to maximise their profits or utility respectively. There are four other conditions required however for perfect competition to exist, the first of which is non increasing production technologies. What this means is that there are no economies of scale and thus no advantages in larger-sized firms. If there were increasing returns to scale, then there would be an in-built incentive for firms to increase in size in order to lower average costs and thus be in a position to undercut smaller rivals and gain a larger share of the market. If increasing returns to scale existed over the whole market size, the ultimate conclusion would be a monopoly, where one firm would face a position of no competition.

Non rivalry in consumption is often confused with non excludability in consumption. What non rivalry basically means is that consumption by one person does not affect the consumption of the good or service by someone else. In simple terms, therefore, if one person consumes the good it does not make it unavailable to others. Hence the market for a rare Picasso painting has rivalry in consumption, as one person's purchase will make the painting unavailable to others. Potatoes on the other hand have non rivalry in consumption; hence one person's purchase of a 5 lb bag of new Ayrshire potatoes is unlikely to impact upon others' consumption of new Ayrshires. Basically, therefore, if consumers want a given product they can get it. This is often confused with non excludability in consumption, where the benefits in consumption cannot be confined to only those that pay for them. Thus consumption of rail services gives some benefit to road users in terms of reduced journey times on the roads. These come under the next assumption, externalities, in this case an external benefit. However, there can also be external costs, where the costs of a given activity fall not only on those that benefit from that activity but also on others who do not. The problem with externalities are that they are not taken into account when making a market-based decision as the externality has no market value. Thus the road user does not consider the costs on the environment when deciding whether or not to use the car. As externalities are a major issue in transport markets, these are dealt with far more extensively later in the text. In this case, however, it is a market failure that may lead to over or under consumption of a particular good or service due to the presence of externalities.

The last assumption, government intervention, is also a major transport issue, hence will also be returned to, but is outlined here in terms of a condition of perfect competition. Government intervention is a form of market failure as it would interfere with market signals and thus lead to an inefficient outcome. For example, consumer sovereignty above was highlighted as a case where consumers, through their market actions, indicate what goods and services they want to be produced, i.e. the ones they buy, and which ones they don't want to be produced, i.e. the ones they don't buy. Government intervention, by for example paying subsidies for certain goods or services, interferes with these signals by encouraging consumers to buy products they do not really want!! To be more rational, subsidies encourage the tying up of resources in the production of goods or services at a higher cost than the benefit derived from the consumption of those goods or services. Such productive resources therefore would be better employed in some other activity, where the benefit gained matched the cost of production. Note however that this rationale is based upon a single perspective of taking each assumption on its own, i.e. only viewing government intervention in isolation. In most instances, intervention in the market is in order to correct for an existing breach of one of the other assumptions, for example that of no externalities. This is why government action to 'correct' for such market failures is often referred to as a second best solution, as the best solution, the market itself, is incapable of delivering economic efficiency due to market failure.

Apart from the previously cited US bicycle industry, however, does perfect competition exist in any of the transport industries? One that is often cited as being close or near to perfect competition is the road haulage industry, thus Case study 6.1 examines the extent to which this industry meets the conditions of perfect competition. The case should also help to develop further the ideas behind perfect competition, particularly the practical aspects, as well as begin to introduce some of the problems that can be associated with highly competitive markets.

Case study 6.1 Road haulage and the economist's model of perfect competition

Road haulage has often been cited as an example of an industry that meets, or is close to meeting, the conditions of the economist's model of perfect competition. This facet of the industry has long been recognised, with Adams and Hendry stating as long ago as 1957 that:

> 'The problem under study here is of interest because these authors hold that the trucking industry epitomises the classical model of perfect competition. Here is an industry where there appears to be no economies of scale, where the number of firms is large and where, in the absence of restrictions, entry would be brisk.'

That premise was used as the main thrust of the authors' argument that at that time the US trucking industry should not be subjected to government control and regulation. Not all authors agreed, however, with Smykay (1958), a strong advocate of continued regulation, in particular showing hostility to this point of view and arguing that such an important industry to the US economy could not be simply left to market forces to decide haulage rates and the level of supply provided. Eight years later Munby (1965), with regard to the British industry, concluded that there was no adequate general case for any licensing system for road haulage beyond control of drivers' hours, the condition of the vehicles used and other safety-related measures. The basis for this conclusion was that the industry would operate along free market principles that would, due to its closeness to the model of perfect competition, ensure economic efficiency.

This case study attempts to investigate the extent to which the road haulage industry does actually adhere to the economist's model of perfect competition by examining industry conditions under each of the four basic assumptions of the perfect competition model, plus the further key assumption of non-increasing returns to scale.

Many buyers and sellers

The first assumption of perfect competition is many buyers and sellers, with the very strong implication that no single buyer or seller is large enough to affect the price, hence the price is set by the market and all firms are price takers.

Examination of the relevant statistics for the UK, taken from a number of different sources, reveals that in 2004/5 there were some 102,000 goods vehicle operator licences, i.e. qualified firms, in the industry. This represented a significant decline over the preceding eleven year period since 1993 when there were some 125,000 licensed operators (FTA, 2008). Nevertheless, this is still a very large number of firms in the industry. Furthermore, a quick look at any local Yellow Pages under 'road haulage services' also produces a large number of firms within the local area, certainly far more than listed under 'bus, coach and tramway'. As regards registered vehicles, the DfT (2007) report that there were some 441,000 registered vehicles in total in 2004/5, an increase of 5.6 per cent since 1993. This would suggest an average fleet size of 4.25 vehicles, which compared to 1993 represents a significant increase from 3.29 vehicles. Average firm size would therefore appear to be increasing over time and most of this would appear to have come through industry consolidation, i.e. company mergers and takeovers.

Despite such consolidation a high number of small firms still appear to exist in the industry. The FTA (2008) cite that three quarters of road haulage operators operate a fleet size of two vehicles or less, with a very high percentage of single-vehicle firms operated by owner-drivers. This on its own would suggest a highly competitive industry that despite some industry consolidation still closely resembles the perfect competition assumption of many buyers and sellers. The FTA also quotes however that 10 per cent of fleets operate half the total fleet, suggesting some significantly larger operators with an average fleet size of around 20 vehicles. Thus although the industry has many firms, this appears to consist of a very clear division of small and large companies. There would thus appear to be a significant number of firms that are of a size to influence the market, i.e. not all firms are price takers.

A homogeneous product

Taking a somewhat simplistic view that many industry experts would undoubtedly disagree with, road haulage firms operate a basic low-tech service to transport goods from one location to another, i.e. a driver and a lorry. This would appear to represent an identical product and as such conforms completely to the assumption of a homogeneous product.

In some ways however there can be deviation from that basic assumption, and certainly an element of product differentiation. One factor that plays a key role in the road haulage industry is the firm's reputation. Hauliers with good reputations for high quality services that deliver on time could feasibly charge higher prices and will almost certainly acquire a degree of consumer loyalty. Although the basic service provided can by argued to be identical, these are not perfectly substitutable between suppliers due to variations in how that basic service is actually provided, i.e. there is product differentiation. Nevertheless, most firms operate under contract to large freight-handling firms or big fleet operators (Lacey, 1990) in which there is strong downward pressure on prices due to the relative ease of substitution between firms. How the industry actually operates, therefore, with a high degree of substitutability between operators, would appear to be a very close approximation to the assumption of an identical product.

Perfect information

In reality, there is always a limit to perfect information. In simple terms, no one can know all relevant market information and in any case the transaction costs involved in actually acquiring such information may be economically inefficient. We therefore concentrate only on three aspects of perfect information – prices, production and performance. Regarding haulage prices, another look at the local Yellow Pages or the Internet would suggest that there exists a position that is near to perfect information. It would be relatively easy to make a round of phone calls to produce a reasonable data set of prices on which to base a rational decision as to which haulier to choose on the basis of price, although it is recognised that this is a considerable oversimplification of the issue.

As regards the production of road haulage services, as highlighted above, at the basic level of the transport component this tends to be a relatively low-tech industry. All that is required is a vehicle and a driver and there are few 'secrets' in the basic production of road haulage services. The wider issues of building a company reputation or in successfully running the business may be different issues; however, in this respect there is no reason to suspect that road haulage should be any different to any other type of business and therefore these constitute basic business skills.

The final aspect considered is information relating to performance of the industry. This would obviously be an important dimension for potential new entrants. Certainly in comparison with passenger-related transport, information appears to be far more difficult to obtain. A simple look at government statistics reveals few related to freight whilst many more related to passenger movements. This may reflect a policy bias where there is far more legislation related to passenger services than freight activities, hence the government collects and publishes far more statistics on the former than the latter. Furthermore, information on profitability in the industry has, perhaps not unsurprisingly, proved virtually impossible to obtain in the course of writing this case study. Whilst both the Road Haulage and the Freight Transport Associations provide some general information and support for those within the trade, this does not include market information, hence in the aspects considered here this falls short of what could be termed 'perfect information'.

Information on market prices and production technologies therefore would appear to be relatively easy to obtain; however, potential entrants to the industry may be limited to those with an inside knowledge of the prevailing business environment. In some respects therefore, this last aspect may be no different to any other industry, where those inside the industry are best placed to take advantage of market opportunities (as exemplified by the numerous insider trading and banking scandals that have occurred in the city over the years!). Thus information may not be 'perfect' as such, but is probably as close as is realistically possible.

No barriers to entry or exit

As with perfect information, the position of no barriers to entry or exit can never be achieved in reality, there will always be some form of cost, either financial or in terms of the opportunity cost, in setting up in business. The issue therefore surrounds the existence of significant barriers to entry that restrict entry to only medium- or large-sized firms. The basic components required for a road haulage firm are a qualified driver, an operator's licence and a suitable vehicle. All of these aspects are in the bounds of possibility for the small firm. The large number of owner-drivers in the industry would also suggest that small firms do enter and survive in the industry. Therefore there would appear to be few barriers to entry and thus this condition of perfect competition in practice would appear to be largely met.

Non-increasing returns to scale

One further crucial element to examine is the assumption of non-increasing returns to scale. In other words, are there any advantages for larger firms with regarded to improved productivity or lower average costs? Most research on the topic relates to the trucking industry in the US because of more readily available data and because it is a crucial element in the operation of the market. It was thus a critical aspect of the whole de-regulation debate in the US before and after deregulation of the market in 1980.

To summarise what is a considerable research area, the balance of evidence would tend to suggest that economies of scale do exist in road haulage, but are not as extensive as in other industries such as rail freight. There are however inconsistencies in the findings. For example Nebesky *et al.* (1995) found no evidence of returns to scale in the less than truck load (LTL) segment of the US market. Giordano (1997) on the other hand examined the 100 largest less than truckload carriers over a period of 20 years. The author found evidence of increasing returns to scale up to firm size that would be consistent with significant fleet sizes, specifically around 28 vehicles.[1] Constant returns to scale were then found beyond that to a point of around 70 vehicles, after which decreasing returns were found. Furthermore, Ying (1990) examined the US trucking industry at three points in time, 1975, 1980 and 1984, in order to assess the impact of the 1980 Motor Carrier Act, the actual act that deregulated the interstate trucking market. With regard to scale economies, a massive swing was found from constant returns to scale in 1975 and 1980 under the regulated market, to very strong increasing returns in 1984 under the deregulated market. The author suggests that the restrictive nature of the regulated market prevented firms from fully utilising their own large networks, hence once the market was deregulated firms exploited the advantages presented with regard to the scale of operations.

As regards the British experience, there is far less evidence and almost all of it dates from the period prior to the Transport Act 1968 which deregulated the UK road haulage industry. As an example, Harrison (1963) reviews studies carried out up to that period and concludes there is little evidence of economies of scale in road haulage. This is despite an apparent increase in firm size; however, the author attributes this to the greater restrictions on market entry than on increasing capacity in what was then the regulated market. A second factor highlighted interestingly was imperfections in knowledge that influenced choices between established and non-established operators in favour of the former.

This inconsistency in the findings on the existence or otherwise of economies of scale in road haulage would perhaps suggest that within certain sectors there are other factors present that may allow smaller firms to compete with larger competitors on a relatively equal basis. In other words, economies of scale do not destroy competition. As such, therefore, this would appear to be consistent with a near to perfect competition model rather than perfect competition per se.

Conclusion

From this albeit simplistic review of the road haulage industry, it would appear that the industry does closely resemble certain aspects of the perfectly competitive model. What this produces is a very competitive industry, even in specialised segments where the number of firms may be relatively small, e.g. the less than truckload market.

In the past, road haulage has been heavily regulated and controlled, not only in Britain but throughout the whole developed world, not because of market failure but rather due to the strategic importance of the industry to the workings of the whole economy. With the subsequent shift in general economic thinking towards far less state intervention in the economy, the poor economic case for intervention has been exposed and the industry largely de-regulated.

Note however that having a highly competitive market in an industry such as road haulage, where there exist operational safety issues, is not without drawbacks. This breaches the assumption of no externalities, as the cost of operations includes the potential human cost to others in terms of injuries and fatalities if things should go wrong. What it produces therefore is a cut throat scenario in which there are very strong pressures to keep costs down and thus a temptation for some to not follow all of the qualitative regulations that exist. This leads to the idea of cowboy operators and fly-by-night type operations. Building and construction is another industry that exhibits the same characteristics, i.e. a high level of competition and the need for extensive safety precautions.

Due to the presence of such externalities, therefore, road haulage still requires effective qualitative regulation, where the chances of offenders being caught are high and the cost of the penalties imposed far outweigh the potential benefits that may arise from getting away with it. The industry therefore cannot be entirely left to the market; however, the state's role is to ensure that minimum operating standards are set at an appropriate level and that these standards are enforced and maintained. Economic forces should then be able to take the industry forward from there. Of increasing concern with regard to road haulage, however, is the presence and impact of another externality, that of air pollution, and that may require stronger market intervention from the relevant authorities in the future.

CHAPTER SUMMARY AND REFLECTION

This chapter has examined the issue of perfect competition in transport markets. That was defined as the position where the level of competition within the market is maximised. For this to take place, a number of conditions or assumptions are required, and if fulfilled, the market will find the 'right' answer in transport markets. In other words, the correct level of transport services will be produced in a cost efficient manner to those that value them. Operators will only earn a 'fair' reward in the form of normal profits for providing such services.

What we also saw however was that transport markets, even in the case study industry of road haulage, breach at least one of the assumptions of perfect competition. Whilst that is probably true of all industries, in certain transport sectors the problem is that it is particularly acute. We examine some of these issues in subsequent chapters; however, the following chapter considers breaches of at least one of the basic four assumptions of perfect competition, which results in the creation of imperfectly competitive markets.

CHAPTER EXERCISES

The two exercises that follow can be completed after reading this chapter, particularly the first; however, you may wish to also read the following chapter before attempting these questions.

Exercise 6.1 Perfect competition in bus markets

If we assume that a given bus market is in perfect competition which charges a flat fare of £1, and if the formula for the total demand (in thousands) in the market is given by the equation:

$$Q_d = 250 - 60P$$

Where Q_d is the quantity demanded in thousands at a given price P.

If we further assume constant returns to scale, then:

a) What is the total market demand at the £1 flat fare?

b) If the market is shared equally by 4 firms, what is the number of passengers carried by each company?

c) If the cost per vehicle kilometre is £1.60, average utilisation 20 passengers per vehicle kilometre and average trip distance 10 kilometres:[2]

    i What is the level of bus kilometres required to service this market?

    ii What profits are being made?

    iii What type of profit is this, normal or abnormal?

    iv What is the cost per passenger carried (as opposed to the cost per vehicle kilometre)?

d) As this is perfect competition, new firms may enter the market and compete these profits away. What price therefore will ensure that only normal profits are made?

e) The answer to part d should be the same as the answer to c(iv), why?

f) At the lower flat fare, why has market efficiency now been achieved?

g) This exercise assumes that the four firms in the market will behave consistent with the perfect competition model, however is that in their own best interests? What does this tell us about market structures where only a few firms exist?

h) Why in this exercise however would the firms be forced to behave consistent with the perfectly competitive market?

Exercise 6.2 Transport industries' market structures

In this chapter we have only examined perfect competition in transport markets. Nevertheless, this was stated as the position where the level of competition within the market is maximised. As we will see in the following chapter, the other end of the spectrum is where there is no completion at all, i.e. a monopoly. From the following list of transport industries given below therefore:

- The British Bus Industry
- Road Haulage
- Domestic Air Services
- Suburban Rail Services
- National Intercity Rail Services
- Long Haul Air Flights originating in the European Union
- All land-based forms of public transport in Britain
- Rail freight services
- Urban taxi services

Place those industries on a spectrum of market structures that should look something like this:

●━━━●

Monopoly   Perfect Competition

where perfect competition represents the position of 'maximum' competition and monopoly the position of no competition.

Questions:

a) What criteria did you use in your assessment of where on the spectrum a particular industry should be placed?

b) On a scale of 1 (very low) to 5 (very high), mark against each industry this (very!) rough indicator of government intervention in that particular transport market. Does there appear to be any particular order in your assessments?

c) What have you learned from this exercise, particularly with regard to the definition of a particular transport market and its associated market structure?

Chapter 7

Imperfect competition in transport markets

Learning Outcomes:

On reading this chapter, you will learn about:

- The imperfect market structures of monopoly and oligopoly and their high prevalence in transport markets
- The main sources of barriers to entry into transport markets
- The disadvantages and advantages of imperfect markets in the provision of transport services
- The tendency for competitive transport markets to veer towards imperfect market structures through company mergers and acquisitions
- One perspective of the process of competition and how industry structure may change and evolve over time.

INTRODUCTION

In this chapter the examination of competition within transport markets is further developed by introducing the idea of the imperfectly competitive market. A simple but highly accurate definition of such a market is one that breaches one or more of the assumptions of perfect competition. What this results in is a market that may have some form of competition, but that competition tends to be flawed in some respect. Consequently, operators within the market generally do not compete as fiercely as they would do in a situation of perfect competition. When left to the free market, historically most transport industries have tended towards these types of imperfect market structures, thus the two main forms, monopoly and oligopoly, are introduced in this chapter. In the course of the chapter we will also see that competition can take several different forms other than being based solely upon the price charged and/or the service offered, some of which are not always obvious as competitive strategies.

In addition to the impact and effect of externalities, the issue of imperfectly competitive markets is the other major issue facing the organisation and provision of transport services. The consequences reach far beyond the direct issues covered in this chapter and extend to other matters such as the payment of subsidy, the regulation of operations and the question of private versus public ownership and control of transport services. This chapter will outline the problems as well as the potential advantages of imperfect markets in the provision of transport services. In the final section, the actual process of competition is examined, which attempts to address the question as to why so many transport markets tend towards this structure even where the best intentions of regulatory authorities have been that these markets should remain competitive. There are numerous examples where reforms have been almost wholly unsuccessful in delivering a competitive transport market in the long run. One of the principal reasons for this is that the underlying market structure, and more importantly market conduct, has proved to be far stronger than any government intervention. Understanding the basics of the competitive process is thus an important part in identifying the underlying characteristics that lead to such undesired outcomes.

MONOPOLY

There is a spectrum as regards forms of market structure and levels of competition within transport markets. At the one end is the highly competitive market of perfect competition as roughly approximated by the road haulage industry. There are then a number of increasingly anti-competitive forms before arriving at the other extreme where no competition exists at all, known as a monopoly. Most rail services are a good example of a monopoly, where there exists only a single operator on a given route. There are also countless examples in the bus sector where all services within a given area are provided by one company. In Britain and elsewhere, however, in the case of railways this has almost universally occurred by design rather than as a result of market forces. This is the regulated market, where a monopoly is legally imposed, and thereby controlled, by the regulatory machinery. This topic will be further examined in Chapter 10. In the second example, however, local monopolies in the deregulated British bus markets have occurred as a result of market forces. In this chapter we consider the free market idea of a monopoly in order to first understand this as a concept in its own right and major issue in transport markets, and then to better appreciate the ideas underlying the regulated market considered later.

In theoretical terms, a monopoly in transport services is said to occur where there is only one supplier to the market, in other words a 'pure' monopoly. Note therefore that this can exist both within a single industry such as bus or rail services or across modes within a single area, such as is the case in London and many other major cities. Note also that this definition refers to the theoretical case; however, in practical terms a monopoly situation is generally considered to exist in Britain where one firm controls more than 25 per cent of the market, or in the EU where it breaks a number of turnover thresholds. Any proposed merger within Britain therefore that would create a company with more than 25 per cent of the market would be investigated by the Competition Commission, or referred to the European Commission in the case of a European cross-border merger that breaks the minimum revenue threshold. This is because at that level of dominance the danger is that such a merger may create an anti-competitive market and thus operate against the public interest. For example, in 2006 the proposed joint venture in the provision of Scottish inter-urban bus services between the two incumbents, Scottish Citylink and Stagecoach, was referred to the Competition Commission on the grounds that it would act against the public interest. Despite a large body of evidence to the contrary, the Commission concluded that the joint venture would result in higher fares, reduced services and increased barriers to entry through network effects. As a result, their preferred remedy was the sale of a number of buses to a rival operator. After two years however the sale had still not happened, highlighting one of the problems with addressing the problems of imperfect markets, in this case finding a company willing to compete in this particular market. The Competition Commission has also investigated the situation of Ferovial owning BAA airports in the South East of England, on the basis that it could be seen as anti-competitive.

Returning to the theory, as there is only one operator supplying the market in a monopoly, then the firm's individual demand and supply curves are the market's demand and supply curves. Unlike perfect competition, therefore, the monopoly profit maximising position is shown on a single graph.

Notice that Figure 7.1 is almost exactly the same as Figure 6.2 in the previous chapter, the only difference being the labelling to identify this as the monopolist's profit maximising position. The monopolist faces a downward sloping demand curve (there is always an alternative to a monopolist's goods or service – go without!) and marginal revenue is less than average revenue at each level of output. Extending the analysis, the firm's profit maximising level of output is found at Q_M, where marginal revenue equals marginal cost. This would produce an average cost of AC_M and at that level of output the price charged would be P_M. Notice that the firm is not producing at the lowest point on the average cost curve, hence this is one reason why monopolies are not as economically efficient as perfect competition.

At the profit maximising level of output Q_M, the monopolist would be making abnormal profits, as shown by the shaded area AC_M, P_M, b, a. In this case, however, unlike perfect competition, abnormal profits would not be competed away in the long run due to the existence of barriers to entry which prevents new firms entering this market. The only change that may occur is in the

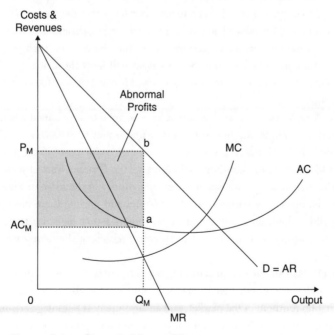

Figure 7.1   *Monopolist profit maximising position*

very long run, as a result of a sustained shift in demand away from the good or service. The monopoly market structure raises a number of important economic issues, the first of which surrounds the key part played by barriers to entry.

Barriers to entry

Barriers to entry are key to sustaining a short-run monopoly into the longer term, as a barrier to entry stops new firms entering the market and competing with the established operator. Often a distinction is made between structural and strategic barriers to entry. The former relates to where there are basic industry conditions that may limit market entry, the latter where organisational barriers are put in place by incumbent firms in order to achieve the same effect.

Structural barriers

Firm size. Firm size as a barrier to entry is directly related to economies of scale. Where there are substantial economies of scale, any potential entrant must be of a size that will enable it to capture all the economies of scale, i.e. operate at the minimum efficiency scale. Any entry at a smaller scale would put the new entrant at a cost disadvantage that could ultimately be exploited should a price war ensue. The sheer investment involved therefore in entering at a large scale of production can be a barrier to entry as only a few firms or organisations will have the ability to undertake the investment. We have already seen in Case study 5.3 that within rail operations, returns to scale tend to be significant due to the high capital requirement in the production of rail services. If left purely to the market, therefore, this would act as a significant barrier to entry to potential new entrants. This is something we shall see further in Chapter 12 and also applies to many if not most of the US rail freight companies. Note that a further barrier is that the new entrant would have to sell the large level of output produced at a profit in order for its operations to be sustainable in the longer term. The prevailing market conditions would thus have to be such that another major operator could be supported in the industry. This again will limit those able, or willing, to enter the industry, and certainly within the rail examples cited is one that is unlikely to apply (see below under natural monopoly).

High sunk costs. A sunk cost is a cost that cannot be redeemed or re-claimed when the firm leaves the market. The best example of a high sunk cost, with no pun intended, is the Channel Tunnel. When this opened in 1995 this represented a very high sunk cost. If the tunnel's operator, Eurotunnel, was to leave the market they could not take the Channel Tunnel with them and set it up elsewhere. This was in direct contrast to their competitors in the form of the ferry operators, who could leave the market by withdrawing their ferries and putting them onto other routes, as many ultimately did. A high sunk cost therefore represents a very high risk to the potential new entrant, and as such would be a strong barrier to entry because if the firm leaves the industry it leaves with nothing.

Moshandreas (1994) lists further structural barriers to entry as product differentiation, where a strong brand loyalty is created, hence making it difficult for any potential entrant to gain a significant (profitable) foothold in the market, and an absolute cost advantage arising from a skilled management team, superior techniques and know how. In more general terms this effect is where existing firms have certain cost advantages due to the experience of being in the industry for a significant period of time. This is sometimes referred to as the learner curve, a well-known phenomenon in aircraft production, where the experience of doing results in less waste and more efficiency in the production of the good or service. Any new entrant would have to go through the same process of the learner effect and may not survive that period as it would be at a disadvantage to the incumbent operator. The learner effect as a barrier to entry could also be expanded to include market knowledge, where a better knowledge of the market served represents a barrier to entry. Hence, for example, the Manchester bus market is not the same as the Sheffield bus market, and hence those serving the Sheffield market would be at an advantage even against established bus operators as they would better know the needs of their customers. Moshandreas (op. cit.) also lists a lower cost of capital due to a good reputation gained over a lengthy period of time and the beneficial effects of vertical integration as further structural barriers, although this latter effect probably falls somewhere between a structural and a strategic barrier.

Strategic barriers to entry

Legal protection. This is the first barrier to entry listed as strategic, as it does not relate to industry conditions but rather is one imposed by a third party, in this case the legal system of the country. A legally protected monopoly arises where the firm has a legal right to be the only provider/producer of a given good or service in a particular country or area, and as such is the most straightforward and the most stringent of all the barriers to entry listed here. The most common legally protected monopolies are normally created through the issuing of patents, where the inventors or discoverers of a drug or process are given a legal right to be the sole producers of that good over a period of time. Others exist however. Regulatory authorities in certain markets may nominate a particular operator to be the only provider of that service. In the London bus market, for example, the winner of the tender to provide a given service has the exclusive right to operate that particular route. Direct competition on the route is prevented through legal protection which stops any other bus company providing an identical competing service.

Control of the factors of production. Where one single firm controls the factors of production, then this constitutes a strategic barrier to entry as it would be very difficult for any other firm to enter the market as it simply would not have access to any production capabilities. This will normally relate to production processes and labour skills, where one company may have all the skilled labour and that knowledge may be protected by some form of covenant. The classic example of control of the factors of production is De Beers, the world's largest producer of diamonds, which controls world supply and distribution through its London-based Central Selling Organisation. This is what would be known as a vertically integrated firm, in which one single firm owns and controls the whole production process from supply of the raw materials right through to the final point of sale to the consumer. In the past, breweries were also a classic example of the vertically integrated firm, as they brewed the product, distributed it throughout the country through their own fleet of lorries and network of depots and then finally sold it to the consumer through their own outlet of hostelries. As such, it would be very difficult for any new firm to enter at any particular stage of this process, and thus market entry would be restricted. Such operations however are far less common today; however, horizontally integrated firms continue to exist. These are firms that are at the same stage in the production process. Thus First Bus, as was, began by operating bus services but then moved into the provision of rail services as well, thus becoming

First Group. Horizontally integrated firms are not a direct barrier to entry to a single market as such, although may operate as a barrier with regard to firm size, as in order to compete with a particular operator a firm may have to simultaneously enter several markets at once.

Exclusive dealerships. An exclusive network of dealerships is where the manufacturer of a given product may choose to only supply a particular outlet in a given area. This therefore gives the manufacturer far more power throughout the whole logistical chain, and in particular, far more control over the actual point of sale. Car manufacturers are a good example of this type of barrier to entry, where the manufacturer carefully controls the number and location of retail outlets. Within the EU, car manufacturers were exempt from EU competition laws which would have prevented such actions. This exemption was used highly effectively as a barrier to entry, and meant car manufacturers could carefully control the network of outlets and prevent local competition in new car sales. This unsatisfactory situation resulted in considerable variations in car prices throughout the EU and the exemption was eventually removed by the European Commission in 2002.

Branding. This is the last strategic barrier to entry listed and one in which a good example is given by the bus industry in the UK. When organised in the public sector, most bus companies were identified with particular regions or areas. Thus Glasgow buses were green and yellow, Edinburgh buses maroon, Bristol buses green and so on. If that way inclined, you could in fact identify where you were in the country by the colour of the buses operating on the streets! In the early days of privatisation, most of the private bus companies kept these regional identities; however, over time most if not all have been eradicated and national 'brands' identified. Thus First Glasgow buses are grey, First Edinburgh buses are grey and First Bristol buses are grey. This is to establish a national brand and thus one that makes market entry for a new entrant more difficult, particularly at a national level.

Disadvantages of monopolies

Monopolies are normally associated with all things that are 'bad' with capitalist (market) based economies. Most of these 'all things' are associated with the fact that monopolies are anti-competitive. This not only results in the charging of higher prices to consumers that are faced with very little alternative other than to do without, but can also result in a general slackness in the working practices of the monopolist due to the lack of competitive pressures. This has led to a whole host of anti-competitive agencies, such as those highlighted earlier, which have been appointed to oversee the structure of not only transport services but all industrial sectors of the economy. In the case of the transport industries, this intervention would be irrespective if the industry had a specific regulator or not, as the roles and functions of the industry regulator tend to be very different from that of the competition agencies. This basic argument of anti-competitive market behaviour however can be expanded in order to look in more detail at the main disadvantages of monopolies.

Production inefficiencies

Unlike perfect competition where in the long run production will always occur at the lowest point on the long run average cost curve, a monopolist is not 'forced' into achieving this position. In simple terms this means that in most cases resources are being inefficiently used in the production of that good or service. Costs, in the form of the prices of factors of production, are a signal to the producer of the best combination of resources to use in the production process. Where costs are not minimised, production resources are not being used in their best combination. Monopoly is therefore almost always economically inefficient, although this will mainly relate to the scale of operations, i.e. scale inefficiencies. This occurs as a result of the monopolist restricting supply in the market, which in most cases will mean that it fails to capture all the available economies of scale.

Higher prices charged and lower output produced

If left to the market, the prices charged will be higher and the output level produced will be lower than a perfectly competitive industry facing exactly the same cost conditions. This is illustrated in Figure 7.2.

In the figure, the monopolist's demand curve is the market demand curve, shown by $D = AR$, and the associated marginal revenue curve is given by MR_M. Faced with average and marginal cost curves as outlined by AC and MC respectively, the monopolist will profit maximise where $MC = MR$, which is at output level Q_M with an associated price of P_M.

If this market was in perfect competition, however, for each individual firm the marginal revenue curve would equate to the average revenue curve as all firms are price takers. As before, the firm would again profit maximise where $MC = MR$, which in this case occurs at output level Q_{PC} with the associated price of P_{PC}. Under monopoly, therefore, the level of supply would be less and the price charged would be higher than if the market was in perfect competition. This

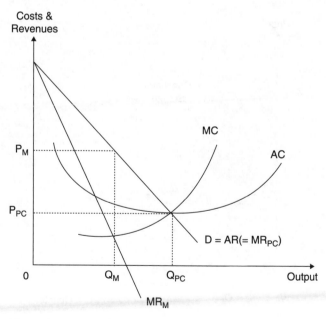

Figure 7.2 *Monopoly versus perfect competition*

restriction of supply in order to induce higher prices is probably viewed as the biggest drawback and fear of monopoly market structures. As highlighted, most transport markets tend towards this very type of market structure, which initially led to their control through public ownership, i.e. to force the (monopoly) industry through direct management to produce at Q_{PC} on Figure 7.2 rather than Q_M. Over time however thinking has changed, and now much of the reform that is ongoing within European Union transport markets is concerned with introducing and maintaining some form of competition into these markets in order to bring about the same result (see Chapter 10).

Reduces consumer surplus and is regressive

Consumer surplus is defined as the level of demand that would have been willing to pay a higher price than the market price. This is the area of consumer demand to the left of the total quantity demanded, as these individuals would have been willing to pay a higher price for the good than the market price. Consider Figure 7.3, where the market price is P_1 and demand found at point a on the demand curve, giving a quantity demanded of Q_1. At that price however those consumers whose demand lies in the area to the left of Q_1, the shaded area, would have been willing to pay a higher price for this service. This is the area of consumer surplus. For example at quantity Q_2, consumers would have been willing to pay price P_2. In a certain sense, therefore, these consumers are in 'profit' as they acquired the service for a lower price than the level at which they valued it. The money 'saved' therefore can be used to purchase other goods and services that will increase their utility, hence net consumer welfare is increased. Now consider what happens to this area of consumer surplus under perfect competition and monopoly market structures. This is illustrated in Figure 7.4.

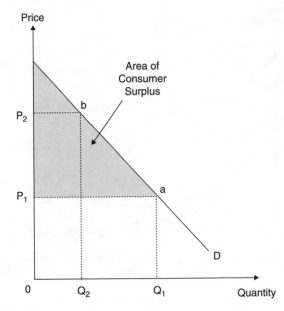

Figure 7.3 Consumer surplus

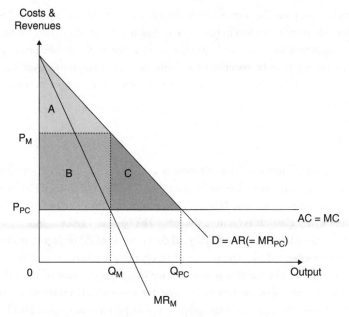

Figure 7.4 *Consumer surplus, perfect competition versus monopoly*

In order to simplify this illustration, costs have been assumed to follow constant returns with no economies of scale, hence the average cost curve is horizontal and thus at each point marginal costs equal average costs. Under perfect competition total consumer surplus is given by a summation of the areas marked by A+B+C, as the price is set at P_{PC}. If this market was a monopoly, however, then the area of consumer surplus would reduce to only that shown by area A. As we have seen, trade should never be a zero sum game, thus both parties benefit in any exchange. This reduction in consumer surplus concerns the balance between the utility received in the exchange of transport services for financial gain between the consumer and the producer. Where there is a monopoly provider of transport services, it is argued that if this remains unchecked the balance is too much in favour of the operator. This is also shown in Figure 7.4. Note that not only has the area of consumer surplus been reduced, but also area B has been transferred from the consumer in the form of lower prices paid for the service, to the producer in the form of higher profits gained from the production of the service. Not only is this a simple 'transfer', however, but is also potentially a regressive measure as bus users will include the less well off within society, whilst shareholders will include the better off. Such actions therefore take from the poor (due to the necessity of many transport services) and give to the rich, thereby increasing the divisions between the rich and poor within society.

Net welfare loss

Monopolies are said to suffer from what is known as a net welfare loss. Basically, the imbalance in the trade between the consumer and the producer in favour of the producer results in a reduction of the total benefits that could be accrued from the exchange. Note that in Figure 7.4, not only has area B 'transferred' to the producer, but area C has been lost altogether. What this actually represents are consumers who no longer use the service due to the higher prices charged under monopoly. If the price was to be reduced back to the perfect competition level, they would again use the service. This therefore is a net welfare loss and society is no longer maximising the uses of its scarce resources.

X-inefficiency

X-inefficiency was briefly introduced in Chapter 5 as a source of decreasing returns to scale. It is also however a major argument against monopolies. The idea of X-inefficiency was originally devised by the American economist Harvey Leibenstein in 1966 (Leibenstein, 1966), and lies outside mainstream neo-classical economic thinking. The basis of Leibenstein's argument was that under certain conditions the average and marginal cost curves would be higher than they should be due to general management slack. The source of this general slackness was most prevalent under two situations. Firstly, where there was state ownership, then the lack of incentives created by providing services for the public interest rather than for profit would create such a situation. State ownership also removes the fear that management under performance would lead to bankruptcy or a take-over and replacement of the management team by the new owner. The other situation is where there is little or no competition to act as a spur to keep management control tight and hence costs slowly drift upwards. Monopolies, therefore, particularly those that are state owned and controlled, would be prime candidates to suffer from X-inefficiency. Until more recent times, virtually all public transport industries were state-owned monopolies and hence fell into this category.

The market no longer regulates itself

This final argument against monopolies is not actually an argument in itself but is rather an accumulation of all of the previous points listed. Where one firm dominates the market, then the market can no longer regulate itself in terms of producing economically efficient goods and services at equitable prices. As such, this is an outcome rather than a specific disadvantage. In most cases, therefore, particularly with respect to many transport industries, external intervention is required to provide this regulatory function, and this will always come at an added cost. This is an example of what was referred to as a second best solution in the previous chapter. Thus within transport markets there exists a massive machinery of bureaucratic regulatory agencies with respect to the rail, air and bus markets that in effect don't actually produce anything.

Advantages of monopoly

Despite the disadvantages outlined above, there are a number of situations where a monopoly market structure may offer several advantages over a more competitively based system.

A higher level of expenditure on research and development

Where there is only one single large firm in the market it is argued that the firm will have more financial resources and a higher level of confidence in the future to enable it to invest in a significant ongoing programme of research and development. Through this activity it can continue to make technological advances in the future that would simply not exist if production was spread around a large number of considerably smaller operators. The nub of the argument, therefore, would be that a monopoly can be economically efficient in the very long run through technical innovations in production techniques and processes. Whilst that argument concentrates very much on the supply side of the market in the form of lower costs, technical innovations may also enhance the consumer's experience from using that good or service, i.e. increase utility. Thus the high-speed train in France, the TGV, has significantly reduced journey times between the major French cities and brought almost airline standards of service to rail customers, whilst Maglev technology offers the potential to reduce journey times by a similar step again.

Market size – a natural monopoly

This is an issue partly examined before. The basic argument is that the market is of such a (relatively small) size, that only one firm can operate in the market and achieve all of the economies of scale. This is shown in Figure 7.5.

The key point to note from the figure is that the market demand curve, D_M, cuts the average cost curve AC before the point of minimum efficiency scale, Q_{MES}. At the maximum market size, therefore, average production costs are still falling. As a result, in order to take advantage of all of the potential economies of scale only one firm should supply the market. If the market was to be divided between a number of different firms, then as the major constraint is the market size, no

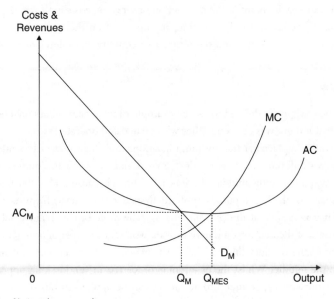

Figure 7.5 *Natural monopoly*

firm would be of a significant size to capture most of these economies. This is known as a natural monopoly, where it makes economic sense that there is only one firm in the market. The natural monopoly argument normally applies where there is some form of network used in the production of the service, such as in gas pipelines. The usual textbook example however is in the provision of rail services. Two companies may be competing between two cities, each company with its own rolling stock and infrastructure, but the total market is of such a size that neither achieves all potential economies of scale. This was the case in Britain in many areas prior to nationalisation of the railways in 1948 and even more so before the big four grouping of 1923. Services were nearly always duplicated between most towns and even triplicated between the major centres of population. As a monopoly provider, British Rail was in a position to ensure that the available capacity was fully utilised and hence capture all possible economies of scale.

Wasteful competition

Although very closely related to the natural monopoly argument, the issue of wasteful competition is worth highlighting on its own. Wasteful competition occurs where effectively double or treble the production resources are used to provide a service. Nash (1982) explains that wasteful competition happens when competition leads to the bidding down of average loads, and consequently average costs rise. While this can easily be confused with a natural monopoly due to a number of similar characteristics, the key difference can be highlighted by drawing a distinction between economies of carriage and economies in the production of services. Natural monopolies occur where there are economies in the production of services, where constraints on the market size mean that only one firm can achieve productive efficiency. Economies of carriage however exist where the cost per passenger carried can only be minimised where there is a single operator. This particularly applies to bus markets where many tend towards monopolies on the basis of economies of carriage. Thus whilst a given bus market may support more than one operator and all may be operating at the MES point in the production of services, costs in the carriage of passengers could be significantly reduced if only one company operated on the route. Due to economies in carriage, therefore, any competition on the route/area could be considered as wasteful.

Hotelling's law

Hotelling's law was originally devised using the example of ice cream sellers on a beach. Hotelling (1929) showed that if there was only one seller who owned and operated two ice cream vendors on a beach, these would be placed at the optimum locations in order to cover the entire beach. If on the other hand two different ice cream sellers owned and operated the outlets, they would be located next to each other in the middle of the beach. This is because each seller would seek to not only cover its 'share' of the beach but also potentially take custom away from its rival. This could only be done if it was located at the centre. Although the price of ice cream would be lower, the added distance users of the beach would have to walk would be the cost of having that competition. Given the nature of the product this may be a critical aspect. More crucially, it may also lead to overcrowding in the middle. Whilst the positioning of ice cream vendors may appear to have little relevance to transport issues, an identical argument can be applied to bus services. Consider the case illustrated in Figure 7.6.

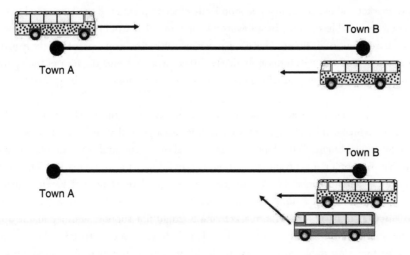

■ *Figure 7.6* *Hotelling's Law applied to buses*

In the upper part of Figure 7.6, say that the Dalmatian Bus company is publicly owned and has a monopoly on the route between Town A and Town B. The time taken between the two towns is 30 minutes, and Dalmatian sends out one bus from A and at the same time one bus from Town B. The service frequency therefore between the two towns would be one bus every 30 minutes. If however in order to introduce competition on this service Dalmatian was privatised and split between Dalmatian Bus and a newly formed rival the Grey Bus Company, the same running pattern is unlikely to be maintained. Whilst Grey Bus 'should' run a service from Town A when Dalmatian sets off from Town B, it is far more likely to run slightly ahead of it. By so doing Grey Bus will attempt to capture all the passengers on the route from Dalmatian. Frequency therefore will have fallen from one bus every half hour to effectively a bus every hour, hence the introduction of competition on the route has halved the frequency of service. This tendency towards a common point of sale is classic Hotelling behaviour. Note also that Dalmatian is likely to retaliate and will reschedule their service to run slightly ahead of Grey Bus. This process is likely to continue and hence the confusion and disruption caused by constant changes in timetables will represent a further deterioration in the standard of service provided.

The theory of contestability (Baumol, 1982)

William Baumol in his *American Economic Review* article of 1982 (Baumol, 1982) was the first to put forward the notion of the 'contestable market'. What Baumol argued was that it was unnecessary for the market to be in perfect competition in order to produce economically efficient market behaviour, what really mattered was whether the market was contestable or not. If a new entrant could enter the market and compete with the incumbent, then the threat of this potential competition would force the incumbent to act as if under a perfect (or near perfect) market structure. Rather than pursue super-normal profits therefore (i.e. profit maximise), the firm would only seek to achieve normal profits in order to deter market entry. Competitive pressures would thus be supplied by the constant threat of entry that force the firm to behave as if it was in a competitive market and hence act in an economically efficient manner. If the firm failed to do so, it would become vulnerable to entry by a lower-cost operator that would eventually take the whole market and drive it out of business. This is a particularly attractive concept, particularly given that transport markets tend towards monopoly market structures, and thus the idea of the contestable market may be seen as one way in which the advantages of a monopoly can be gained without the drawbacks.

A perfectly contestable market is said to exist where entry to the market is free and exit is costless, hence no financial barriers to entry exist. It is also argued that there must be no structural barriers to the entry of firms in the long run. As noted above, structural barriers relate to industry conditions that prevent a new entrant competing with existing firms in the market. This particular point however is perhaps debatable, particularly with regard to structural barriers that relate to market conditions. For example, demand conditions in the market may act as a structural barrier to entry, as in basic terms the market simply could not support another major operator. As such, the market would not be contestable. This however appears to miss the whole point of the idea of the contestable market, as the basic premise is not that the monopolist would lose market share to a new entry but rather that the monopolist would lose the whole market to a new entrant. In other words, the market cannot support two firms; thus if truly contestable the threat is that a new entrant would take the whole market from the existing operator. On their own, therefore, structural barriers would not appear to be a barrier to the contestable market. The financial risk involved in such a venture however certainly would be, thus the presence of structural market characteristics considerably increases the financial risks associated with market entry.

The same argument however would not apply to strategic barriers to entry. Where strategic barriers exist, then this does act as a clear barrier to the contestable market. Thus, for example, the branding of airline services would make it far more difficult for a new entrant to gain customers from an established firm, and hence the incumbent's position would be far more secure and the contestability of the market significantly reduced.

Pulling all of these ideas and assumptions together, the market position of the perfectly contestable market firm can be illustrated graphically.

The basis of Figure 7.7 is Figure 7.2 above which compared perfect competition with monopoly. In this case, however, if all of the assumptions of the contestable market fully apply to the monopolist then the firm will not pursue a strategy that profit maximises at output level Q_M with the associated market price of P_M. Rather, it will act like the perfectly competitive firm and set the output level at Q_{CM} with the associated price of P_{CM}. This would therefore map directly onto the position of the perfectly competitive firm illustrated in Figure 7.2 above.

In simple terms, however, very few truly contestable markets exist in practice as the assumptions of the contestable market are highly restrictive, particularly those relating to zero entry and exit barriers. Like perfect competition, the assumptions are virtually impossible to find in reality. Low-cost airlines are said to be near such a model of competition, as aircraft can be leased on entry and returned to the leasing company on exit, hence significantly reducing the entry and exit costs. Whilst that may overcome the major financial entry barrier, others still remain with regard to the availability and attractiveness of airport landing slots and various other factors concerning the infrastructure. Even in such a market, therefore, there will always be a cost associated with market entry and exit.[1] In reality, therefore, a monopolist in a potentially contestable market will set its

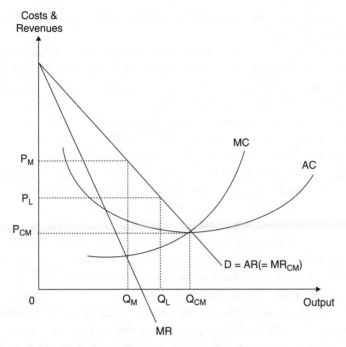

Figure 7.7 *Pricing and output levels in the contestable market*

level of output somewhere between Q_M and Q_{CM} dependent upon the level of barriers to entry. In order to illustrate this idea, a Q_L level of output has been added to Figure 7.7. If entry and exit barriers are relatively low, then this would indicate that the market is highly contestable and the output level Q_L will tend towards the perfectly competitive market position of Q_{CM}. If entry barriers are relatively high, however, then the contestability of the market is severely compromised and the firm's output level will tend towards the monopolist position of Q_M. This is Bain's idea of a limit price (Bain, 1956), where the firm will not set a price that maximises profits but rather set the price at a level that will deter market entry. The extent to which the limit price P_L deviates from the perfectly competitive market price of P_{CM} will be directly related to the scale of entry and exit barriers. In most situations, however, some degree of abnormal profits will still be achieved and maintained in the long run due to such barriers.

Another important aspect of contestable markets is that they are said to suffer from hit and run entry. If the full assumptions of contestability are met, then with a zero entry and exit cost firms can enter the market and cream off abnormal profits while they are available and then exit the industry when market conditions tighten up and eradicate such profits. This is because if incumbent firms restrict market capacity in order to maintain prices at a level that produces abnormal profits, new firms can easily enter the industry in pursuit of the profits being made. Following entry, however, established firms will be forced to protect market positions by lowering prices and driving new firms out (at a zero exit cost to the exiting firm) to re-establish their former market dominance. Related to hit and run entry, contestable markets are also said to suffer from cherry-picking. This is where the new entrant rather than entering the whole market will only enter those segments where the highest returns are to be made. This is particularly true in service industries, such as transport markets, where there are clear market divisors that allow such market behaviour to take place.

Whilst low cost airlines were said to be a possible example of a contestable market, another example from the transport industries would be the bus market. There is, for example, nothing, in theory at least, stopping one firm entering a given city and competing with the incumbent operator. This is further reinforced by the fact that one of the criticisms of privatisation of the industry in Britain was that many firms cherry-picked, which created a situation of intense competition on the most attractive corridors and a complete dearth of services on the less attractive routes. As regards the British market, however, in the current climate the fear of retaliatory action may act as a significant barrier to market entry. Stagecoach for example would be unlikely to enter the Bristol bus market in direct competition to First for fear of retaliatory action by First entering one of Stagecoach's strongholds, such as Newcastle. This is something akin to the view that in a price war, all are losers. Where a 'stand alone' operator may dominate the market, however, as is the case in Edinburgh with Lothian Buses and Nottingham with Nottingham City Transport, the incumbent faces quite a different situation. This is almost solely because retaliatory action against an established new entrant is virtually impossible, hence those bus markets can be viewed as being contestable. That said, such market entry can only be pursued by firms of a size to 'take on' the incumbent, as was the case with First's intrusion into the Edinburgh market in 2002/3. Nevertheless, despite Lothian's successful repelling of First's intrusion, the Edinburgh bus market and others like it remain potentially contestable markets, which in part regulates the incumbent's market behaviour. It is thus perhaps no surprise that Lothian buses have won the industry-sponsored 'Bus Operator of the Year' award in 2002, 2003 and 2007!

A final consequence of contestable markets highlighted here is that contestability may affect the strategy of the company. In a more general sense, Microsoft are said to defend their monopoly position in the provision of operating systems for computers on the basis of a contestable market – the costs of entry are very low, all that is required is a personal computer (Rodda, 2001). This however raises an important aspect of contestable markets, as the counter argument to such a claim is the market behaviour of Microsoft. The market actions of Microsoft will be to maintain its market position through acquisition, hence establishing strategic barriers to entry. Thus if any rival firm was to gain a technological advantage it may then become vulnerable to a take-over by Microsoft. The strong market position and financial resources of Microsoft would allow them to make the new entrant an offer that the directors of the company simply could not refuse. The extent to which the market is truly contestable therefore is highly questionable, as the strong market position of Microsoft effectively allows it to quash any potential competition without resorting to illegal measures (such as predatory pricing). This highlights the more general point that in such markets the incumbent will act to make the market less contestable, through tightening up the market. It may also seek to gain over-capacity, and hence in the event of market entry it could very quickly flood the market and thereby drive down the price. This would almost immediately eradicate any profit opportunities available to the new entrant and result in their market exit. Directly with respect to transport markets, this over-capacity may take the form of over-coverage of the market served in order to ensure no gaps from which any potential rival could get a foothold in the market.

The importance of contestable markets in the analysis of transport markets cannot be over-stressed. As should be realised from the analysis of the advantages of the monopoly market position, many of these apply to transport markets, particularly the ideas of natural (local) monopolies and the eradication of wasteful competition. The ideas behind contestable markets have been applied almost universally in transport markets as an alternative to the free market position in an attempt to capture these advantages without the drawbacks normally associated with monopolistic market structures. Nevertheless, there can be some confusion regarding contestable markets. This usually arises from the misconception that a contestable market is one that is only imposed by an authority that 'awards' the market to a particular operator for a period of time based upon some form of tender. This however is contestability through regulation, which by and large is how it has been introduced into transport markets and is more commonly known as Demsetz competition. What has been outlined here, however, is a free market solution, i.e. one devoid of regulation and working entirely along market principles. Nevertheless, most contestable transport markets are through regulation, a topic that will be taken up further in Chapter 10.

Whilst the analysis above has detailed reasons as to why the airline sector may not display the characteristics of the pure contestable market there is a view (Button, 2006) that the sector has become more contestable in recent years, i.e. firms within the industry have increasingly moved away from Q_M and more towards Q_{CM} on Figure 7.7. The main arguments of this view are briefly summarised in Case study 7.1.

Case study 7.1 Contestability and the airline sector

Within the airline sector there are a number of factors that have changed or are in the process of changing that suggest that the sector has become or is becoming more contestable. Specifically, these are:

- Control over landing slots is becoming less of an issue for a number of reasons. Firstly, landing slots have become available with the demise of certain airlines, most notably Sabena. Secondly, there has been a growth in the use of less congested regional airports which represents competition to the major hub airports such as Heathrow. An example of this is the growth in passenger numbers at Stansted, Luton and East Midlands providing competition to Heathrow on certain European routes, with operators such as Ryanair and easyJet.
- The internet has provided an important source of detail to potential passengers in terms of flights, prices etc which was previously only in the domain of travel agents. Thus websites such as www.expedia.co.uk, or the airline's own website, have considerably expanded access to information regarding the price and frequency of flights. As a consequence of this more readily available service information, this has proved less of a barrier in terms of new airlines entering a particular route.
- The frequent flyer initiative, which was a mechanism used by airlines to tie passengers into using their services, is now less of a benefit to passengers than it has been in the past because the savings to be made on low cost fares in many cases more than offsets the free air miles.

- The growth in low cost carriers such as bmibaby, easyJet and Ryanair along the principles of operation outlined in Case study 5.2 have illustrated that it is possible to enter and compete with incumbent operators. In some cases this has even resulted in incumbents being driven out of particular market sectors, as exemplified by British Airways 'sale' of its regional airline, BA Connect, to low cost carrier Flybe in 2007. This effectively resulted in the termination of all previous BA Connect services.

Whilst it is difficult to give any real world examples of perfectly contestable markets, not least because most markets experience sunk costs, it is more realistic to imagine an industry approaching perfect contestability. Whilst there are clearly barriers to entering the airline sector, not least in terms of the restrictions on landing slots, the role of the travel agent and the frequent flier initiative, there are signs that the sector is becoming more contestable.

OLIGOPOLY

To this point we have outlined the two most extreme positions of competition: perfect competition where the level of competition is at its maximum and monopoly where absolutely no competition exists at all. In most market-based situations, however, particularly within transport industries, some form of competition exists. Indeed the market structure of most transport industries would be broadly classified as either oligopoly or tending towards monopoly. The provision of bus services for example in Birmingham is almost entirely the preserve of National Express through its subsidiary National Express West Midlands, and hence constitutes a near monopoly. Similarly, Glasgow is largely dominated by First Glasgow, but some competition on the key radial routes comes from Stagecoach. This latter market would constitute an oligopoly (or duopoly to be exact), albeit one dominated by a single operator.

Oligopolies however are difficult to define. Unlike the first two market structures which were quite straightforward from a theoretical perspective, i.e. came to definitive answers, oligopoly tends to be one of the more messy pieces of economic theory. This conclusion can be drawn because whilst there is only one type of perfect competition 'model' and one type of monopoly 'model', there exist different theories or different forms of oligopoly. This is because the theory largely involves two or more firms, thus market structure is not only dependent upon the number of firms in the industry but also how they react to each other's market behaviour. In this section we will simply outline the basic ideas behind oligopoly most applicable to transport markets, beginning with the common characteristics of an oligopolistic market.

Basic assumptions of oligopoly

As highlighted above, oligopoly lies somewhere between perfect competition and monopoly if assessed on the basis of a scale of competitiveness in the market. Nevertheless, it is undoubtedly far closer to monopoly than perfect competition, as the number of competitors tends to be small in number and barriers to entry high. Virtually all public transport markets would therefore probably be classified as an oligopoly. The underlying general assumptions of oligopoly are:

1. Few sellers, many buyers

In an oligopoly market, there exist few sellers and many buyers. The main implication from this assumption is that when making market conduct decisions such as the pricing of fares or the level of service to provide, firms will take into account rivals' likely reactions to their market conduct. This contrasts both with perfect competition, where there are so many other sellers in the market place that the firm cannot take such actions into account, and monopoly, where there are simply no other firms in the industry to take into account.

2. Barriers to entry are significant

With significant barriers to entry such as those outlined above, firms within the industry have a degree of protection from new entrants. When considering market conduct decisions, therefore, little account needs to be taken of any potential competition that may enter the market. Contestability of the market is thus limited.

3. Non price competition

Where there are very few sellers, price wars tend to damage all firms in the industry and benefit none. This is something that we saw in Exercise 6.1. What tends to happen under oligopoly therefore is that firms compete on factors other than price, thus all charge similar prices but differentiate the product or service that is offered. This has led to the development of the idea of the kinked demand curve (Sweezy, 1939), illustrated in Figure 7.8.

At the market price P_O, the firm's demand curve is kinked at point b, which in reality is the intersection point of two different demand curves. These in turn represent different reactions from rivals to a firm's change in price. The demand curve D_E represents relatively more elastic demand, whilst D_I is relatively more inelastic. The basic theory is that if a firm was to increase its

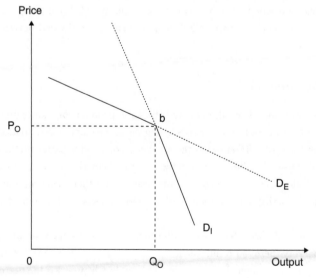

Figure 7.8 *The kinked demand curve*

price from P_O, demand would follow the path of D_E. This is because it is assumed that no other firm will follow suit in increasing prices, hence the firm will be alone and experience a substantial drop in quantity demanded. Some consumers will be retained due to brand loyalty; however, many will switch to what are now less expensive rival products. As demand is relatively elastic, then any increase in price will actually lead to a decrease in total revenue, hence there is little incentive to take such actions.

If, on the other hand, the firm was to cut its price, the theory is that other firms will follow suit for fear of losing market share. Demand would therefore follow the demand curve D_I. Although the lower price will encourage more consumers to purchase the product, because other firms have matched any price reductions these 'new' consumers will be the only increase in the quantity demanded for the individual firm's product. The firm's demand curve is therefore kinked at the market price of P_O.

The inevitable conclusion of the theory of the kinked demand curve is that all firms will charge the same price and thus not compete on the basis of price. What the kinked demand curve does not explain however is how the price came to be at that level in the first place. This is normally assumed to be set by some form of price leader, which would be a company that either has an ultimate cost advantage (hence could eradicate the competition if necessary) or one that has a very large market presence. Under such a scenario, the market leader sets the price and all other firms follow suit.

What the kinked demand curve leads to is non price competition normally based upon product differentiation. Other forms of non price competition exist, however, most notably company acquisitions and mergers; such actions are taken in order to gain a positional market advantage over a rival operator.

Note finally however that whilst non price competition is generally regarded as a characteristic of oligopolistic markets, not all forms of oligopoly operate on this basis. Some oligopolistic markets have pretty vicious price competition, the parcels market being a case in point. Energy providers are the same, where most compete on the price paid for electricity and gas and few on the actual service provided, which becomes particularly critical if things should go wrong. Oligopoly models of market structure therefore can normally be divided between price and non price competition forms.

4. Product differentiation

Unlike perfect competition, where all firms sell the same product, or monopoly, where only one product is sold, under oligopoly there exists a degree of product differentiation. This differentiation can take the form of differences in the frequency of service patterns, the flexibility of the tickets sold, the role of special offers and even the company's market position. As noted above, this can be one of the main bases of competing with rivals. The other main consequence of product differentiation however is that firms in their market conduct decisions can expect a degree of brand loyalty to exist.

This aspect of oligopoly however is where the theory begins to become 'messy'. In reality, in many oligopoly markets there is no difference in the products that are marketed, i.e. there is no product differentiation! One such classic example we saw in Chapter 4 is the petrol market, where what you put in your tank is an identical product whether it is Shell, Esso, BP, Morrison's, or

Sainsbury's. Bus and airline journeys are exactly the same, where the basic products offered are fundamentally the same. Coke (the drinking kind!) is exactly the same – it's black, fizzy and bad for your teeth! These however are all examples of oligopolistic markets. The important characteristic therefore is not actual product differentiation but rather perceived product differences, and hence in turn what becomes important under oligopoly is advertising and branding. Through advertising, firms build up a perception of differences in competing products and thereby build up brand loyalty. This gives the firm a degree of power over the market and hence more flexibility in setting the price.

5. Tacit collusion

Oligopolistic industries are said to experience what is known as tacit collusion. Tacit collusion means there is a hidden degree of co-operation. This does not mean hidden from regulatory authorities, etc, but rather that under such a market structure there is a strong incentive for firms, to a certain extent, to co-operate rather than compete with each other. Under oligopoly, in an ideal situation firms should fully co-operate and take decisions as a single group of companies. This is what would be known as a cartel, which would enable firms in an oligopoly to act like a monopolist and hence maximise the profits of all. This is where the OPEC countries were highly successful in increasing the price of oil in the mid and late 1970s. Such actions however are anti-competitive and illegal under European Union competition laws. Tacit collusion however does not refer to such illegal 'active' co-operation but rather to unspoken or 'passive' co-operation where it makes sense for firms to relax competitive pressures against each other in certain situations. The bus industry in Britain is a very good example of this, where the period of intense competition (the bus wars) was followed by consolidation and the emergence of three large operators. In many bus markets it made economic sense for these firms to not compete intensively with each other, as once firms became established price wars became far more detrimental than they had been before, e.g. damaged profits rather than eradicate the competition. Furthermore, certain bus 'territories' were ceded to rival operators through market withdrawals, in order to allow concentration on the 'home' markets without the distraction of potentially damaging competition. Under such a scenario, all the major firms benefited, hence the idea of 'tacit' collusion.

The market position of the oligopoly firm

Using these assumptions, we can construct the oligopoly market position. Rather than produce a further simple variation of Figures 6.1 and 7.1 (which would be appropriate for an oligopolistic market based on price competition), Figure 7.9 shows the position for a non price competition oligopoly. Thus the market demand curve is kinked at the market price, P_O. Under oligopoly, whilst there is a degree of consumer loyalty, the firm faces a downward sloping demand curve from left to right; however, this is kinked at the market price, being more inelastic below the market price than above. As with a monopoly, however, in order to sell more units in any given time period the firm must sell all products at a lower price, hence at each level of output MR < AR (although we will relax this assumption in Chapter 8), and this again is kinked (or broken) at the market price. Costs behave as before.

Our overriding assumption of firms behaving as profit maximisers still applies, hence the firm

165

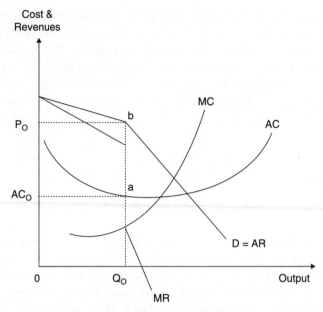

Figure 7.9 *Profit maximisation position of the non price competition oligopolistic firm*

produces at that level where MC = MR. In Figure 7.9, this is at output level Q_O, which gives an average cost of AC_O and a price of P_O. Note that at this level of output the firm is not only making abnormal profits of AC_O, P_O, b, a, but also is not producing at the lowest point on the average cost curve as AC_O is above the MES point. As with monopoly, it is therefore not economically efficient. Furthermore, this will be the long run position, as oligopolistic markets, similar to monopolies, have significant barriers to entry which prevent new firms entering the market and competing away abnormal profits.

This is the basic neo-classical position, in which the firm sets the output level at the profit maximising position, and then charges a price that the market will bear (as shown by the demand curve). Note however that the firm influences the market primarily through its output level supplied to the market, and that by restricting output it can increase price.

The process of competition in oligopolistic markets

Whilst neo-classical theory tells us of different market structures and the form of market behaviour that may be expected, in most cases it falls short of giving an explanation as to how such market structures come about. For this we need to consider the process of competition. This is particularly pertinent in the case of transport markets, as most tend to evolve over time towards an oligopolistic structure even where the 'design' had been to attempt to produce a competitive industry. An early example of this was the US Deregulation Act 1978, which removed price and capacity controls from all US domestic airline services. Following the passing of the Act, there followed an intense period of merger and acquisition activity, from which emerged eight large dominant operators and the complete control of particular airports (or hubs) by a single operator. This whole process was almost exactly repeated seven years later with the UK Transport Act 1985, which removed price and capacity controls from all British bus services and led to an intense period of acquisition and merger activity, out of which eventually emerged three dominant operators and the (virtual) complete control of particular areas of the country. This took place against a backdrop of competitive authorities with a remit from government to install and maintain a competitive bus industry. Many other transport industries appear set to follow the same pattern, with for example rail operations within Britain experiencing a significant reduction in franchise holders since privatisation in 1997 and European airline reforms producing some merger and alliance activity amongst the major European airlines, the most notable being the purchase of KLM by Air France in 2004.

This aspect of anti-competitive market structures is a major concern in the reform of public transport markets and one for which there appears to be no answer. Much academic, practitioner and policy advisory thought has gone into this issue and has not yet provided a definitive solution. Here we attempt to explain why this type of market behaviour should happen by combining a number of different theoretical perspectives that go beyond the neo-classical theory of the firm. The main basis is provided by Downie's little-known theory of the competitive process (Downie, 1958). This theory examines the competitive process over time and is primarily based upon the ethos of the survival of the fittest, the 'fittest' in this case being the most efficient firms. Further theoretical perspectives of oligopoly and economic theories of managerial enterprise are also introduced in an attempt to explain transport markets' tendency towards supply side consolidation. You should carefully note however that oligopoly theory has many different variants, thus what is presented is only one possible theoretical perspective/framework from which this process could be viewed.

Figure 7.10 attempts to outline the basic process of Downie-type competition over four time periods. Beginning in the first period there are five bus companies all competing in the market. Due to the geographical nature of bus operations, direct competition involving all five seldom occurs, with most competing in different combinations of two's and three's in different parts of the country. In Figure 7.10, in each time period the five companies are always arranged in

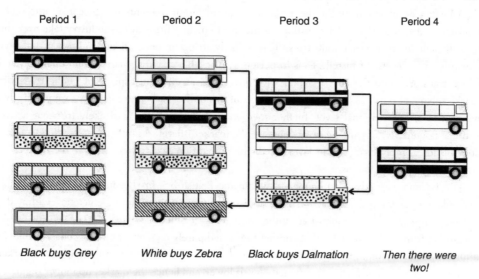

| Period 1 | Period 2 | Period 3 | Period 4 |

Black buys Grey White buys Zebra Black buys Dalmation Then there were two!

Figure 7.10 *Downie competitive process applied to buses*

167

efficiency order, thus in time frame 1 Black Bus is the most efficient and Grey the least. Due to its relative inefficiency, Grey is not fulfilling its full market potential, providing the owners, either in the form of shareholders or private investors, with a level of returns or dividends that are smaller than they could be. As a consequence, in the case of a listed company its stock market value to asset base ratio would fall and hence it becomes vulnerable to a takeover. With a privately controlled firm, if returns are less than they could be then the opportunity cost of being in the bus business is rising, i.e. better things could be done with the funds invested. As Grey continues to underperform, therefore, it will ultimately be acquired by another company, in this case the most efficient firm, Black Bus. As a result in the second time frame there are now only four bus companies, with Black Bus now slipping to second in the efficiency rankings due to its purchase of the inefficient Grey, which results in a larger but less efficient company. White Bus are thus now the most efficient, with Zebra the least. In a similar cycle to period one, Zebra now becomes vulnerable to a takeover, which is completed when White buys it. This reduces the competition down to three in the third time frame, but Black Bus has now again become the most efficient as it integrates and rationalises the operations of Grey in the enlarged 'Big Black' bus company. It now buys the least efficient firm in the industry, Dalmatian, and hence in the final period there are only two bus companies left competing in the market. This motivation to purchase other companies is primarily driven by the desire for growth in the market, a view consistent with Baumol's idea of revenue maximisation (Baumol, 1959), and similar to Williamson's Theory of Managerial Enterprise (Williamson, 1963), which also puts growth, albeit through internal company expansion, as a prime motivation of both managers and investors.

Note in the Downie model of competition rather than the industry becoming less efficient as it consolidates over time (which would be consistent with neo-classical theory), it is actually becoming more efficient as the operations of the less efficient firms are rationalised and taken over by the more efficient ones. Note also that this is more likely to occur in markets where there is wasteful competition, as these operations can be easily consolidated in the enlarged company and hence the efficiency of both improved.

A further development of the theory is that efficiency improvements will be spread into other industries through horizontal acquisitions as the most efficient firms in this industry take over the less efficient firms in other industries. This is likely to occur once all possibilities of industry expansion have been exhausted. Thus in period 5, Black Bus may purchase a train operator, and hence transform into the Black Group with operations in different aspects of public transport markets. Note also that as the definition in terms of size of the market changes, for example from a national to an international level, further mergers and consolidations are likely to occur across national boundaries. Expanding or opening up the market, therefore, rather than leading to more competition, simply changes the level at which competition takes place, thus at the local level competition may well be lost.

This is almost exactly what happened within the British bus market in the period following deregulation, as mergers and acquisitions took place at a national level, efficiency within the industry improved and competition at the local level declined (Cowie, 2002). The inevitable conclusion from such a model is that competition based purely on market forces is unattainable, as ultimately in the medium to longer term this will lead through mergers to an oligopolistic market structure. Prices will be higher and capacity levels lower, and hence the market no longer regulates itself, requiring some form of external control in order to attain economic efficiency.

All of these issues are explored further in Case study 7.2, which examines the impacts of reforms in the British bus industry and in particular the issues arising out of moving an industry from a publicly owned monopoly to a privately owned competitive industry.

Case study 7.2 The British bus industry

This case study takes an extensive look at the British bus industry over the last thirty years. Whilst one of the longer cases in the book, the British bus industry over the period reviewed provides an interesting study of changing market structures, competition levels, competitive processes, ownership issues and regulatory failures, and underpins many of the key issues examined in not only this but other chapters. Although covering a thirty-year period, the case is not intended to be a lesson in economic history, but rather an examination of reform in public transport markets, a subject that remains an on-going issue today and one that we return to in Chapter 10.

Until the industry reforms of the early 1980s, the provision of bus services in Britain had been largely governed by the rules and regulations laid down by the Traffic and Transport Act 1933. That Act regulated all bus services with regard to market entry, the level of service frequency and the fare charged, as well as qualitative regulation regarding driver behaviour, operators' licences and the standard of the vehicles used.

The structure of the supply side of the industry was effectively a state-controlled monopoly, with all major bus companies publicly owned, with very few private operators on staged services. Two national operators existed, the National Bus Company (NBC) covering England and Wales and the considerably smaller Scottish Bus Group (SBG) in Scotland. These companies operated services in outlying areas and the smaller towns as well as inter-city bus services between the major centres of population. In addition to the two national operators, there were over 70 local-authority-run bus operators, which in most cases were provided as a function of the local administration, i.e. a local authority department. All of these operators had exclusive rights to operate in their respective towns and cities, while the NBC and SBG had exclusive rights to operate everywhere else. There was very little direct competition except on the main radial routes into the main towns and cities, but even here the intensity of that competition was low, with each operator having its own distinctive remit. Prices and frequencies were strictly controlled, thus the two main mechanisms by which to effectively compete were nullified.

With the coming to power of the Conservatives under Margaret Thatcher in 1979, this situation dramatically changed. Thatcher and her deputies encompassed the economic beliefs of Milton Friedman and what became known more generally as 'New Right' ideologies. At the very heart of this ideology is the belief in the power of the market to find the optimal solution to produce economic efficiency, equity and general well being – exactly the issues that have been examined in this and previous chapters. 'Non-staged' express routes, i.e. town-to-town, were deregulated by the Transport Act 1980. This removed all economic regulation from the long-distance bus market, thus any operator was free to compete with the NBC and SBG on these routes and charge whatever price they wished. This Act in itself was wholly successful, with increased patronage, reduced prices and a significantly increased network of cross-country bus services.

Following that success, the Transport Act 1985 took the issue considerably further. The main problems perceived with the bus industry at the time were a long-term decline in patronage, rising costs and considerable increases in subsidy. In an attempt to reverse these trends, the 1985 Act removed all economic regulation (i.e. price and capacity constraints) from staged services throughout the country except in London, reform of which we examine in Chapter 10. Outside of London, the Act re-organised the supply side of the market, resulting in the creation of around 150 new bus companies. The NBC was divided into 72 regionally based operators and the SBG into nine. These were sold to the private sector in the form of a share issue (for National Express) and private sales, either to the existing management of the company or to existing bus companies such as Stagecoach. In order to encourage and maintain competition, sales were restricted to no more than 3 NBC subsidiaries and 2 SBG subsidiaries to any single buyer.

The 1985 Act also required local authorities to organisationally separate their bus operations from the authority. Bus operations were to be set up at 'arm's length' to the local authority, initially as wholly owned private limited companies, which in simple terms means a complete organisational separation from the authority. They were to no longer receive direct subsidy, as most had run at a loss with the authority making up the net difference at the end of the year. These new companies were expected to operate at a profit and be driven primarily by the profit motive. Most were then sold to the private sector from 1986 onwards, with the last of the majority of sales being in 1995.

Local authority powers in the planning and control of bus routes was thus severely limited. Before the 1985 Act, local authorities acted as a single authority in the planning and operation of services in their respective areas, as well as dictating the fares to be charged and making up any losses by a lump sum payment. After the 1985 Act these powers were severely restricted and the planning and operating functions transferred to the private sector. Local authorities' only function under the new structure was to specify individual services not already provided by the free market on the grounds of a social necessity. These would then be put out to competitive tender. Bus companies would lodge bids to run the service for a given amount of subsidy over a period of time, hence where competition in the market was not possible, competition for the market was introduced, i.e. contestability through regulation, or what is more commonly known as Demsetz competition.

Finally, unlike other privatisations, there was to be no industry regulator. It was felt that the existing regulatory competition agencies, in the form of the Monopolies and Mergers Commission (now the Competition Commission) and the Office for Fair Trading, would be able to handle all regulatory issues arising from the industry.

The important part in this whole case study is to consider the rationale behind these industry reforms, as these are the lasting issues that continue to this day. The rationale was almost exclusively based on the premise of the power of competition, with the 'vision' being of a bus industry made up of a large number of small- to medium-sized operators. Many of these would be managed by the owners themselves, i.e. would be owner-controlled firms, which in part reflected the times – this was the 1980s, apart from many other things, a time where there was a strong belief in the entrepreneurial spirit. Bus companies would compete with each other in order to better meet the needs of passengers in terms of price, quality and the overall standard of the service provided. This view is very much in line with the theory outlined in this and the previous

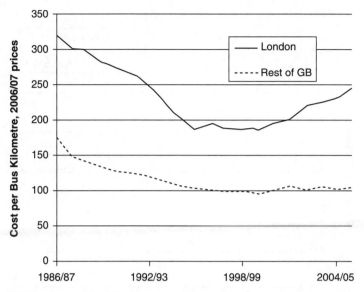

Figure 7.11 *Cost per bus kilometre, 1986/87 to 2005/06, constant 2006/07 prices*

Source: Compiled from DfT Statistics

chapter, where effectively the reforms moved the industry from a tightly controlled monopoly to one of a highly competitive industry. Consistent with the theory, therefore, costs would be expected to fall, supply and patronage increase and the need for subsidy outside of socially necessary services would be eradicated. Not only that, but there were also ownership aspects, not covered until Chapter 10, which surrounded the issue of public v private ownership. In this context the main concern related to costs, where the belief was that the private sector would be better able to control costs through the profit motive than the public sector had managed under a public interest motive. Note an important deviation from the theory outlined above; this is not about forcing firms to produce at the lowest point on the average cost curve (as with perfect competition), but rather a lowering of the whole average cost curve itself. This is consistent with the views of Harvey Leibenstein and his idea of X-inefficiency (Leibenstein, 1966) outlined in the main text, hence average costs may be higher than they should be due to general management slack and a lack of incentives in public sector companies.

What happened after 1985?

All bus services outside of London were de-regulated on 23 October 1986, known at the time somewhat unimaginatively as 'D' day. This caused massive disruption in most major cities, with Glasgow suffering particularly badly as the streets were swamped by buses of various vintages. There then followed the period of what became known as 'the bus wars', where some cut-throat competition took place in order to gain market share. One of the worst examples of this occurred in Darlington, where the local authority bus company was driven out of business by a rival operator after the authority had announced a preferred buyer for its bus company. The Monopolies and Mergers and Mergers Commission report (MMC, 1995) into wider issues concerning bus services in the north east, found that the experiences of the worst elements of the

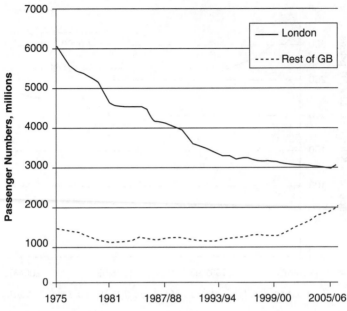

Figure 7.12 *Bus patronage, 1975 to 2006/07*

Source: Compiled from DfT Statistics

bus wars in Darlington to be predatory, deplorable and against the public interest. This is just one example, but the bus wars period included constant changes in timetables (i.e. classic Hotelling behaviour), wasteful competition in the form of duplication of well-served routes, the withdrawal of rural services, dangerous driving behaviour and some dubious business practices. Although significantly reducing costs and subsidy, the privatisation/de-regulation measures failed to stem the decline of passenger numbers, and with rising prices and the creation of considerable confusion of bus services, the downward spiral continued unchecked. For illustrative purposes, Figures 7.11–7.14 show the trends in four key indicators, namely the cost per bus kilometre, bus patronage, bus kilometres and bus fares in real terms, over the period 1995 to 2005/06. This unsatisfactory period for the bus industry came to an end with the emergence, through acquisition, of four major operators, Firstbus, Arriva, Stagecoach and Go Ahead. These bus companies now dominate the market, with around 70 per cent of passenger revenue in the staged bus market. What has emerged is now a series of territories, where one bus company dominates in one area with limited competition from another. In many cases these markets constitute local monopolies and certainly are far removed from the planned highly competitive market perceived by the 1985 Act. As stated earlier in the chapter, this need not necessarily be a 'bad' thing as long as the market is contestable; however, these markets are neither competitive nor contestable.

Whilst painting a very negative picture of the bus industry in Britain, it is not all bad news. Whilst companies were expanding through merger and acquisition, company growth as such could be gained relatively easily. Opportunities for growth in firm size through such measures however are now severely limited and companies have to examine other methods of maintaining

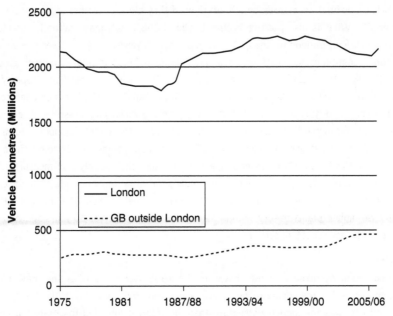

Figure 7.13   *Bus kilometres, 1975 to 2006/07*

Source: Compiled from DfT Statistics

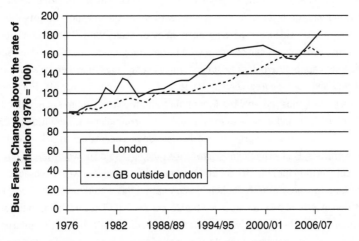

Figure 7.14   *Bus fare increase in real terms, 1976 to 2006/07*

Source: Compiled from DfT Statistics

and increasing market share, i.e. more focus on the consumer. Some success has been achieved with bus quality partnerships, where the local authority agrees to install bus priority measures such as bus lanes and generally improve the infrastructure (bus stops, bus stations, real time passenger information etc.). The company in return agrees to invest in new buses and provide an overall higher quality of service. The second positive issue to arise is increased investment, where fleet average ages have fallen considerably in recent years. It is also worth stressing that

173

higher prices need not necessarily be a 'bad' thing if they allow operators to fund investments out of profits. What is also positive is that in year 2006/7 patronage actually rose for bus transport outside of London for the first time in almost 40 years.

In more recent times, bus costs have begun to rise again. This once more would be consistent with the theory outlined above, as the industry has become far less competitive. Property rights theories, however (Parker, 1994), would suggest that because all of the major operators are Stock Market listed, this on its own should apply strong downward pressure on costs. This pressure is applied through the needs of the Stock Market for reasonable financial returns in the form of dividends and strong company growth. These basically replace direct competitive forces in the market. Cowie (2008) however suggests that rather than supply side measures driving such factors, it is now demand side factors that have a far larger influence. Major social change, in particular rising real incomes and increased general affluence, mean that today's bus users demand a far higher quality of service than their predecessors of 20 or 30 years ago, and this in simple terms is more costly to provide.

Reflection

Bus deregulation occurred in 1986; however, the 1985 Act remains as the main piece of legislation overseeing the supply of bus services in Great Britain today. What however went wrong, and why was the industry structure that the reforms intended to create not actually achieved? In some ways it actually was, in the form of the bus wars, a period of low investment and intense competition. The problem however is that the market is not perfectly competitive, particularly with regard to an homogenous product, hence whilst low price services may be achievable using vintage bus stock, this is not really what the consumer wants. Furthermore, whilst there is mixed evidence regarding economies of scale, with Cole (2004) for example arguing that small companies can compete with larger companies by achieving cost savings that larger companies cannot, there does exist economies in carriage. Thus there are cost advantages to larger firms and to a degree certain aspects of the natural monopoly. Furthermore, the competition agencies, most notably the Monopolies and Mergers Commission, failed to prevent the consolidation of the industry, with most problems surrounding the definition of 25 per cent of the market. For example, as a prelude to privatisation bus operations in Bristol were split into two separate entities, Badgerline and Bristol City Line, and sold to two different buyers, hence introducing competition into the Bristol bus market. When Badger however subsequently bid for Bristol City Line (or more exactly, its holding company), this would have effectively eradicated the competition in Bristol and far exceeded the 25 per cent market threshold. In the subsequent investigation, however, the market was defined on a British scale, hence the enlarged Badger would still have considerably less than 25 per cent of the total British market. As a result, the merger was allowed to proceed. This gave Badgerline a strong base from which to compete on a national scale, which it did highly successfully through its merger with Grampian Regional Transport based in Aberdeen to form FirstBus.

Far more is understood today about the wider aspects of bus operation economics and the effects of removing all forms of economic regulation, i.e. price and capacity controls, from the market. Most reforms now tend to introduce Demsetz competition for the market with only limited cases of direct competition in the market. The British market is still extensively studied today as an example of bus reform, both with regard to the short-run impacts and now the longer-term consequences of complete economic deregulation.

As a final point of reflection, it is very easy to forget the problems facing the industry at the time of reform, namely falling patronage, rising costs and rising subsidies, hence the perceived danger today is that re-regulating the industry would bring these aspects back to the forefront.

CHAPTER SUMMARY AND REFLECTION

This chapter has examined imperfect competition in transport markets by introducing the ideas of monopoly and oligopoly. In the course of this, we looked at the drawbacks and advantages of these market structures, and importantly also considered the important idea of the contestable market.

We also saw that most transport markets tend towards these market structures. However, imperfect markets tend towards economic inefficiency, which at a wider level leads to the need to pay higher subsidies for transport operations. In a changing macroeconomic environment, particularly debt issues, governments have no longer been able, or willing, to continually subsidise transport operations based upon an open ended regime. Rather than cut services, however, reform through the introduction of market principles have been introduced into the operation of public transport services. This has not been without its problems, particularly the inevitable tendency for such markets to veer towards imperfect market structures. Open-ended market reforms based upon perfect competition principles therefore would appear to be unattainable, hence some other form of reform is required. This has tended to be based upon Demsetz competition through franchising or bidding for the market, which in turn brings in the need for control of operations in the market through market regulation. These issues are considered further in Chapters 10 and 11.

CHAPTER EXERCISES

Exercise 7.1 Spectrum of competition in British transport industries

Exercise 6.1 asked you to place a number of British transport industries on a spectrum ranging from monopoly on the one hand to perfect competition on the other. In light of this chapter, you may now wish to re-consider some of your placements. Having done so, now

a)   Mark roughly on your spectrum that range of oligopoly, placing an upper and a lower boundary on the diagram.
b)   Have you re-evaluated any of the criteria you used to come to your original placements?

What have you learned from this exercise?

Exercise 7.2 Barriers to entry in transport markets

For the following transport industries:

- Bus production
- Provision of rail services
- Provision of the rail infrastructure
- Road haulage
- Air services
- Parcels market

Identify the main barriers to entry into each of these markets for a potential market entrant under the headings of structural and strategic barriers. Then place these industries on a scale, where 1 represents the industry with the lowest barriers to entry and 6 the industry with the highest. What does this tell you?

Exercise 7.3 Low cost airlines and the contestable markets

Using a template similar to that laid down in Case study 6.1 in the previous chapter which examined the extent to which road haulage met the conditions of the perfectly competitive market, examine the extent to which you believe that the low cost airline market meets the conditions of the contestable market.

Exercise 7.4 Case study questions

Re-examine Case study 7.2 and then consider the following questions:

a) To what extent do you think that the 'vision' that was foreseen through the 1985 Transport Act meets the conditions of perfect competition?

b) Why was the 'vision' not maintained after deregulation and the industry revert to effectively a series of local monopolies?

c) What is 'different' about the bus industry in Case study 7.1 compared to road haulage in Case study 6.1, which results in competition in one but only limited competition in the other? What therefore can be learned about competition from these case studies?

d) Do you believe that any of the advantages of monopoly apply in this case study?

e) What could be learned from the British experience of bus industry reform to other European and North American countries?

Chapter 8

The pricing of transport activities

Contributed by Stephen Ison

Learning Outcomes:

On reading this chapter, you will learn about:

- Price discrimination in the pricing of transport services
- Pricing malpractice, namely predatory pricing, as it has been applied in transport services and price fixing, and thus what constitutes 'fair' and 'unfair' pricing policies in the pricing of transport services
- A closer examination of private transport services with a particular focus on the pricing of such services.

INTRODUCTION

Pricing is a vital component in the economics of transport services. As we have already seen, not only does the price determine who gets and who doesn't get a particular service, but also determines the distribution of the 'rewards' between the provider and the user of transport services, with imperfect market structures characterised by higher rewards for the providers of such services. That of course assumes that transport services operate along purely free market principles, which of course in most cases they do not. Although most are subsidised and/or regulated, a basic understanding of these issues is required before we go on and examine the issues of transport regulation in Chapter 10.

In this chapter therefore we examine further the issues surrounding the pricing of transport services. Earlier chapters have already outlined the theory behind the price, with in simple terms the price being dependent upon the market conditions facing the individual firm. An important finding from that analysis was that in order to achieve economic efficiency the price should equal the marginal cost. This chapter will also consider how people actually pay for their transport services, as in many ways the pricing of transport is very different from a typical consumer good. With say a basic commodity such as groceries and general foodstuffs, the price is displayed and people hand over cash or some other form of payment and consequently obtain the groceries that they desire. With regard to the payment for transport activities, however, it is far from straightforward. Individual bus or rail journeys tend to follow that basic pattern of payment of a fare followed by consumption of the service through undertaking the actual journey; however, more regular travel brings with it a host of other issues, such as season tickets, the use of smart cards etc. Furthermore, the pricing of private transport services is more complex again, as that is 'paid' for through a combination of different mechanisms – not only directly by the user through vehicle purchase, vehicle licensing, fuel and other running costs, but also through the tax system, which in most developed countries makes a significant contribution to the upgrade, maintenance and renewal of the road system. This is an area which is likely to see considerable change in the near future, with far more emphasis placed on a direct user charge, and this chapter will consider the key points surrounding this issue.

PRICING IN PUBLIC TRANSPORT SERVICES

The price set by public transport operators, particularly if they are operating under conditions of monopoly, will depend on 'what the market will bear'. The reason for this is that the market does not consist of homogeneous consumers. Different parts, or segments, of the market will comprise of customers who will respond differently to changes in price, advanced booking requirements, ticket flexibility and so on. Thus market segmentation. When considering pricing under a monopoly situation then the various segments will have differing levels of elasticity, and this can be used to the operator's advantage when deciding what price to charge. As such, individuals undertaking work-related journeys during peak times, with inelastic demand, can be charged a relatively higher fare as can be seen in Table 8.1. Individuals however for whom the journey time is somewhat less important, and therefore where demand is relatively more elastic, will be charged a lower fare in order to stimulate travel. What is known as price discrimination will therefore be undertaken, in order to maximize revenue and this is likely to take place at the national public transport level, namely with respect to rail and airline travel.

In terms of local public transport, then, passengers tend to purchase their tickets at the 'point of use', that is, at the time of departure and in such a situation it is not possible to segment the market. In addition, local public transport passengers are likely to be more sensitive to waiting and journey times than they are to the level of fares.

Price discrimination

Price discrimination refers to a situation where a company charges particular consumers a higher price than others for the same product for reasons unrelated to cost. Price discrimination is extensively used in the transport sector with bus, coach, rail and airline operators charging a range of prices for the same service depending on the time of the day, when the tickets are booked or the particular period time of the year. It does not simply refer to transport services, however, but can also be applied in other areas of transport operation, such as the pricing of car parking spaces. An example of this can be seen in Table 8.1 where the car park tariff varies depending on the number of hours parked, which is simple market pricing, or whether it is a weekday or Saturday, which is a classic case of price discrimination.

The basic principle of price discrimination is to increase an operator's total revenue and earn higher profits, and as a result reduce consumer surplus. Consumer surplus is a concept that

Table 8.1 *Weekday and Saturday opening times and daytime charges, Grand Arcade 7.30am – 5.00pm, Cambridge, from April 2008*

Hours	Weekday tariff £	Saturday tariff £
0–1	1.60	1.80
1–2	3.20	3.60
2–3	4.80	5.40
3–4	8.00	8.80
4–5	14.50	16.50
5+	21.00	21.00

Source: Cambridge City Council (2008)

has been dealt with in the previous chapter, but given its importance to price discrimination it is worth recapping here. Consumer surplus refers to the difference between the actual price a consumer pays for a product and what they would be willing to pay. As such, in Figure 8.1 the actual market price is P1 but some consumers would be willing to pay a price as high as P2, some would be willing to pay a price just below P2 and so on. There is thus consumer surplus equal to the area abc and this is something that transport operators are keen to exploit by price discrimination.

In order to practise price discrimination and reduce the consumer surplus certain conditions must prevail. First, the seller must possess a degree of market power, although the operator does not have to be a monopolist. Possessing a degree of market power means that the seller faces a downward sloping demand curve. Second, the seller must be able to divide the market into individual segments and thus separate different customers within a particular market, such as peak and off-peak. These segments must be clearly divisible and there must be no mechanism through

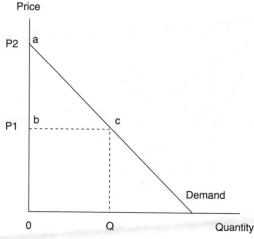

Figure 8.1 *Consumer surplus*

which high-yield premium charge consumers can 'down trade' to the lower-charge segment. Such market dividers are known as inhibitors and prevent trading between different market segments from occurring. This tends to mean that price discrimination is more likely to be practised in service industries, such as transport, where the market can be divided relatively easily in terms of time. Indeed, divisions tend to be on the basis of time of day, day of the week or season of the year. Other inhibitors can be based upon geographical location, age and time of purchase (booking).

Third, each market segment must have differing elasticities of demand. There is no point in dividing up the market into different segments if all segments have identical elasticities of demand, as each could only be charged the same price and hence there would be no price discrimination.

Ideally, an operator would like to sell each unit (or ticket) separately, charging the highest price that each consumer is prepared to pay and if this was achievable the seller would obtain the entire consumer surplus from the consumer. This can be illustrated by the use of Figure 8.2 and is known as perfect price discrimination.

To undertake this form of price discrimination the seller must know the exact shape of each consumer's demand curve and perhaps with more difficulty charge each consumer the maximum price they are prepared to pay. In Figure 8.2 if the supplier was a profit maximiser then it would charge a price of Pm, earning abnormal profit of bcde, with the consumer obtaining consumer surplus of abc. If the seller was able to perfectly price discriminate then the consumer willing to pay the highest price would be charged P1. Having sold that unit the second unit would be sold for a slightly lower price and so on. As such, the seller would charge down the demand curve, which would thus become the marginal revenue curve. The operator would continue to sell the product until point f is reached, with a quantity of Q1 sold. The operator would be profit maximising (producing where MR=MC) and would have obtained the entire area of consumer surplus.

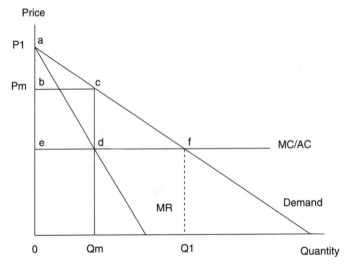

Figure 8.2 *Perfect price discrimination*

This type of price discrimination is an ideal from the point of view of a transport operator, but for obvious reasons is not very common. While it is not a common practice airline operators by practising yield management are aiming to get somewhere close to such as situation, and this is illustrated in the following case study.

Case study 8.1 Sale of airline tickets

On a typical airline flight there are three classes, namely First, Business and Economy. Figure 8.3 refers to travel in a particular class and the assumption is made that the marginal cost (MC) of one extra passenger is constant up to the point where the aircraft reaches full capacity, which is represented by Q5. At this point the MC curve becomes perfectly inelastic.

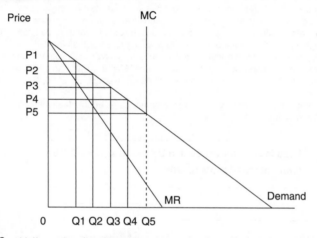

Figure 8.3 *Airline price discrimination*

If the airline operator was to profit maximise it would set a price equal to P2 and sell a quantity of Q2 tickets. As can be seen however this would mean that the airline would be operating at below full capacity, with Q5-Q2 seats empty at the time of departure. As such, the airline operator would seek to price discriminate and release seats onto the market at different prices at different time periods. This it is able to do because consumers will purchase their tickets at different times. For example, certain passengers will have a low ability to pay but will be able to book well in advance. As such, they may be able to buy their tickets at a price of P4. Others who are only able to finalise their travel plans close to the time of departure may be willing to pay P1. As these consumers have different price elasticities, this allows the airline to price discriminate. This it does by pricing along the demand curve and although they may not be able to perfectly price discriminate they are obtaining additional areas of consumer surplus and are therefore adding to their level of profit. Technically this is known as 3rd degree price discrimination, as each group of consumers is charged a different price. 1st degree on the other hand occurs where each individual consumer is charged a different price, hence perfect price discrimination would be an example of this.

Airline operators are able to price in this way since they are able to separate their customers and prevent arbitrage and this is possible since tickets when purchased are not transferable. When purchased the passenger needs to give a particular name and when checking in this is matched against the name in the passport and this prevents arbitrage taking place.

Airline operators have become highly sophisticated in determining how many tickets to issue onto the market at any one time, providing them with the opportunity to maximise their yield. Yield management is an important strategy for the airline sector be it traditional carriers or low-cost operators. The following relates this to load factors, yield management and airline pricing as outlined by the Eddington Study (2006).

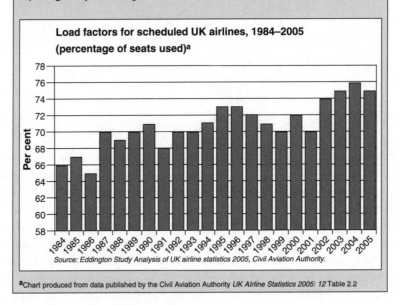

Yield management in the aviation sector

Airlines are already using pricing very successfully through yield management, which involves a sophisticated and flexible approach to pricing. Using historical sales information to allocate some seats to price-sensitive, low-paying non work/leisure travellers, while holding others for time-sensitive, high-paying business travellers, airlines aim continually to find the best product mix of differently priced seats, to gain the highest possible revenue from the fixed capacity of each airline flight.

Widespread use of yield management techniques allowed dramatic efficiencies to be achieved in the airline industry throughout the 1980s and 1990s. In 1984, UK airlines sold only 66 per cent of seats on each flight on average. By 2005, this figure had risen to 76 per cent.

In recent years, technological improvements have enabled airlines to continue improving their yield management.

Load factors for scheduled UK airlines, 1984–2005 (percentage of seats used)[a]

Source: Eddington Study Analysis of UK airline statistics 2005, Civil Aviation Authority.

[a]Chart produced from data published by the Civil Aviation Authority *UK Airline Statistics 2005: 12* Table 2.2

Source: Crown Copyright Eddington Report (2006)

Airlines therefore profit maximise through revenue maximisation by practising price discrimination. In so doing, airlines attempt to obtain the largest level of passenger revenue for a fixed level of capacity.

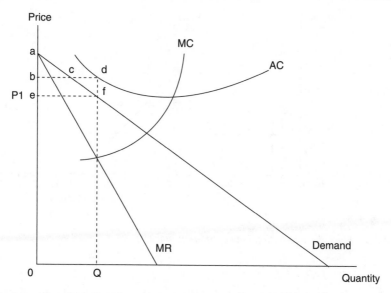

Figure 8.4 *Loss making operator and perfect price discrimination*

Pricing along the lines outlined in the above case study can actually be of benefit to consumers. Figure 8.4 illustrates a situation in which a transport operator charging a single price of P1 is making a loss of bdfe. This could represent an airline operator serving a remote sparsely populated area and as can be seen it is not covering its average cost and consequently it would cease operating in the long run. If however it were to charge more than one price it might be able to make a profit and continue to operate the service. If, as explained above, the operator was to price down the demand curve starting at point a, then those airline tickets sold would be profitable as they would be sold at a price above the average cost. Tickets sold beyond c up to point f and the output of Q however would represent loss-making sales to the airline operator. Nevertheless, as long as area abc is greater than area cdf then the strategy will lead to a profitable outcome and the passengers will continue to find the service is in operation.

Whilst perfect price discrimination is an ideal strategy from the operator's point of view it is very difficult and costly to practise. As such, operators may practise a more crude form of price discrimination dividing the market into two or more segments based on different price elasticity conditions. This is a policy of charging different prices to consumers in different markets and is a common type of discrimination characterised by such things as discounts to students and senior citizens and peak and off-peak rail use. In each case some characteristic has been used to divide consumers into distinct groups such as students and non-students who have a different ability and willingness to pay. In this situation the student union card is used as a means of enacting price discrimination.

The idea behind this more common form of price discrimination can be seen in Figure 8.5.

In this situation there are two markets, markets A and B. The demand in market A is less elastic than it is in market B. This could represent the peak and off-peak nature of rail travel, with the split between the commuter and the leisure rail user. The overall quantity in Figure 8.5(c) is derived by the horizontal summation of the demand in market A and B. If only one price were to be charged,

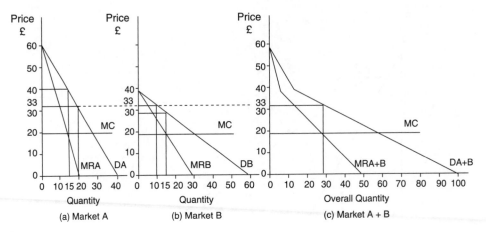

Figure 8.5 *Price discrimination in two different markets*

under conditions of profit maximisation (MR=MC), then the price charged would be £33 and 30 units would be sold. If the MC/AC is constant at £20, then the abnormal profit earned would be £390. In terms of markets A and B this would represent 20 units sold in market A and 10 units sold in market B.

If an operator were to practise price discrimination and charge a price where MR=MC in each market separately then it would be possible to increase its level of profit. Thus a price of £40 could be charged in market A with 15 units sold (which is where MRA = MC in market A) and a price of £30 charged in market B with 15 units sold (MRB = MC in market B). This would result in abnormal profit of £450 representing an increase in profit of £60. Clearly this is at the expense of consumer surplus, but the passengers who make up market B do in fact benefit since the price charged to them is less than it was before price discrimination was undertaken.

It might not however be worthwhile for the operator to sell to more than one group of consumers. In fact it may be that demand is so low in one market and so costly to provide to that market that the operator may be better off charging a single price and selling only to the larger group, since the additional cost of serving the smaller group could outweigh the additional revenue.

While the above relates to price discrimination and charging passengers what they are prepared to pay, transport operators may also use predatory pricing in order to achieve an objective of higher profit in the long run.

Predatory pricing

Predatory pricing is said to occur when a firm, normally with market power in more than one market, reduces its price below cost in the short run so as to obtain abnormal profit in the long run. Predatory pricing is aimed at either achieving or maintaining a monopoly situation, with the price set so as to bankrupt competitors, 'encourage' them to merge or in fact collude. Clearly, the market power comprises barriers to entry, since a failure to prevent new entry would make it difficult for the operator undertaking predatory pricing to raise their prices once an incumbent operator had been removed from the market. Thus whilst the consumer may benefit in the short run from lower prices, such activity may not be in the public interest in the long run.

While it would seem relatively straightforward in theory to show that predatory pricing has occurred (by ascertaining whether the price charged is below average variable cost), in practice it can be very difficult to prove that such an activity has taken place. For example, small firms may accuse larger firms of predatory pricing when in reality it may be no more than robust competition based upon lower operating costs. Where the confusion can occur is in the allocation of costs between different aspects of operation in larger firms. This results in it becoming very difficult to establish the actual average cost for a particular aspect of the firm's business, and thus in turn it becomes very difficult to prove that a firm is pricing at below the average cost. Predatory pricing is an appealing strategy in a segmented market. The reason for this is that the dominant firm is able to impact a rival firm without changing the prices it charges in other markets that it serves. Because of the destructive effect of predatory pricing, it is illegal in most developed countries. Thus in Britain, for example, it can result in investigation by the competition agencies, such as the Competition Commission, and if a case of predatory pricing found to be proven will result in the imposition of severe financial penalties. Some of the issues surrounding predatory pricing are developed further in Case study 8.2, which surrounds acquisitions against EWS, the main British rail freight company, of predatory pricing and other anti-competitive practices.

Case study 8.2 EWS and predatory pricing

EWS (English, Welsh and Scottish Railways) has been at the centre of a number of accusations of predatory pricing, two of which are highlighted in this case study – one which was upheld and one for which it was cleared. This case study attempts to develop the ideas outlined in the chapter with regard to predatory pricing and more general anti-competitive practices.

Case 1 – The heavy haul sector
EWS is the main heavy haul operator in the UK, and by far the largest rail freight company in Britain. A major part of its business is in coal haulage, and for this Enron Coal Services (ECSL) acted in the role of a freight forwarder and offered customers in the sector end-to-end services in the transportation of coal. It thus acted both as a partner for EWS (for the business with which it contracted EWS as the rail haulier) and as a competitor to EWS (for the business it contracted with other rail freight operators). In early 2001 Freightliner bulk, the other main rail freight company in Britain, entered the heavy haul sector of the market in direct competition to EWS, having previously concentrated on the market it inherited on privatisation, namely the carriage of containers. Between February 2001 and August 2002 EWS became the subject of a number of referrals to the industry regulator, the Office of the Rail Regulator (the ORR), in respect of its coal haulage operations. In particular, some of its actions in the market came into question and the issue arose as to whether this constituted 'fair' competition or was action in contravention of UK and EU competition laws. Specifically, EWS was accused of:

- Discriminatory pricing practices in relation to ECSL by offering selective price reductions to various customers. These rates were significantly lower than quoted by ECSL for the same flows. This severely compromised ECSL's competitive position, particularly its ability to offer end-to-end services to some of its customers.

- Predatory behaviour towards Freightliner. The ORR found that EWS had offered prices to two electricity generators that were significantly below its average costs for these flows.
- Exclusive contracts – several power generator customers were required to sign long-term supply contracts with EWS (in one case up to a period of ten years), in which part of the contract was an exclusivity clause in which the contractor could not engage other rail freight companies in the haulage of coal. These came in different forms, thus in one case it was a straightforward exclusion clause, in another a discount scheme was offered which was dependent upon continued use of EWS services, and the third in the form of a minimum annual payment which represented around 60 per cent of the contractor's haulage requirements.

The fine imposed on EWS by the ORR was £4m; however, similar to the OFT's 'leniency policy' highlighted later in this chapter, this represented a 35 per cent 'discount' due to EWS's cooperation in the investigation.

Case 2 – Chartered passenger trains
A second case involving EWS was referred to the ORR in 2003 which surrounded the passenger charter market. For information, although principally a rail freight operator, EWS is the main owner and operator of locomotives in Britain because all of the British passenger rolling stock is of the multiple car or trainset variety. Its services are thus in demand for one-off type operations such as tourist trains on the West Highland line in Scotland that require the hauling of passenger coaches. The complaint against EWS highlighted a number of issues:

a) EWS had offered prices to certain customers that were significantly below its published terms and that these were designed specifically to undercut the prices offered by a competitor.
b) EWS had offered certain concessions on its usual terms of trade to specific customers, conditional on those customers continuing to deal exclusively with EWS – these concessions were, in effect, also designed to exclude a competitor.

After its investigation and review of the 'factual' allegations contained in the complaints, the ORR found that in this case it had no grounds to conclude that EWS had engaged in predatory pricing or anti-competitive behaviour. Interestingly, very little information surrounds this case, and hence the actual reasons behind the ORR decision are not clear. It may have, for example, found that EWS did indeed have a degree of exclusivity clauses, but these may have been based upon the start up costs of providing these services to particular customers and thus EWS was simply ensuring recovery of these costs rather than engaging in anti-competitive behaviour.

In many respects what this case study shows is actually nothing at all, but that in itself underlines the difficulty with predatory pricing and issues surrounding anti-competitive behaviour. It also stresses the point raised in the main text that whilst in theory predatory pricing may seem quite straightforward, in practice there is a very narrow line between what constitutes competitive market behaviour and what constitutes anti-competitive behaviour. For example it could be argued that the key objective of any firm is to either eradicate the competition that exists or protect its current market position by preventing any potential competitor from entering that market. As in sport, however, the competition should be won through fair means and not foul, and hence the 'best' competitor succeeds. The two cases in some ways show where this dividing line lies, with in the first case exclusivity contracts simply being designed to keep the competition out. In the second (which we can only speculate on), if similar exclusivity contracts were found these were in place for a different reason – to ensure recovery of costs, for which any rival operator could have put an initial bid in to run these services.

An alternative strategy to predatory pricing is for an operator to collude with a competitor, fixing a price which is in the interests of both operators, but works against the public interest.

Price fixing[1]

Firms in oligopolistic markets such as the airline sector often face a dilemma as to whether to compete with each other in order to increase their market share and hopefully their profits or to collude. Collusion allows firms to act as a monopolist with the aim of maximising their joint profits. There are clearly benefits from collusion not least in that by agreeing on what price to charge or what market to serve organisations can reduce the level of uncertainty. Competition on the other hand can lead to price wars, predatory pricing or retaliatory action from which all organisations could find their profits reduced. Formal collusion whereby all firms in a market are part of a cartel means that they are acting as a single monopoly as in Figure 8.6.

In the figure demand is the industry demand curve and the marginal revenue curve represents the summation of the marginal costs of the firms operating in the cartel. The profits of the cartel are maximised since MC=MR and they are providing Q output which is sold at a price of P.

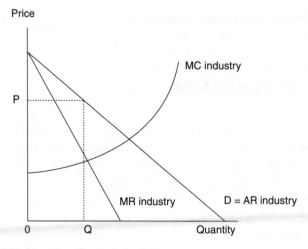

Figure 8.6 *Cartel based profit maximisation*

Price fixing is one such collusive activity, a situation where firms within a market agree on the price they are going to sell their goods or services at in order to remove price competitiveness and thus increase their profits. In such a situation organisations could compete in terms of non-price factors such as the level of service offered or the routes served rather than in terms of price. This is a feature which can be found in oligopolistic markets and can represent a situation in which an organisation might think that if it increases its price other organisations will not follow and it will lose market share. We saw an example of this in Chapter 7 which led to the kinked demand curve. If, however, all the organisations in the cartel agree to set a particular price (whilst demand may be reduced) all organisations may benefit through an increase in revenue if demand is price inelastic. As such, price fixing is a form of collusion which enables organisations to increase their profit levels, but it can be seen to act against the public interest since the organisations are behaving as if they were a monopoly. As with predatory pricing, therefore, active collusion (as opposed to tacit collusion – see Chapter 7), in most developed countries, is against competition legislation and thus is illegal.

Collusion by organisations is more likely to occur if:

- There are only a few organisations operating in the market
- The organisations trust each other, so that the agreement reached is not reneged on
- The organisations have similar costs and as such are likely to agree on the proposed price change
- The organisations provide similar products so there is little scope for competition based on the quality or level of service
- The market is fairly stable in that neither demand nor costs are changing dramatically. If they were, then agreement on the price to charge would be difficult
- There are barriers to entry into the market such that new firms will find it difficult to penetrate the market in order to take advantage of the increased profits.

Collusion can take a number of different forms with members of the cartel agreeing on courses of action such as: what price to charge or level of output to set, what customers to supply or what discounts to give.

Collusion is difficult to prove since it is usually undertaken in secret behind closed doors, is often informal and the discussions are verbal.

Case study 8.3 BA price fixing

Introduction

In August 2007 the Office of Fair Trading (OFT) fined British Airways £121.5m for illegally fixing fuel surcharges levied on its passengers undertaking long-haul flights. The fine, which represents 1 per cent of BA's turnover, was the result of investigations by the OFT (which began in June 2006) into collusion between BA and Virgin Atlantic in terms of setting fuel surcharges over the period August 2004 to January 2006. BA and Virgin are said to have discussed or informed each other about their proposed changes to fuel surcharges, as opposed to independently setting levels which is required by Competition Law over that period. Competition Law forbids firms agreeing prices since competition is seen as a prerequisite for cheaper goods and services for consumers. Fuel surcharges on passengers were introduced in May 2004 as a way of aiding airline operators offset the rising cost of aviation fuel and have subsequently become a significant component of the price of an airline ticket. This case study seeks to outline BA and Virgin Atlantic's anti-competitive price fixing behaviour.

The Competition Act 1998

Under the Competition Act 1998 organisations are prohibited from entering into agreements, practices and conduct which could be damaging to competition in the UK. In addition to this the Enterprise Act 2002 gave the OFT additional powers in order to investigate people suspected of price fixing.

The OFT leniency policy grants immunity from penalties for reporting particular categories of infringement of the Competition Act and for assisting the OFT in its investigation. The financial penalty depends on such things as how serious the infringement is and the turnover of the organisation and can be as much as ten per cent of their worldwide turnover.

Price fixing of fuel surcharges

The investigation of BA price fixing was undertaken by the OFT alongside the US Department of Justice who were investigating allegations of illegal price fixing on air cargo long haul fuel surcharges. Over the period August 2004 to January 2006 the fuel surcharge of BA and Virgin Atlantic increased from £5 to £60 for a long haul return ticket.

It can be quite difficult to distinguish between price fixing which is illegal and legal price setting that constitutes price leadership. In this case of fuel surcharge price fixing, Virgin Atlantic contacted the OFT in order to report the collusive activity and as such escaped a fine itself since under the OFT 'leniency policy' it was granted immunity.

Price fixing in terms of the fuel surcharge is said to have taken place on a number of occasions as spelt out in Table 8.2

Table 8.2   *The price fixing activity*

Date	The collusive activity
August 2004	BA and Virgin Atlantic exchanged information on the 6th August 2004 regarding the intentions of their respective organisations to increase the fuel surcharge (FS). BA told Virgin Atlantic of its intention to increase its FS to £6. On 9th August both announce an increase in their FS to £6 with effect from 11th August 2004.
October 2004	BA understands that there may have been attempts by Virgin Atlantic to contact BA prior to the second increase, but these were not successful. BA announces an increase in its FS on 8th October to £10. On the same date Virgin Atlantic announced a corresponding increase in its FS to £10.
March 2005	In two sets of calls on 21st March BA and Virgin Atlantic exchanged information concerning proposed increases in their respective organisations' FS. On 21st March Virgin Atlantic announced an increase in its FS to £16 with effect from 24th March. On 22nd March BA announced the same price increase in its FS with effect from 28th March 2005.
June 2005	BA informs Virgin Atlantic on 23rd June that it is going to announce an increase in its FS to £24. On 24th June 2005 BA announced an increase in its FS to £24 with effect from 27th June. That same day Virgin Atlantic announced the same increase in FS to £24.

■ *Table 8.2 — continued*

Date	The collusive activity
September 2005	On the 5th September Virgin Atlantic informed BA that it intended to increase its FS and be the first to announce the increase on this occasion. On 6th September 2005 Virgin Atlantic announced an increase in its FS to £30 with effect from 7th September. On 8th September BA announced an increase to £30 with effect from the 12th September 2005.
November 2005	On 18th November Virgin Atlantic informed BA that it was about to announce a reduction in its FS to £25. Shortly afterwards Virgin Atlantic announced a reduction to £25.
January 2006	On 6th January Virgin Atlantic informed BA that it intended to increase its FS to £30. Later that day Virgin Atlantic announced an increase in FS of £30. BA did not change its FS in response.

Source: Adapted from Times Online (2007)

It is unlikely that the fixing of the fuel surcharge undertaken by BA and Virgin Atlantic will have led to joint profit maximisation as outlined but the collusive price fixing activity is however likely to have increased their profit margins, otherwise it would be a futile exercise. It is however a risky activity, as shown by BA's experience since it is illegal and liable to financial penalty if exposed.

The whole episode reflects negatively on the reputation of BA and Virgin Atlantic. In saying this, the ability to claim immunity acts as an incentive for any sector to police itself, to the benefit of the consumer.

So far this chapter has dealt with pricing with respect to public transport, detailing the possible practices of price discrimination, predatory pricing and price fixing. What follows relates to pricing in terms of private transport, which in many respects is a far more complex area.

PRICING OF PRIVATE TRANSPORT SERVICES

The pricing of private transport services, namely, cars, vans, motorcycles and the like, is multi-faceted as stated above, being paid via a combination of mechanisms starting with the purchase and licensing of the vehicle, the purchase of fuel; and running costs and also a range of taxes most notably Vehicle Excise Duty and Fuel Duty. In various locations there is also road user charging in operation, most notably in Central London and further a field in Singapore and Stockholm. These prices can be seen placed under various headings as illustrated in Figure 8.7.

Acquisition costs

Acquisition costs are those incurred when a vehicle is obtained. These refer to the purchase price of the vehicle including VAT. The private motorist will typically ignore these costs when under-

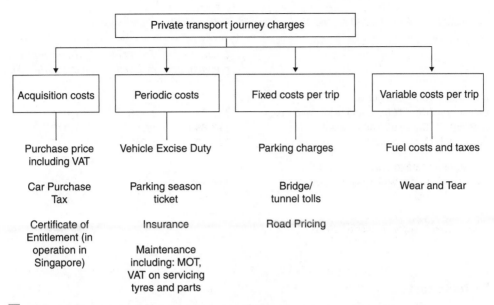

Figure 8.7 *Charges incurred when undertaking a private transport journey*

taking an individual trip, but they can be substantial particularly when new vehicles are involved. There can be other acquisition costs involved in certain countries such as car purchase tax and the Certificate of Entitlement which is a system in use in Singapore.

Car purchase tax is to be found in most EU countries and is paid in addition to VAT on new cars bought. Car purchase tax of 10 per cent was abolished in the UK in 1992 and replaced by an increase in fuel duty. This was a move welcomed by the motor industry who had long canvassed for its abolition regarding it as a discriminatory tax applying only to cars, with all other consumer goods being only subject to VAT.

The Certificate of Entitlement (COE) is a system used in Singapore in order to limit car ownership and as such the number of vehicles on the road. The system requires Singaporean residents to bid for the right to purchase a vehicle, with a limit placed on the number of COE. Typically, COE bidding starts on the first and third Monday of each month and lasts for three days. There are various categories as seen in Table 8.3. A bid can be submitted anytime during the three-day process with a reserve price being the maximum that the bidder is prepared to pay for a COE. If the current COE price is above the bidder's reserve price then the individual will be out of the bidding unless they revise their reserve price. It is important to note that the reserve price can only be revised upwards and not downwards. Clearly this is to prevent bidders from submitting an initial bid for a COE which is somewhat higher than they would actually be prepared to pay. In the event of an unsuccessful bid then the bid deposit will be credited to the bidder's bank account.

As can be seen in Table 8.3 6,038 bids were received by the Land Transport Authority in the second open bidding at the end of August 2008. Of these approximately 80 per cent (4,800) were successful. The non-transferable COE are linked to specific vehicles, but both the COE and the vehicle can be sold to a new owner. In terms of Transferable COE they can be changed from vehicle to vehicle. As can be seen, the Quota premium ranged from $14,001 for Category E to $1,310 for Category D.

Table 8.3 *August 2008 second bidding exercise for certificates of entitlement*

	Quota premium	Total bids received	Number of successful bids
Non-transferable categories			
Category A (Cars 1600cc and below, and taxis)	$13,289	2,318	2,036
Category B (Cars 1601 and above)	$13,890	1,362	1,071
Category D (Motorcycles)	$1,310	548	445
Transferable categories			
Category C (Goods vehicles and buses)	$12,989	492	370
Category E (Open)	$14,001	1,318	878

Source: Land Transport Authority (2008)

Periodic costs

These can also be called standing charges and are the basic costs of owning a car for use on the roads network. They refer to charges that have to be paid whether or not the car is used and as such include the annual registration tax (Vehicle Excise Duty) and insurance.

The majority of developed countries operate an annual registration tax, called vehicle excise duty (VED) in the UK. In the majority of cases this is related to the power of the car or engine size but in a number of cases, including the UK, it is linked to addressing environmental issues and to encourage fuel efficiency. This can be seen in Table 8.4 below with a range of VED Bands based on carbon emissions, with band G being the highest emitting band in 2008–09.

In the UK vehicles which are more than three years old require a Ministry of Transport (MOT) test each year. This is to ensure that the vehicle complies with a minimum road safety and environmental standard. There are various test fees depending on the type of vehicle, but at the time of writing, the fee for a car with up to 8 seats is £53.10.

Table 8.4 *UK vehicle excise duty rates (£12 month rate), 2008–09 (for private vehicles registered from March 2001)*

VED band	CO_2 (g/km)	Petrol and diesel cars	Alternative fuel cars
A	100 and below	£0	£0
B	101–20	£35	£15
C	121–50	£120	£100
D	151–65	£145	£125
E	166–85	£170	£150
F	186–225	£210	£195
G*	Over 225	£400	£385

Source: Directgov (2008)

Note: *For cars registered on or after 23 March 2006.

Fixed costs per trip

The fixed costs which may be incurred by those undertaking a journey include parking charges whether that be public on-street, through pay and display or off-street in public or privately owned car parks.

The journey may also involve a river crossing for which a charge or toll is made. For example at the time of writing the tolls shown in Table 8.5a and b were in operation at two such river crossings in the UK:

■ *Table 8.5a*   *Severn River crossing westwards toll only*

Vehicle Category 1 (Up to 9 seats)	£5.30
Vehicle Category 2 (Small bus up to 17 seats, Goods vehicles up to 3500KG)	£10.60
Vehicle Category 3 (18 seats and more, Goods vehicles from 3500KG)	£15.90

■ *Table 8.5b*   *Dartford River crossing: charges in operation 0600–2200*

Between 2200–0600 charges are £1.00 for each category	
Motor Car: including Motor Car with three wheels or taxi	£1.00
Light or Medium Goods Vehicle: Motor Coach, Omnibus or tractor: having more than two axles	£1.80
HGV, Motor Coach or Omnibus or Tractor having more than two axles	£2.90
Special Type Vehicles	£2.90

Road pricing is designed as a measure to reduce congestion (see Chapter 3). As such, it will impact on the price of a journey, since it represents a charge for the use of road space. There are a small number of schemes worldwide including the Electronic Road pricing scheme in Singapore and the congestion charging schemes in Stockholm and Central London. Case study 8.4 considers the London congestion charging scheme in more detail.

Case study 8.4 Central London congestion charging

The first major congestion charging scheme in Britain was launched in Central London in February 2003, the aim of the scheme being to reduce congestion.

Motorists entering the congestion charging zone between the hours of 7am and 6pm Monday–Friday (excluding public holidays) are charged £8. 700 video cameras enforce the scheme via the scanning of the rear number plate of the vehicles that enter the area during the charging period. The information obtained is matched against a database of motorists each evening in order to ascertain who has paid the charge. Payment can be made via the Internet, by phone or at shops or petrol stations. If the motorist has failed to pay the charge before midnight a fine of £100 is imposed and if the offender pays within 14 days then the fine is reduced to £50. In relation to the charge certain groups are exempt or given a discount from part or all of the charge:

193 ■

- Certain vehicles receive a 100 per cent discount including alternative fuel vehicles, namely those powered by an alternative fuel, bi fuel or dual fuel, and not solely by petrol or diesel. They are exempt on environmental grounds but must also meet strict emissions criteria.
- Blue and orange badge holders are also exempt.
- Certain NHS staff, patients and emergency vehicles (police vehicles, fire engines, and ambulances) are exempt.
- Certain vehicles such as those with more than 9 seats and two-wheeled motorbikes (and sidecars), mopeds, black cabs licensed with the Public Carriage Office (PCO) and mini cabs licensed with the PCO are also exempt.

Advantages of the scheme
- Congestion in urban areas can be viewed as market failure with the actions of road users in Central London affecting other road users. Congestion has a cost associated with it not least in terms of the increased time taken to undertake a journey and the opportunity cost that involves. The charge is aimed at reducing congestion, thus freeing up the road network and so reduce the time taken to complete a journey.
- Economics is concerned with the optimum use of scarce resources and since road space in Central London can be viewed as a scarce resource then charging for its use will mean that it can be used more efficiently. Thus those that value the time most will pay the charge.
- The revenue raised from congestion charging is to be used to improve the alternatives, namely, public transport.
- Individuals tend not to like being charged and as such the use of regulation has tended to be more acceptable. The use of regulation however tends to be a 'blunt instrument', something which cannot be fine tuned to tackle varying demand conditions and unlike congestion pricing it produces no revenue.
- Encourages efficient transport systems in terms of land use space, i.e. mass movers of people.
- Unlike measures such as enhancing public transport services in the area, one major advantage with a congestion charge is that the charge can by varied at very short notice. It is therefore very flexible.
- In simple terms it works. If set at the right level, a congestion charge will impact on congestion.

Disadvantages of the scheme
- Clearly one issue with congestion charging is the invasion of privacy given that the system relies on taking a photograph of vehicle number plates.
- The charge can be viewed as a regressive measure as those who pay the charge and are on lower incomes pay a larger proportion of their income than those on higher incomes in order to drive in central London. In order to negate this claim, the use of the revenue generated from the scheme is all important. If the revenue is used to subsidise and enhance public transport as an alternative to the car, then the charge can be seen as more equitable.

- The cost has been seen as a disadvantage. It has been estimated that the cost of setting up the scheme has been £200m and it costs an additional £80–90m to operate per year.
- The scheme utilises a rather simplistic technology. Namely cameras on all the roads into the central area and a fixed price of £8, the charge not changing in line with the level of congestion experienced. This may however change over time and as the scheme evolves it could see the use of global positioning satellites (GPS) and cars fitted with satellite receivers in order to allow a charge to be made based on distance, time and location.
- Ideological argument – in urban areas individuals already pay for the roads through local taxes, hence why should they pay again?

Variable costs per trip

The last main item shown in Figure 8.7 is the variable costs per trip. These are costs that are incurred on each trip and which vary in accordance with one or more of the characteristics of the trip. For example, trip length, trip destination, timing of the trip and traffic conditions. The major element of this cost relates to fuel.

In addition to VAT fuel is subject to fuel tax, called Fuel Excise Duty, which is charged as a rate per unit of fuel, i.e. per litre/gallon (Potter 2008). The rate will differ depending on the type of fuel, whether it be petrol, diesel, LPG or low-sulphur.

The fuel duty rates vary across the European Union, thus impacting on the retail price, as seen in Table 8.6.

Table 8.6 *Retail price of premium unleaded petrol and tax (2008)*

	Tax as % of retail price	Retail price (Eurocents per litre)
Netherlands	64	1.69
Denmark	62	1.58
Germany	65	1.57
Finland	64	1.57
Italy	61	1.54
Belgium	61	1.53
France	64	1.51
United Kingdom	67	1.51
Portugal	60	1.50
Sweden	63	1.47
Irish Republic	57	1.34
Austria	56	1.33
Luxembourg	54	1.32
Greece	47	1.27
Spain	53	1.23

Source of data: Potter (2008) based on www.aaroadwatch.ie/eupetrolprices/ (accessed 12.08.08) and Transport Statistics Great Britain, 2007, Table 10.8.

Note: This data covers all tax on petrol (including VAT).

A change in the tax structure?

There has been a debate in the UK about the potential implementation of a national road pricing scheme although this seems unlikely at the present time. If it were to be seriously considered then one of the key issues would be the type of technology used. It would need to be flexible enough to charge based on time, distance, and place as well as being able to target the environmental costs (DfT 2004). The motoring taxes as outlined above are not able to match that of a national road pricing scheme in terms of sophistication in addressing the issue of congestion when and where it occurs (DfT 2004) – but then this is not the prime function of motoring taxes.

If a national road pricing scheme were to be introduced then important decisions would be required in terms of whether it should replace fuel duty – whether in whole or in part. If it were to be totally replaced then it would require a change in European law. Equally, it would not be possible to abolish fuel duty until the whole country was operating distance charging.

CHAPTER SUMMARY AND REFLECTION

This chapter has examined the issues surrounding the pricing of transport services. In a free market economy, the price is set by and large by the type of market structure, and hence is generally determined by the forces of demand and supply. As will be seen later in Chapter 10, in mixed markets the price is a combination of the market and intervention by transport authorities in the form of regulating the price and/or capacity. This chapter has therefore considered 'deviations' from these two positions in order to gain a better understanding of pricing issues in transport markets. Firstly therefore price discrimination was introduced as this is an important aspect of public transport pricing being extensively utilised by bus, rail and air operators. The aim of price discrimination is to increase the operator's profits by eroding the passengers' consumer surplus. Airline operators, in particular, have been astute when it comes to price discriminating with respect to price or practising yield management – charging varying prices to their customers with differing time-sensitive elasticities in order to increase the number of seats sold. It should also be noted however that price discrimination may be used by public transport authorities to better manage the demand for a given transport system and thus spread the demand for the service across a larger time range. In addition to price discrimination public transport operators have been known to use predatory pricing, charging a price below cost as a means of undercutting competitors in order to create a monopoly situation. An alternative strategy to predatory pricing is one of price fixing, where operators collude, fixing the price at an artificially high level, in order to increase profit. An example is given of airline price fixing of fuel surcharges between 2004 and 2006. Both measures however are illegal as they are anti-competitive and act against the public interest. Finally, pricing of private transport services has been detailed, being multifaceted in nature, with acquisition, periodic, fixed and variable costs.

CHAPTER EXERCISES

Exercise 8.1 Price discrimination

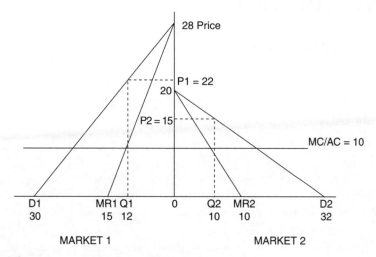

Figure 8.8 *Price discrimination in two rail markets*

Figure 8.8 refers to a rail operator that is practising price discrimination, charging a different price to the passengers in market 1 compared to those in market 2. It is assumed that costs are constant, therefore MC = AC.

a) What does Figure 8.8 reveal about the type of passengers using the service and their relative elasticities?
b) Calculate the abnormal profit earned by the rail operator by price discriminating.
c) Based on the information presented in Figure 8.8 sketch out the diagram for the rail operator if it were not to price discriminate.
d) Are there any beneficiaries from price discrimination and what happens to consumer surplus when price discrimination is practised?

Exercise 8.2 Pricing behaviour

Transport operators in oligopolistic markets practise predatory pricing and price fixing from time to time. Outline what you perceive to be the benefits to transport operators of such practices and the reasons why they are illegal in many countries world-wide.

Chapter 9

Transport and the natural environment

Contributed by Stephen Ison

Learning Outcomes:

On reading this chapter, you will learn about:

- The relationship between the macro economy and the environment
- The impact which transport has in terms of the environment
- The main issues surrounding the carriage of freight and its impact on the environment from a balanced perspective
- How economics can aid in our understanding of how transport affects the environment
- The economic options which can be considered as a means of addressing environmental issues.

INTRODUCTION

The link between the demand for transport and economic growth and thus the need for travel has been detailed in Chapter 2. This link has environmental implications and if left unchecked these will impact on economic activity. Vehicle emissions impact on the quality of life both at the local level in terms of air quality and hence individual health, and at a more global level in terms of CO_2 emissions, an important source of greenhouse gases which impact on climate change. This chapter seeks to utilise economic theory as a means of analysing the relationship between transport and the environment. It starts by outlining the background to the general environmental problem, before detailing the various transport emissions and their impact and then specifically examines freight transport's impact on the environment. The chapter then develops an economic model of pollution and explores the types of measures which could be implemented as a means of dealing with the problem.

The macroeconomic concept of the circular flow of income relates to the flow of income and expenditure between households and firms and can be used in order to set the scene in terms of transport and the environment. With respect to the circular flow of income households receive income for the factor services they have undertaken and with that income they buy goods and services, including transport. This can be seen in the upper portion of Figure 9.1.

We have seen part of this diagram already as Figure 2.3 in Chapter 2. What it did not take

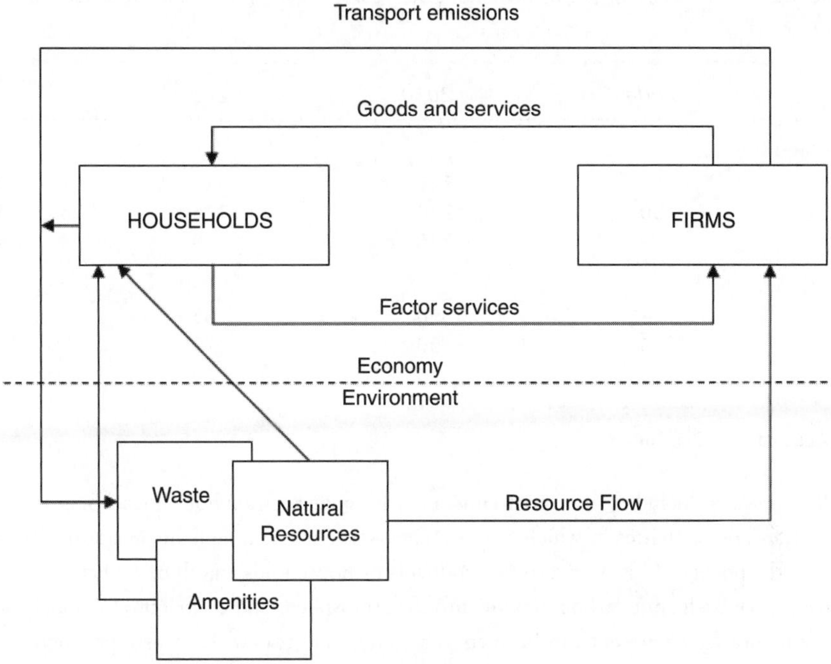

Transport emissions

Goods and services

HOUSEHOLDS

FIRMS

Factor services

Economy
Environment

Waste

Natural
Resources

Resource Flow

Amenities

Figure 9.1   *The macro economy and the environment*

account of however was the constraints imposed on the economy by environmental factors, of which transport plays a significant part. These can be seen on the lower part of Figure 9.1 and includes aspects on which transport impact. For example, if you take the period 1996 to 2006 car passenger transport has increased from 622bn to 686bn passenger kilometres (a 10 per cent increase), with car transport comprising 85 per cent of all passenger kilometres (DfT 2007b). As for domestic freight then the road also dominates, representing 64 per cent of all domestic freight transported, increasing from 153.9bn tonne kilometres in 1996 to 163.4bn tonne kilometres in 2006, a 6 per cent increase. (DfT, 2007b). In terms of air transport movements there has been an increase from 0.9bn passenger kilometres in 1996 to 1.2bn passenger kilometres in 2006, which represents a 33 per cent increase. All of these increases in transport activities impact on the environment. In addition, whilst air transport is still relatively small it is a significant contributor to climate change. The reason for this is the release of greenhouse gases into the upper atmosphere (Chapman, 2006). A concern is the projected growth in air transport as seen in Table 9.1.

The environment, transport and the economy can be linked in three ways as illustrated in Figure 9.1.

a) *Natural resources*: transport makes use of natural resources most notably oil which is in fact the most dominant source for transportation (Chapman, 2006). According to the International Energy Agency (2002) the transport sector accounts for 54 per cent of the primary oil demand in OECD countries.

199

■ *Table 9.1*   *Forecast of air traffic demand: 2004–2030 (Million terminal passengers at UK airports)*

	2004	2010	2020	2030
International				
Low	–	225	310	370
Mid	180	230	325	400
High	–	235	340	435
Domestic				
Low	–	50	65	80
Mid	40	50	70	85
High	–	50	70	95

Source: Adapted from DfT 2007a

b) *Waste products*, including transport emissions, are generated by both households and firms in the transport activities in which they are engaged. For example firms in transporting goods from the ports of East Anglia to the Midlands or households travelling by private car to and from work both emit carbon dioxide into the atmosphere and contribute to global warming. The natural environment can be seen as a 'dumping ground' for waste products, and one that apparently comes at a zero economic cost.

c) *Amenity services* relates to the natural environment which provides households with benefits such as recreational space and areas of natural beauty such as National Parks, accessed predominately by the private motor vehicle. These can clearly be affected by economic activity and the related transport decisions made by both households and firms in terms of transport emissions.

In terms of waste output and transport emissions there are a range of pollutants associated with transport and passenger cars in particular. These include emissions of carbon dioxide, carbon monoxide, nitrogen oxide, particulates, benzene and 1,3-butadiene. The pollutant emissions are given in Table 9.3 and it can be seen that transport, and road transport, in particular, are major contributors particularly in terms of carbon monoxide and nitrogen oxide.

Transport is a major consumer of energy. In fact in 2004, 36 per cent of all United Kingdom energy consumption was used by transport.

Case study 9.1 Transport emissions

Carbon dioxide: the largest source of carbon dioxide in the UK is combustion of fossil fuels and in terms of domestic transport accounts for 23 per cent of carbon dioxide emissions which is not insignificant at 23.3 million tonnes of carbon. The non-transport source of carbon dioxide includes sectors most notably domestic, industrial, commercial, agricultural, and the military. Globally, the transport-related emissions of carbon dioxide are growing rapidly with the use of petroleum as a major source of fuel. Carbon dioxide is an important greenhouse gas and one which is estimated to account for in the region of two thirds of global warming. As for the direct health implications the impact is rather less than for other emissions detailed below. In fact, carbon dioxide is all important for the internal respiration in the human body. In saying this, if the levels of carbon dioxide are not in balance then it could lead to health implications, such as asphyxiation.

Carbon monoxide is the product of internal combustion engines, and domestic transport accounts for approximately 50 per cent of carbon monoxide emissions, representing 1,199 thousand tonnes per annum in the UK. It is a toxic substance which impacts, amongst other things, on an individual's respiratory and central nervous system. Catalytic converters have been important in reducing the amount of CO in car exhausts by oxidising CO to CO_2.

Nitrogen oxide is caused by combustion engines and other industrial, residential and commercial sources that burn fuels. It can impact on the environment in a number of ways, once emitted it can be transported many miles before being deposited as acid rain impacting on forests, lakes, wildlife, crops and buildings. This means that buildings and historic monuments can deteriorate and lakes can become uninhabitable in terms of wildlife. The increased nitrogen in rivers and lakes accelerates eutrophication, which leads to a depletion of oxygen thus reducing the stock of fish. It can also react with 1,3-butadiene in the atmosphere with sunlight to form ground level ozone which is a major component of summer time smog. It is also harmful to human health impacting on the functioning on the respiratory and lung system and can in fact cause premature death. Domestic transport comprises 684 thousand tonnes per annum within the UK and accounts for 42 per cent of nitrogen oxide emissions.

Particulates (PM10) also impact on health including effects on both the respiratory and cardiovascular systems. It particularly impacts on asthma sufferers. 27.3 per cent of particulates are the result of domestic transport which represents 40.9 thousand tonnes per annum within the UK.

Both **benzene** and **1,3-butadiene** emitted from car exhausts are seen to be a human carcinogen, which means it is an agent that is directly involved in the promotion of cancer. It can also suppress the immune system, increasing the risk of infection. Benzene is present in vehicle exhausts and evaporative emissions of gasoline-dispensing systems. As for 1,3-butadiene it arises from the combustion of petroleum products. The introduction of catalytic converters in 1991 had a major impact on the emissions of 1,3-butadiene from road transport. In terms of emissions then domestic transport accounts for 25 per cent (3.5 thousand tonnes) of benzene emissions and 63 per cent (1.7 thousand tonnes) of 1,3-butadiene.

Lead has historically been a major source of emission from motor vehicles and industry. With the prohibition of lead-based petrol (four star), however, lead emissions have fallen dramatically from the transport sector, with domestic transport now only comprising 2.3 per cent of all emissions, at 2.1 thousand tonnes per annum. Lead has an impact on health in terms of damage to the kidneys, liver, brain and nerves. Exposure to lead can also lead to osteoporosis and reproductive disorders.

In terms of Figure 9.1 there is a need to break the link between the economy, and its related transport activity, and the environment, which could be argued is unsustainable. Sustainable transport can be defined as 'the ability to meet society's need to move freely, gain access, communicate, trade and establish relationships without sacrificing other essential human or eco-logical values, today or in the future' (WBCSD, 2002). The Eddington Study (2006) reports that transport sector emissions are a 'significant and growing contributor (around a quarter in 2004) to the UK greenhouse gas emissions' and these emissions are seen to have an impact on long-term UK economic growth. This is reinforced by the Stern Review (2006) which provides evidence of the negative impact climate change will have on economic growth. The UK Government is of the opinion that climate change is 'the greatest long-term challenge facing the world today and that transport policies can make an important contribution to tackling climate change' (DfT, 2007a).

Case study 9.2 Aviation and the environment

There has been a growth in air transportation in the past 40 years and Table 9.2 illustrates that growth, in terms of airport traffic over the period 1990–2006. It reveals an increase in international and domestic air transport movements, both landing and take-off, of 86 and 42 per cent respectively.

The table also reveals that while all airports have experienced growth in air transport movements some have shown greater growth than others, such as Stansted, with significant low-cost airline development, Manchester and Edinburgh. There are undoubted benefits in terms of the growth in passenger and cargo movements, not least in terms of employment opportunities created and the enhanced mobility of the population. For example, there were 85,071 employed directly by UK airlines worldwide in 2006 positions such as pilots and co-pilots, cabin

Table 9.2   Traffic (in thousands) at UK airports: 1990–2006

	1990	1994	1998	2002	2006
International:					
UK operators	479	529	655	753	808
Foreign operators	340	403	480	543	713
Domestic:	301	308	331	364	427
TOTAL:	1,120	1,240	1,476	1,660	1,948
Of which:					
Gatwick	189	182	240	234	254
Heathrow	368	412	441	460	471
Luton	40	17	44	55	79
Stansted	24	58	102	152	190
Birmingham	66	71	88	112	109
East Midlands	29	33	39	49	56
Manchester	122	146	162	178	213
Edinburgh	48	61	72	105	116
Belfast	38	33	37	38	48

Source: Adapted from DfT statistics

attendants, maintenance and overall personnel, tickets and sales personnel. In addition, there are thousands employed in areas such as cargo handling and travel agencies. Like other modes of transport however there are negative effects of aircraft movements in terms of the environment.

Table 9.3 illustrates the emissions from civil aircraft over the period 1995–2005 with resulting effects on health and the quality of life. The figures for civil aircraft are insignificant when compared to road transport but as can be seen pollution emissions from road transport and non-transport end users have been declining over the period in question, unlike civil aircraft. In addition, by definition air travel is a major generator of road traffic as passengers and cargo need to get to and from the airport.

Aircraft noise is an additional external effect of aviation. Aircraft noise is measured as an equivalent continuous sound level (L_{eq}) averaged over a 16-hour day (0700 to 2300) and is calculated during the peak summer months. 57 L_{eq} is seen as the onset of disturbance, 63 L_{eq} and 69 L_{eq} as moderate and high disturbance respectively. The 471 thousand air transport movements based on Heathrow in 2006 affected a population of 258,000 within the 57 L_{eq} contour. For Gatwick the figure was 45,000 population within the 57 L_{eq} contour (DfT, 2007b).

Table 9.3 *Pollution emissions from transport and other end users in the UK: 1995–2005*

Thousand Tonnes/percentage

Pollution type:	1995	1997	1999	2001	2003	2005	% of 2005 total
Nitrogen oxides:							
Road transport	1,098	1,014	900	749	636	549	34
Civil aircraft	4.4	4.9	6.3	7.3	7.5	9.1	0.6
All transport	1,204	1,127	1,004	840	756	684	42
Non transport users	1,180	1,030	965	988	972	983	58
Carbon monoxide:							
Road transport	4,180	3,664	3,003	2,128	1,594	1,124	46
Civil aircraft	31	39	47	59	47	58	2.4
All transport	4,224	3,717	3,065	2,200	1,655	1,199	50
Non transport users	2,072	1,957	1,875	1,691	1,292	1,218	50
Sulphur dioxide:							
Road transport	52	28	14	4.2	4	3	0.4
Civil aircraft	0.3	0.5	0.4	0.5	0.5	0.6	0.1
All transport	83	58	39	23	31	43	6
Non transport users	2,239	1,583	1,188	1,096	960	660	94
Particulates (PM_{10}):							
Road transport	54	47	43	38	36	34	22
Civil aircraft	0.1	0.1	0.1	0.1	0.1	0.1	0.1
All transport	59	53	48	42	42	41	27
Non transport users	179	161	149	136	113	109	73

Source: Adapted from DfT (2007b)

Overall therefore, there are global impacts and local environmental impacts associated with aircraft movements. At the global level there is the effect of aircraft emissions on climate change. Aviation emissions are small but growing, as illustrated in Table 9.3, and it is estimated that by 2050 aviation's contribution to man-made climate change will be somewhere between 3 and 7 per cent. At the local level there is the local air quality effects of emissions from aircraft at airports, the effect of aircraft noise, the noise, emissions and congestion resulting from surface access to airports as well as the land take and urbanisation as a result of airport development.

FREIGHT TRANSPORT AND THE ENVIRONMENT

This short section will consider the main issues surrounding freight transport and its impact upon the natural environment. As shown in Chapter 2, over time levels of freight transport activity have been very closely related to economic growth as measured by GDP. As we will see later in Chapter 12, however, the levels of both factors have also been affected by the reduction in trade restrictions between nations over the period. This is no more so present than within the European Union, which since the introduction of the Single European Act in 1986 (which introduced the single European market) has seen a considerable rise in the movement of goods between member states. With that has come increased freight transport activity and concern over the impact this has had upon the environment. This has been particularly true in geographical areas that have seen large increases in freight transport flows but that are also regions of particular environmental sensitivity, the most obvious example being the Alps. Perhaps surprisingly, although air pollution is an international issue, this has led to strong national policies rather than policies at the EU level. This is particularly true in Switzerland, which introduced a through truck 28 tonne weight limit, and Austrian decisions on night and weekend road haulage movements. What exactly however is the problem with freight transport and the environment?

We have already seen earlier in this chapter the impact of road transport on the environment. With regard to freight, these issues are also generally tied up with road haulage; however, two particular problems for the road haulage sector is that its relative share of nitrogen oxides has been growing considerably as more private cars have been fitted with catalytic converters. The second problem is that its share of carbon dioxide will also probably become a relatively greater problem as cars become more fuel efficient. As a consequence, over time the issue with road haulage's impact on the environment will become more acute as the impact of the car is lessened.

Nevertheless, actual figures on the impact of freight transport upon the environment are difficult to obtain. Given in Figure 9.2 however are the relative levels of road transport by type of transport and the level CO_2 emissions for each (road-based) mode.

This in many ways highlights the problem with road haulage, specifically that it has a far larger share of CO_2 emissions (and NO_X emissions) than its share of road transport, thus it has a disproportionately high polluting effect. Road haulage is also particularly high in the emission of particles, with DfT statistics (DfT, 2007b) quoting values of emissions per vehicle kilometre some nine times higher than that for a diesel private car. Since the introduction of Euro emissions standards, however, particularly Euro III,[1] these have been considerably reduced by just over a factor of two; however, this is still considerably less than the impact of Euro standards on private vehicles

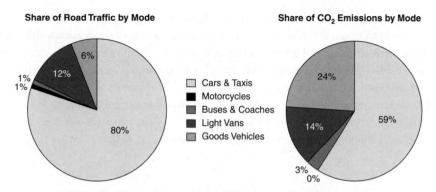

Figure 9.2   *Road transport 2005: modal share and share of CO$_2$ emissions*

Source: Drawn from DfT (2007b)

– for a diesel motor car, the effect has been to reduce the emission of particles by a factor of just under five, hence highlighting the problem that road haulage share of emissions is increasing.

In terms of comparisons with other modes of freight transport, Short (1995) cites figures from Befahy (1992) who calculated comparative differences in pollution rates per road and rail tonne kilometre moved. For three measures of air pollutants, nitrogen oxide, hydrocarbons and carbon monoxide, the levels of emissions for road were four times higher per tonne moved than by rail in the case of the first, forty-five times higher for hydrocarbons and thirty-five times higher for carbon monoxide. These however appear to overstate the issue, with similar comparisons made by the Strategic Rail Authority in 2005 as quoted by the Freight on Rail campaign (FoR, 2008) revealing smaller differences. Their figures suggest that emission per tonne kilometre of freight moved were 12 times higher for PM10 (particles), ten times higher for carbon monoxide, five and half times higher for nitrogen oxides and 12 times higher for carbon dioxide. The main reason for the considerable differences in the two studies cited however is due to the advances made in controlling the emissions of road vehicles over the intervening periods. These have resulted in a substantial decrease in comparative differences, although differences still remain significant. Schipper and Fulton (2005) however make the important point that the composition of freight drives the modal mix. Hence low-volume high-value commodities tend to go by road, whilst high volume low value commodities by rail. Unlike passenger transport, therefore, where such comparisons are based upon (roughly) the same unit of measurement in the form of passenger kilometres, the different composition of freight tonne kilometres make such comparisons far more problematic. Thus for example a significant modal shift from road to rail would change the freight composition on the relative modes (particularly rail), and this change would in turn impact on emissions per tonne kilometre hauled.

As the impact of transport on the environment is an international issue, we end this short section with a brief international comparison of freight carbon emissions per capita for a number of developed countries. Research by Schipper *et al.* (1997) found that the US had a figure of over twice as many freight carbon emissions per head than seven countries of the European Union. Norway also had around an output 50 per cent higher than the EU countries. This suggests that there exist considerable variations around the world of the impact of freight transport on the environment in relation to the size of the population.

To conclude this short section and bring it into focus with the economics of transport, relating freight transport to Figure 9.1 it would appear that road haulage has a disproportionately high call upon environmental resources highlighted in that figure, and thus the total cost of that mode of transport is relatively more understated than the other freight transport modes. As environmental concerns heightened, this is likely to have a more detrimental impact on the use of the mode. How this might be brought about is considered later in the chapter under policy options for addressing environmental concerns; however, to put some of these issues in perspective we end this section with a case study titled 'is it really road haulage that is bad for the environment?'.

Case study 9.3 Is it really road haulage that is bad for the environment?

We saw above that road haulage is a major contributor to the deterioration of the natural environment, far more so than any other land-based individual transport mode. If road haulage is so bad for the environment, therefore, why don't we just get rid of it? That would, after all, be the ultimate conclusion of such a finding. What this highlights is that what has been presented so far is only one side of the argument, but this issue should not be looked at in isolation. This case study attempts to give some insight into the wider problems that may result as a consequence of significantly reducing the reliance on the mode, as this in turn brings into focus the issues involved in attempting to lessen transport's impact on the environment. What follows however is pure speculation on the author's part; this is designed merely to give some idea of the problems that this would involve rather than act as a highly accurate scientific study. In compilation of this case, thanks are due to Professor Alan McKinnon on whose research some of this case rests (see McKinnon (2006) for further details). That research was a scientific study aimed at developing a scenario for a temporary disruption in road haulage services of a week. In this case, we speculate on some of the issues involved in a more long-term modal shift.

We begin with the basic question that if the reliance on road haulage is to be eradicated or significantly reduced, then how would all of the freight that is currently transported by the mode be moved? Currently within the UK some 1.936bn tonnes of freight are shifted 167 billion kilometres over a road network that is 398,350 kilometres in length. In comparison, 108 million tonnes of freight are moved 22 billion kilometres on a rail network 15,795 kilometres long. In simple terms, therefore, the rail network simply could not cope with a significant increase in freight loads, particularly given that in certain parts the network is already at or close to capacity. To bring these figures more clearly into understandable terms, for each head of population in the UK some 33 tonnes of freight are moved annually by road, compared to just under 2 tonnes on the railways. Whilst railways were described in Chapter 2 as the driver of the Industrial Revolution in the 19th century, road haulage is undoubtedly the mainstay of the economy of the 21st century.

The modal split of freight however is not a straight division between the various modes involved, but rather particular modes tend to specialise in certain sectors which results in an uneven division of freight moved across the whole sector. Road haulage has an almost complete monopoly at the lower levels of the supply chain in the delivery of retail supplies, hence any impact of reduced road haulage levels would be most acutely felt at that end of the supply chain, i.e. by the consumer.

McKinnon (2006) evaluates four forms of substitution that could occur in the face of an absence or reduction of road haulage levels. These are used below to examine the potential longer-term consequences of a major modal shift.

Product substitution

One of the main issues with road haulage is that the greater flexibility that it presents has led to the development of the concept of the whole logistical supply chain, with one direct result being that inventories levels have been considerably reduced. Product substitution would effectively involve a reversal of that position, where greater stocks would be held at all levels from production through to consumption. Simple examples would be the substitution of fresh produce for frozen and greater reliance on electronic communication rather than traditional postal services. Major shifts would have to occur however in consumption patterns towards goods with a longer useable life and a significant shift away from the consumer-orientated society. The impact on production would be considerable, and this is considered further under locational substitution.

Modal substitution

This has been hinted at above where the substitution is in the mode of transport used. Thus road haulage would be replaced by rail and maritime transport, with most of the emphasis falling on rail. In simple terms, the rail network would have to change beyond all recognition in order to cope with any increase in demand. This not only relates to the actual length of the network, which would have to expand in size well in excess of pre-Beeching levels, but also would require considerable enhancements in terms of loading gauges in order to accommodate larger and heavier trains and in signalling to reduce headways in order to accommodate more traffic. Such enhancements would not come cheap.

Vehicle substitution

Vehicle substitution is different from modal substitution in that it involves using the existing road infrastructure, however, with vehicles that are far less polluting. A number of alternatives to fossil-based fuels currently exist, the better known ones being biodiesel, bioalcohol (ethanol, methanol, butanol), electricity and liquid gas. These alternatives however have a considerable way to go before they could substitute fossil fuels. Whilst undoubtedly a biased viewpoint, the AFCG (2003) nevertheless state that only natural gas could compete economically with existing fuels and gain a market share in excess of 5 per cent by 2020.

Locational substitution

As with product substitution, locational substitution involves a reversal of long-term trends. Over time there has been a major shift from high density living to a greater geographical dispersion of the population and a general de-centralisation of activities. This not only refers to the American concept of 'urban sprawl', but has occurred in many other countries where new housing developments have generally been of the low density form. Location also relates to the whole structure of industry, which is very different today to how it was 30 years ago. Logistics play a major part in the whole industrial activity, and this has led to a centralisation of activity. McKinnon (2006) highlights the case of agriculture and the requirement for the distribution of winter feed and the centralisation of slaughterhouse capacity, which now involves both feed and animals being transported far greater distances. This change in industrial patterns is also very true of manufacturing, where there is now a far greater tendency for movement through the logistical chain of component parts. Whilst perhaps not a good example in the current context, motor cars do nevertheless provide a good example of this change; in the past cars were built in a single factory and components sourced locally; however, today different parts are built in different locations, many not even in the same country.

This case study began by attempting to speculate on what life would be like with a significant reduction in road haulage transport driven by environmental concerns, but in many respects it has failed to do so because such a scenario is simply outside of current terms of reference. In other words, it cannot be contemplated. Road haulage will never be replaced; however, any move to significantly reduce the reliance on the mode will have to be done over a very long period of time and will come at a very high cost (in terms of living standards). In many respects it would be akin to returning to the 1930s, the only problem however is that the global population is far larger today than it was then, hence effectively a 1930s transport system could not support today's population, never mind at current living standards.

AN ECONOMIC MODEL OF TRANSPORT AND POLLUTION

The effect that transport has on the environment can be studied by the use of an economic model (see Figure 9.3). In the figure the horizontal axis measures the level of transport activity and its related pollution, which is assumed to be directly related to the level of transport activity. This could relate to an airport and the number of aircraft and passengers who use the airport over a period of time. Since transport can be seen as a derived demand, as outlined in Chapter 3, then transport activity can be firmly linked to the level of economic activity. The vertical axis measures the costs and benefits, both to transport and society.

Marginal private benefit (MPB) measures the additional benefits, in terms of satisfaction received by the road user or airline passenger from undertaking journeys, or road haulier, cargo

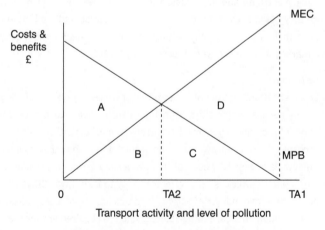

Figure 9.3   An economic model of transport activity and pollution

handler or airport authority in terms of profitable activity. The marginal external cost curve (MEC) measures the additional environmental cost of transport activity, in terms of air pollution, noise and so on. If the transport user/sector is not constrained in terms of their level of activity then they will consume or provide an amount equal to TA1. This means that the area under the MPB curve, represented by A + B + C will be maximised. At that level of activity (TA1) however there are external costs in terms of the impact of the emissions detailed above of B + C + D. The optimum level of pollution, therefore, is achieved at a scale of transport activity TA2, where the MPB = MEC. If the transport user operated at a level of activity above TA2 then the additional environmental costs would be greater than the additional benefits accrued from undertaking the transport activity. This represents what is termed a 'welfare loss' to society, whereas at a level of transport activity below TA2 the opposite is true. Here the MPB is greater than the MEC and as such, activity should be allowed to increase to TA2, in order to take account of these additional benefits. Note further, however, that continuous production above level TA2 will result in a significant negative impact upon the environment. As can probably be gathered from Figure 9.3 the benefits accrue to the road user or airline passenger in terms of moving between destination A and B for work or leisure activities, or to road hauliers, bus operators, airport operators or the like in terms of profitable activity. The costs (MEC) in terms of airport pollution and so on are not incurred by the same group. For example, aviation activity is likely to lead to profit for the airport operator, but the costs are incurred by those who live in the vicinity of the airport and who suffer, in particular from the noise and air pollution, not simply from aircraft but also the surface access traffic. These can be viewed as external costs since transport users or organisations do not normally include them in their decisions as to what output level to produce. The costs are actually incurred by third parties who are not involved in the transport activity but who suffer from the 'spill over effects'. In terms of our airport example, the first two parties are the airport operator (the producer) and the airline and airline passengers (the consumers).

There are a number of policy options which can be considered as a means of addressing the issue of the environmental impact associated with road and air transport.

It is important to state that the options detailed below are by no means exhaustive but provide an indication of possible measures, namely a bargaining solution, a tax-based solution, the role of tradable permits, the setting of standards, technological change and the encouragement of alternative modes of transport that can be considered. These options need to be considered as part of a package of measures, although note that we have already seen some of the impacts such actions may have in Case study 9.3.

Bargaining

The basis of this particular approach is that if property rights are assigned then bargaining will occur naturally between the various parties that suffer from or are the source of external cost, the externality, and the optimum level of pollution will be the result. Based on Figure 9.3 the two parties are airline operators and the airport who generate environmental pollution and those who suffer in terms of that pollution, namely those who live close to the airport. The notion of bargaining is based on the idea that if property rights are assigned to either of the two parties, thus giving the airline operators or airport the right to pollute or to those who are affected by the pollution to clean air, then via bargaining agreement will be reached so that pollution is reduced.

209

If the property rights were assigned to the airline/airport operator then in terms of Figure 9.3 the level of transport activity would be TA1, with profit maximised and no account given to those affected by emissions. It would however be in the interest of those suffering from the emissions to pay the polluter if they agree to reduce their level of activity and thus their level of pollution. In this situation the sufferers would pay as long as it was less than the value of the pollution from which they would otherwise suffer. The bargaining solution states that payment would be made to the airline/airport operator by those that are suffering so long as it is below the valuation of the damage they incur. In terms of Figure 9.3 therefore the sufferers may be willing to offer the polluters a maximum amount of C+D, which represents the total external cost incurred by the sufferer as a result of the transport activity TA2–TA1. The airline/airport operator would have been prepared to reduce their scale of activity from TA1 to TA2 for an amount no less than C, an amount which represents the total profit gained from activity undertaken TA2 to TA1. As such, there is a basis for 'bargaining' between the two parties. For this option to work, the amount paid by the sufferers would be somewhere between C and C+D, and as might be expected the amount actually paid will depend on the relative strength of the two parties involved.

If on the other hand the 'property rights' were to be assigned to the sufferers, who therefore have a right not to be affected by aviation pollution, that is a right to clean air or no noise, then the airline operators and thus the airport would have to cease operation, thus being at point 0 in the figure, with no airline or airport activity or related pollution. In such a situation the polluters may find it to their advantage to offer the sufferers compensation that allows them to undertake activity and its related pollution. The polluters would offer compensation so long as it is less than the private benefits they receive from undertaking their activity. In terms of Figure 9.3 it would be worth the polluters offering the sufferers an amount equal to B or a little more, so that they could operate and obtain profit of A, or a large portion of A. Any activity beyond TA2 would not be sensible since the amount of compensation paid would outweigh the satisfaction received. The result would therefore be the optimum level of pollution, at TA2. Under either scenario economists such as Coase (who developed the idea of bargaining) reveals that assigning property rights can result in bargaining which brings about an optimum solution.

There is however an issue of equity, which varies greatly depending on which of the two scenarios is adopted. In addition whilst the theory of bargaining seems relatively straightforward it may not be possible to adopt such an approach when addressing traffic-related pollution. There are a number of issues raised when considering the bargaining solution which would seem to favour the 'polluter pays principle'.

- Those affected by pollution will often find it difficult to organise themselves. This is certainly the case in terms of those who suffer from transport-related pollution, since there may be so many individuals they will find it difficult to coordinate their activities and thus may not be able to offer the appropriate monetary amount in order to induce polluters to reduce their level of activity.
- Those who suffer from pollution may not have sufficient funds to compensate those who pollute for the cost of reducing pollution. As such, the optimum level of pollution consistent with a level of activity TA2 will not be attained.
- Certain individuals who suffer from transport-related pollution or noise may be reluctant to contribute to the monetary payout to the polluter, not because they are unconcerned about

the situation, but because they assume others will take responsibility and they will reap the benefits without paying a penny. They can be termed 'free-riders'.

- If polluters were aware of the fact that they would have to make payments to sufferers then it is likely they would curb their activities or would encourage research and development into more environmental friendly technology, such as quieter aero engines.

The success of the bargaining solution depends in part on the numbers involved, and even with two parties an agreement is not automatic. As such, the government may resort to alternative methods of dealing with the problem.

A tax-based solution

This would involve setting a price which places a monetary value on the environmental costs of transport using taxation and imposes these upon the polluter. Such a solution is likely to reduce the demand to travel and therefore the environmental impact.

In terms of the economic model in Figure 9.4, then, if an environmental tax of t (known as a Pigouvian tax, which is a tax imposed upon an externality) is imposed on the transport user/ operator/polluter it has the effect of shifting the MPB curve to MPB−t. The tax would be paid on each unit of pollution and the transport operator would now maximise their marginal private benefits at a level of activity equal to TA2. If the transport operator undertook a level of activity between TA2 and TA1 then the benefits received (in terms of profit) would be less than the amount of tax paid.

Using an environmental tax is a way of internalising the external cost and the tax of t can be viewed as the optimum tax.

The use of this kind of measure is based on the notion of the 'polluter-pays principle', with the polluter being responsible for the cost of measures to reduce pollution.

There are a number of advantages and disadvantages with the use of an environmental tax on the transport user/operator.

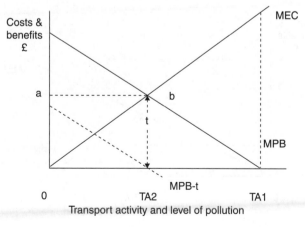

Figure 9.4 *Imposition of an environmental tax*

Advantages

- With an environmental tax, then, the road or air transport user or airport/airline operator has to pay a price for the pollution caused. As such, the polluter has an incentive to reduce their level of activity to the optimum level of TA2 in Figure 9.4.
- The introduction of an environmental tax allows the transport user/operator to decide how they will respond, unlike the use of a standard which sets a particular limit.

Disadvantages

- There may be difficulties in establishing the optimum tax of t, although in reality the aim may be to get as close to the optimum as possible. If the tax is underestimated then it may lead to a problem as illustrated in Figure 9.5 below.
- There are often political difficulties when introducing a new tax, say with a passenger tax on airline users. There may be resistance in that the belief is that the tax will be raised above t in Figure 9.4 once it is introduced – the tax being seen simply as a revenue-raising measure.

  In Figure 9.5, if the optimum tax rate t is established then there is no problem. This may not however be the case. The tax rate could have been set too low, say at t_1 and this could be problematic. At a tax t_1 then the level of transport activity would be TA3 and this would equate with an external cost of b which is higher than that at the social optimum of c. This may be acceptable, but if the MEC were to rise more sharply as with MEC2 then the MEC would be significantly larger at a, which may be far more problematic. What this scenario illustrates is that small miscalculations can result in far larger deficits.
- It could be argued that the transport user is penalised twice. First by virtue of the fact that the level of transport activity has been reduced from TA1 to TA2 in Figure 9.4 with the resulting loss in profit given by the triangle TA1TA2b, and second by having to pay tax equal to the area TA20ab.

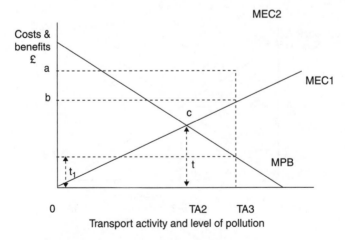

Figure 9.5 *The problem with underestimating the optimum tax rate*

Case study 9.4 Fuel tax

A fuel tax increase can be seen as a somewhat crude method for dealing with the problem of the environmental fall-out from transport. Their impact in the short run may be slight other than provoking a very short-term knee-jerk reaction to the increase in price. In the longer term however it could influence the choice of vehicles with a smaller engine capacity and a reconsideration of either the place of employment or residential location. In terms of Figure 9.6 following a rise in the price of fuel from P1 to P2 in Figure 3 the demand in the short run may reduce from Q1 to Q2, a movement from point a to point b along the short run demand curve (D_{SR}), as motorists use their car less. In the long run demand could reduce further to point c on D_{LR} with a quantity Q3 through the purchase of vehicles with smaller engines or because of the relocation of households to be nearer their work.

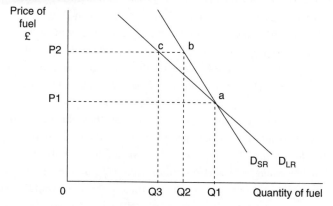

Figure 9.6   *The potential impact of an increase in fuel prices*

Clearly, the objective of fuel tax is not environmental even though as stated by the Royal Commission on Environmental Pollution (1994) that:

- The amount of tax paid varies with the environmental cost with the amount of fuel duty used in the main proportional to the amount of CO_2 emitted and (for any given vehicle) is closely reflected in the quantities of other substances emitted.
- It is simple to administer, it costs little to collect, is difficult to avoid or evade, and can easily be modified.
- Road users have discretion about how to respond: road users may respond either by reducing the number or length of their journeys or by reducing their use of fuel in other ways, such as switching to a smaller or more fuel-efficient vehicle or driving in a more fuel-efficient way.

Tradable permits

The idea behind tradable permits is that polluters are presented with a number of 'permits' which allow them to emit a particular level of CO_2. The number of permits which exist clearly limits the amount of emissions. The permits are tradable in that they can be bought and sold to other polluters who are participating in the particular tradable permits scheme. The basis of such a scheme is that those organisations who are able to achieve a lower level of emissions are then able to sell their superfluous permits to organisations that are not able to meet the emissions target set and are therefore forced to buy permits to emit if they do not want to curtail their activity.

The tradable permits market is illustrated in Figure 9.7. The body responsible for setting the level of pollution will issue a number of permits in line with a predetermined level of pollution, such as Qp, which at the level of demand would give a market price of Pp. If there is an increase in demand and thus a shift in the demand curve to the right then clearly the equilibrium price will increase. Figure 9.8 illustrates how the market operates in a hypothetical situation, with two airline operators A and B. In the figure airline operator A emits 100 thousand tonnes of CO_2 annually, and airline operator B emits 80 thousand tonnes of CO_2 annually. MAC refers to the marginal abatement cost curve and represents the additional cost to each airline operator of abating pollution. As can be seen operator A's curve is flatter than operator B's, thus abatement is more costly for B than it is for A, and as such there is a basis for trade in permits to take place between the two operators.

Without the existence of the permit scheme, then, 180 thousand tonnes of CO_2 would be emitted, namely 100 thousand tonnes from operator A and 80 thousand tonnes from operator B. If the body responsible for setting CO_2 emission targets wanted to see a 50 per cent reduction then this could be achieved by issuing 90 tradable permits. Allocation of those permits is an issue, but if they were issued based on previous emission levels, then operator A would receive 50 (one for each thousand tonnes) and operator B would receive 40 (also one for each thousand tonnes). Clearly the merits of allocation can be debated, but if this were the case then operator A would reduce its emissions to 50 thousand tonnes, and operator B to 40 thousand tonnes.

In order to conform to the reduced emissions levels, there will be a cost involved for both airlines, and this is known as the marginal abatement cost. This would include all aspects involved

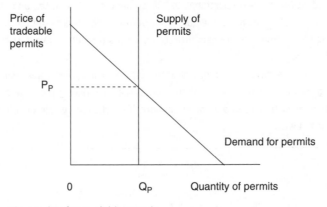

Figure 9.7 *The market for tradable permits*

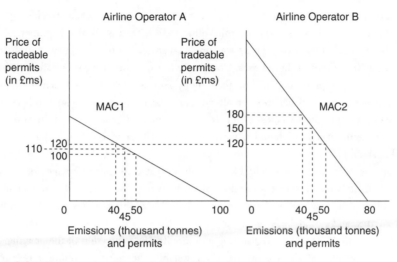

Figure 9.8   *The operation of a tradable permits scheme*

in conforming to the new standards as a consequence of the tighter restrictions placed on pollution levels. Say therefore that for airline operator A the total cost of cutting its emissions from its previous level of 100k tonnes to its 'new' level of 40k tonnes was £100m, then that would represent its marginal abatement cost (MAC). Furthermore, if we know the level of emissions at a zero MAC and at a level of 40k tonnes, then assuming a linear relationship we can sketch out the marginal abatement cost curve (MACC) for firm A. This is done on the left of Figure 9.8. Note however that in practice this would be a curve, and concaved towards the origin – hence as the level of pollution needed to be reduced by ever greater amounts, the relative increase in the marginal abatement cost would increase by far greater relative values. However, to return to our example, if we assume that the cost to airline operator B to reduce emissions from its current level of 80k tonnes down to its allocated permits of 40k tonnes to be £180m, again this represents its marginal abatement cost. By applying the same logic as above then again we can draw the marginal abatement cost curve for operator B, which is shown on the right of Figure 9.8 as MAC2. Due to the difference in the marginal abatement costs facing the two firms, there would thus be a basis for trade between the two operators. For example, say in the following time period operator B wished to increase its emissions (due to the profitability attached to them – see Figure 9.1) by 5k tonnes to 45k tonnes, then reading off the MACC it would be willing to pay up to £150m in order to do so. At that level, however, the MAC to A is £110m in order to bring its emissions down by 5k from the previous time period. It is therefore worthwhile for A to cut its emissions to 45k as the revenue they would earn from the sale of the excess permits (in this case 5k) to B would be in excess of what it would cost them in additional abatement costs. This is because B will buy these permits because the price will be lower than its own abatement costs at that level of emissions. The net difference between the two values therefore (£150m v £110m) represents the basis for the trade. This process of exchange will continue until the two MAC's are equal to each other. Referring to Figure 9.8 this would occur with the price of permits at £120m, hence operator A would emit 40k tonnes of CO_2 and operator B 50k tonnes of CO_2.

215

There are a number of issues that require careful consideration when developing a tradable permit scheme. First, how are the permits allocated? In terms of the hypothetical situation outlined above the allocation of permits was undertaken on the basis of current emission levels, each receiving 50 per cent of those levels. Companies however may have successfully reduced their levels of pollution, by investing in new technology and as such they are penalised for this by receiving a lower number of permits. An alternative measure could be equal numbers of permits to each participant, but the weakness of this is that they may differ in terms of the amount of CO_2 they currently emit. Second, should permits be freely allocated or should they be auctioned? Third, what should be the overall number of permits in circulation? It could be the case that the supply is greater than would be ideally liked simply so that company acceptance of the scheme is gained. Fourth, it is possible that a number of participants may corner the market in permits, making it difficult for new companies to enter a sector. If this situation developed it would act as a barrier to entry and could be seen as anti-competitive. Fifth, there are administrative costs involved in a scheme of this type, registering and monitoring ownership of the permits. Finally, a tradable permit scheme allows the owner of the permits the right to pollute, a permit to emit pollutants and this is possibly a strategy that can be questioned.

There are a number of advantages however with a scheme of this type:

Advantages
- A tradable permit scheme affords the companies that participate flexibility in terms of the way in which they address the reduction in their emissions. Do they reduce emissions by the manner in which they operate or do they purchase permits?
- Environmental taxes require polluters to pay for emissions, something they once undertook for free. As such, it might be politically easier to get companies to agree to a tradable permit scheme, since a new 'marketable' permit has been created.
- A tradable permit scheme is cost effective in that incentives are provided to address emission levels since lower abatement costs will allow permits to be sold whereas higher abatement costs require permits to be purchased.
- Unlike a Pigouvian tax which needs to estimate the cost of the pollution, with tradable permits it is the market (in tradable permits) that will find the optimum price.

The EU is operating what it calls an Emissions Trading Scheme (ETS), a scheme which is seen as a major economic instrument in addressing greenhouse gas (GHG) emissions. The scheme seeks to make sure that companies operating within specific sectors which are responsible for GHG emission, reduce their emissions or buy permits from other participants within the scheme with lower levels of emissions. The scheme commenced in January 2005 initially covering carbon dioxide (CO_2) emissions. The first phase ran from 2005 to 2007 covering companies of a certain size in sectors including energy (with activities such as oil refinery and coke ovens), production and processing of ferrous metals, the mineral industry (including cement, glass and ceramic bricks), pulp and paper. Overall in the region of 10,000 installations are included covering in the region of 50 per cent of the EU CO_2 emissions. Participants, or what are called installations, obtain their allowances (or permits) for free from the EU member states. The second phase began in 2008 and runs until 2012 and a number of non-EU member countries have joined. It is expected that the UK Treasury will auction off a percentage of their ETS permits rather than is currently the process of issuing them to companies based on their current emission levels. To date aviation has not been included in the ETS even though it represents 3 per cent of carbon dioxide emissions in the EU. The reason for this has been concern over the impact inclusion would have on the sectors' ability to compete in international markets. Aviation is however going to be included in the EU ETS from 2012.

The setting of standards

Whilst not an economic instrument, it is important to introduce the notion of setting standards, since these form a major part of environmental policy and can have a considerable impact on the economics of transport. Polices such as the requirement for an annual vehicle inspection for road trucks and private vehicles (with the latter known as the MOT test in the UK) and vehicle exhaust emissions tests or limits on noise from aircraft come under this category.

Setting a standard of S1 would achieve the optimum level of transport activity TA2 in Figure 9.9. If achieved this would result in the optimum level of pollution. Clearly as with taxation it could be the case that the standard has been incorrectly set. It could be too harsh, thus a point to the left of S1, or too lenient, a point to the right of S1. Not only does the standard have to be set correctly but the penalty for not meeting the standard has to be established. The optimum penalty will be Penalty 1, for if a penalty such as Penalty 2 were to be set then the polluter would be tempted to pollute up to TA3 because the penalty (if ever administered) would be less than the level of additional satisfaction obtained between TA2 and TA3.

Technological change

This can take a number of forms. First, transport emissions of carbon monoxide have been reduced through technology-related initiatives such as cleaner fuels with reduced carbon content, cleaner, more efficient car engines and electrified public transport. Catalytic converters fitted to petrol-driven cars have reduced emissions in pollutants such as nitrogen oxide and benzene and in the UK new cars are 10 per cent more fuel efficient, on average, than they were 10 years ago. In addition,

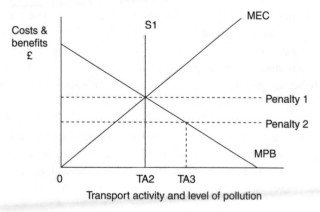

Figure 9.9 *Setting a standard*

in the UK, by 2010 as part of the Renewable Transport Fuels Obligation 5 per cent of fuel sold in the transport sector will have to come from renewable sources.

Second, technological advances have improved the ways in which individuals can make choices about transport modes, through in-car information and real-time information at public transport stops.

Third, through video conferencing meetings can be undertaken without the need to travel. This is also another aspect of technological change which leads to a reduction in transport emissions.

In the figures illustrated above it is hoped that technological change will have the effect of reducing the gradient of the MEC curve.

Promotion of alternative modes of transport

This policy option involves encouraging alternative modes such as public transport, walking, cycling, rail freight and shipping. The private car has the advantage of convenience and flexibility whereas public transport tends to be confined to fixed routes. As will be seen in Chapter 12, much the same applies with respect to road haulage in the carriage of freight in comparison to the other available modes. Measures can be undertaken in order to make public transport more competitive through things like dedicated bus lanes; however, as we have seen the options with regard to freight transport alternatives to road haulage are far more limited and problematic.

Trams are in many respects a more environmentally-friendly, although expensive, alternative to the private car. In recent years a large number of UK towns and cities and other European cities have invested in the tram, such as Croydon, Manchester, Nottingham and Sheffield in respect of Britain and Karlsruhe, Grenoble, Bordeaux and Genoa on the European continent. Improved cycling and walking facilities are also seen as an important alternative to the private car. The aim of providing alternatives to the private car is to reduce the gradient of the MEC curve in the figures above.

CHAPTER SUMMARY AND REFLECTION

The aim of this chapter has been to highlight the link between the macro economy and the environment and the impact of transport on that relationship. It has detailed a number of transport emissions and the effect that they have in terms of individual health and on a more global scale. The chapter has used economic theory in order to analyse the relationship between transport and the environment. This has allowed various policy options to be studied. In terms of the bargaining solution, although theoretically attractive, it raised a number of issues in terms of the practicalities of implementation. The tax-based solution also raised issues not least in terms of establishing the optimum tax although it would allow the transport operators/users to decide how they respond. Tradable permits also allow flexibility and may also be politically easier for the market to accept. The measure too has issues not least in terms of the allocation of merits, whether they should be issued free or auctioned, their supply and administration. Alternatives, namely the setting of standards, technological change and the promotion of alternatives, have also been examined.

CHAPTER EXERCISES

Exercise 9.1 The use of an environmental tax

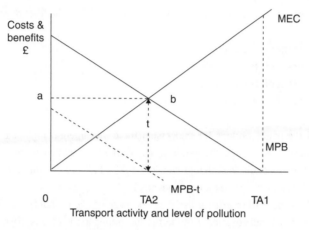

Figure 9.10   *The use of an environmental tax*

Use Figure 9.10 in answering the following questions:

a) If the transport activity carried on at TA1 following the imposition of a tax equal to t, then how much tax would be paid by the polluter?

b) Why will the polluter reduce their transport activity level to TA2 from TA1 following the imposition of an environmental tax?

c) What is the external cost saving to be made by reducing transport activity from TA1 to TA2?

d) What will be the implication if tax is set at a level greater than t?

e) Why is zero output unacceptable from an economic perspective?

Exercise 9.2 Trends and implications

Based on Tables 9.1, 9.2 and 9.3:

a) Outline the trends in terms of traffic at airports, the forecast for air traffic demand and pollution emissions from transport and other end users.

b) In terms of Tables 9.1 and 9.2 what are the likely implications both at the local and global level?

c) Based on the information to be found in Chapter 13 on forecasting the demand for transport services, outline the difficulties inherent in forecasting air traffic demand.

d) Referring to Table 9.3, outline what you think are the reasons for the trends presented in terms of road transport and civil aircraft.

e) What do you see as the advantages and disadvantages of the various options for addressing the environmental impact of transport.

Exercise 9.3 Is it really road haulage that is bad for the environment?

Reconsider Case study 9.3 and then attempt the following questions:

a) Who is responsible for the large increase in road haulage transport that has occurred over the last 50 years?

b) How would we start to estimate the costs involved in reducing the level of road haulage by:

    i 20 per cent of its current level

    ii 50 per cent of its current level

    iii 80 per cent of its current level

    iv Who would have to pay for these reductions?

c) In terms of the policy options for addressing the environmental impact of transport on the environment outlined in this chapter, how would these be applied to road haulage? Note in addressing this question, you should consider that what you do not want to produce is an overnight collapse of the road haulage industry!

d) Of all of the substitution effects listed in the case study, probably the most far reaching would be locational substitution. Outline the full implications of this effect, both in terms of society and the economy.

e) This case only considered the impact of addressing a long-term modal shift at a national level; however, in today's global economy such unilateral action is simply not feasible. How might long-term change be brought about internationally? (Note: you may wish to briefly view the first part of Chapter 12 on the internationalisation of freight transport before considering this issue.)

Transport regulation and ownership

INTRODUCTION

In many respects this chapter is concerned with 'control' and specifically the control by relevant transport authorities on the levels and behaviour of transport users and operators under their authority. Whilst at first sight this may appear to be only related to public transport, it concerns all areas of transport, whether that be public, private or freight. Government control of transport markets can be achieved through one of two measures – in the first instance the transport authority can own the assets and the means of production. In this case the market is brought into the public sector and thus it does not have to operate along market principles. This it would mainly do in the pursuit of the public interest. This however is not the only reason for public ownership, and others are examined later in the chapter. Alternatively, rather than control through ownership the authority could exhibit its control through direct command, i.e. by telling operators what to do. This would be through regulation of the market, which again would be undertaken on the premise of the public interest, although once more other reasons exist for regulation.

The chapter begins by examining the different forms of regulation before going on to look at the issues surrounding ownership and operation of transport assets by public bodies. It then considers different ownership forms in transport activities and outlines the various models under which transport services are delivered to the market. In some ways, regulation is a lesser form of ownership, and thus examining regulation first gives a better understanding and leads into the issues surrounding public ownership.

FORMS OF TRANSPORT REGULATION

The main forms of transport regulation can be generally categorised under the broad headings of qualitative and quantitative regulation.

Qualitative regulation

Currently most forms of movement, irrespective if a mode of transport is involved or not, constitutes regulated behaviour. This is for the simple reason that all forms of movement, if completely unchecked, can result in potentially hazardous outcomes, particularly where others are involved. Even the simple act of walking can result in broken limbs and scraped knees. Individuals therefore need to be able to move around with a reasonable level of confidence that this will not result in serious injury to either themselves or to others. If this was not the case, many individuals would simply not travel at all. This is the basic rationale for qualitative regulation.

Qualitative regulation therefore is where the regulatory authority intervenes in the market in order to stipulate minimum criteria that regulate behaviour within the market. This tends to come in the form of direct legislative measures that lay down the laws to be followed by users of the transport system. Such actions need to be enforced and breach of any of rules penalised, either through financial penalties or by the withdrawal of the right to use the system. Thus speed restrictions for example are a form of qualitative regulation, as these regulate the speed of vehicles on the roads, with different speed limits applying to different types of roads. Breach of those rules will normally result in the imposition of a financial penalty, whilst a continuous breach of speed limits leads to the withdrawal of the driver's licence. The same type of conditions apply to operators of public transport services or road haulage operators, where there are clear minimum criteria relating to driver behaviour and vehicle condition and a major breach of these rules can lead to the suspension or removal of the operators' licence.

Quantitative (Economic) regulation

Quantitative regulation, more commonly known as economic regulation, is where the regulatory bodies intervene in the market in order to place economic controls on the operation of the market. This is either in terms of restrictions with regard to the price or restrictions or minimum specifications with regard to the supply. Dealing firstly with price regulation, this comes in a number of different forms:

Specify the price to be charged

In theory, this is the simplest form of price regulation and is illustrated in Figure 10.1.

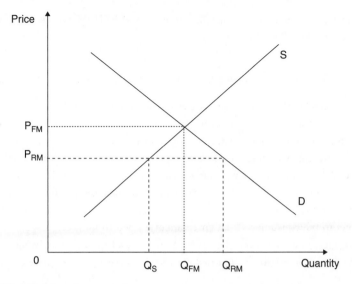

Figure 10.1 *Simple price regulation*

In the figure, the free market price is given where supply equals demand, hence P_{FM}. The transport authority however sets a maximum price below the equilibrium price at P_{RM}. Note it only makes sense to set a regulated maximum price below the equilibrium price, otherwise it would have absolutely no impact on the market. As can also be seen from Figure 10.1, however, a price at the regulated fare will create excess demand, i.e. there will be more wanting to use the service than is being supplied to the market. This is shown by the difference between Q_{RM} and Q_S. The authority would therefore have to address this problem. What it would have to ensure is that the supply curve moved to the right. This can be done in several ways, with the 'simple' solution being to pay the operator a subsidy. Alternatively the whole rationale for imposing a maximum fare may be to motivate the operator to lower its cost. Hence the supply curve would shift to the right thereby eradicating the excess demand. In practice this has normally been done over time by regulating price increases, as outlined below.

Specify the maximum increase in price allowed

Rather than state a specific price, the authority limits the extent to which the operator can increase its prices over time. In the UK this has normally been done through an 'RPI-X%' formula, where RPI relates to the prevailing rate of inflation and X the value to which price increases are restricted to. Hence in theory prices should rise at lower than the rate of inflation, thereby falling in real terms. Hence if the rate of inflation is 3 per cent, and X is set at 2 per cent, then the maximum fares can rise by is 1 per cent. In real terms, therefore, this would be a 2 per cent cut in the fare. As stated above, this would primarily be used to motivate efficiency improvements, as it is only through reducing costs, and not increasing prices, that operators can maintain or increase profitability.

Nevertheless, where price increases are expected to rise by well in excess of the rate of inflation, these can be limited through an 'RPI+X%' formula. Thus fares on most of the rail franchises in Britain are currently regulated on the basis of RPI+1% with some of the franchises allowed to raise fares by RPI+3%.

Regulate the (final) price through the tax charged on the good or service

Varying tax levels can be used to regulate the price in the market, and these can be specified either as a percentage or set at a specific value. In most case such taxes are used as general tax-raising measures in which the government acquires public finance to spend on the provision of public services. In the UK, for example, all goods except exempt items are charged Value Added Tax (VAT) at a rate of 17.5 per cent. Hence this adds 17.5 per cent to the price of the good with this additional tax revenue passed on to the government. Additional or specific taxes however may be imposed to regulate the price in the market, thus fuel duty has the effect of significantly increasing the price of fuel to the consumer. If the government wished to limit car usage, it could do so by increasing fuel duty, thus increasing the price. As seen in Chapter 9, this would be a form of a 'Pigouvian' tax, which is one that is imposed in order to correct for a negative externality.

Specify the rate of return (profit) to be gained

Prices charged by transport operators can be regulated based upon the level of profit to be gained. Hence a 'reasonable' rate of return may be set and then prices regulated accordingly to achieve that rate of return. This will normally take place where the level of demand can be estimated to a very high level of accuracy, and hence the only real variation in total revenue will be as a result of the price charged. Network Rail for example is regulated by the Office of Rail Regulation with regard to the level of track access charges it imposes on the train and freight operating companies on this basis. The charge is based upon a rate of return on the assets employed. Given that the level of train movements on the network are known a year in advance, then the level of revenue gained can be accurately predicted by the price. This however is a considerable oversimplification of the problem, as obviously operating costs as well as efficiency gains also need to be estimated in advance. If efficiency gains are not taken into account, then the level of the access charge, or fare in more general terms, would be set at a rate that would provide a higher level of profits than had been deemed to be a 'fair' return. In order to fully illustrate these principles, the whole issue of regulating the former British infrastructure provider, Railtrack, is covered in more depth in Case study 10.1.

Through introducing yardstick competition

Yardstick competition exists where direct competition in the market is not feasible but is introduced indirectly through regulation, and is normally used to control price levels. This is achieved by linking the performance of different firms in different markets to each other. If it was conceived today, therefore, 'yardstick' competition would probably be termed 'benchmark' competition, as effectively the performance of each firm in the industry is benchmarked against one another. As an example, if two firms A and B faced similar cost and market conditions, then under yardstick competition the price that A could charge would be dependent upon the level of costs in firm B. Thus if B was to lower its costs, the result would be that under the regulatory system A would be forced into charging a lower price in its market and vice-versa. Such regulatory measures are said to be appropriate where the potential for cost savings is unknown and difficult to estimate in either market, and where cost and demand conditions in each market are very similar. Exercise 10.2 explores further some of the ideas behind yardstick competition.

These are the five main mechanisms through which the price charged in the market can be controlled; however, price regulation is only one form of economic regulation. The other main form is where the level of available capacity is controlled through regulatory measures, normally in the form of specification of minimum frequencies and/or through the control of market entry.

Specify a minimum frequency

In the simple case the authority specifies the minimum level of frequency to be provided. This will normally be in the form of actual frequencies and operating hours; however, it can take other forms such as total vehicle kilometres supplied. This is shown below in Figure 10.2.

In the figure the free market position is shown by supply curve S and demand curve D. In this case no market would exist for this transport service as the highest price that consumers are willing to pay, as shown by the demand curve, is below the lowest price that suppliers would be willing to provide a service, as shown by the supply curve. There is no market equilibrium and thus no transport service is provided. In this case, the transport authority specifies a minimum service frequency in order to create a regulated market where none existed before. This is set at level Q_R. Note however that such action taken on its own would be entirely pointless; even if an operator did, for whatever unwise reason, enter the market it would quickly go out of business as the level of demand would be insufficient to support the level of supply. As with simple price regulation, therefore, such regulatory action cannot be taken on its own. The regulatory authority would need to have some belief that supply will increase and result in a shift of the supply curve from S to S_1.

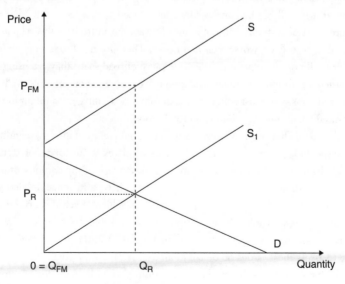

Figure 10.2   Simple quantity regulation

Thus it may again pay a subsidy or alternatively 'package' the non-existent service with other more profitable routes and put these out to tender to the highest bidder.

Limit market entry

We have already seen in Chapter 7 the legal control of market entry as a barrier to entry, but it is one that would usually be imposed in transport markets as a form of capacity regulation. This is where the regulatory authority will set clear limits on those operating in the market and thereby directly restrict supply. Taxi services in most locations are a good example of this form of regulation, where the regulating authority sets a limit on the number of licences issued. Such measures were originally imposed to avoid street congestion and to limit the competition to public transport services.

The rationale for the regulation of transport services

In most cases regulations, both qualitative and quantitative, are imposed due to some form of market failure, with the main reasons outlined below.

To overcome the market failure of imperfect/dissymmetry of information

The first rationale for the regulation of transport services covers most forms of qualitative regulation, where these are imposed in order to regulate user behaviour and to impose minimum standards on the operation of the transport system. This is directly to overcome the market failure of imperfect information, or more generally because a dissymmetry of information exists where some know more than others. In many ways this is akin to the view that every other driver on the road is an idiot apart from me, and in many ways, there is actually some truth in that statement. In general, users of a transport system need to have a level of confidence in others' movements in order to feel more secure when undertaking their own. Hence when walking on the pavement, pedestrians need to feel reasonably assured they will not be run over by a high-speed vehicle. Similarly, drivers need to feel reasonably assured that pedestrians will not aimlessly walk out in front of the vehicle, hence causing them to swerve dangerously or, worse, run them over! They also need to have confidence in the fact that other drivers will not attempt to use the same piece of road space they are using at that point in time, hence causing a collision. Through regulating behaviour, e.g. you can only walk on pavements, you must obey road signs, you must adhere to maximum speed limits etc, a minimum overall level of behaviour is assured when moving around and total chaos avoided.

Not only individual behaviour however needs to be regulated, but also the condition of vehicles used in the transportation of people and freight. This relates to all forms of transport, private, public and freight haulage, and through this a minimum standard of the equipment used is ensured. None of us when boarding a bus, or an airline, or a train, have sufficient knowledge to be able to assess the skills of the driver/pilot or the condition of the vehicle. Even if we did, the practicalities of doing so would make the whole system completely unworkable. Such knowledge however is not necessary, as that is one of the main functions of the regulatory authorities. They have the skills and the knowledge to assess these issues on behalf of all users of the transport service. In simple terms, qualitative regulation overcomes the market failure of imperfect information and makes the whole system work.

The market can no longer regulate itself

If the market can no longer regulate itself, then external regulation is required to ensure that economic efficiency is achieved. Why this occurs is because most transport industries tend towards anti-competitive market structures, namely monopoly and oligopoly, hence regulation is required to attempt to minimise the disadvantages associated with such market structures.

To correct for externalities

Even where the market can regulate itself through strong competitive pressures, it may still not produce the 'right' answer in terms of modal splits that maximise economic welfare. This is due to the high level of externalities present in transport markets, hence all decisions are based on private costs and benefits and do not take into consideration the wider implications of these decisions. As a result the 'wrong' society maximising decision is reached. External intervention in the form of regulation, which although a further breach of the conditions of perfect competition, is required to rectify this situation on the basis that two 'wrongs' will make one 'right'. The extent to which this has been successful or not in actual transport markets is considered later in the chapter.

To ensure the quality of the service provided

Ensuring the quality of service provided in the market relates directly to qualitative controls on the standards of service to be provided. Whilst relating to 'qualitative' controls, however, most of these are imposed through economic and not qualitative regulatory measures. Thus for example in Britain, Statutory Bus Quality Partnerships are agreements between the local authority and the bus operators, where the local authority can limit entry to the market to only those bus companies that meet the vehicle standards specified in the agreement. Other examples exist where the quality of service is regulated even more directly. British passenger rail franchises agreements for example specify the minimum level of service to be provided and the investments in new rolling stock to be made by the operator over the course of the franchise.

Regulation may also be used to ensure the quality of service in the longer term. For example market entry may be restricted in order to provide market protection and hence maintain the profitability of those already in the market. It is out of profits that investments are funded; hence restricting entry gives current operators the business confidence to make future investments in new vehicle stock and thus maintain or improve quality levels. A similar reason may be to protect the livelihood of those in the industry. The most well-known example is the EU's Common Agricultural Policy, which was originally conceived to lend support to farmers within the industry through regulating the prices of agricultural produce. Regulated prices were set above the market price in order to ensure future livelihoods and thus the future of the industry.

To provide a transport service where none existed before

Rather than leave entirely to the free market, transport authorities may decide to intervene and package routes in order to ensure that all necessary services are provided. It may therefore restrict entry on certain (profitable) routes in exchange for the protected operator providing services on unprofitable routes. This is known as cross subsidisation, where the revenue earned from profitable services is used to fund the losses incurred on unprofitable routes. Whilst such measures prevent the cherry picking of 'good' routes and can provide a far more overall balance in the provision of transport services, there are generally far better measures that can be used to ensure that all necessary services are provided. This is a topic that is developed further in the next chapter.

To improve efficiency within the industry

As outlined above, the regulatory framework can be used in an attempt to bring about efficiency improvements within the industry, normally through restraining price increases. This was a measure that was extensively applied in the British privatisation programme of the 1980s, where charges relating to telecommunications, electricity, gas, water and so on were carefully monitored by an industry specific regulator. After privatisation, rail fares in Britain were also regulated on an RPI − X% basis, where X first equalled zero and then subsequently one. These measures are used to not only instigate efficiency improvements, but also to ensure that productivity improvements result in lower consumer prices rather than higher shareholder dividends. As noted above, however, the British rail franchises are now regulated on an RPI+X% formula, which hardly provides an incentive to improve efficiency but has been introduced for other reasons mainly surrounding investments in rolling stock.

The drawbacks of economic regulation

We have looked above at the rationale behind the regulation of transport activities; however, it does not always result in the desired outcomes and has a number of drawbacks.

Limits free enterprise

Often cited as the biggest drawback of economic regulation, the issue of the limitation of free enterprise was often put forward as a reason for the removal of economic regulatory measures during the enterprise culture of the 1980s. Acting out of self interest, whether that be at a company or at an individual level, is said to be a far stronger motivator to 'do the right thing' than a regulator acting in the public interest. This is related to the free market ideology of consumer sovereignty, where those that profit most are those that are able to give the consumer what they want. In a transport context, the argument would be that not only would an entrepreneur be far better positioned to identify users' needs and provide services users want, but also would be far more motivated to do so by the profit motive, i.e. direct benefit to themselves. This contrasts with a regulatory authority that would plan such networks at a distance and be motivated by the public interest, i.e. simply doing the job they are employed to do. Closely related to limiting free enterprise, regulated markets are said to also limit innovation, as it dampens the free enterprise spirit. This is because there are clear limitations imposed upon the market and consequently less room for the operator to use entrepreneurial flair and innovative solutions in the provision of transport services.

Inefficient, second best solution

As will be developed further in the next chapter on subsidy, issues of subsidy and regulation are what are termed 'second best solutions'. The best solution is that the market itself regulates the performance of operators. This would be an internal/automatic type of regulation. As we saw in Chapter 6 with perfect competition, any operator that cannot offer services at the lowest price and produce these at the lowest possible cost will be driven out of business, hence the market regulates itself. The problem with an external regulatory body is that this leads to added costs in the operation of the market, as the administrative burden of the regulatory mechanism adds to the overall cost of providing the service. The annual costs of running the Office of Rail Regulation (ORR) in the UK for example came to a total of £30.5m in financial year 2007/8 (ORR, 2008). Whilst these are not all additional costs, as for example if the ORR did not exist then a number of its duties would need to be amalgamated into other government bodies, a large part of it is, particularly those concerning economic regulation. Thus transport services are provided at a higher cost due to increased administration costs.

Also under this heading is the time issue, and in particular the time gap between changes in market conditions and changes in the provision of services. It has often been argued that due to the added layer of regulatory bureaucracy, a regulated market does not act as quickly as the free market in responding to changing conditions in demand and supply. A classic case of this would be the bus industry in Britain, where during the period of the bus wars (see Case studies 6.1 and 8.2) a large number of mergers and acquisitions were referred to the relevant regulatory body, in this case the Monopolies and Mergers Commission. By that time, however, the act of merger/acquisitions had already occurred, hence many of these referrals ended in purely nominal measures and the upholding of the merger. Cowie (2002) for example highlights that of 33 cases referred to the Monopolies and Mergers Commission[1] between 1986 and 1998, only 3 resulted in dissolution of the merged company.

Asymmetry of information

In order to regulate efficiently, the regulator needs a high level of information in order to plan and control operations. Whilst sounding obvious, the major drawback with this is that the regulator will undoubtedly be the authority and not the operator, and hence the operator, unsurprisingly, knows more about their own business than the regulator does. There is therefore a need for a flow of high quality information between the two. It may however be in the interests of the operator to withhold important information from the regulator if they believe this may be used against them. There is thus an imbalance of information, with the operator often holding the key information that the regulator needs to regulate effectively.

The issue of regulatory capture

The theory of regulatory capture was originally put forward by George Stigler (1971) and after the negative effect on entrepreneurial flair is often cited as the second biggest drawback of economic regulation. The issue of regulatory capture is where the regulator, who is supposed to oversee and control the industry on the grounds of the public interest, is in effect not as 'tough' on the industry as they perhaps should be in the public interest. The consequences are that the regulator better serves the interests of the industry than the interests of the consumer. Whilst the term 'capture' suggests that the regulator is enticed in some manner, 'capture' also refers to capture with regard to the prestige that goes with being an industry regulator. In simple terms, the status and overall prestige of the regulator rises with the importance of the industry. What happens therefore is that instead of regulating the industry, the regulator becomes the protector of the industry. A more direct form of regulatory capture is where the regulator becomes dominated by the vested interests in the industry, where political pressure may be applied from above forcing the regulator to take a 'soft' stance in regulation of the industry.

Cumbersome regulatory procedures make avoidance of regulatory measures possible

This is the most basic drawback of regulation where it simply fails to regulate the actions or behaviour it is designed to regulate through avoidance. This is because regulatory measures are by their very nature cumbersome processes that can be avoided or ignored by those they are designed to affect. As a result, the expected outcomes are not achieved. Case study 10.1 shows how difficult and costly it can be to regulate an industry, and such cumbersome processes can make it very difficult to get it 'right'. An obvious example is the issue of the regulation of rail fares highlighted above. These were initially regulated on the basis of RPI-0%, thus in theory rail fares should not have risen above the rate of inflation, and fallen in real terms when the base moved to RPI-1%. Nevertheless, the process used to regulate fares was, and still is, to have a collection of 'regulated' fares and 'unregulated' fares. Hence train companies are at liberty to increase the price fares of unregulated fares. More obviously, given the diverse range of train tickets available for a given journey, companies were at liberty to withdraw lower fare tickets, hence effectively bypassing the regulatory mechanism and increasing the price of the rail ticket above the rate of inflation.

Note that whilst these major drawbacks of regulation have been listed separately, they all in some form relate to the issue of it being a second best solution – in simple terms, the only problem with regulation is that it is needed at all. If there are thus problems with regulating the market for transport services, the alternative is to take it into public ownership. The issues surrounding the public ownership of transport assets are considered after Case study 10.1, which attempts to put some of the issues outlined into practice through examining the process of regulating the British rail infrastructure provider.

Case study 10.1 The practicalities of industry regulation – regulating the British railway infrastructure provider

Whilst in theory the process of regulation can appear reasonably straightforward, the practice is almost always far more complicated. This case study attempts to illustrate this through the examination of regulatory mechanisms surrounding the former British railway infrastructure provider, the private sector company Railtrack.

Under British rail privatisation, the single nationalised operator, British Rail, was divided into 104 separate companies with the main purpose to introduce competition at all levels of railway operation. Competition would exist not only between train operators in the passenger and freight sectors, but also between industry suppliers. Thus there were three rolling stock leasing companies and 14 infrastructure maintenance and renewal companies. The one exception was the infrastructure provider, where it was considered that the advantages of having a single national network operator significantly outweighed the drawbacks of splitting the network up into separate geographical areas. This therefore left a monopoly provider of the infrastructure throughout the country. This was organised into a company called Railtrack which was floated on the stock exchange. The company was expected to operate primarily on a commercial basis; hence all infrastructure access charges were to be at full cost. As a result, the firm would return a profit and receive no direct subsidy except to assist the funding of railway investment.

Being in a monopoly position, therefore, the access charges levied on the train-operating and freight-operating companies required to be regulated in order to avoid abuse of this market position. The Office of the Rail Regulator (ORR) was thus established as an independent regulator to oversee the market actions of the infrastructure provider, Railtrack. This however was not only in terms of the access charge levied on train companies but also to ensure that the conditions under which Railtrack had gained its network licence, which gave the company the right to be the infrastructure provider, were upheld. The ORR was thus empowered to set the contractual and financial framework under which Railtrack operated the network, ensure that the company carried out its activities efficiently and finally had an obligation to see that the company was adequately funded to enable it to discharge its responsibilities effectively. This in many respects underlines the balancing act that a regulator has to achieve between the needs of the company and the needs of the customer. The company needs to have sufficient profits to be in a position to undertake investments whilst at the same time leaving a reasonable level of profits to satisfy shareholders in the form of dividends. This would tend to suggest higher prices, whilst the interests of the consumer are obviously best served by lower prices. The regulator therefore needs to set a price that strikes a 'fair' balance between these two parties. In this particular case, however, the situation is further complicated by the indirect payment of subsidy. Although Railtrack was not directly subsidised, its principal customers, the train-operating companies, were, and in most cases to fairly substantial amounts. Failure to regulate correctly therefore could have serious knock-on effects in terms of the whole industry supply, i.e. increase subsidy, and the imposition of financial penalties difficult to impose given the contrasting nature of the responsibilities of the regulator, i.e. to regulate Railtrack and ensure it had sufficient funds for investment.

Figure 10.3 illustrates the independent nature of the rail regulator in the privatised rail industry structure created by the Railways Act 1993. Whilst OPRAF was delegated responsibility for the awarding and the overseeing of the passenger rail franchises (and hence was directly accountable to the DfT), the Office of the Rail Regulator was an independent body outside of the direct control of government. It could therefore, in theory at least, act in the public interest without fear of political interference or pressure.

How therefore was regulation to be achieved?
The key to the whole regulatory structure was centred upon the setting of the access charge to be paid by the train- and freight-operating companies. This would then ensure that sufficient revenue was raised through the charge to cover operating and maintenance costs, depreciation charges and provide a return on capital (i.e. profit) of 8 per cent, which was the agreed form of regulation. The 8 per cent rate of return and depreciation charges were set on Railtrack's

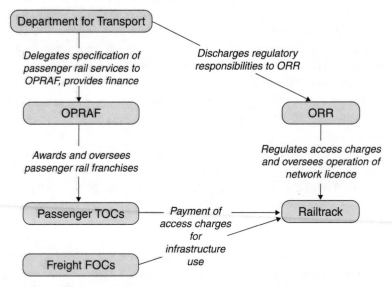

Figure 10.3 *Rail industry regulatory structure 1997–2001*

Regulatory Asset Base (the RAB), which in simple terms was a list and valuation of all assets to be included for regulatory purposes in order to determine the level of profit. Valuation of the RAB was initially based upon a Modern Equivalent Asset Value (MEAV), in other words how much would it cost to replace all the assets in the RAB? This by and large was a highly questionable basis from which to value the asset base (Stittle, 2002), and most agreed one that would produce an artificially high valuation and consequently an over-inflated profit. For the purposes of regulation, the RAB was to be revalued every five years, which divided the regulatory periods into the first control period, running from 1995 to 2001, the second control period from 2001 to 2006 and the third control period from 2006 to 2010.

To recap, therefore, in order to set the access charge the regulator needed to calculate the 8 per cent return on capital (the RAB), estimate Railtrack's operating and maintenance costs over 5 years and its depreciation charges over these periods. Around that basic figure then arose questions of Railtrack's investment needs, its borrowing requirements (and more importantly associated interest payments) and its possible efficiency gains (see next paragraph). This would then produce a figure that amounted to Railtrack's financial requirements over the 5-year period. In (very) simple terms, this would then be divided by total track usage to derive the access charge. Through such a pricing regime, therefore, the infrastructure provider would recover the full cost of the use of the network and its investment requirements to which it would add an 8 per cent mark up for its profit – sound simple?

During the process of regulating Railtrack several highly contentious points arose. The first concerned Railtrack's investment needs. If Railtrack was to be regulated on the basis of an 8 per cent rate of return on capital, then higher investment needs would push up depreciation charges and interest payments, and thus if not properly accounted for would literally eat into the 8 per cent rate of return. This debate also included questions over the cost of capital to Railtrack, as higher costs of capital would again reduce profit if not appropriately accounted for. The second and perhaps greatest disagreement between the ORR and Railtrack was over the issue of efficiency gains. Again if Railtrack was to be regulated on the basis of profit, then the question of the extent to which Railtrack could lower its unit operating costs over time became crucial. As mentioned above, this is because the level of access charges required to produce the 8 per cent return needed to be set in advance, and if efficiency gains were not taken into account then even modest improvements would increase the level of profit and push it above the 8 per cent regulated limit. The regulator therefore commissioned an independent report from NERA to examine the potential for efficiency gains in the infrastructure provider. One of the problems facing any such assessment however was a lack of empirical evidence of other systems, as very few rail systems at the time had such a vertical separation of infrastructure from services. Nevertheless NERA (2000) estimated potential efficiency gains of between 3.3 to 3.9 per cent per annum. Railtrack on the other hand, in their own evaluation (Railtrack, 1999), forecast significantly lower efficiency gains of around 1.5 per cent per annum (Railtrack, 1999). A second group of consultants, Booz, Allen and Hamilton (BAH), were then commissioned by the ORR to examine Railtrack's own estimates. BAH (1999) derived a target figure of between 4 and 5 per cent for efficiency gains for Railtrack in the period 2001–2006. Other stakeholders, notably the freight companies, also commissioned a separate report into potential cost savings in the provision of the infrastructure company, and one that estimated potential efficiency gains of a higher order, at around 6 to 7 per cent (LEK, 2000). In very broad terms therefore, there were three estimates of Railtrack's potential efficiency gains, ranging from 1.5 per cent (Railtrack), around 4 to 5 per cent (ORR commissioned studies) and finally 6 to 7 per cent (a Railtrack 'customer'). Eventually, the efficiency target was set at 3.6 per cent per annum (Pollitt and Smith, 2002).

One of the problems however was that Railtrack had effectively very little control over its own costs. Under the structure created at privatisation, sub-contractors carried out all of Railtrack's maintenance and renewals. This was further compounded by a loss of railway engineering expertise in the company that could either evaluate the need for the work or the standard of the work completed. Thus most efficiency gains were not under the direct control of Railtrack but rather were dependent upon the structure created on privatisation delivering a competitive market in rail infrastructure maintenance and renewal.

To worsen problems, a train derailed at Hatfield resulting in four fatalities and seventy injuries. This was as a result of a broken rail that had been known for some time to be 'at risk'. The fear that more rails on other parts of the network might be similarly affected led to the imposition of temporary speed restrictions in many parts of the network whilst these were checked, resulting in widespread disruption. Under the terms of the track access agreements, Railtrack then had to pay more than £500m to the train-operating companies as a result of the disruption caused. This combined with major cost overruns on the company's major infra-structure project at the time, the upgrade of the west coast mainline between London and Glasgow, led to the company being placed in administration by the then Minister for Transport in October 2001.

This case study not only shows some of the difficulties with industry regulation, but also the failure of Railtrack raises the question if this was a case of regulatory failure? In other words, did Railtrack fail due to failure of the regulator to sufficiently protect it and enable it to continue in profitable operation? Whilst regulatory failure can come in a variety of guises, such as regulatory capture highlighted in the text, Lodge (2002) only finds some evidence of what is known as regulatory 'drift'. This occurs when there has been an insufficient upholding of the policy by the regulator. In this case, this was as a result of agenda selection where certain areas of the regulator's remit were overly focused upon at the expense of other aspects which were also under the regulator's control. Lodge, however, suggests that the failure of Railtrack was more as a result of a far more complicated and widespread set of circumstances, many of which are connected to the general reform of public transport services. In simple terms, implementing reforms into transport markets is not easy.

THE ISSUE OF OWNERSHIP IN TRANSPORT MARKETS

If you have read the book up to this point, then you should realise by now that transport markets except with one or two exceptions cannot be left entirely to market forces to resolve economic transport issues. In most cases, therefore, they need some form of external intervention in order to correct for market failures. One way that this can be achieved, as seen above, is through regulation of the market. The alternative is far more direct and is where the state effectively takes control of the market by bringing it into state ownership. The market therefore does not have to follow market principles, i.e. be subject to the forces of supply and demand, nevertheless the economics of the whole operation still need to add up.

Reasons for the public ownership of transport assets

The issue therefore of ownership within transport markets in most cases comes down to the simple choice of whether services should be provided by the public sector or a regulated private sector. The 'old' view was that transport services, both passenger and freight, were vital services to the national and local economies that they served. Rather than questions surrounding issues such as the standard of service to be provided or the fare to be charged being left to the private sector to decide, these should be resolved by the state on the basis of the public interest. The 'best' way to achieve this was through direct ownership and control of the assets required to produce such services. This view is best exemplified with what eventually developed into the 'Morrisonian model' of public ownership, named after one of the leading Labour politicians of the time, Herbert Morrison. In the early 1930s, London's public transport services comprised of buses, trams and the underground, and all operated as individual transport modes by 89 mainly private sector operators. Morrison's view was that these individual services could only be fully exploited (in terms of public benefit, not profitable reward) as part of a single unified system that was controlled and operated by a single transport authority. The authority should operate 'at arm's length' to the local authority with the remit to provide economic and efficient transport services. This was the origins of London Transport, which was enacted by the London Passenger Transport Act (1933) that established the London Passenger Transport Board to bring all passenger modes in London into public ownership and under the Board's direct control.

However, the public interest argument is not the only reason why assets should be taken into the public sector, or nationalised, the main other ones being:

Eradicate wasteful competition

Wasteful competition has already been outlined in Chapter 7, and is where two or more services exist where one would be sufficient. One way that this can be eradicated is to bring competing services under the control of a single operator. The problem however with such a re-organisation is that the eradication of competition would leave a monopoly provider with all the associated problems of such a market structure. One way these drawbacks can be overcome is through direct control of the operator via public ownership. The operator could then be managed on the basis of the public rather than the profit interest. If managed correctly, this should result in economic efficiency. Alternatively, wasteful competition could be removed through regulation, thereby replacing the free market with a planned or regulated market and ensuring that capacity matched demand.

Military significance

The industry is seen to have important military applications that mean it cannot be simply left in private hands. In some ways the rail industry is an example of this, where during WW2 the 'big four' rail companies were jointly managed in order to better assist the British 'war effort' and to co-ordinate troop and equipment movements.

Public goods

If left to the market certain types of beneficial goods, known as public goods (see Chapter 1 for a description), would not be provided as no single firm could make a profit out of doing so. One way to ensure that such goods are provided is through state ownership.

Essential to the economy

This is an extension of the public interest argument. Certain industries were viewed as under-pinning the whole economy and hence could not be left to market forces because if the particular industry suffered the whole economy would suffer. Hence for example the coal industry was nationalised in 1947 and steel in 1965 as at that time these were important raw materials to the whole British economy. Many transport industries came under this same argument, hence the railways nationalised in 1947, road haulage and the major ports in 1948 and most of the bus industry taken into public ownership in 1968.

A large employer

Very much a rationale of the times of mass production, where firms were major employers and thus their potential collapse could not be contemplated in unemployment terms. As an alternative, they were nationalised. Hence British Leyland, a major British car manufacturer and mass employer at the time, was nationalised in 1975 following its bankruptcy. This was and remains a particularly acute threat in certain areas or localities, where certain firms may be the only major employer in the area, and hence its collapse would have implications far beyond the direct loss of employment. The aerospace industry in South West England for example is a major employer, and hence the collapse of the industry would result in considerable economic hardship throughout the whole region.

Key industry

A key industry is different from an essential industry to the economy as it is one that is seen to be of vital importance to the country. Hence for example Rolls-Royce was nationalised in 1971, the only firm to be taken into the public sector by a Conservative government, for reasons that primarily related to it being a key industry. This is because firstly retention of the skills and knowledge employed in the company were seen to be important to the country and secondly, it was and remains one of a small number of 'prestigious' companies that stand for excellence in British engineering. Note also that the Rolls-Royce example falls under the military rationale, as most Royal Air Force and Royal Navy aircraft are powered by Rolls-Royce engines. Retention of such engineering skills and knowledge was therefore also of military significance.

High project development costs

Any major project requires considerable financial outgoings before any revenue is forthcoming. In many instances these can be of such a size that the whole company is put at risk. In the case of Rolls-Royce, for example, the company ran into major cash flow problems over the development of the civil RB211 aero engine that ultimately forced it into liquidation. Because of such high business risks, projects of this nature would not be undertaken by the private sector regardless of any wider benefits that may follow completion. Consequently under 'normal' circumstances, only a publicly owned company could take on such a project.

In the 21st century many of these arguments are outdated and reflect different times. In several cases, other alternatives to public ownership can now be used to overcome many of the issues. In other instances, however, reasons for public ownership still apply. For example, the net outcome of the reform of ferry services to the islands off the west coast of Scotland, which was required under EU competition laws, resulted in the services being provided by a combination of two heavily subsidised public sector companies rather than previously where they were only provided by one heavily subsidised public sector company. All private sector bidders withdrew in the course of the bidding process as they were unwilling to bid under the terms of the tender. As the ferries are essential to the economy and social foundation of these islands, if no private sector company was willing to take the risk in providing services they could only be operated by a public sector concern. Whilst this is not a typical example, it does nevertheless lead into the more general issue of public ownership reform.

Reasons for reform

If transport services should or can only be provided on the basis of the public interest, which can be 'best' guaranteed under the direct control of public ownership, then why reform? Some of the reasons for reform are outlined below:

Increasing discontent with the model of public ownership

Over the years there has been increasing discontentment with the model of public ownership for a number of reasons. The first is the basic efficiency argument, where such organisations are perceived to suffer from general management slackness and thus are not as efficient as private enterprise. This is the classic x-inefficiency argument. The second relates to the constraints that operating in the public sector imposes on such concerns, which may limit options and overall performance. This particularly surrounds financial constraints, where because all borrowings count as part of the National Debt, these are closely scrutinised and controlled. For companies and organisations working in the public sector this limits planning horizons and investment plans, and consequently leads to much shorter planning frameworks.

Changing macroeconomic environment combined with social change

A changing macroeconomic is mainly as a result of changing global economic conditions (see Chapter 12). As a consequence, the economic power of governments and their ability to influence markets has been considerably reduced due to the rise of multinational and transnational companies. Governments therefore have found it increasingly difficult to intervene directly in markets, and hence the government's role in certain markets has changed more towards that of one of a facilitator. Reduced economic power has also meant that governments can no longer afford to simply give public transport operators an open budget with which to provide services. Over this time there has also been major social change, with changing mobility patterns and overall increases in levels of personal travel. In particular, less people are now reliant on public transport services, thus the gap between costs and revenues have grown substantially causing an increased subsidy requirement. One 'solution' to this was to cut transport services, a view best encompassed by the 'Beeching' approach, where unprofitable railway lines were closed in the 1960s in the UK in search of the profitable railway. An alternative approach is to attempt to run the existing network but at a reduced cost, hence the motivation for reform.

The desire to introduce competition into the provision of transport services

This is partly connected to increasing discontentment with public service provision. The Morrisonian view of transport provision is that of a public corporation being the sole provider of transport services. Apart from the x-inefficiency argument cited above, reform may be motivated because of social change and the increased desire for choice and options. Whilst fifty years ago people would generally put up with the bus service provided by the local city corporation regardless of the quality of the service, now they won't. Choice is more a part of today's society than it has been in the past, hence introducing competition into the market gives the consumer more viable choices.

Ownership forms in the provision of transport services

Even where considerable market reforms have been enacted in the provision of transport services, there still remains a wide range of ownership forms within the sector: public ownership is far from being completely removed from the provision of transport services. Ownership structures range

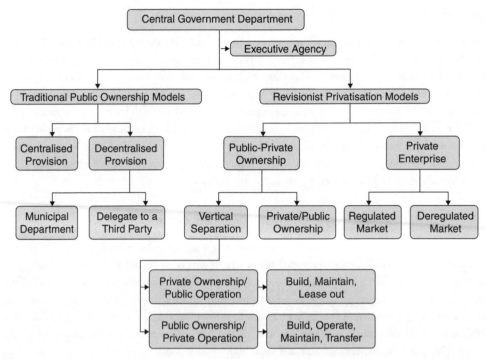

Figure 10.4 *Ownership forms in the provision of transport services*

Source: Adapted from Jain *et al.* (2008) and Cowie (1995)

from a tightly controlled government department to a free market profit maximising company. In many ways the issue of the ownership of transport assets is very closely associated with the issue of transport governance, as those empowered by the state to provide transport services are generally those that own or control transport assets. This close relationship is very similar to the old adage that possession is ninth tenths of the law. Nevertheless, Figure 10.4 attempts to summarise the main ownership forms with focus on the economic rather than the legal issues. Some cross over between the two however is inevitable.

Central government department

Beginning at the top of Figure 10.4, a central government department is where the provision of transport services or the management of transport assets, such as national roads, remains directly a responsibility of central government administration. The department receives an annual budget from central government funds to enable it to fulfil this obligation. Rather than perform all of these duties internally however, it may delegate a specific task or aspect of these responsibilities to an external body in the form of an Executive Agency. As an example, the Highways Agency is an executive agency of the Department for Transport (DfT) and is responsible for the management, maintenance and development of the national road network in England. The running of the British passenger rail franchises was also formerly under the control of an executive agency, the Strategic Rail Authority. This however was abolished in 2006 and the function brought directly back under central government administration in the shape of the DfT Rail Group.

In many other instances, responsibility may be delegated to other bodies further removed from central government, which leads into the traditional forms of public ownership.

Traditional public ownership forms
These are subdivided into centralised and decentralised provision.

Centralised provision
This is where transport services are provided on a national basis, usually by a nationalised operator in the form of a statutory corporation. These are legally constituted bodies given the authority by the state to perform a public service. Within the transport sector, this has normally related to rail services. Thus in Britain, for example, until 1996 all rail services were provided by the nationalised British Rail. Statutory corporations still exist in other countries in Europe and other parts of the world. Interstate passenger rail services in both Canada and America for example are provided by statutory corporations, VIA Rail in the case of the former and Amtrak in the latter. These bodies will generally plan and operate all transport services for which they have been given the legal authority.

Decentralised provision
Rather than run on a national basis, under this form of public ownership transport services are owned and controlled at the local level. This is usually done either directly by the local council or responsibilities are delegated to a third party.

The municipal department
This is where the local council plans and directly provides transport services. In Britain prior to the Transport Act 1985, this form of public ownership was widespread in bus operations, where buses were part of a transport department that was no different to any other local authority department such as housing, education, refuse collection, libraries, social services etc. Under this model of ownership, the transport department is given a budget and for that budget expected to provide local transport services. Many transport assets in Britain are still managed in this way, such as urban and county roads, bus stations and many ports and harbours.

Delegate to a third party
As with central government, the local council may also transfer specific responsibilities to a third party. This can come under a multitude of legally constituted forms, from the wholly owned subsidiary through to an executive agency or statutory corporation. Thus for example Transport for London is a statutory corporation responsible to the Greater London Authority for most aspects of the city's transport system, whilst Highlands and Islands Airports Ltd is a wholly owned company of the Scottish Government. As a very general rule, at the local level planning and co-ordinating bodies are normally constituted as statutory corporations, whilst operating arms as wholly owned subsidiaries. Thus London Underground Ltd is a wholly owned subsidiary of Transport for London. In all cases, however, the level of public control is very high as the third party is wholly responsible to the local council.

One of the major reasons for this type of public ownership structure rather than it being part of the local administration is that it allows the organisation with the responsibility to focus entirely on the specific activity. A further reason is that a degree of competition can be more easily introduced into operational activities rather than simply giving a budget to an internal department. Thus subsidised transport services can be put out to competitive tender, and even (if desired) competition introduced on profit-making routes. The performance of the publicly owned company can thus be 'benchmarked' or even more directly set against private operators in the market. For example Lothian Buses in Edinburgh, by far the largest publicly owned bus company remaining in Britain, not only openly competes in the market against private sector companies for patronage, but also has to tender for local authority contracts. It receives no direct funds from the council, and profits made on operations are paid to the council in the form of dividends. Nevertheless, in Britain this form of public ownership is a peculiarity left over from bus privatisation in the 1980s. Most of these companies were organised separately from the council as a prelude to privatisation, hence the ownership type transitory, as it was never intended that they should remain in public ownership. Nevertheless, there are many examples in Europe and other parts of the world where either publicly owned transport firms compete with private sector companies or perform specific transport functions for the local authority.

Revisionist privatisation models

Under revisionist privatisation models, aspects of the private sector are directly involved in the provision of transport services and/or the management and operation of transport assets. This would be consistent with what Swann (1988) termed as a 'wide' form of privatisation, in which any measure designed to refocus the public enterprise towards market-based principles can be described as privatisation. The main forms of revisionist privatisation models to be found in the delivery of transport services are also shown in Figure 10.4 and outlined below.

Public–private partnership

As the name clearly indicates, this is where there is some form of partnership between the public and private sectors. The most straightforward is where a joint company is set up to operate the service or transport facility. In France for example some bus companies are jointly owned by the public and private sectors. Other examples exist of joint public–private operation of airports. Under this model of ownership, this is a straightforward partnership, where a hypothetical case would be where Lothian buses, rather than being entirely owned by City of Edinburgh Council, was partially owned by a private sector operator. Interestingly, however, research has consistently shown that in terms of operational efficiency, this tends to be the worst form of ownership. Roy and Yvrande-Billon (2007) for example in a study of French bus operators found that privately owned firms were technically more efficient than publicly owned companies, but that the worst form of ownership was the mixed public–private model. This they attributed to three possible reasons. Firstly, that it led to opportunistic behaviour due to responsibilities being difficult to attribute between the two partners. Secondly, public administrations were 'captured' by their private partners so that their performance was even worse than if acting alone. Thirdly, that those public administrations that had retained the direct management of their public transport systems were particularly proactive in this respect, i.e. were keen to see, and highly active in providing, a high-quality public transport service. This last argument is particularly valid, especially when it is considered that technical efficiency assessments completely ignore the quality of service as they are solely based on quantitative measures of service output. This research as a whole, and this aspect in particular, illustrates very clearly some of the major issues in the reform of public transport services.

The other form of public–private partnership is far more complex and is where there is a clear division of responsibilities between the public and private partners. The first of these forms highlighted is where the private sector constructs and owns the transport assets, which it then leases to the public authority to use. Examples of such ownership structures in transport however tends to be limited, but does include some bus stations where the station may be part of a larger development that is owned by a private sector company and leased to and operated by a public authority. It has however been extensively applied in other areas of public service provision, such as schools and hospitals. The advantage of this model of delivery is that the authority may be able to bring forward investments in transport facilities, because the private sector will carry the debt, hence by-passing the financial constraints of the public sector.

The second form of vertical separation is where the private sector operates the service; however, the assets are effectively owned by the public authority. Such structures are fairly common in light-rail schemes, where the infrastructure and vehicles are constructed and built by the private sector, but ultimately owned by the public sector. One of the first examples of this model of delivery was the Manchester light-rail scheme, Metrolink, which was constructed in the late 1980s and opened in 1991. Construction was undertaken by a private sector consortium, which then had a fifteen-year concession on the operation and maintenance of the system. After that period, ownership of the assets reverted back to GMPTE, the local transport authority, who then re-let the franchise.

Private enterprise

The last main heading given in Figure 10.4 is private enterprise. This is where the service is provided entirely by the private sector. The constitutional forms of private sector companies are far more straightforward than public sector concerns, and are outlined below:

Stock market listed

This is the public limited company (plc), where shares are quoted on the stock exchange. Any investor therefore can purchase shares in the company. Most of the major private operators in transport markets are of this form, as the ability of plcs to raise finance and the options to spread financial risks are considerably enhanced. Liability is limited to the amount invested in the shares in the company. Plcs can and normally do have wholly owned subsidiaries, which are in the form of private limited companies.

Private limited companies (Ltd)

Private limited companies are similar to plcs in that shares are purchased and liability limited to the level of investment in shares; however, the difference is that shares cannot be sold openly on the stock market, any share transfers will be in the form of private sales. These therefore tend to be smaller transport operators as financing levels tend to be limited to the financial reserves of the (private) shareholders in the company. As stated above, however, many bus companies are wholly owned subsidiaries of plcs. Hence for example First South Yorkshire Ltd was previously Mainline Partnership Ltd, which was a private limited company owned by the management and employees of the firm. However, after a majority of the shareholding agreed to sell their shares to First Group plc, the company then became a wholly owned subsidiary of First.

In terms of how private sector companies provide services to the market, two possibilities are outlined. The first is under a regulated market, where normally a private operator will run services to the specification of a public transport authority. This is the model found in many urban areas, notably London Buses, and other examples are given in Case study 10.2. The second is the deregulated market, where any operator that meets the requirements of business start up can operate services. This is the most extreme form of revisionist privatisation model where the whole transport market is privatised and operates like any other normal good. Better known examples of such markets are buses and road haulage in Britain and air, trucking and rail freight services in America.

What this discussion shows is that even with major reforms, such as bus deregulation in Britain, there is still a significant element of public provision in deregulated transport markets. The only possible exceptions are freight specific railways such as in America; however, even these are subject to minor forms of economic regulation from the US Surface Transportation Board, particularly in the area of proposed railroad mergers. What should not be taken from this discussion however is that Figure 10.4 presents a definitive set of discrete forms of ownership and operation in the provision of transport services. There are not only many other variants that exist, but also a high degree of cross over between a number of the structures outlined. Hence for example public ownership/private operation is normally tendered on a regulated market basis. Ownership forms are thus very difficult to specifically pigeonhole into a number of well-defined and discrete categories.

Some of the issues surrounding reform through introducing private sector practices into the running of publicly owned transport services are explored further in Case study 10.2, which examines three different models of reform, two in urban-based systems and one in a national railway.

Case study 10.2 The move away from control through ownership to control through regulation in public transit markets

'*Regulatory reform is often seen as a road paved by good intentions, but leading to "policy hell"*' (Lodge, 2002, p. 271).

We have already examined in Chapter 7 the impacts of reforms on the British bus market outside of London. Whilst that is an example of reform, it is only one example of reform. In this case study we underpin a number of the ideas outlined in this chapter by considering other examples where there has been a reform away from a traditional public ownership model towards some form of revisionist approach. Three examples are given, two from major European cities and one state railway. The case begins with the London example, as this picks up from the Morrisonian model of public transport provision outlined earlier in the chapter and the reforms enacted in London have been broadly followed in other major cities.

Prior to reform, as we have seen public transport in London was provided by a single at arm's length authority, London Transport, which planned and operated all services. Under the provisions of the London Regional Transport Act 1984, these functions were divided and separated out of a single unitary authority. The planning function was transferred to a new body, London Regional Transport, which was formed to take responsibility of the public transport network under the direct control of central government. In 2000 this was replaced by Transport for London (TfL), who now report to the Greater London Authority and have wider responsibilities that also include implementing transport strategy. The bus operating arm of London Transport, London Buses Ltd, was divided into ten subsidiaries and these were then eventually sold to the private sector in the mid 1990s. TfL put individual bus routes out to tender and private sector bus companies operate the service to fare levels and service patterns specified by TfL. These contracts are purely on an operational basis (to be examined further in the following chapter), hence the tender is for the cost of operation and all revenue returned to the authority. TfL also lay down other service specifications, such as the standard of vehicles to be used and importantly in the case of London, that all buses are red. The London Underground remains in public ownership and is operated by London Underground Ltd, which since 2003 has been a wholly owned subsidiary of TfL. Like the private sector bus companies, London Underground runs services to a pattern specified by TfL. In 2003 responsibility for maintenance of the trains, stations and infrastructure was transferred to two private sector companies, Tube Lines and Metronet, who supplied these under contract to London Underground Ltd. Following financial difficulties, however, in May 2008 the Metronet companies, which were responsible for mainten-ance on 9 of the 12 tube lines, were transferred to new companies within Transport for London. Hence maintenance responsibilities on these lines are now back in the public sector. As all urban public transport services within London are under the direct control of a single transport authority, TfL, an integrating ticketing scheme is operated where tickets are valid on all services as well as some rail services. This is the well-known Oyster card seen in Chapter 8, where debit is built onto the card and the 'fare' deducted from the value on the card.

This model of urban public transport provision whilst not the first of its kind is probably the most well known. In essence, the buses have been privatised and are run under contract to the local transport authority, whilst urban rail remains in public ownership. Very similar characteristics to these are to be found in other major cities; however, under slightly different delivery models. Using Helsinki as an example, the city has a wide range of different public transport services that include the bus, the tram, two ferry services, mainline rail services and an underground. The overseeing transport authority, Helsinki City Transport (HKL), was formerly the operator of all of these modes outside of mainline rail, which was the preserve of Finnish State Railways. Bus services however were merged with another city-owned bus company in 2005 and privatised to form a new private sector operator. HKL now specify the bus services to be run, and as in London these are contracted out to private sector companies on an operational basis with a similar model of the passenger revenue being returned to the authority. HKL however remains as the direct owner and operator of the trams, metro and ferries in Helsinki. Public transport services to the outlying areas of Helsinki are overseen by the regional transport authority, the Helsinki Metropolitan Area Council, YTV, who plan and specify bus services in the same manner as the HKL. Again an integrated electronic ticketing system is used and is valid on all modes operated within the city. Whilst very similar to the situation in London, this model of delivery is more consistent with the traditional form of public ownership, particularly in character, where operation and management of all transport assets except buses remain directly within the local transport authority.

The final example given is of reform in state railways. British privatisation has been well covered elsewhere in this text, but this is only one example of the approach taken in the reform of European railways. Britain however was not the first country in Europe to radically restructure its railway. In the late 1980s, Sweden divided its rail operations between infrastructure and services. Infrastructure was separated out into the National Rail Administration, Banverket, which is a government agency directly responsible to central government for the maintenance and development of the national rail network. To carry out this responsibility, it receives a budget every year directly from state funds. Operator track access charges are paid directly to the Swedish government and are levied on the basis of the marginal cost, hence do not meet the full cost of the network. At the time of the split, services remained the responsibility of the Swedish State Railway (SJ). The rail network however was notionally divided between a commercial sector, mainly intercity routes, and a contract sector, made up of local and interregional services. On the commercial sector SJ had a monopoly over the provision of these services and was expected to cover the cost of operations out of passenger revenue. Note that it only pays the marginal and not the full cost on infrastructure. SJ now however faces some direct competition on parts of these routes in the south west of the country following the loss of the Oresund train contract to DSB First, a joint venture between the Danish state railway and First Group. For information, the Oresund is the sea strait between Malmo in Sweden and Copenhagen in Denmark and was bridged in 2000 by a combined bridge/tunnel fixed link. SJ may also face further competition in the commercial sector as a result of EU-wide rail reforms, specifically the opening up of the market for international passenger rail services that includes cabotage rights, i.e. the right to pick up and put down passengers along the whole route.

On the contract sector of the network, train services are run under contract to regional government transport authorities on regional and local lines on the basis of operational contracts where the authority pays for the cost of providing the service and takes all the revenue, and the Swedish National Public Transport Agency (a government agency) on interregional services under net cost contracts, which is the net difference between cost and passenger revenue. Contracts are normally awarded for five years. Here SJ faces competition in the bidding for these contracts from other rail operators, such as Arriva and the French operator Veolia Transport and other state railways, specifically Norwegian, Danish and German. In 2005, SJ had around 74 per cent of the total Swedish passenger rail market.

After the reforms of the late 1980s, freight operated as a separate division within SJ. In 2001, however, SJ was further divided into six separate operating companies, all wholly government owned. The two main ones are passengers, which remains as SJ, and freight, named Green Cargo. In 2002 Green Cargo returned heavy losses and the government contemplated privatising the company in the form of a private sale to another rail freight operator. The company now however appears to have returned to reasonable profit levels and remains state owned.

As with Britain, however, Swedish rail reform has not been without its problems. Alexandersson and Hultén (2006) report many similarities between the two, with over-optimistic bids, disruptions in services, several cases of bankruptcies of the train operators, problems with co-ordinating and integrating tickets between services supplied by different operators, monopolistic behaviour by SJ and ticket prices up 43 per cent in real terms since the beginning of the reforms in 1988. On the positive side, passenger numbers have risen by 32 per cent since 1995 and subsidy levels have usually decreased by 10 to 20 per cent. Over time however with subsequent re-tendering, the general trend has been for the level of reduction to fall and even in one case, to increase.

What this case study shows is that whilst it is relatively easy to talk about models of reform of public transport services, in practice implementation is far from straightforward. It also shows some of the general dangers of involving the private sector in the provision of public services, in this case specifically public transport. The biggest danger is that failure of the company will result in withdrawal of the public service, a situation that the relevant authorities simply cannot allow to happen. Many other facets are related to the original reasons for taking public transport services out of the private sector and thus no longer subjected to market forces in the first place. This is particularly relevant to the eradication of wasteful competition, that services should be run on the basis of the public interest and finally that these are vital industries to the economy. Whilst these and other objectives can be achieved successfully with private sector involvement, such as shown in the case of London and Helsinki buses, further involvement appears to become more problematic and hit or miss. Why for example should Tube Lines deliver London Underground maintenance and network enhancements on time and to budget and Metronet not? This raises the question of when does private sector involvement 'work' and when does it not? This case study, in common with many learned transport professors, cannot provide an answer to this question as this is a multifaceted topic and one of the major issues in transport economics today. One reason however why bus services have been the most reformed and rail services the least is that any private bus company is fairly easily, i.e. cheaply, 'replace-able' by another bus company. In the case of mainline and urban-rail-based operations however it becomes far more problematic, i.e. expensive and disruptive.

CHAPTER SUMMARY AND REFLECTION

This chapter has examined the issues of regulation and ownership in transport organisation and operation. As should have been seen in the course of the text, there is a balance somewhere between the regulation of transport markets through the mechanisms of ownership and regulation. The old style model is encompassed in the ideas of what became known more generally as the Morrisonian model, where a national public corporation is a publicly owned company that operates at arm's length to the state with a remit to act in the public interest and break even. Such a model originated from a transport problem, i.e. London's public transport. Various drawbacks however were identified and encountered with this approach in public ownership, and much transport provision across the globe has been privatised or reformed. Much however still remains in public ownership, with buses normally privatised but metros, trams and rail services in most cases still remaining in public ownership. The problem now has switched from trying to overcome the problems with public ownership to trying to steer the private sector towards doing what the public authorities want it to do through the regulatory mechanism.

CHAPTER EXERCISES

Exercise 10.1 Regulating the price

In the following exercise, you are given some basic information for a local bus operator for the first year of operation and then asked to find the regulated average price over the following two years. In the following calculations, you should round all figures to the nearest whole unit (i.e. nearest £000s, 1000 journeys or the nearest pence in terms of the actual price). Information on the first year of operation is thus given below:

	Year One
Operating Costs (£000s):	500
Journeys in thousands:	600
Profit Margin:	16%
Average Fare Charged:	0.97
Revenue (£000s):	580
Profit (£000s):	80

As seen above, the level of profit margin in the first year is 16 per cent at an average fare of £0.97. You are given the following information below in order to set the regulatory price:

Expected inflation in prices and operating costs in each of the next two years:	3%
Rise in passenger traffic in each of the next two years:	1%
Expected annual efficiency improvements:	2%

Increases in passenger numbers are expected to arise from other external factors that impact on the local bus market, therefore you should assume that this growth is not dependent upon the final price that will be set. It is also anticipated that this increase will be incorporated on existing available capacity, thus any changes in passenger numbers will have no effect on costs, therefore any increases in costs are purely as a result of inflation.

a) You should calculate the regulated average price (to the nearest pence) for the following two years on the following two bases:

    i On a straight RPI-X% basis where X is set at 1 per cent

    ii On a return on capital employed basis, where the regulatory asset base is set at £1.2m and the rate of return at 8 per cent.

b) Now re-calculate both a(i) and a(ii) on the basis of an anticipated rise in passenger traffic of 2 per cent over the next two years.

c) Using your answers to parts a and b, outline the advantages and disadvantages of regulating based upon RPI-X% as opposed to a return on capital basis in an expanding and a declining market.

d) The company proposes to undertake an increased investment programme in order to enhance existing bus services. It estimates that it will invest £500k up front and write these investments off over a ten year period. It will fund this investment initially from increased borrowings, which on average will be borrowed at a 5 per cent rate of interest over the first two years. It forecasts however that these enhancements will have a major impact on demand, increasing it by 12 per cent in each of the first two years. The authority agrees that £300k of this new investment can be added to the regulatory asset base. Using your original calculations for part a(ii), what would be the revised regulated price over the first two years that would maintain an 8 per cent return if the proposed investments were made? Should the regulator agree to this investment plan – note that whilst a 'good' thing as it will increase passenger numbers, are there any other reasons why the regulator should agree to this investment plan?

Exercise 10.2 Yardstick competition

Yardstick competition as a principle is not extensively applied in transport markets, nevertheless as a subject it does raise a number of issues concerning the economic regulation of transport operators. This exercise will therefore take the ideas of yardstick competition and illustrate some of the principles involved in using such a system to regulate the price of transport operators and then examine some of the issues raised.

Consider the following two transport operators:

Unit costs and prices:		
1st Period	Company A	Company B
Average Revenue	2.00	2.00
Average Costs	1.75	1.75
Profit per unit	0.25	0.25

The level of the price for these two companies in Period 2 is to be based on a straight percentage of the reduction in the other's costs. Thus, for example, a 10 per cent reduction in B's average costs will cut the price in Period 2 for firm A by 10 per cent. Using that as the basis of regulation, you should now calculate the respective prices and associated unit profit levels for each of the following three scenarios:

Scenario 1: B cuts its average cost to £1.60; A fails to make any cost savings
Scenario 2: Both A and B cut their average cost to £1.60
Scenario 3: B undertakes a massive cost-reduction exercise and cuts its unit cost to £1.40; A fails to make any cuts in costs

Questions:

a) What is the basic equity problem created by scenario 1 and how may the regulatory formula be adjusted to partially overcome this issue?

b) If we assume equal numbers in both markets:

   i which scenario is the best possible outcome from the passengers' perspective?

   ii would that answer still apply if B was a deprived area and A a relatively prosperous one?

c) Although unrealistic as a scenario, what are the problems that are likely to arise from scenario 3?

247 ◼

d) From undertaking this exercise, what is the basic assumption underlying operator behaviour that is required for yardstick competition to work? As probably a very big hint, in this market there will only ever be a small number of firms 'competing'.

e) Why can yardstick competition only be practised in markets in which there is inelastic demand?

f) What do you see as the main problems in introducing yardstick competition:

   i in general?
   ii specifically in certain transport markets?

g) Compare and contrast yardstick competition with competitive tendering and outline the main strengths and weaknesses of the two approaches.

h) Whilst yardstick competition may not be extensively practised in transport markets, what role might such a model of competition play in the contracting of transport services through a negotiated contract?

Other questions

1 Outline the main roles and responsibilities of a regulator in the transport industries.

2 What do you see as the main advantages and disadvantages of public ownership in transport markets?

3 What do you see as the main advantages and disadvantages of involving the private sector in the provision of public transport services?

Transport subsidy

INTRODUCTION

Subsidy plays a vital role in the operation of transport markets, possibly more so than in any other industry. This is because transport markets are made up of a combination of market forces and the actions of transport planning authorities, with subsidy playing the pivotal role in reconciling these two 'forces' in the actual market place. An understanding of the uses of subsidy in transport industries, and perhaps more importantly the issues that surround the payment of it, is therefore vital to any analyst of transport markets.

Nevertheless, the payment of subsidy is closely related to aspects of regulation in transport markets. With the general move away from transport provision through traditional forms of public ownership towards far more private sector involvement, many argue that it is no longer a 'subsidy' but rather a payment for the performance of a contract for providing a service. In other words, like university lecturers, doctors and nurses and policemen and women, they are simply providing a service for the state. Irrespective of that argument, in return for the payment of the contract these operators are 'regulated', i.e. required to provide a certain level of transport provision. Thus in many areas the regulation and subsidisation of transport services are very closely linked. Furthermore, with greater private sector participation more regulation is required as direct control between the authority and the operator is lost with the loss of public ownership. Regulatory issues have been examined in the previous chapter, and this chapter takes aspects of that topic forward and deals specifically with the matters surrounding the actual transfer of funds between the state and the operator.

At first sight, the payment of subsidy may appear to be a fairly straightforward process. For example, if a transport authority wants a service provided that cannot be run at a profit, it would appear to be a simple case of paying an operator to provide the service. The subsidy paid would be the net difference between the cost of the service and the revenue gained from passengers. However, that raises many issues and questions, such as how much subsidy should actually be paid to the operator to run the service? What is the best way to pay that subsidy, i.e. simply hand over the cash, or is there a better way? Should the operator that provides the service be publicly owned to increase 'account-ability' or would that require more subsidy than a private operator? What is the likely impact of the subsidy payment on what the authority is trying to achieve, i.e. what are the side effects of paying subsidy on the standard of service provided and the efficiency of the operator providing it?

None of these questions are easily resolved. Taking the first point, how much subsidy should be paid for a particular transport facility, this would be dependent upon a number of factors. Firstly, how much it is decided that it is 'fair' to charge direct users of the facility and thus how much should be paid by the state. That in turn will be dependent upon the costs of actually providing that facility and the level of non-monetary benefits and costs associated with it. Finally, in the case where a private operator is to be contracted, then is it right that they should earn a profit from its operation, and if so, just how much profit should they earn? This raises the issue of what would be a 'reasonable' level of profit for the operator and to what extent should that be dependent upon performance?

The issue is further complicated as the payment of subsidy is not a straightforward economic issue, but also has a very strong political dimension, both in terms of the levels of subsidy paid and how it is to be paid. Some governments or authorities for example may continue to operate certain transport services irrespective of the costs involved and thus go way beyond any rationale economic argument. For example, it could be argued that the provision of night sleeper rail services from Fort William to London falls into such a category as its continued operation has little to do with the economic realities of the costs and benefits of the service.

As can be seen from this brief introduction, there are far more issues surrounding the payment of subsidy than actual subsidy itself. Nevertheless, without it the transport system of any country would come to a grinding halt. It is the essential cog in the wheel that keeps the whole system moving and is usually used to guide transport behaviour towards more land use efficient modes of transport or to underpin, in whatever form, economic development of a particular region or locality.

In this chapter we explore these issues and hopefully provide some insights into the points raised above. We begin by outlining the economic argument for the payment of subsidy to transport operations and this should dispel any thoughts that subsidies are used simply because transport services, particularly the train, are unprofitable because they are run inefficiently. We then consider what are known as demand and supply side measures and the main drawbacks of paying subsidy, before finally looking at the actual forms that subsidy payment can take and how this contrasts with the idea of cross subsidisation. In reading this chapter, however, you should also see that within the economics of transport it is very difficult to look at a single issue in isolation. For example transport services are often subsidised because the service that is provided is seen to be of a high 'external' value (e.g. provides a socially necessary service) but cannot be operated profitably by private companies. The inevitable consequence therefore is that when subsidised there will only be a single operator, i.e. a monopoly, and this in turn raises the problems associated with such market structures highlighted previously in Chapter 7, particularly the strong position of the operator. Part of the system used to pay subsidy therefore is to ensure such drawbacks are minimised.

THE RATIONALE FOR PUBLIC SUBSIDY

In most market-based economies, if a firm or industry cannot make a profit from selling its goods or services then it simply goes out of business. This in a nutshell is what is known as the efficiency of the market. Basically insufficient numbers valued the goods and services that were being produced at the prevailing market prices, hence the continued employment of resources in the production of those goods and services could no longer be supported. By going out of business, the resources previously used are now 'freed' to be put to other purposes more in line with society's wants and needs. Why, therefore, should transport be any different? In order to address this issue, we need to first introduce the basic idea of an externality using non transport examples before applying this to the transport context. This is because the arguments that surround the payment of subsidy for transport services are equally applicable to any other good or service, transport is no different or no 'special case' with regard to this issue.

Externalities

We have come across externalities several times before in this text; however, it is one of the main reasons for paying transport a subsidy. To quickly recap, externalities are often called 'spill-overs' and occur when the costs of producing a good or service fall not only on the producer of that good or service but also on others that are not involved in the activity in any capacity. The full cost of an activity therefore can be divided into two categories. Firstly, private costs, which are those that fall on the producers or users of that product, and secondly public costs, which are those costs that fall on others who are not involved in the activity and consequently do not benefit from it. The full cost, i.e. private and public costs, is normally referred to as the social cost.

External costs and over production

The main implication of externalities is that they are not taken into account when individuals make private production and consumption decisions, as only the private costs of that decision are considered. In terms of an external cost, this leads to over-production of a given good or service, as illustrated in Figure 11.1.

As only private decisions are taken into account in this market, the market would be in equilibrium at point b with a market price of P_{PRI} and quantity traded given by Q_{PRI}. When externalities are brought into the analysis, however, in this case an external cost, the effect would be that the supply curve should be further to the left,[1] as now all costs are brought into the analysis. Hence the market should be in equilibrium at point a, with a higher market price (P_{PUB}) and lower quantity traded (Q_{PUB}). This is a case of over-production, as not all of the costs associated with this good or service are taken into account in the production/consumption decision.

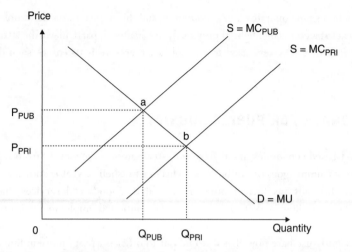

Figure 11.1   *Over production due to an external cost*

External benefits and under consumption

Externalities however not only work in relation to costs, but there may also be benefits that are not registered in the market place. For example, if an individual chooses to undertake a programme of physical fitness and also changes to a healthy diet, then a number of benefits will arise. Most of these will accrue directly to the individual concerned, but others in society will also benefit from the individual's new healthy lifestyle. Firstly because of their actions they will probably be less of a drain on health resources and consequently less of a drain on the tax resources used to pay for those health services. Secondly, the individual's employer will benefit in the form of less days off sick and a more 'wide awake' employee. These 'additional' benefits are shown graphically in Figure 11.2.

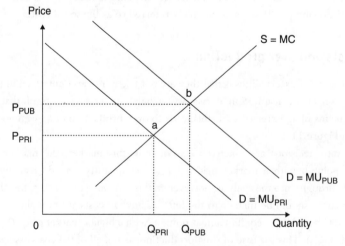

Figure 11.2   *Under-consumption due to an external benefit*

252

As above, if only private decisions are taken into account in this market, the market (in this case for exercise and healthy diets) would be in equilibrium at point a, with a market price at P_{PRI} and quantity traded given by Q_{PRI}. When externalities are introduced into the analysis, however, because in this example these are benefits that are not taken into account by the individual, this would have the effect of increasing demand at each and every price. This is because there is a higher level of common utility (benefit) than is being registered in the market place by private individuals. Once these are taken into account, the market demand curve should be further to the right. Hence when all benefits, both private and public, are taken into account the market price should be higher (P_{PUB}) and the quantity traded higher (Q_{PUB}). This is therefore a case of under consumption, as not all of the benefits associated with this good or service are taken into account in the production/consumption decision.

Both over production and under consumption are cases of market failure, as the presence of externalities breaches one of the conditions of perfect competition. Thus the market does not find the 'right' answer in terms of production and consumption decisions. Hence in the first case more is produced than is optimal and in the second less is consumed than should be (note however that over production equates to over consumption and vice-versa). Also note however that virtually all goods and services to a greater or lesser extent have an externality associated with them. For example, even a simple chocolate bar may provide a benefit to the person eating it but not to the person sitting next to them who is on a diet! The presence of externalities on their own therefore are not sufficient to justify the subsidisation of transport services; however, the issue is the extent and far reaching consequences of such spill over effects.

The economic rationale for the subsidisation of transport services

Outlined below are the main economic criteria that support the idea of payment of a subsidy for transport services. All however are related to the idea of market failure, where the market as such is either providing too much (over production) or too little (under consumption). Correction of such market failures is the strongest rationale for the payment of subsidy, and as highlighted in Chapter 10 this is primarily on the basis that two 'wrongs' make one right. More precisely, where a second breach of the conditions of perfect competition in the form of government intervention is 'justified' in order to compensate for the effects of a first breach in the form of the presence of externalities. The following economic criteria should also move away from the idea that subsidy is paid simply because transport firms are inefficient or ineffective. Such views are still a hangover from the 1970s where industrial problems were widespread and many key industries and employers effectively bailed out by government due to financial difficulties. This led to a general perception that subsidy equated to inefficient operations. Supporting inefficient operations however is not one of the criteria for the payment of subsidy, the four main ones being:

In support of land use efficient modes of transport

Some forms of transport are far more land use efficient than others. The private car for example is said to take up some 30 metres of land space per vehicle. Whilst in many occasions this may not be a major issue, there are certain areas and certain times where such inefficient use of land does create major problems, commonly known as traffic congestion. Where such instances arise, authorities have basically two choices. Firstly, they could penalise users of the land inefficient modes of transport through some form of tax. That however may have certain political drawbacks. Alternatively, they could attempt to make the alternative land efficient modes of transport more attractive to car users. This could either be in the form of directly reducing the fares charged, hence directly subsidising the services, or through increasing the quality of the service provided. This may be either through increased frequencies, hence again a direct subsidy on services, or alternatively through the quality of the vehicles or the reliability of the infrastructure on which it runs, hence subsidy would be used to encourage investment. Subsidies therefore can come in the form of supporting the service or in providing financial support in investment in the service, commonly known as capital grants.

To lessen the impact of environmentally unfriendly modes of transport

Not only are certain modes of transport less space efficient, but as illustrated in Chapter 9 some have a far larger impact on the environment than others per passenger journey or tonne of freight hauled. This is one of the major externalities associated with the use of the private car and road haulage in the carriage of freight. As regards the solutions, these are almost identical to those outlined above for land use purposes, hence in simple terms either tax the more environmentally unfriendly forms of transport and/or subsidise the less environmentally harmful modes.

Both points one and two can be reinforced and explored further by the use of an example. Rail travel is known to possess an external benefit, or to be more exact, both an external benefit and avoidance of additional external costs. Those using rail services are not using private transport, therefore road users directly benefit through reduced congestion, faster and less stressful journeys and a reduced number of accidents on the roads. These are the direct external benefits of rail travel and all relate to the land use issue. However, the train also reduces the overall impact of movement, and more exactly private transport, on non road users for the simple reason that many who need to travel are using the train and not the car. Thus the external costs of private motoring on non users, such as noise, pollution, intrusion etc, are reduced because people are using the train to travel. The train, as such, would therefore be a case of under-consumption, as it is valued only by those that directly use the service, not by those that also benefit but whose benefits are not registered in the market place.

To support economic development or regeneration of an area

As outlined in Chapter 2, transport can be viewed as the vital component in promoting and sustaining economic growth. This relates to both enhancing the quality of the transport network and also maintaining existing services at a desirable level. Whether a demand-led or supply-led view is taken of the relationship between transport and economic development, economic development is normally associated with improved or upgraded transport links and services. There may be a political responsibility to take such projects forward; however, there are other reasons as to why this provides an economic rationale for the subsidisation of transport services. These mainly surround the idea of what are known as public goods, which we examined in Chapter 1. In this example, no single individual or firm is ever going to finance the upgrade of transport services into a particular area on economic development grounds. This is because (a) it probably could not afford to do so entirely on its own and (b) once the services were upgraded it would not be the only firm to benefit from the improvements because of the free rider problem associated with public goods. In this particular case, therefore, the payment of subsidy may be justified on economic rationale grounds on the basis that such an upgrade of services and/or transport infrastructure will boost the local economy. All individuals in the area will therefore benefit from this improved wealth and the aggregated level of 'benefit' will be greater than the level of subsidy paid. This is a topic which is developed further in Chapter 14 on Transport Appraisal.

To support socially necessary services

Grouped under this heading are a range of social considerations which can be commonly regarded as issues concerning equity. Not everyone in the country either owns or has access to (as a driver or as a passenger) private transport, i.e. the car. The 2004 National Travel Survey (DfT, 2004) for example showed that 20 per cent of individuals that were 17 or over lived in a household with no car. Car availability was found to be strongly related to income, with 47 per cent of those on the lowest quintile living in a household with no car compared to a mere 8 per cent in the highest quintile. Furthermore, 50 per cent of single-parent families did not have access to private transport. Even these figures tend to underestimate the scale of the problem because an individual may live in a household that does have a car, but it may be in constant use by other household members and hence access may still be a major issue. This may be a particular issue in rural areas.

In today's modern society, Barr (2004) views transport as a 'participative requirement', i.e. it is required in order to fully participate within society. Education is a similar need, where a lack of education will not kill you but it may make it difficult to 'get on' in the world. Contrast this with an 'absolute requirement', which relates to food, shelter and health services. These are the basic necessities required to sustain life, without access to which you simply could not survive. With a participative requirement, however, the basic assumption is that some kind of minimum standard is required. In other words, not everyone requires an Oxbridge education and a Ferrari but rather requires access to some minimum level of provision. With regards to transport needs, public transport fulfils this role. Many instances exist however where the very nature of these transport operations means that they cannot be operated on a commercial basis. This would therefore be termed a 'socially necessary' service and provides the rationale for the payment of subsidy, i.e. to provide some minimum standard of living.

Some may question however whether the provision of a socially necessary service should be listed under an economic rationale for the payment of subsidy, as essentially this may be viewed as a purely political decision, and one based on maintaining the social fabric within society. Thus for example it could be argued that within a civilised society all its members should have access to a reasonable level of transport provision to enable them in turn to access their work, shops, recreation and various other activities considered as essentials. That in essence would be the political argument and furthermore that ultimately, it is politicians and not economists who decide which transport services should be provided and which should not. The economic argument however would surround the issue of equity (not to be confused with equality), and in particular the equity of opportunity. Wealth-creation opportunities, such as employment, should be open to all and thus those best qualified are those that benefit the most. Furthermore, if the best qualified attain such positions, this will also have wider economic benefits. Transport depravation should not debar such a process from taking place.

255

As regards specific services that relate to 'socially necessary', this normally refers to the provision of public transport in socially and economically deprived and/or rural areas. As seen in Chapter 2, there is a very high level of correlation between the level of GDP and the level of passenger transport. Whilst that relationship related to the whole of Great Britain, it also exists at a regional, local and district level. Hence within economically deprived areas, the demand for transport services tends to be far lower than in more prosperous ones. If left to the market, therefore, very few transport services would be provided. The perceived danger is that the lack of transport will only worsen the problems facing the area. Whilst extreme, this could almost be termed the 'ghetto' syndrome. Transport services therefore need to be subsidised to assist in the development of such areas and prevent a massive imbalance appearing between the 'haves' and the 'have nots' within society.

With regard to the rural transport problem, most services are provided on the basis of socially necessary services where transport is supplied on the grounds of basic accessibility. It thus gives those that do not have access to private transport a minimum level of transport provision. This is even more acute in rural areas that are particularly remote. Thus for example the island communities off the west coasts of Scotland and Norway simply could not be sustained at their present population levels if ferry services were not subsidised. Faced with the full cost of transport to the island, many important economic sectors, particularly tourism, would be severely affected and the cost of living would also increase significantly as goods and services brought over from the mainland paid the full transport cost. This would almost certainly lead to a massive depopulation of the islands, especially of those on medium and lower incomes. This is a classic example of a 'socially necessary service', where without the service the local society would simply disintegrate.

INTERVENTION IN THE MARKET

In order to pay subsidy to correct for the market failures outlined above, subsidies from transport authorities can either be 'injected' into the supply side of the market or the demand side, known conveniently as supply side and demand side measures.

Supply side measures

A supply side measure is where the subsidy is paid directly to the operator, not the consumer. This then enables the operator to supply a level of service that it would otherwise not have been able to in the absence of the subsidy. Services that are provided as a consequence of supply side measures are open to all potential users and not specifically targeted at or restricted to certain groups within society. The direct effect of a supply side measure is to increase the supply of that service to the market. This is illustrated in Figure 11.3, which is an extension of Figure 11.2 outlined earlier. You may also notice that this is basically one of the answers to Exercise 3.1 in Chapter 3.

In Figure 11.3, prior to the payment of a subsidy then as in Figure 11.2 the market is in equilibrium at point a with a market price of P_{PRI} and a quantity of Q_{PRI}. As illustrated, however, due to an external benefit the 'true' market value, i.e. when all costs and benefits are taken into account, would be at point b with a quantity traded of Q_{PUB}. In order to correct for this market failure, one option for the transport authority is to increase the level of supply so that the market

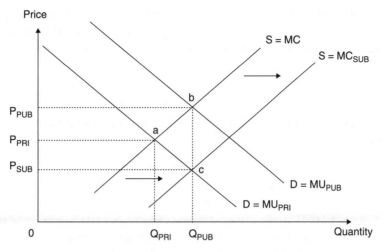

Figure 11.3   *Subsidy to operators to correct for under-consumption*

will be in equilibrium with a quantity Q_{PUB}. Using a supply side measure, this it does through the payment of a subsidy to transport operators, hence producing a shift in the supply curve from $S = MC$ to $S = MC_{SUB}$. The market would therefore be in equilibrium at point c, with a quantity traded of Q_{PUB}. The difference in the prices between P_{PUB} and P_{SUB} is the effect of the subsidy, with the state effectively paying the operators the value of the external benefit. Note also that the extent to which subsidy impacts upon either reducing fares or increasing the level supplied will be dependent upon the elasticity of demand. Where demand is inelastic, the effect will be to mainly reduce the price with little impact upon the quantity traded. In markets with elastic demand on the other hand, most of the impact will be on quantity with little effect on price. This has major implications on transport markets, where as seen in Chapter 4 demand for most transport services tends to be inelastic. This is one of the reasons why it is very difficult in general for authorities to produce a modal shift from the car to public transport services using subsidies alone, as the biggest impact is on the price and not on quantity demanded.

Note finally in this example, although an external benefit was identified as a demand side problem (under consumption), the easiest 'solution' in most cases is a supply side measure (pay a subsidy to operators).

Demand side measures

In theory these are far more straightforward, as a demand side measure is used to correct for a demand side market failure and exists where specific groups or individuals are 'targeted' to receive the subsidy. Unlike supply side measures, therefore, these are not open to all. In effect the individual is given a 'concession' (a reduced fare) to use a transport service, either public or private, but in reality most if not all concern some concession on the use of public transport. This usually requires some proof of entitlement to the reduction and should not be confused with commercial initiatives taken by operators such as the Young Persons Railcard. These are a form of price discrimination and are offered purely for commercial purposes to fill spare capacity. Concessionary fares are given to individuals that the state has decided should receive some

257 ■

form of discount on their travel needs. These are normally taken on social inclusion grounds and are specified at the minimum level. Whilst in theory the ideas behind concessionary fares are straightforward, the practice of actually bringing such schemes into operation are far from straightforward and the situation in Britain is considered further in Case study 11.1 below.

Case study 11.1 Issues surrounding concessionary fare reimbursement

Perhaps the most common form of demand side measure found in transport markets are concessionary fare schemes. Within the UK, this type of subsidy has seen considerable reform over recent years, which partly reflects the devolved nature of government in the UK. The original Transport Act 1985 allowed for voluntary concessionary fare schemes to be operated for the elderly and registered disabled, thereby leaving it entirely up to local authorities to specify their own schemes for these two groups, including the option of not having one. Local authorities would then allocate a budget that was available to run the scheme. This led to considerable variations between different local authority areas regarding the level of actual fare concessions given, with Scottish local authorities tending to be more generous than their English and Welsh counterparts. Most schemes consisted of either the purchase or the free issue of a pass that entitled the holder to some form of discount on bus travel, but not on train services – as highlighted in the main text, any rail schemes that did exist were entirely on commercial grounds. The actual concession was either set at a straight flat fare irrespective of distance travelled or some form of percentage discount on the full fare. Hence in the Glasgow area, those entitled to the scheme applied for a free bus pass and then paid a flat fare of 25p on all bus services, whilst in West Berkshire a free bus pass entitled the holder to a 50 per cent discount. A final example was in Darlington, where entitlement holders could pay an annual flat charge for the pass, £80, which then entitled them to free travel in the Darlington area and half fare in the outlying rural districts. These arrangements remained in place until the devolution of political power to a Welsh Assembly and a Scottish Parliament, with transport being one of the devolved powers. Wales was the first to introduce an area-wide free concessionary fare scheme in April 2002, covering essentially all of Wales. Scotland followed with first a free travel scheme within local authority boundaries and then a nationwide free concessionary fare scheme that allowed the crossing of local authority boundaries. England followed suit in 2006 with a free local travel concession and then a national scheme in 2008. As can be seen from Figure 11.4, the move to free travel concessions has led to a significant increase in the level of subsidy paid through these initiatives.

Until the last few years shown, there had been a fairly constant pattern in concessionary fare reimbursement. The general trend in the early part of the period shown was upwards, but a squeeze on local authority finances in the early 1990s led to a decrease, although differences are relatively small and the figure hovered around £600m in 2008 prices. The sharp increase in the later years is entirely due to the introduction and expansion of free concessionary fare schemes throughout Britain, firstly in Wales (in 2002), then Scotland (2003 and 2005) and England (2006). In Wales the annual subsidy rose from £14m in 2001/2 to £38m by 2004/5, and in Scotland from £39m in 2001/2 to £92m by 2004/5. The final year shown is the

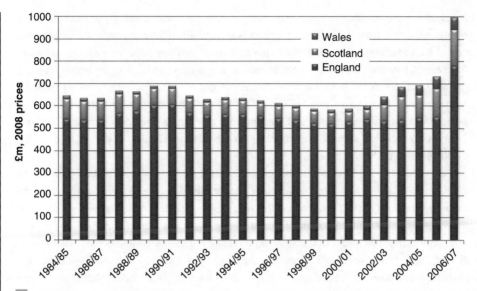

Figure 11.4 *Concessionary fare reimbursement, 1984/85 to 2006/07, at 2008 prices*

Source: Compiled from DfT Statistics

impact of the free local travel English scheme, which led to a 42 per cent increase in the level of concessionary fare reimbursement.

How these schemes are administered is a confusing and far from straightforward matter, but in many ways tie in closely with the economics of bus operation. There are a number of ways such schemes could be operated:

a) As an entirely demand side based scheme where the concession holder pays the full fare to the operator. The traveller would then reclaim all fares at a later date from the authority. The problems with such an arrangement however are considerable and would almost certainly render such a system unworkable.

b) A voucher or token system could be used, where tokens are issued to entitlement holders, who would then use these instead of paying the fare. Prior to 2006, this was an option in the Cumbria concessionary fare scheme and a number of other English counties. Operators would then reclaim the loss of fares from the authority on production of the vouchers received. Such a system however would be open to exploitation, and thus would also require some form of identification confirming that the user of the tokens was entitled to the concession.

c) The third option is a pass system, where the entitlement holder shows a pass on boarding and the operator records the number of concessionary passengers. The operator is then reimbursed for every recorded concessionary passenger carried.

As highlighted above, within Britain a pass system is used. However, how operators are then compensated by the authority raises many issues. What complicates the process is that the underlying principle is that the operator should be no better and no worse off as a result of the scheme. In other words, company profits (or losses!) should be unaffected by the running of the concessionary fare scheme. At first therefore the easy solution would appear to be simply to reimburse the operator for each concessionary fare passenger carried. For example, say a 50 per cent concession is introduced, and there is a hypothetical bus company that charges a flat fare of £1, consequently those entitled to the concession only pay 50p. For each concessionary fare carried, therefore, should the operator receive 50p as compensation for the loss in revenue? The not so simple answer is no, due to the concept of 'generated traffic'. The following examples illustrate the idea of generated traffic and the process of operator reimbursement firstly where a reduced fare is imposed and then where a completely free concession is introduced. Figure 11.5 therefore shows the demand for bus services specifically from the sector of the market entitled to the concession.

Beginning with the diagram on the left of Figure 11.5, this is the situation prior to the introduction of the concession. The operator charges the full fare, P_M, and at that fare the quantity demanded for this sub group is Q_M. All revenue accrues directly to the operator. Once the concession is introduced, however, the fare falls to P_{CF} in this market sector, i.e. 50 per cent, and sector demand increases to Q_{CF}. $Q_{CF} - Q_M$ therefore represents the additional travellers who did not travel before and this is known as the 'generated traffic'. These individuals are now paying the operator the concessionary fare, in this case 50p. These extra 50ps therefore are fares the operator had not received before and are due to the increase in bus use, or generated traffic, brought about by the introduction of the concession. This represents a net gain to the operator's revenue and needs to be taken into account in any fare reimbursement. The loss in revenue on the other hand, i.e. those concessionary travellers who would have travelled at the full fare, is shown by the area mapped out by P_{CF}, P_M, a, c. It should be clear now that the amount of compensation due to the operator would be the loss in revenue minus the revenue gain from the generated traffic, i.e. area P_{CF}, P_M, a, c minus area Q_M, c, b, Q_{CF}. There is however a further complication. This would still not leave the operator no better or no worse off as there is an additional cost connected with carrying more passengers. This will generally slow down boarding times and hence more buses may be required to maintain route frequency. The operator therefore also needs to be compensated the extra costs incurred as a result of carrying the generated traffic and this is shown in Figure 11.6.

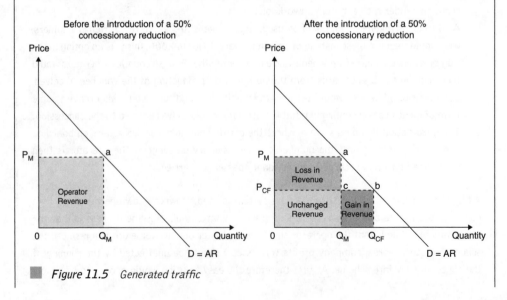

Figure 11.5 *Generated traffic*

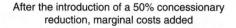

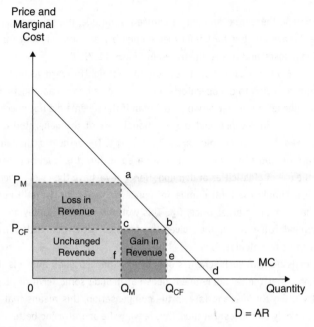

Figure 11.6 *Generated traffic with marginal costs added*

Figure 11.6 shows the marginal cost, and these are shown by adding the line labelled 'MC' which for simplification assumes constant non varying economies of scale. Thus the operator also needs to be compensated by the area Q_M, f, e, Q_{CF} in order to cover these added costs in order to be no better or no worse off as a consequence of the concessionary fare scheme.

In practice operator reimbursement has caused much confusion and resentment amongst operators as to what the actual level of 'generated' traffic should be, as may be imagined this is difficult to determine and even more so with the passing of time. Furthermore as most of these reduced fare schemes were only valid at off peak times, the expectation was that concessionary travellers would only use spare capacity and thus marginal costs would be minimal. This would still be the case however where no such time restrictions applied.

Even under a free concessionary fare scheme, the issue is still not straightforward as to how much the operator should be reimbursed. In Figure 11.6, demand for the concessionary group would now increase to point d and whilst the level of generated traffic will be significant, the level of generated (operator) revenue will be zero. DfT guidelines (DfT, 2008) on the introduction of the English national scheme gives the following measures that should be taken into account in the process of operator reimbursement:

- The average number of pass holders
- The average bus fare for the concession group, or where this is not available, the average bus fare charged
- The expected fare reimbursement revenue

- The expected number of concessionary fare trips
- The expected additional costs.

In order to determine the actual amount of compensation due, the critical elements of those listed above are the average bus fare, the expected number of concessionary fare trips and the expected additional costs, and this is illustrated in Figure 11.7.

After Figure 11.6, Figure 11.7 should be a lot more straightforward, as under a free scheme there is no revenue accruing to the operator from the concessionary passengers. Hence in order for the operator to be left no better or worse off than if the scheme did not operate, they should be reimbursed the loss in revenue and the additional cost of the generated traffic, which is simply given by area 0, P_M, a, Q_M plus area Q_M, f, e, Q_{CF}. Nevertheless, the whole process of concessionary fare reimbursement is still a messy area, as how the level of generated traffic is estimated is by the use of elasticities of demand. Hence if we have the level of demand at a zero price, Q_{CF}, which is simply the total number of concessionary trips, we still need to estimate the level of demand at the market price, Q_M. This would be done by applying an appropriate elasticity of demand value which then gives the level of generated traffic from which the additional costs could be calculated.

Another major issue with such schemes only briefly touched upon above is the question of whether it is 'right' that the reimbursement does not include some form of normal profit for the operator? By using the average fare in the compensation, this means that it will include operator profit, but only on the lost revenue, thus leaving the operator 'no better or worse off' as a result of the scheme. Many bus operators argue that the full fare should be compensated on all passengers carried, as in effect they are providing a service to the government in putting such

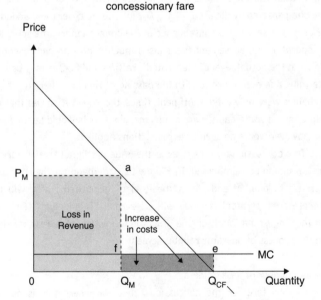

Figure 11.7 *Concessionary fare reimbursement, free concessions*

schemes into operation. For example, in the case of socially necessary services, services are operated on behalf of the government where operators will bid on the tender that will include a profit element, as in simple terms they will not do it for nothing. Why therefore should concessionary fare schemes be any different? The problem with full fare reimbursement however is that operators could increase profits by simply increasing the average fare, hence the level of reimbursement would automatically increase. This would be a particular danger where there is inelastic demand and a high number of concessionary passengers. The compromise solution would be to agree some rate, and this indeed is the case in Scotland and Wales, where all operators receive a flat rate of 73 per cent of the average full fare for each concessionary passenger carried. Rye and Carreno (2008) argue however that this is over-generous and thus provides an indirect form of subsidy to bus operators, and furthermore that such negotiations should be far more localised to reflect local bus market conditions. Nevertheless, regardless of the form of compensation arrangements in place, concessionary fare schemes are critical to the economics of the local bus market – Rye and Scotney (2004) estimated that the revenue from this market segment accounted for around 20 per cent of bus operators' revenue, and that at a time prior to the widespread introduction of free concessionary schemes.

All of the grey areas outlined in this case study are the main reason why such schemes tend to be limited in scope and there is far more reliance on supply side measures. The actual costs of administrating such schemes tend to be very high and thus should only be implemented where a true 'need' exists. It also highlights the problems when involving the private sector in public transport (i.e. a follow on from Chapter 10), as in the days of public ownership bus operators could simply have been ordered to carry concessionary travellers and the whole reimbursement process included in a single budget. Furthermore, given the criteria of 'no better or no worse off', the success of such schemes in meeting the targeted group are very much dependent upon market forces. If there are insufficient numbers of full paying passenger to support a bus service, then it will be cut, even if it is carrying a high level of concessionary travellers as they in theory do not contribute to operator revenue. In a deregulated transport market, this is always going to be the case with demand side measures, as those targeted can only use the services that are available, which in this case are in the main only those that can be sustained commercially. The fallback position of course is that if cut, the service could then be subsidised by the local authority by being deemed to be a socially necessary service. This clearly shows the areas of cross over between demand-side and supply-side measures in the support of transport services. That is, target specific groups through demand-side measures, and then ensure that a satisfactory level of transport provision is available to such groups through supply-side measures.

Drawbacks of paying subsidy

As highlighted in the introduction, there are many more issues that surround the actual payment of subsidy than subsidy itself. Most, if not all, agree it is a 'good thing'; however, most if not all recognise that there are many issues that need to be considered first before supporting transport services in such a manner. There are thus several potential shortcomings from an economic perspective when subsidy is paid. In this short section the four main drawbacks of paying subsidy are outlined, although there are many more.

It is always a second best solution

As we saw with regulation in the previous chapter, the payment of subsidy to a transport operator to provide a service is what is known as a second best solution. The best solution is always provision of the service by the market under the conditions of perfect competition. When subsidy is introduced into the market, however, this will usually be accompanied by some form of regulation in order to specify the conditions under which the subsidy is paid. With regulation comes the associated added costs of the additional bureaucracy needed to measure and monitor performance. The payment of a subsidy also interferes with the market signals generated by the forces of demand and supply. In a free market situation (and again assuming perfect competition), the market will ensure that the 'right' services are provided in the 'right' quantities. If consumers desire more of one type of service over another, then demand for the former will rise and for the latter fall. This will be signalled to producers through the price mechanism and they will ensure that more of the former is provided. When subsidy is paid however this interferes with that process and it becomes dependent upon accurate forecasting and planning in order to ensure that subsidy is used where it is most needed. This procedure will never be as efficient as the market, although note that it should be more effective.

Can lead to inefficient operations

In many ways, this is the most often cited case against paying a subsidy. The basic idea is that because the organisation is not working to strict market principles (i.e. primarily survival of the fittest), then costs are not as low as they should be. This is the x-inefficiency argument again. As a result, public subsidy is used to support inefficient operations rather than providing the service for which it was intended. Those more astute readers will realise that it is very difficult to isolate the subsidy component in such an argument, as in most if not all cases such subsidises will be provided in a monopoly type situation. In other words, if one operator cannot make a normal profit out of such operations then it makes little sense subsidising two!! Hence it is very difficult to split inefficient operations as a result of paying a subsidy or as a result of being the monopoly provider of services, and as highlighted, the two are invariably linked.

Whilst the general perception is that paying an operator a subsidy will lead to inefficiencies, is there any evidence to support that general view? Most research on the topic has indeed found that operators with higher levels of subsidy tend to be less efficient, although one problem in this research area is that some transport operations by their very nature are technically inefficient to provide, hence require subsidy. A classic example would be a rural railway, where frequencies will be low but the necessary inputs, particularly the infrastructure, relatively high. There is thus a problem of the direction of causation, where in many cases it is the inherent inefficient nature of operations that requires higher subsidy in order to sustain the service, i.e. inefficient operations, rather than higher subsidy sustaining inefficient management. Whilst most research has found an inverse relationship between subsidy and productive efficiency, several other factors have been found to impact upon that basic underlying relationship. For example, research on US public transit operators (Pucher *et al.*, 1983) suggested the source of the subsidy was an important factor in this relationship: federal subsidies had a large adverse effect on productivity whilst state subsidies had a small positive effect. This suggests that the nearer the transport authority is spatially located to the operator then the better targeted the subsidy can be on the use for which it was intended. It is thus less likely to result in productive inefficiencies. Other US research (Karlaftis and McCarthy, 1998) also found that the size of the firm was an important determinant. Larger firms were more vulnerable to the effects of higher subsidy levels on efficiency than smaller firms, with the source of the inefficiency being specifically x-inefficiency. Further studies (Sakano *et al.*, 1997) have also suggested that the source of the inefficiency is related to over-staffing, with those firms with higher subsidy payments tending to employ unnecessary staff.

Understanding these basic underlying factors is important in ensuring that subsidy is used for the purpose for which it was intended, rather than resulting in productive inefficiencies. This whole area of research, however, whilst considerable, still has some way to go before this relationship is fully understood, particularly in identifying the conditions under which paying a subsidy will not have a detrimental effect on efficiency.

The winner's curse syndrome

The idea of the winner's curse is used in auction theory to explain why winning bids may be based upon judgmental failures where the auction is ultimately won by the most optimistic valuation of the auction's item (Alexandersson and Hultén, 2006). Adnett (1998) further argues that winner's curse is more prevalent in tendering situations where the number of bidders is low and inexperienced in the first round of tendering. In terms of the payment of transport subsidy, the idea of the winner's curse is highly relevant, particularly with the general movement towards competitive tender. In these situations, the transport operator would bid for potential transport contracts based upon market information, and this information would tend to be optimistic in its forecasts of the potential market. The winner of the contract therefore would be that operator with the most optimistic revenue figures, hence, all else being equal, requiring the lowest subsidy to operate the service. The net result would be that when successful, the winning bidder would find out the optimism of their forecast and encounter losses on the service (hence the idea of a winning curse). For the transport authority, this would at first appear to be a beneficial situation, as basically they have secured the service at a lower price than would have otherwise been the case. The problem however is that such an argument completely overlooks the very the strong position of the incumbent operator. In a worst case scenario the operator would go out of business due to the losses being incurred, at best look for an early termination of the contract or finally they would provide the required services to the very minimum of standards with a danger of defaulting on the contract. Experience has shown that all of these scenarios are entirely unsatisfactory. In all instances the authority would either be faced with or potentially be faced with refranchising the service. The refranchising process would not only incur an added cost but would also undoubtedly end with the authority paying a higher price for the contract. What usually happens therefore is that the contract is re-negotiated with the existing operator being paid higher levels of subsidy, as that is the lower cost option. There is strong evidence that this was the case with many of the British passenger train operating companies (Cowie, 2009), which resulted in significant increases in subsidy at the time of contract extensions. The real problem with the winner's curse is that it is not the 'best' or most efficient operator that wins the contract, but rather the one with the most optimistic bid, but that it is the authority that ultimately has to address this problem. In simple terms, even as a second best solution this is not market efficient in any sense of the word.

265

Subsidise a service that doesn't actually need a subsidy

This drawback in some ways is a bit unclear, as many proponents of public transport would be of the view that all public transport services should be subsidised, even where a financial profit could be made. Such a view would be based on the premise of market failure caused by externalities (particularly public benefits) resulting in such services being undervalued by the market (see Figure 11.2). Therefore, accepting a political view that only loss-making services should be subsidised, the fourth and final drawback in paying a subsidy is that it may lead to the subsidisation of a service that on strictly financial criteria grounds does not actually need a subsidy to operate profitably. Hence rather than being used to provide an essential service, the subsidy is being used to bolster the operator's profit and increase the shareholder's dividend at the end of the financial year. The opportunity cost of these increased dividends therefore is the necessary service that is not being provided, and hence such measures are highly regressive. Undoubtedly having a two-tier system, where some services are subsidised and some are not, will affect operators' behaviour in transport markets. There is for example some circumstantial evidence of operators in Britain withdrawing a marginal service in the knowledge that the local authority would have to re-instate that service with the incentive of paying a subsidy. This in many ways is a consequence of a second best solution, because under a highly competitive market such an occurrence simply would not arise as the market would regulate itself.

As with point 2 above, there is far more to this argument than the simple provision of a single service and whether or not it requires subsidy. One factor such an argument overlooks is the systematic nature of public transport networks, and the extent to which one service 'supports' the whole system (note, not to be confused with cross-subsidisation – see below). This is best illustrated in the case of the Beeching closures on the British rail network of the 1960s. It has been argued by Henshaw (1995) that closure of branch lines led to a reduction in patronage on the lines to which they fed into, and thus those lines then became vulnerable and eventually closed. Public transport networks should therefore be viewed as complete systems and the contribution to overall revenues not based purely on whether each individual service covers its full costs or not. A further complication arises as many transport services have shared costs, such as maintenance and administrative overheads, hence how these are apportioned between the various services will determine the extent to which services are profitable or not.

OTHER ISSUES SURROUNDING TRANSPORT SUBSIDY

We end the chapter with a look at some other issues surrounding the payment of transport subsidy. The second, actual methods of payments, outlines the methods open to the authority for the payment of transport subsidy; however, the first issue considered, cross-subsidisation, also relates to how subsidy is paid. In simple terms should it be paid for a group of services which in total fail to make an economic return or should they be subsidised individually?

Cross-subsidisation

Cross-subsidisation occurs where the profits of one route or service are used to pay for the losses on another route or service. Why this idea is covered here under subsidy is that cross-subsidisation has often been used in the past as an alternative to a transport authority paying an operator a subsidy, or has been used to at least reduce the level of subsidy to be paid. This is particularly true of local authority owned and run bus companies, where the profits from high-density well-defined bus routes were used to recover some of the losses from little used low-density routes, hence reducing the overall reliance on subsidy.

In some ways, and to the general public at large, cross-subsidisation appears to be a 'good' thing. This is because there seems to be some balance in such a system where profits from one part of the operation are used to cover losses in another. As such, the system would appear to be self-contained, and where wholly cross-subsidised, the system entirely self-funded with no reliance on public subsidy, i.e. tax payers' money. Furthermore, in a regulated transport market where an operator may be protected from competition through the regulatory system, then it may seem only 'fair' that in return for this regulatory protection the operator sacrifices a part of their profit to provide some unprofitable routes for the authority.

The biggest argument against cross-subsidisation, however, particularly from an economist's point of view, is that it hides the true costs of providing a particular service. If profitable services are used to support loss-making routes, then the true costs of providing these services is completely hidden. In turn, if the true costs are not known then there is no way to judge if those routes are worth supporting or if the money could be better spent on other transport services. Direct accountability is therefore lost, which can lead to bad decision-making due to incomplete and aggregated data.

A second argument against cross-subsidisation is that rather than the operator being 'penalised' by using potential profits to fund loss-making routes, it is the users of the profitable routes that are being 'penalised' as they are paying for the users of the poorly used routes. This may well be a regressive measure, particularly given that some of the high-density routes may serve less prosperous areas, nevertheless the fares facing those individuals will be higher than they would otherwise be. As a result, the market as such is not as efficient as it should be. More may well use profitable services if fares were reduced to reflect their true market value, and hence it is also those potential users that are also paying for unprofitable routes. In many ways, therefore, cross-subsidisation is again in the realm of second best solutions, in which market signals are distorted by such measures. Importantly, however, in this case the best solution (i.e. the market) is an option that is available but simply not taken.

A final argument against cross-subsidising transport services is that there are other and better measures and policy instruments available to ensure that necessary services are provided to those that need them. Why should, for example, the users of profitable bus routes pay for the users of non-profitable bus routes whilst car drivers make absolutely no contribution? Or put the other way around, why should those dependent upon loss-making routes be reliant upon users of profitable bus routes for their bus service? What happens if bus patronage falls and the number of loss-making routes increases, are the number of bus routes cut? If a transport service is deemed to be a social necessity but is a loss maker, it should be the whole society that pays for the provision of that service, not just those existing users on profitable routes. This relates to the argument that transport should be provided on the basis of need rather than financial means. The 'best' mechanism for doing this is through the tax system, as this takes a far wider view than simply concentrating on the users of the system.

Other instances arise which may be confused with cross-subsidisation, where a loss-making route is continued but it can be justified on purely economic grounds. This can occur where there are short and long run factors or network effects present. In the first case, a route may be covering its short run costs but is returning losses as it is not covering the capital costs. In such instances, it makes economic sense to continue the service in the short run but when it comes to replacing the capital stock to then withdraw it. This is because in the short run the route will be returning a profit; however, the future return could never justify the investment required to continue operating the service. The second instance may be where an individual route is making a loss; however, in total it is adding to profits through network effects. This is because the service is making a positive contribution to the network as passengers brought in are then using other services in the network, hence if the route was cut these passengers would not use the service. Neither of these instances however should be confused with cross-subsidisation.

Methods of payment of subsidy

Today transport subsidies increasingly come in the form of a contractual payment for a service and may be applied to a specific route or a batch of routes or network. Where these are paid to a private sector operator, this would normally be in the expectation that the operator could provide the service at a lower cost than a publicly owned firm and that cost savings would more than offset the operator's profit from providing the service. Consequently, the total cost (i.e. subsidy) to be paid by the transport authority would be reduced; however, practice has shown that this has not always been the case. Moreover, such methods of subsidy payment are not the only ones open to transport authorities and outlined below are the five main methods used to pay subsidy to transport operators, irrespective of if the operator is publicly or privately owned. These virtually all concern supply side measures used to provide a service where one would not exist under free market conditions.

Deficit subsidy

This is the simplest form of subsidy and as suggested by the name, this is where the authority pays the difference between the revenue received from the service and the cost of providing that service. In the past these have been in the form of open-ended subsidies, where the authority covers the size of the deficit irrespective of how large that subsidy is. Increasingly, however, authorities have moved to a form of an allocated or negotiated budget. In many respects these forms of subsidy are consistent with the traditional view of the nationalised operator where the operator is allocated a budget, usually on an annual basis, to provide public transport services. Being publicly owned, the operator would be expected to provide the service in the public interest rather than for profit and hence break even (after the payment of subsidy) at the end of the year. This could be paid either through a straight allocation, as happened in the pre 1985 Transport Act with local authority bus operators/departments, or alternatively through negotiation. Many, if not most, of the Swiss independent railways operate along similar principles, where the standard of services to be provided is agreed and an annual budgeted figure negotiated.

The modern day equivalent of the deficit subsidy is what is known as a management contract. In simple terms, this is where a transport operator will run the service for a transport authority and then invoice the authority for the cost of running that service. This will consist of the difference between passenger revenue and operating costs in addition to a management fee. This will be subject to a negotiated budget beforehand and may be put out to tender. Such contracts may be used where there is a high degree of uncertainty involved, both in terms of future demand and future production requirements, and hence no operator willing to take on the business risk.

Net cost contract

Under such agreements, the operator in effect acts as a sub-contractor to government to provide transport services within a given area. This also reduces cross-subsidisation and produces greater visibility as to the actual cost of providing a given service/batch of services. Such contracts are normally for a set period of time, after which point the contract is then re-tendered. This basically is the idea of the contestable market outlined in Chapter 7 and it is over the last point highlighted, the length of the contract, that much debate exists. This is because the length of the contract ultimately determines the extent to which the market is actually contestable. In order to increase contestability, contracts should be for relatively short periods, because a short contract length puts added pressure on the incumbent to provide the best service. Under such a scenario, if they fail to perform then they can be replaced in a relatively short period of time or alternatively strong performance will increase the likelihood of success in any imminent re-bidding. However, there are several problems with short contracts. Firstly, the cost of having to re-bid the contract on a regular basis becomes a financial drain on the money available to actually spend on the service. Secondly, constant changes of operator may become disruptive in the provision of the service and hence not represent 'best value'. Thirdly, the longer the contract then the more likelihood that the operator will invest in new vehicle stock and a general organisational investment in the whole operation which may lead to a better understanding of users' needs and improvements in the service provided. The length of the contract therefore is a question of finding the optimum time period that maintains the contestability of the market but does not discourage investment in the service being provided. Due to the heavier investment requirements in the rail industry, this has tended to lead to longer contracts in the provision of rail services than for bus services. In Britain standard rail franchise lengths are seven years, whilst as seen in Case study 10.2 in Sweden it is five. For bus services, however, experience from around Europe shows that local transport author-ities offer bus contracts in most instances for two to three years.

Full cost contract

Under a full cost contract the operator's bid for subsidy is based on the full cost of running the service or network specified by the transport authority. This is what was referred to as an operational contract in Case study 10.2. Under such a contract, the fares charged are specified by the authority but collected by the operator who then returns the revenue to the authority. The net subsidy paid under such a contract by the authority is therefore the cost of the operator's contract less the revenue received from passengers. All revenue risk therefore rests with the authority and none with the operator. The operator thus knows exactly how much they will receive whilst the authority's revenue is dependent upon patronage levels. As with a net cost contract outlined above, such contracts will normally be for a set period of time, with the same issues over short versus long contracts. Several of the British passenger rail franchises operate under full cost contracts, Merseyside for example, whilst again as seen in Case study 10.2 both

Transport for London and the Helsinki Transport Authority operate a system of full cost contracts for the provision of bus services.

Design, Build, Operate and Maintain (DBOM)

DBOM contracts usually surround a major infrastructure project, such as the construction of a light-rail network such as the Nottingham Tram or a new (relief) motorway, such as the M6 Toll around Birmingham. Under these contracts, tenders will be based upon the price required to design, build, operate and maintain the infrastructure over a set period of time. Due to the high level of investment required, in most cases these will tend to be long-term contracts. The actual price bid in most cases is the difference between the revenue received from the operation of the service over the contract period minus the cost of designing, building and maintaining the system during that time. Therefore, once the lump sum is paid, the operator will be expected to make a profit out of the operation of the service (i.e. cover its short run costs). The revenue risk in this case therefore is with the operator of the service. Once the contract is completed the ownership of the infrastructure will return to the transport authority and then the contract re-tendered based upon either a franchised subsidy contract or a full cost contract. This is how the first phase of the Manchester LRT system (Metrolink) highlighted in the previous chapter was financed, where Serco won a DBOM contract for 15 years' operation. Once that contract expired in 2007, the facility was then re-tendered with Stagecoach winning it under a fixed term management contract (see above). Many other variations of DBOM contracts exist, however, for example in some specifications the revenue risk remains with the authority or others specify only operate and maintain. The distinguishing feature of these types of contracts is that the assets used in the provision of transport services are ultimately owned by the transport authority.

As we have seen, the payment of subsidy to a transport operator has seen considerable reform in the recent past, with several different methods and models of delivery (see Figure 10.4) introduced in the process of reform. Case study 11.2 considers the success in introducing these reforms into the provision of transport services.

Case study 11.2 Success in the payment of subsidy

This case study examines the actual mechanisms used in the payment of subsidy to support public transport services and the evidence of success or otherwise of these different approaches. As will become apparent from the case, in many instances how subsidy is paid can be dependent upon what is 'in vogue' rather than being based on any objective criteria. One problem when examining the different methods that have been used to inject subsidy into transport markets, is that there is a danger it can dissolve into an economic history on the payment of subsidies to transport industries. In this case, some historical background and precedent is useful, as how subsidy was paid in the past in some ways shapes how it is paid in the present. Nevertheless, this case will particularly focus on the movement away from open ended lump sum subsidies to more contract-based approaches.

Subsidies have been around for many years in one form or another, although there has always been differences regarding the extent to which the state should intervene in transport

---

markets with the support of public finance. Even back in the 19th century many railways around continental Europe were constructed with heavy state backing due to their perceived strategic importance, whilst in Britain all railways were constructed using only private finance (although required state legislative approval). Even within Britain, however, the idea of subsidising transport services was not a completely alien notion. In the 1930s the big 4 'private' railways received substantial payments from government and the 'national' airline, Imperial Airways, was allegedly supported by an annual subsidy of around £1m (a relatively large sum at the time) to support air services that connected the Empire. The subsidisation of transport services however never really became a major issue until the 1960s when the last of the major state railways, Swiss Federal Railways, fell into deficit for the first time in 1969. With the rise of the private car, the financial viability of bus services also became increasingly marginal and ultimately required subsidy to support existing networks. The US experience for example shows that subsidy for public transport from all levels of government (local, state and federal) rose from $318m in 1970 to $9.27bn by 1990 (Karlaftis and McCarthy, 1998).

The first form of subsidy payment used was deficit subsidy, where subsidy bridged the gap between passenger revenue and the cost of providing the transport service. This was given legislative backing by the then European Community with the passing of directive 1191/69 in 1969 that introduced the idea of Public Service Obligations (PSO). This recognised that there were certain transport services (mainly bus and rail) for which the then largely state-owned operators were 'forced' to operate but which would never make a viable economic return. The directive required the relevant authorities to re-compensate the operators for such public service obligations in the form of a lump sum payment. When Britain joined the EC in 1973, the PSO was introduced into the railways by the Railways Act 1974, which required that the then state-owned British Rail provide services 'broadly consistent with that provided at the moment'. In subsequent years this was generally interpreted as a level of train kilometres consistent with that run in 1974 (British Railways Board, 1988). The PSO was paid on the basis of a lump sum subsidy for the whole of the British network. In the 1980s, however, under the Organising for Quality initiative, BR was re-organised more along market-focused principles and thus the PSO was split between the three passenger sectors of Regional Railways, Network South East and Intercity, and negotiated annually. By far the largest part of the PSO was taken by Regional Railways, which consisted of all non Intercity routes outside of the south east. The Intercity sector however was set a target of zero subsidy, a position it duly achieved in the years 1986/87 and 1987/88, whilst the Network South East sector (NSE – London commuter routes) hoped to reach a target of zero subsidy by the early 1990s. A major change in the economic climate however brought about a major re-think, in which it was realised that the Lawson Boom of the late 1980s had been the prime driver behind the strong performance of NSE. Consequently it was also realised that NSE would always require subsidy if it was to provide a valuable transport service to the London commuter network.

The first country however to adopt full market principles in the payment of subsidy was not Britain but New Zealand, with full deregulation of bus services in 1983 and railway reform between 1986 and privatisation in 1993. The first large land-based passenger transport market to be deregulated however was the British bus industry. The topic of transport industry reform has been covered in the previous chapter, hence this case study only concentrates on the reforms in the payment of subsidy to operators. The Transport Act 1985 put an end to open ended lump payment subsidies and all services were expected to make a profitable return, even where provided by a local authority company. The one exception, as noted previously, was that local authorities could specify a service where none was provided by the free market on the basis of a social necessity. This would then be put out to competitive tender, hence creating competition for the market rather than in the market. The impact these reforms had on subsidy payments can be clearly seen in Figure 11.8, which outlines subsidy payments in constant 2008 prices from 1976/77 to 2004/05.

Figure 11.8 shows the total subsidy paid for services for all of Britain up until 1984/85, and then due to availability of the data, splits this between London and outside of London after that period. The rise in the level of subsidy paid throughout the mid 70s and early 80s is very clear, primarily caused not only by falling passenger numbers, but also a suspicion of decreasing efficiency in operations. With the change in the system of subsidy brought in by the 1985 Act, subsidy levels fell considerably, so that by 1990/91 for supported services outside of London the subsidy paid to operators had fallen to almost 40 per cent of its previous level. This should not however be taken as an indication of simply moving from an open-ended-type payment to a contractual payment, as other reformatory principles were also put into effect, principally the requirement that fares could no longer be directly subsidised by local authorities.

The British experience is fairly consistent with that in other countries. Most of the research cited below comes from the Thredbo series of conferences on 'Competition and Ownership in Land Passenger Transport' led by Professor David Hensher of the University of Sydney and held biannually since the first conference in Thredbo, Australia, in 1989. This has been a major forum that draws on a wide range of international experience for the discussion of reforms in the organisation and operation of public transport services, including, of course, the payment of subsidy. For example, Hauge (1999) found considerable savings in the subsidies required to maintain Norwegian ferry links, where the introduction of competitive tendering on a limited number of routes had led to reductions in subsidy, improved efficiency and a better organised

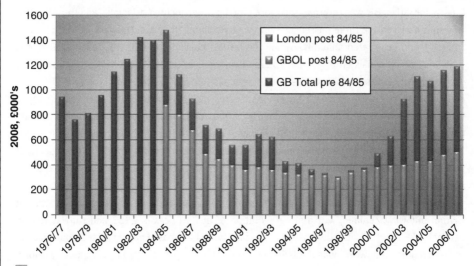

Figure 11.8 Public financial support for services, 1976/77 to 2005/06, 2008 prices

Source: Compiled from DfT Statistics

transport ferry operation. The author also found some evidence however of winner's curse. Johansen (1999), in an examination of the Norwegian bus industry, found that the movement away from net cost contracts, i.e. lump sum subsidies, to contracts based on cost norms and competitive tendering had had a major impact on the bus market in Norway. The main findings were that costs had decreased by around 20 per cent, the reliance on subsidy had fallen from 37 to 24 per cent and finally that the reforms had sparked off major restructuring of the supply side of the industry. This had seen the number of bus operators reduce from 220 to 83 and the emergence of two dominant operators through mergers and acquisitions who held around 40 per cent of the total market. Van de Velde (2003) not only found that the introduction of market reforms had led to considerable supply side consolidations across a number of countries examined, but also strong evidence of the 'internationalisation' of public transport operations. This was no more acute than in Denmark, where two foreign-owned companies held almost two-thirds of the bus market. This had led to an upward trend in contract prices; however, subsidy levels had stabilised at around 10 per cent under pre-reform levels. Finally Preston (2001), in a review of bus and light-rail systems across Europe, estimated that the dependence on subsidy for fully competitive transport markets, at 37 per cent, was considerably lower than for either limited competition markets or fully regulated markets, where the level for both was found to be 53 per cent. Competitive bus markets also had costs per vehicle kilometre some 23 per cent lower than limited competitive markets and 51 per cent lower than regulated markets.

Whilst the evidence would undeniably support the view that the move away from open ended lump sum payments towards more competitive and public sector contract agreements has considerably reduced subsidy levels, there remains a question mark and debate over how far such reforms can be taken. There is clearly a limit as to how little subsidy can be paid before the low finance levels impact upon the quality of the service provided. Paying low subsidy levels to sustain a poor quality service with little patronage could never be described as 'value for money'. Considered opinion is therefore moving back towards the idea of negotiated contracts, where in the first instance, the transport authority will re-negotiate the contract with the incumbent operator. This overcomes the problems of the transaction costs of having to re-tender the contract as well as what can potentially be a disruptive period as one operator takes over from another. The evidence suggests that where such initiatives have been put into place, then potentially the added advantages are that it can lead to less conservative approaches to the provision of public transport services and contract renewal can be directly linked to key performance indicators and appropriate benchmarks. Hensher and Wallis (2005) clearly see a greater role for negotiated contracts under a particular set of circumstances. Namely, where the incumbent is recognised as an efficient supplier, where a greater focus needs to be placed on innovation to grow patronage and finally where incentives need to be provided to encourage the required investment to support such activities. Around the globe, such circumstances are hardly uncommon. Rather than the authority/operator as a contractor/contractee relationship, this encourages far more of a genuine partnership arrangement between the authority and the operator. Much debate and inconsistencies however remain over this whole issue. The European Union for example require that in certain transport sectors all public service contracts over a given threshold be put out to competitive tender irrespective of the circumstances facing the particular transport mode.

This case has provided a review of the development and changing trends in the payment of subsidy and would appear to outline a clear evolutionary process in the structure of subsidy payments. Starting from a simple open-ended lump sum payment, regulatory reform has tended to move the operator towards a more market-driven focus and subsidy usually paid on a negotiated or cost norm basis with clear 'targets' set. The next stage would be to introduce competition for the market through competitive tender, where the market for the payment of subsidy is 'opened up' to other operators. Research suggests however that whilst both these regulatory reforms can produce considerable reductions in subsidy, these appear to be one-off effects and are not continued into the medium to longer terms; in fact if anything, such trends are reversed in subsequent rounds. Under such circumstances, therefore, negotiated contracts may produce better results, where the authority negotiates with the incumbent, rather than continue with a system of competitive bidding.

CHAPTER SUMMARY AND REFLECTION

This chapter has directly followed on from the previous chapter on regulation and ownership in transport markets, and examined the issue of where the state directly funds transport operations or investments in a specific location. It has considered the main issues surrounding this topic in the form of the reasons for doing it and the associated drawbacks in doing so. Whilst this has generally been from a 'pro' perspective, i.e. under certain conditions transport services should be subsidised, alternative views do exist. For example Karlaftis and McCarthy (1998: 359) state that while capital subsidies to transport industries can be justified on the grounds of achieving returns to scale, '. . . there are no economic grounds for providing operating subsidies'. To a certain extent such a view may reflect a far narrower definition of what constitutes 'economic grounds', as 'revitalizing cities' for example is considered as a social objective, but it is nevertheless a statement that few would agree with. What we have seen in the course of this chapter is that the rationale for the payment of subsidy mainly surrounds issues of market failure, thus in a mixed market economy one of the roles of the state is to correct for such market failures. It cannot however correct for all market failures, as the resources at its disposal are limited. It therefore has to ensure that when such action is taken, the financial resources are used in the appropriate manner, i.e. to correct the market failure, and are not wasted in the process due to inefficiencies. It is thus this second point around which most of the issues surrounding subsidy revolve.

CHAPTER EXERCISES

Exercise 11.1 Options in the payment of subsidy

A transport authority seeks to produce a modal shift from the car to public transport services in order to encourage local economic development and reduce traffic congestion. Outline in a variety of diagrams the main options that are open to the authority to achieve this aim and come to a conclusion as to which you believe to be the 'best' approach or combinations of approaches that should be used.

Where subsidy features in your solutions, you should outline the main drawbacks that stand in the way of a successful outcome and what measures you propose to take to minimise the impact of these drawbacks.

Exercise 11.2 Which type of contract to use

As the recently appointed leader of your local transport authority, you are given a blank sheet of paper with which to re-organise urban based public transport services in your local area. Assume that the national legislation allows for any of the models of delivery outlined in Chapter 10 to be used, but nationalisation is out of the question.

Using Figure 10.4, which related to ownership forms in the provision of transport services, consider for each of the following scenarios which 'model' of ownership would be most suitable for the particular situation:

i   A pro public transport council that has a strong policy stance on encouraging more people to use public transport.

ii A council that is facing possible budget cuts in the medium to longer term and seeks to reduce its budget for public transport services.

iii A council that is expecting strong economic growth in the medium and long runs and is concerned that the current public transport provision, which is mainly bus based, will limit this economic growth.

iv Where public transport services have been run directly by the local authority department, however, the last ten years have seen a significant decline in patronage and low investment levels.

v   Public transport services are currently run by private sector companies; however, the overall perception is of poor quality services that have seen significant passenger declines in the last ten years.

vi A publicly owned and run urban rail metro that is badly in need of refurbishment; however, budget constraints means that the local authority do not have the funds available to undertake the investment required.

Then consider under what type of the following contracts should be used in delivery of these services:

a) Complete deregulation with contracts only for socially necessary services
b) Tender all services on a full cost basis
c) Tender all services on a relative cost basis.

Exercise 11.3 Blue bus company's bid for a local authority contract

This exercise concerns the costing of a bid for a local authority specified bus service contract. The case surrounds a local operator, The Blue Bus Company, that is a very traditional local operator with a reputation acquired over a number of years for providing an excellent service. Blue Bus has won several Local Authority contracts in the past. It has however recently experienced a small dip in its share of the local market.

The Contract

The contract is for a new route of 6 kilometres in length that will operate from 7am in the morning (first service) until 7pm in the evening (last service) from Monday through to Saturday. Total annual revenue is expected to be in the order of £85,000 and you should assume a 50 week operating period.

New buses will have to be purchased if the company is successful in its bid for this contract. These will cost £110,000 each and will be written down to their scrap value of £10,000 using the straight line method over a period of ten years. The company expects that the buses operated on this route will broadly match the company's current average annual mileage per bus.

The specific costing figures for Blue Bus are:

Fixed costs:	£350,000
Variable costs, per kilometre run:	£0.95
Annual vehicle Km:	1,200,000
Number of buses operated:	27
Profit Mark Up:	12%

The variable costs per kilometre run include all the costs associated with the running of the buses, including staff costs, fuel and maintenance and so on. Fixed costs include depreciation, interest payments and fixed depot costs. For the purposes of this exercise, assume that the only fixed costs associated with the new contract will be the depreciation of the vehicles used.

Competition

The company is likely to face competition for this tender from two other bus companies, with some brief details given of these below:

The Go By Red Bus Company

Go by Red is a bit of a pushy company known for its aggressive marketing campaigns and cut-throat competition in the market place. A well-known local operator, the company was acquired by a major UK and international bus company with a similar reputation of aggressive and rough market tactics. Since the take-over, the company has not bid on any Local Authority contracts.

Black and Gold Platinum Bus Services

Part of a major UK bus group, Black and Gold are looking to expand operations and have not previously run bus services in this area, either commercially or under contract to the local authority.

You should price this contract in the first instance based upon the Blue Bus Company's current costs and profit mark-ups. Having done so, you should then consider the competition and whether there are any 'adjustments' that you feel should be made to the contract price before putting in the final tender. Note in making these decisions your figures should still make economic sense, i.e. running the company into the ground to win this contract is not an option!

Exercise 11.4 Concessionary fare reimbursement

Consider the following exercise below which concerns compensation for the implementation of a concessionary fare scheme.

The transport authority wishes to implement a concessionary fare scheme on the basis that the operator should be 'no worse or no better off' as a result of the scheme. The current demand for bus services from those that would benefit from the scheme is estimated to be in the order 3,500 passengers daily and the flat fare charged by the operator is £1.20. The authority is considering the following options.

Scheme 1: The concessionary fare to be implemented would be a flat 25p charge. This would be expected to increase demand of those entitled to the concession by 10 per cent and the authority agrees to pay 20p to the operator to cover the cost of each additional passenger carried.

Scheme 2: An entirely free concessionary fare scheme which would be expected to increase demand of the entitled group by 25 per cent with again the authority agreeing to pay 20p to the operator for each additional passenger carried

a) Calculate for both schemes the expected level of compensation that will be due to the operator on an annual basis, where the schemes are assumed to operate for 360 days a year.

b) Having looked at the figures, which of the two schemes do you think the authority should introduce?

c) An alternative form of reimbursement is proposed, where the operator receives a straight compensation of 75 per cent of the full fare for each concessionary passenger carried. Rework the levels of reimbursement under this proposed form for both the flat 25p and free concessions.

d) Using these figures and comparing them to the values given in Figure 11.4 and Case study 11.1 regarding increases in compensation levels in Wales and Scotland (which is on a straight 73 per cent of full fare compensation), what possible reasons can be given for the considerable increases in the levels of reimbursement being paid with the move to a completely free scheme?

Exercise 11.5 Questions for discussion

Discuss the following simple statements, which should help to build on and develop some of the issues discussed in this chapter:

- 'Low subsidy is "good", high subsidy is "bad".'
- 'Transport should only be subsidised on the basis of what can be afforded by the relevant authorities.'
- ' "Public" Transport is a "public" good, therefore should be subsidised.'
- 'Road networks, because they are provided and maintained by the state, are therefore provided free of charge.'

Chapter 12

The economics of freight transport

Learning Outcomes:

On reading this chapter, you will learn:

- The overall trends of freight carriage in Great Britain
- Reasons why nations trade and the major institutional developments that have occurred since 1950 that have led to a significant increase in international freight transport
- Some of the major economic issues surrounding road haulage, rail freight, air cargo and maritime transport.

INTRODUCTION

The economics of freight is an often overlooked and considerably under-researched area. One of the main reasons for this is that freight transport conforms far more to the principles of the free market than passenger transport. In simple terms, if a profit cannot be made from the sale of the goods in a different location because for example of high transport costs, the freight won't go anywhere, and in fact will not even be produced in the first place. Even this book is a case in point of far less attention being paid to freight than passenger transport. The importance of freight transport however should not be understated. In purely financial terms, the carriage of freight and distribution services was estimated to be something in the order of £74.45bn in 2006 to the British economy (Keynote, 2007), which compares for example to some £3.7bn in passenger receipts from the bus industry or £6.6bn from passenger rail.

This chapter will examine the overall issues surrounding freight transport, beginning with an overview of the trends in freight carriage. Considerable space however is given to the major external factors that have impacted upon the freight transport industry since the 1950s. Freight, even more so than passenger transport, does not operate in a vacuum and external factors can and have had a major impact upon freight transport levels. This is particularly true of the international dimension, thus the chapter will introduce a very simple theoretical explanation of why nations trade before going on to consider institutional and economic developments that have led to considerable increases in trade, and thus international freight transport, since the 1950s. The second part of the chapter examines some of the economics involved in the individual modes of freight transport. The form and content of this chapter is very different to those that have gone before, as it deals far more with practical developments rather than theoretical issues; in many respects this chapter is about using the tools of economic analysis to examine freight transport modes in order to come to a better understanding of some of the issues facing these modes of transport.

AN OVERVIEW OF FREIGHT TRANSPORT

The 18th and 19th centuries saw firstly the rise of the canal network in Britain and then the railways. Railways historically carried most of the freight in Britain, certainly all freight that needed to be transported over a relatively long distance. As has been highlighted in Chapter 2, railways were the driver of the Industrial Revolution in Britain, which saw a shift from an agricultural-based to a manufacturing-based economy. All of these lines were built using private finance, and a large number constructed based upon the freight-carrying potential (although one that often was never realised).

These are the origins of today's freight transport industries, and Figure 12.1 outlines the trends, by mode, of freight transport in the UK since 1953.

With regard to the overall figures for total freight tonne kilometres hauled, this has been seen before in Figure 2.1 in Chapter 2. Across the whole period shown, the overall level of freight transport has risen by a factor of almost three, with most of this increase coming from increases in road haulage. At the beginning of the period, road haulage had a 36 per cent market share, and this had almost doubled to 64 per cent by 2006. More revealingly, road haulage accounted for around 80

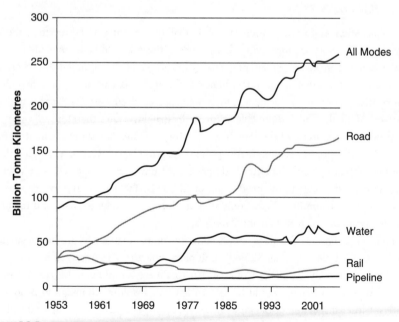

Figure 12.1   *Trends in the carriage of freight, 1953 to 2006*

Source: Compiled from DfT (2007)

279

per cent of the total increase in all freight moved over the period, and even this figure understates the dominance of this mode. This is because if the impact of North Sea Oil (see below) is taken out of these figures, the total would be nearer 100 per cent. Rail freight over the period has been in long-term decline, with tonne kilometres falling from 1953 onwards, making a minor recovery in the late 1980s as a result of the aforementioned Lawson boom, and then increases again in the period immediately after privatisation. After that initial increase, however, freight levels on the railways have remained fairly constant with about 8 per cent of total freight hauled in the last year shown. Transport by pipeline rose in the 1970s, almost exclusively due to North Sea Oil, but accounts for only 4 per cent of the market. Waterways is the only mode that has held its market share constant over the whole period, at around 22 per cent. Most of this however is again due to North Sea Oil, as around 80 per cent of freight moved by water is petroleum-related products. This increase occurred in the late 1970s to early 1980s when the North Sea oil fields came fully on stream, from which point it has hovered around 60bn tonne kilometres per year. As will be seen later in the chapter, water-borne freight transport has an even stronger market share at the European Union level.

The internationalisation of freight transport

Ever since the beginning of the 1950s there has been a constant and steady growth of international freight transport. This in some ways reflects the times and one that has seen the ongoing globalisation of the world economy. This growth is due to significant political and institutional developments, mainly in the form of the lessening of international trade restrictions. Before we examine these, however, it is worthwhile to consider why nations actually trade, as this has a significant impact on the level of international freight transport.

Why do nations trade?

A simple explanation as to why nations trade is that one country is better than the other at producing a certain good or commodity, hence where there is a 'double coincidence of wants' then it makes sense to make some form of exchange. This could be in commodities where it is very difficult for one or the other to produce; hence for example Britain may trade Scotch whisky, which it is relatively good at producing due to certain natural advantages, for bananas with Jamaica, which are very difficult if not impossible to grow in Britain. Trade therefore allows nations to specialise production in areas where they have an advantage and this should benefit both parties to the trade. An early piece of economic theory however from David Ricardo expanded this simple idea to consider the case where a country had only a comparative advantage. This differs in that one nation may have an advantage in the production of all goods. Table 12.1 attempts to illustrate this idea, where the basic assumption is that only two products are produced, food and manufactures, and the trade occurs between Britain and America.

What Table 12.1 shows is that in Britain it takes five units of labour to produce a single unit of food, and 2 units of labour to produce a single unit of manufactures. In America, however, it takes 6 units and 12 units respectively, thus it would appear that there is nothing to be gained from Britain trading with America as Britain would be said to have an absolute advantage in producing both commodities. Closer inspection of the table however reveals that there are comparative differences between the two nations. This is based on the principle of the opportunity cost of switching production from one commodity to the other. If Britain was to switch its labour from the

Table 12.1 *Ricardo's Law of comparative advantage*

Labour per unit of output in	Britain	America
Food	5	6
Manufactures	2	12
Total	7	18

Total: 25

Table 12.2 *Ricardo's Law of comparative advantage*

Labour per unit of output in	Britain	America
Food	–	12
Manufactures	4	–
Total	4	12

Total: 16

production of food to manufactures, then for each unit of food not produced 2.5 extra units of manufactures would be produced. In America, however, if the same switch were to occur, then each unit of food not produced would only increase the production of manufactures by 0.5. America therefore has a comparative advantage in food. This is because food is less 'valuable' in terms of labour productivity in America than it is in Britain, as it is only 'worth' half a unit of manufactures as opposed to 2.5 units in Britain.

There is therefore an advantage to be gained for both nations if each was to specialise in the commodity that has the lower opportunity cost in terms of the other. Put another way, each nation should specialise in the commodity in which it has to give up the least in terms of production of the other. The results of such specialisation are shown in Table 12.2.

In this simplified example, all production in Britain has been switched to manufactures whilst in America concentration is on food production. However, in both cases each country now requires double the labour input, as it is assumed that only one of the produced units is for domestic consumption whilst the second is exported. Before this specialisation, 25 labour units were required to produce 2 units of food and 2 units of manufactures across both countries; however, after specialisation only 16 labour units are required to produce the same quantities. Note also that not only has the total labour requirement fallen, but both countries will benefit from the trade. In Britain before trade a total of 7 labour units were required and this has now fallen to 4, whilst in America a total of 18 labour units were required and this has now fallen to 12. This should result in a net increase in benefit to both societies, thus it makes sense for both nations to trade even although Britain has an absolute advantage.

Note however that the biggest limitation of Ricardo's theory is that it does not consider the terms of trade, which can have a significant impact upon the trade question. Although both nations benefit, the key is how that benefit is distributed between the two and it is the terms of trade that will by and large resolve the issue. In the previous example, Britain has almost doubled its production capacity as a result of the trade, where as America has only increased it by half. Whilst this may at first appear to be 'fair' as Britain had an absolute advantage in both commodities, such an argument completely ignores the key issue that both countries need each other and hence why should Britain apparently benefit by far more? Despite such limitations, the theory nevertheless clearly illustrates that trade can be of major economic benefit to the parties concerned and this has been one of the main drivers behind reducing trade restrictions.

The rise of international trade

Figure 12.2 clearly shows the increase in world trade since the Second World War, basically the period 1948 to 2005, all of which has had a direct impact on transport levels as these goods have needed to be transported from one country to another. Interestingly, in all periods percentage increases in trade have exceeded percentage increases in production; however, this in some respects is slightly misleading, as in terms of absolute amounts the total level of production by far exceeds the total level of commodities traded. Consequently, although output has risen by smaller percentage increases, the absolute increase in production will considerably outweigh the absolute increase in trade. Nevertheless, over the whole period shown, goods for export have taken a progressively larger share of total output. The graph is broken down into six time periods, and whilst all have seen strong growth, this was particularly true in all periods up to 1973. This rate of increase however significantly tailed off in the next three periods shown, almost certainly as a result of the oil crises of 1973/4 and 1978/9. This had a dramatic effect on most of the world's developed economies and also to a certain extent led to the pursuit of more protectionist policies. Even given such factors, however, trade still increased in the period 1973 to 1983 by an average of around 5 per cent per year. When compounded over the whole period, this produces an overall increase of 65 per cent. The last period shown shows a return to strong growth, at levels considerably in excess of those of the 1950s and 60s; however, more recent economic events almost guarantee that this will not be sustained over a longer period.

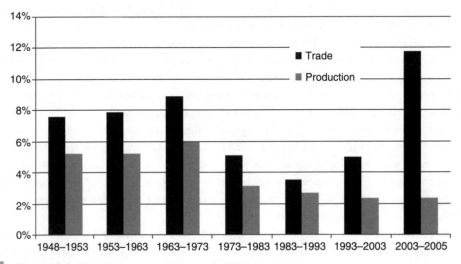

Figure 12.2   Trends in international trade, 1948 to 2005

Source: Drawn from World Trade Organisation Statistics

282

The question arises as to why such strong growth has occurred over this time, which is considered below under the two headings of institutional and other developments.

Institutional developments

With regard to international trade, major institutional and political reforms began even before the Second World War had ended. All institutional developments that have occurred since have their origins in the Bretton Woods Conference held between the Allied powers in 1944. At that time, the outcome of the war was clear; what remained unknown was how long it would take to resolve and the human cost involved. Bretton Woods therefore was convened to discuss the shape of the monetary and financial order in the post-war world, and in particular consider the issue of international trade in an attempt to end economic nationalism. It was recognised that pre-war economic conditions had played a significant part in the origins of the Second World War, particularly the effect of the Great Depression on the appeal of extreme politics. The Bretton Woods Conference laid down the foundations for the development of three organisations which would enhance global trade, of which the main one was the General Agreement on Tariffs and Trade (GATT). This was established in 1948 and originally signed by 23 member states. One of the principal reasons that Bretton Woods specifically considered international trade was the world-wide economic depression of the late 1920s/early 1930s. During that time the declining or negative rate of economic growth led to most nations adopting highly protectionist policies such as increasing import duties, a reduction in import quotas or even complete embargoes, which resulted in trade 'partners' taking retaliatory measures. Instead of improving the economic situation, therefore, such measures only succeeded in making economic matters worse (as trade is never a zero sum game). At Bretton Woods the importance of non-restrictive trade agreements was recognised so that previous mistakes were not repeated.

The main mechanism through which this was to be done was the GATT. The precepts of the GATT are that all trading partners are treated equally and that imports are treated the same as national goods. Negotiations are in the form of 'rounds', the most significant being the Tokyo Round (1973 to 1979) and the Uruguay Round (1986 to 1993), with the latter leading to the creation of a permanent body to supersede the GATT, the World Trade Organisation (WTO). The latest round of trade talks, known as the Doha Round, began in 2001 and includes 141 nations, although at the time of writing these are currently suspended due to various disagreements between the developed and the developing nations. Negotiations were expected to resume in 2009.

The other two bodies created at Bretton Woods were the International Monetary Fund (IMF) and the International Bank for Investment and Re-Development (IBIR, later the World Bank). The IMF was set up to oversee the global financial system after the war, whilst the World Bank now provides assistance to debt-ridden countries that may have no other means of raising the significant levels of capital funds required to help get them out of current economic difficulties.

Other developments

- Increasing sophistication of international financial markets.
  This has been a major driving force behind the trends in international transport created by increased trade. As highlighted above, exchange rates have moved from a system of fixed

exchange rates with a wholly cumbersome and costly process of changing currencies to the situation today where all major currencies are floated on the free market. Whilst that concerns simple spot exchange rates, e.g. how many Euros will I get for £1 today, there is also a system of forward exchange rates where currency can be bought or sold forward at a rate agreed today, thus overcoming any exchange rate risk. There are also far more complicated international payments systems such as credit swap agreements (for investments) and other such measures.

- Development of the concept of the whole supply chain.
  This is the whole idea of logistics, and the entire process of moving goods from the factory to the market is now viewed as a single process. Whole markets and industries have developed around these ideas and the net effect has been to significantly reduce costs and increase efficiency. This not only includes the transport element, but also relates to issues such as warehousing, packaging and the integration of all elements in the supply chain.
- Improvement in political/economic stability.
  Generally speaking major firms are not going to trade or invest in a politically or economically unstable country. Over the period reviewed, however, for a variety of reasons ranging from democratic revolutions to the external overthrowing of political dictators, there are far more politically stable places in the world today than there were fifty or sixty years ago. Many areas however still remain politically unstable.

These are the main drivers behind developments in world trade and thus the rise of international freight transport; however, note that this list is far from exhaustive and there have been many other developments that have led, and continue to lead, to the increasing globalisation of the world economy. It is important to end this section with a reminder that 'globalisation' is not something that happened in the 1990s, but rather is a process that continues to evolve today and consequently is a process that will continue to have a major impact on levels of international freight transport.

MODES OF FREIGHT TRANSPORT

From this and previous chapters, we have seen that the economic environment in which freight transport has been operating is one of a world of continually rising real incomes and increasing levels of globalisation. In this section we take these ideas forward and examine the impact that these and other factors have had upon the main modes of freight transport. As may be expected in a book on the economics of transport, particular emphasis is given to the economic characteristics of each mode where these have not been considered before in earlier chapters. This should also further reinforce some of the economic principles already examined, as well as giving a practical perspective to these concepts. We begin with road haulage, which has already been extensively studied in Case study 6.1 in Chapter 6.

Road haulage

Development of road haulage in the UK

Road transport first emerged as a serious competitor to what had been the premier position of the railways during the 1930s, in the main due to advances in the technology of road vehicles and the development of the road network. At that time, railways were heavily regulated in terms of the prices they could charge for the carriage of freight. These were published in advance and were fixed, hence there was no 'market pricing'. Perhaps more significantly, railways had a duty to carry, which meant that any freight that was presented for carriage had to be accepted and charged at the published prices, no matter how difficult, inconvenient or unprofitable such loads were for the railway to transport. Road haulage was also heavily regulated under the provisions of the Road and Rail Traffic Act 1933 which empowered area Traffic Commissioners to broadly set fares, the rules of carriage and restrict market entry. It is generally agreed however that such regulations were far less restrictive than for the railways (see for example Glaister *et al.*, 2006). This gave those in the industry a degree of competitive advantage over their rail counterparts.

Large segments of the industry were nationalised along with the railways in 1947 as part of the Attlee post-war Labour government's extensive nationalisation programme. All long-distance road services of over 40 miles came under the control of the British Transport Commission (BTC); however, local hauliers remained largely in the private sector. Under the provisions of the 1947 Act, the BTC had a remit to provide 'an efficient, adequate, economical and properly integrated system of public inland transport and port facilities within Great Britain for passengers and goods' (Lloyd Wilson, 1950). The overall aim of the nationalisation was thus to produce a unified and planned network of road haulage services in Britain. When this failed to materialise, most of the component parts were transferred back to the private sector, interestingly labelled as 'de-nationalisation' measures (i.e. as opposed to privatisation).

The parts that remained in the BTC had their own executive under the title of British Road Services (BRS). With the passing of the Transport Act 1962, however, the BTC was abolished and its constituent parts split into separate organisational bodies, with road haulage passing into the control of the Transport Holding Company (THC), along with the nationalised bus companies, shipping lines and bus manufacturers. The THC was relatively short lived, with the 1968 Transport Act transferring control of road haulage over to a new dedicated body, the National Freight Corporation (NFC). The 1968 Act also abolished all economic regulation from the industry, effectively deregulating the market. The only regulation that remained related to qualitative measures over driver qualifications, driving standards, the condition of the vehicles and (in 1977) operator qualifications and business practices. Following the passing of the 1968 Act, the number of operators in the industry rose sharply as a direct result of the abolishment of market entry controls; however, they levelled off after 1977 following the introduction of the professional competence requirement (Lacey, 1990). This largely continued to be the position of road haulage until the election of the Conservative government two years later under Margaret Thatcher.

The privatisation of the nationalised road haulage sector was one of the early privatisations under the Thatcher government and probably one of the few taken for purely economic ideological reasons. The initial proposal was to privatise the industry through a stock market flotation; however, this was dropped due to the prevailing economic recession at the time. The company was therefore sold to a management–employee buyout. Some 37 per cent of employees initially bought shares in the company, rising to 80 per cent by 1989, at which point the company obtained a stock market listing. Profits rose throughout the 1980s but the 1990s proved far more difficult, with profits falling and the share price dropping considerably. This was largely due to increasing competition within the industry brought about in part by the increasing globalisation of the whole logistics market, causing prices to fall dramatically.

By 1998 the NFC had changed its name to Exel plc and had developed into a full logistics provider, not only providing road haulage services but also all aspects of supply chain management. Pickfords, the removal company, was sold to Sirva Inc in 2002. Exel itself was then subsequently acquired by DHL and integrated into their existing operations from December 2005 onwards.

Market segments

As has been highlighted before, road haulage tends to be split into two distinctive market segments – truck load and less than truck load. The truck load sector is characterised by a very high number of small firms that operate local haulage services or point-to-point carriage over longer distance. This market sector tends to be dominated by small companies with a high proportion of one person owner-driver operations; the classic 'loneliness of the long distance lorry driver'. This sector we have already identified in Chapter 6 as being near to the conditions of perfect competition. The less than truck load (LTL) sector is far more sophisticated, and these days increasingly operates at an international level and hence necessitates the inclusion of modes other than road. A large part of the LTL sector is the parcels or small packet market, which requires a nationwide network of depots and local collection/delivery services, in which loads for longer distance carriage are assembled at the depot and made up into full consignments. These are then sent to the depots in other parts of the country where they are then broken into local loads and added to other longer-distance loads coming from other parts of the country.

Cost structures

For the road haulage industry, the main fixed costs are licence fees for vehicles, property taxes, management salaries and the cost of terminals, with the highest capital cost related to the vehicle. This cost however is relatively low in comparison to other modes such as the railways or air freight carriers. Variable costs are the same as those associated with any form of road transport, hence includes drivers' wages, depreciation, maintenance, fuel, lubricants and some marketing costs. Clearly in LTL markets, fixed costs will tend to be a higher proportion due to the network of depots required to service the market. Nevertheless, the few past studies of the road haulage industry that have been carried out suggest that fixed costs tend to be relatively low. Whilst very dated, the ICC (1954) found fixed costs to be only around 10 per cent of all operating costs. Fifteen years later, however, Shirley (1969) estimated fixed costs to be in the order of 25 per cent, which strongly suggests an increase in the capital intensity of the industry over the intervening years, which was mainly attributed to the increased sophistication of terminals. Another reason for the difference however may be the considerable rise in the LTL market between the two time periods.

Economies of density

Economies of scale in road haulage have been examined in Chapter 6; however, what was not considered was economies of density. Whilst scale relates to firm size, density relates to the size of the vehicle. With regard to truck size, there exists the two thirds rule where the outer dimensions of the vehicle will increase by considerably less in size than the volume, and in the carriage of freight it is of course vehicle capacity (volume) that is important. Furthermore, due to the high proportion of variable costs in the operation of road haulage, the marginal costs of operating a larger lorry will be relatively small in terms of the additional operating and capital costs. A second important consideration is that what is important in terms of costs is the cost per tonne carried, not the cost per vehicle km. If larger trucks are operated the cost per vehicle km will increase; however, if fully laden the cost per tonne carried should fall. There is therefore some scope to reduce average costs through economies of density. The extent to which such economies can be exploited however is limited by what the actual infrastructure, i.e. the roads, can take in terms of the weight and dimensions of vehicles. These tend to be heavily regulated with regard to road haulage.

Road haulage summary

As highlighted in Chapter 6, of all of the transport industries studied in this text truck load road haulage is the one that most closely resembles perfect competition. With significant barriers to entry, economies of scale and few sellers, the LTL market on the other hand clearly fits into the oligopoly model, although one in which competition is fairly intensive and heavily based on the price charged. Due to the relatively low proportion of fixed costs and high level of variable costs, road haulage is one of the most flexible forms of freight transport. Combined with the highly competitive nature of large sectors of the industry, this means that over time the economic characteristics of the mode have been well suited to the changing industrial environment, and hence road haulage has made very large gains in market share. As we will see, other modes, particularly rail freight, have found it difficult to adapt to such changing business conditions.

Rail freight

Of all of the transport modes examined in this text, rail freight operations around the world contrast the most in terms of form and structure. Unlike for example buses or road haulage, where some differences may exist but the basics of operation are broadly similar, this is not the case for rail freight. Whilst the underlying economic characteristics are common to all freight railways, the extent to which these affect the structure and form of the industry is largely determined by organisational considerations and even more so by historical precedent. In Europe, for example, due to the nationalisation of the railways in the first half of the 20th century, rail freight has operated as part of a nationalised state operator that has had to share most of the rail network with a high volume of passenger traffic. Because of state ownership and the desire to enact reforms, more recent years have seen many European countries restructure their railways by separating infrastructure from operations. Rail freight in Europe has also increasingly faced strong competition from road haulage which has resulted in a considerable loss of market share. This is probably best exemplified by Britain, where as we saw above rail's market share fell from 30 per cent of tonne kilometres hauled in 1960 to 8 per cent in 2006. Whilst severe, such declines in market share are not unusual in a European context. This situation contrasts quite radically to rail freight in other parts of the world, particularly North America, where market share has always been considerably higher mainly due to the sheer distances involved. For example, statistics for

2002 show that in America rail carried 3 per cent of the value of freight, 10 per cent of the weight and 31 per cent of the tonne miles (US Department of Transportation, 2006). This last figure contrasts with a 34 per cent share for road. The actual type of operation in the US is also very different, consisting of privately owned freight-dedicated operators, each with their own network of rails and depots.

Key economic characteristics of rail freight

Rail freight is characterised by a number of features that are outlined below.

Barriers to entry

Within the rail freight industry there are very high barriers to entry. In Europe these have been in the form of legislative measures, where the state-owned operator has had a legally protected monopoly on all rail operations. This was the case in most European countries up until the early 1990s. With the passing in 1991 of the first EU Directive aimed at railway reform, 91/440, this partially removed this particular barrier to entry for freight operations in all EU member states. Further reforms followed in 2003 with the implementation of the Trans European Rail Freight Network which opened up 50,000 route kilometres to freight operations. While this removed the legal obstacles to access, without further measures control of the infrastructure by the existing operator would remain as a barrier to entry. As noted above, in some countries therefore this has led to an organisational separation of infrastructure from operations, where the infrastructure is owned and operated by a separate state-owned company. Alternatively where the infrastructure has remained in the control of a single company, normally the state-owned railway, regulatory measures have been introduced to lay down access rights and control the infrastructure charges imposed.

A second major barrier to entry is that rail freight operations usually incur very high start-up costs. Investment requirements in railway technology, whether relating to infrastructure or rolling stock, tend to be very high and this may deter potential new companies from entering the industry. Furthermore, because rail freight has increased advantages over a certain distance, this also has implications on firm size, suggesting that small firms may find it difficult if not impossible to enter the industry unless under some form of partnership agreement.

Despite the reforms outlined above, few new entrants have entered the rail freight market in Europe. The main reasons cited for this lack of entry is the difficulty in assembling the required inputs and the problems faced with conflicts in technical standards and regulations across continental Europe (Gómez-Ibáñez, 2004). This in many respects reinforces the point made in the opening statement of this whole section, and further suggests that radically different operational differences are a further barrier to entry.

Outside of Europe, the major barrier to entry is also high start-up costs; however, because in virtually all cases these are vertically integrated railways (i.e. track and services), a new entrant would have to construct a complete railway in order to compete in the market. In most countries outside of state-run passenger services, there is also no legal right to access as the infrastructure is privately owned. Even in the case of the small Class III railroads in America, where the largest line lengths are somewhere in the order of 500 kilometres, such a barrier would prove insurmountable. This is because of a very high level of sunk costs and market structural barriers, where most if not all of the existing railroads were built over a hundred years ago and simply would not be constructed today. In simple terms any new entrant could not compete with the incumbent due to the very much higher capital cost associated with new line construction. Even without direct rail competition, due to such costs any new line would fail to produce a profit. Consequently, the only competition that these railroads will ever face is from other modes of transport. This has led to moves for some form of reform of the US rail freight industry under the provisions of the Rail Competition and Service Improvement Act of 2007, which attempts to clarify the policy position of ensuring effective competition between rail carriers and eased the standards used when shippers challenge the reasonableness of carriage rates.

Cost structures

As has been highlighted before, railway cost structures are such that given the very high level of capital costs, fixed costs tend to be very high. Nash (1985) for example estimated the proportion of fixed costs for railways in Europe to be in the order of 53 per cent. Although this was based on both passenger and freight operations, freight-only railways will have considerably higher fixed costs than a combined passenger/freight railway due to the added cost of depots and freight marshalling yards. Variable and marginal costs however tend to be relatively low. As a result, there is a considerable separation of outgoings from revenue, a high break-even point and a need for the careful planning of operations.

Economies of scale and scope

We have already seen in Chapter 5 that there are significant economies of scale in railway operation due to the high level of fixed costs. There is also however some evidence of economies of scope; these are said to exist when the unit cost is reduced due to common costs being spread across two or more outputs. Thus passengers and freight trains can share the same track, which spreads the fixed costs of the track across both types of operations. As a consequence a lower unit costs for each type of service is achieved than if either one was operated on its own. At a very basic level such as the construction of a new railway, this is obviously true as the costs of construction can be shared between the two types of operation, hence producing lower average costs in each. There are other shared facilities however not only associated with the permanent way that also lead to some economies of scope, the most obvious one being a network of stations/depots.

High break-even point

As briefly highlighted, a further economic characteristic of freight railways is that the break-even point is very high. If fixed costs are very high then it follows that a large volume of output (i.e. freight services) must be sold before any profit is made at all. This may even suggest that a profit can only be achieved if there is only one firm in the market, i.e. a natural monopoly. It is worth highlighting however that profitability above the break-even point is highly inelastic. This is because any additional revenue generated from sales will be virtually all profit as the marginal costs are close to zero.

These economic characteristics such as high barriers to entry, economies of scale, very high break-even points etc has meant that rail freight has been a highly concentrated industry with very few firms in the market. For example, following the Stagger's Act of 1980 which deregulated rail freight in America, a series of mergers and acquisitions resulted in industry consolidation to the point where now there exist only four 'Class I' US railroads, i.e. major railways. Canada has only two Class I railroads and although at a much smaller scale, in Britain after privatisation there are now only two 'national' operators, EWS for Wagons and Freightliner for containers (although some much smaller companies do operate on parts of the network). Railion on continental Europe is a combination of the freight operations of the German, Dutch and Danish state railways, and has since expanded its European operation by acquiring rail freight companies in Switzerland, Italy, Spain and finally the aforementioned EWS in Britain. Rail freight markets therefore would appear to follow the pattern we saw earlier in Chapter 7 of industry consolidation following reform and hence similarly move towards imperfect market structures.

Advantages and disadvantages of rail freight

Advantages

Environmental impact – the first advantage of rail freight is its impact on the environment. Of all of the available freight transport modes, rail, particularly when hauled by an electric loco, is probably the least environmentally detrimental. This is something we have already touched upon in Chapter 9. Note however that this first advantage is not recorded in the market place as this is an externality. Furthermore, because in many countries rail freight operations are run entirely on a profit basis with little or no government support, this is an advantage that currently presents limited opportunities in which to be exploited. It is nevertheless one that does position it well in the face of increasing environmental concerns.

Distance – rail has a major advantage over medium to longer distances over road transport. This is shown in Figure 12.3.

What the figure shows is that as distance increases, average cost per unit moved by rail falls whilst average cost per unit moved by road increases. This is almost entirely due to the division of costs between fixed and variable in the two modes; road has few fixed costs, thus average costs increase directly with distance. Rail however has a very large proportion of fixed costs, thus as distance increases these costs are spread over more tonne kilometres and average cost per unit falls. The cross-over point between the two is usually quoted as somewhere between 300 and 500 kilometres, thus shown at 400 kilometres on Figure 12.3. To a certain extent, however, this advantage of distance is limited by the size and form of many countries – Britain for example is a long/thin island, hence such advantages can only be exploited on north–south flows. In other countries, natural geographical barriers may also limit the extent these advantages can be achieved. As an example, Denmark consists of a large number of islands and the north Jutland peninsula, with most of the population located on the island of Zealand. These factors however can be overcome by large infrastructure projects, such as was the case with the Channel tunnel in Britain and the construction of two fixed links to Zealand in Denmark. In these examples capital has been substituted for land in the production of rail services and thus some of these distance advantages can be exploited. Nevertheless, few actually have been due to other factors covered under disadvantages.

This advantage of distance however is what TSSA (2008), the rail union for salaried staff, describes as one of the myths of rail freight transport, as the implication is that over shorter distances rail has a disadvantage, as indeed shown in Figure 12.3! What they argue however, similar

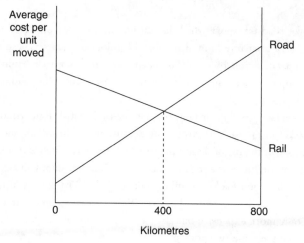

Figure 12.3 *Average cost per unit moved, rail versus road*

to Erickson (2001), is that whilst rail does have advantages over longer distances in certain sectors it can also have advantages over shorter distances, particularly where there are regular flows of freight traffic. The key to these counter arguments is that fixed costs need to be spread over something before the average cost of rail freight becomes competitive; however, distance is only one 'thing' that it can be spread over. The other of course would be volume, thus over high volumes, irrespective of distance, rail freight may also have a cost advantage.

Capacity – capacity to some extent is both an advantage and a disadvantage of rail freight, but the advantages are considered first before the drawbacks are examined below. Unlike road transport, rail has a far higher level of capacity which can extend up to a whole train size. Train size however tends to vary from country to country, with Germany for example limiting the length of its freight trains to 700 metres, countries in Eastern Europe to 1000 metres but in the US and Canada freight train size tends to be considerably longer. Irrespective of any restrictions on length, the capacity of a freight train is considerably larger than that of road trucks. Rail therefore has the potential to move large volumes of freight over short and long distances quickly and efficiently.

Power costs – in simple terms, rail transport per tonne hauled has a very low power cost. This is due to the very high level of capacity of rail, hence relatively speaking less power is required to carry a big load. The implication of these two factors (capacity and power costs) is that rail is good for carrying low-value high-volume freight such as coal, aggregates, shale etc. This is something that has already been seen in the case of the US, where 3 per cent of value goes by rail but 31 per cent of tonne mileage. A further myth highlighted by TSSA however is that the carriage of such traffic is all that rail is good at. It should be thus noted that although it does have certain advantages in the transport of such cargo it does not mean that it cannot also compete for other more general cargo.

Weather constraints – a final advantage briefly highlighted is that of all of the alternative modes that are realistically available, rail tends to be one of the least weather constrained. It is thus the least subject to delay due to poor weather conditions.

Disadvantages

Accessibility – unlike road transport which has an infinite number of access points to the road network, rail only has a relatively limited number of points of access. These essentially are the marshalling yards and collection points. This means that in order to be fully competitive, rail companies need to employ other transport modes to increase accessibility and offer point-to-point carriage.

Shipment size – certainly within Britain, the nationalised British Rail withdrew from the less than wagonload market in the early 1990s simply because it was becoming increasingly unprofitable. This highlights one of the major disadvantages of rail freight, which is that in order to capture the benefits of rail transport there is a requirement for a minimum shipment size. For direct access this will either be a full wagon load or a full container load. Third parties in the form of freight forwarders can make up such shipments; however, the process becomes far more complex and difficult – it is not only more expensive but also needs a variety of shippers who all want to send items of cargo between the same two points.

Security – trains have been known to lie in marshalling yards for days on end and hence can become subject to vandalism and pilferage. This could almost be viewed as an externality of rail freight, where those that benefit (the thieves!) do not pay directly for the cost of the activity, unless of course they are caught in the act! Road haulage on the other hand is generally viewed as more secure as the driver usually accompanies the vehicle at all times.

Frequency – due to high capacity levels, rail freight services tend to be fairly infrequent. To simplify, once a lorry is full it can depart. Considerably more tonnage however needs to be loaded or assembled on a train, and thus by implication such services will be less frequent. As a consequence, regular rail freight services tend to occur only on routes where there is strong demand between the locations. This can lead into intermodal services based around some form of hub and spoke operation. In theory intermodal takes the advantages of rail over long distances and combines these with the advantages of road over shorter distance. The rail terminals act as the hubs with road haulage servicing the spokes. Intermodal freight however is an issue that tends to be much discussed at government level but one that in reality has seen little major movement. The Marco Polo II programme for example, the main EU initiative on intermodal transport, has a relatively small total budget of 400m Euros to spend over the period 2007 to 2013. This is used to provide financial assistance with the start-up cost of intermodal operations.

Key issues facing rail freight

We end our examination of rail freight by considering some of the major issues currently facing the rail freight industry in Europe. Some of these arise as a result of the economic characteristics of the mode, others as a result of more general economic change.

Firstly, the industry has been facing falling or stagnate freight tonnage. Even over a relatively short period from 1995 to 2005, rail's market share within the EU fell from 12 per cent to 10 per cent (Eurostat, 2007). The development of road transport has over time taken much of the market away from the railways. However, whilst now historical, the point has wider implications. With the development of the Single European Market, road hauliers have been able to take more advantage of the opportunities presented, in particular the development of European-wide road haulage networks. Railways on the other hand have tended to have a national focus and there is only recent evidence that some are now beginning to respond to the effective removal of political and economic barriers across Europe (Lewis *et al.*, 2001). The previously highlighted Railion rail freight company is one of the few examples of a pan-European focus to rail freight; nevertheless, even its operations are still very much centred upon the German market.

Passenger oriented rail networks. European railways are much more dependent upon passenger traffic and in many cases view the movement of freight as a secondary business. Austria for example is at the top end of the spectre with 55 per cent of customer receipts in 2007 coming from freight activities. This however is very much the exception, with the Norwegian state operator, NSB, nearer the norm with 27 per cent of all rail revenue coming from freight. Others have considerably lower figures again. Passenger trains tend to receive priority on the network and move uninterrupted across national borders and any major developments in rail networks appearing to mainly concentrate upon passenger services. For example, the TGV in France, ICEs in Germany, the Eurostar (Channel Tunnel services) between Britain and France and the Thalys between Germany, France, Belgium and Holland are all mainly passenger focused. Only one of these projects has a major freight element (the Channel Tunnel). This is an area in which there appears to be some shift in thinking, however, with the Swiss AlpTransit project very much freight driven, as is the Lyon–Turin tunnel project. Both projects surround the construction of lengthy rail tunnels through the Alps. Finally the Betuweroute is a 4.7bn Euros investment in a new freight-only line between Rotterdam and Germany which opened in June 2007.

Lack of harmonisation of standards, regulations and standards in the EU. Freight trains (more so than passenger trains) face a complex patchwork of conflicting standards and requirements for rolling stock, locomotives, signalling and information systems. Whilst road also faces differences in standards across borders, with the most basic being driving on different sides of the road in some European countries, such differences tend to be inconveniences. This is not the case with rail, where different operating practices impede the cross-border movement of goods by rail and act as major barriers. Even where these are overcome there still remains a high variation in the level of infrastructure development in the international context. This has resulted in a number of bottlenecks appearing in the system, such as around Milan, Vienna, Munich and Rotterdam to name but four. These are major problem areas and as regards a European wide network are ones that need to be addressed before rail can be seen as a major competitor to road over these distances.

Structural economic change. As has been stressed in this chapter before, freight transport cannot be looked at in isolation and this point in particular relates to on-going structural change in the wider economy. Over the last thirty years there has been a significant move away from traditional heavy industries such as steel and coal to more advanced lighter industries such as electronics etc. Whilst rail is well suited to be the transport provider for heavy industry, i.e. low-value bulk commodities, it has been far less suited to the new industries. Going hand-in-hand with this development is also a change in production processes, with a movement away from Fordism-type big fixed production to Post-Fordism flexibility in production and the implementation of systems such as just-in-time inventory. These practices tend to be less suited to rail transport and more suited to road. This is one of the main reasons that rail has lost market share throughout most of Europe.

Rail freight summary

Rail freight is one of the great areas of potential to reduce road congestion and its impact upon the environment by switching large volumes of freight from the roads to the railways. That however is far easier said (as it often is) than can be done. In this section we have looked at some of the key economic characteristics of rail freight and the ensuing advantages and disadvantages that follow from these. Rail freight in recent times has existed in a period of outright decline in tonnage carriage, that even after major reformatory measures such as privatisation in Great Britain have failed to address the situation. Operating under purely free market principles the changing industrial structure has not suited rail. Much more requires to be done, such as increasing capacity on certain parts of the rail network and rail gauge enhancements, to allow freight to be carried on more of the network. In a purely free market environment, whilst there is some potential for rail in a hub and spoke type operation with rail taking the long haul in the operation, other opportunities appear to be limited.

Air freight

Many air services have their origins in freight-orientated services. In North America, for example, many companies began operating air mail services where the mail could be transported in a much reduced time than had been previously achievable by overland transport. In other parts of the world where natural geographical obstacles considerably slowed transit times, air services also developed very quickly. For example, the air services route map around the west coast of Scotland, which is made up of a large number of islands, had been quickly established by the early 1930s. This was initially based around mainly mail and newspaper carriage, and the route map as such has remained little changed since that period. Despite such early origins, of all of the modes examined in this chapter air freight has by far seen the largest growth in recent times. This is due to many different factors, but the two strongest drivers have been increases in international trade and technological advances in civil aviation, particularly lifting capacities. As a result air freight is far more international in its focus than the passenger market (Gardiner and Ison, 2007), and thus has generally grown in size with the growth of international trade, assisted by the vast increases in the lifting capabilities of civil aircraft. This phenomenal rate of growth in air freight is clearly shown in Figure 12.4, which expresses revenue tonne kilometres (RTK) on scheduled flights since 1970.

At the start of the period outlined the level of freight moving by air was negligible. At that time most of this carriage would have been mainly related to specific mail or newspaper cargo type activities in addition to small levels of international air freight. Not only was the total low, therefore, but also very low levels of 'freight' were carried on each flight due to limitations on gross weight. Since 1970, however, the market has grown considerably as a result of the development of specific freight-dedicated aircraft, considerable increases in the cargo-carrying capacity of passenger aircraft and the establishment and development of international logistical networks and specific package-related carriers. This has taken place with a backdrop of continuing evolution of the globalisation of production and sales in consumer goods. The net result has been that shippers have tended to move shipments in smaller consignments, more often and require faster delivery times. All of these characteristics suit air freight transport. Boeing (2007), in their regular 'World Air Cargo Forecast' series, forecast that such trends are likely to continue well into the foreseeable

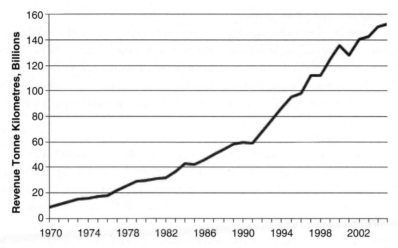

Figure 12.4 *Growth in air freight, international RTK 1970 to 2005*

Source: Compiled from IATA statistics

future, with rates of growth estimated at a low of 5.3 per cent per annum and a high of 6.9 per cent. Even at the lower value of 5.3 per cent this would represent an increased rate of growth in the future and would result in almost a trebling in the size of the market. This section will examine the economic characteristics of air freight operations in order to help explain the phenomenal increase in this sector of the market.

Structure of the air freight industry

In very general terms there are three types of operators that provide air freight transport services:

Line haul operators

Line haul operators only move cargo from airport to airport, relying on third parties in the form of freight forwarders and consolidators to deal directly with customers and cater for their overall requirements. This is the classic transport firm that only deals with the transport leg of the whole logistical chain. These line haul operators can be divided into three further sub-categories:

- All cargo operators

  All cargo operators move freight in dedicated cargo aircraft and mainly specialise in large-volume, long-distance flows. Better known examples of all cargo operators are companies such as Cargolux, who base their operations at Luxembourg-Findel International Airport and are one of the largest all cargo air operators in Europe. The company operates a fleet of 15 Boeing 747-400F with a further 15 747-8Fs on order, and a global network consisting of 45 destinations throughout the world. It works with other operators to provide worldwide coverage based upon a hub-and-spoke network centred upon three core airports – Luxembourg, Hong Kong and Glasgow Prestwick. The company operates both regular scheduled freight services as well as ad-hoc one off type operations.

- Combination passenger and cargo operators

  These companies tend to be large multinational airlines, such as Lufthansa, United Airlines and so on, that use both dedicated cargo planes as well as the cargo hold of passenger aircraft that operate on an extensive worldwide network of air routes. Operations are mainly long haul, with interlining to and from short haul feeder services. This is the classic hub-and-spoke type operation, and hence in some ways the freight operation is piggy backed onto the passenger service.

- Passenger only operators

  All other air operators that carry some form of air freight fall into this last category. These operators only carry freight in the cargo hold of passenger aircraft, and this often means little attention paid to the requirements of the cargo, although the revenue generated from such operations should not be underestimated. Various reliable sources estimate this to be in the order of 15 to 16 per cent of all revenue (Lobo and Zaira, 1999; Boeing, 2007), which although a relatively small proportion does represent a very strong contributor to profitability, particularly given the relatively low marginal costs of carrying this cargo.

Integrated operators

These are specialists in the door-to-door consignment market, generally with guaranteed time delivery services; the main carriers in this sector of the market include UPS, Federal Express, TNT and DHL. These companies operate land modes in addition to air services and thus offer an integrated service aimed to fully meet customers' demands, they will therefore both collect and deliver consignments. To meet the requirements of next-day deliveries, many of the flights operate at night time, particularly those meeting regional demands and again most are based around a hub-and-spoke type network. Of all of the air freight operators these companies have by far the largest fleet sizes, with many fleet sizes larger than most recognised passenger airlines. FedEx, for example, is the largest integrated operator, and with a fleet size of over 670 aircraft, has the largest civil aircraft fleet in the world.

Niche operators

The final sector of the market relates to niche operators. As the name suggests, these operators cater for extraordinary demands, usually of large and heavy items that the standard operators are unable to carry. These tend to be non-scheduled services and are provided on a one-off basis.

Market shares

The ten largest air freight operators in 2004 are given in Table 12.3 along with, where these were available, equivalent figures from 2001.

As can be seen from Table 12.3, the largest carriers of air freight mainly consist of line haul and integrated operator airlines. FedEx are by far the largest single company, having around 10 per cent of the total global market, with the other nine airlines shown accounting for a further 40 per cent of the total market in 2004. The difference between the two years underlines the strong growth that this particular market has experienced in recent years, with growth rates averaging just under 30 per cent over a very short three-year period. Interestingly, however, the top 10 air freighters experienced considerably larger growth than the actual market size, hence its share

Table 12.3 10 largest air freight carriers, revenue tonne kilometres, 2001 and 2004

Operator	2001	2004
FedEx Express	11.0	14.6
Korean Air	5.6	8.3
Lufthansa Cargo	7.1	8.0
United Parcel Service (UPS)	5.9	7.4
Singapore Airlines Cargo	5.9	7.1
Cathay Pacific	n/a	5.8
China Airlines	n/a	5.6
Eva Airways	n/a	5.5
Air France	5.1	5.4
Japan Airlines	4.2	4.9

Source: Compiled from IATA statistics

increased from 40 per cent in 2001 to 48 per cent in 2004, thus the market appears to be consolidating.

Despite such a high level of market concentration and consolidation, Boeing (2007) report that yield levels from air cargo have been falling, with close to a 3 per cent per annum decline since 1985. Yield levels today are thus some 50 per cent of the size in 1985. This however does not necessarily mean stronger competition in the market, as basic economics would dictate that as supply increases, then the price, and hence the yield, will fall. Nevertheless, there are clear indications of increased competition and a renewed focus by passenger airlines on the carriage of freight.

Air Freight – key economic characteristics

Goods in joint supply

In terms of the economic characteristics of air cargo, goods in joint supply are undoubtedly the most defining feature. These exist because a large percentage of air freight goes in the cargo hold of commercial passenger aircraft; therefore, the production of more passenger services automatically produces a higher supply of freight operations, as these 'extra' passenger aircraft all have cargo holds. Therefore strong demand in the passenger market will result in increased capacity in the freight market. Boeing estimated in 1998 that 70 per cent of freight was carried in passenger planes (Boeing, 1998); however, now due to a significant increase in freight-only operations, that figure is probably nearer 60 per cent. Not all passenger airlines however carry cargo; low-cost airlines for example in general do not carry freight, and most of this joint traffic tends to be on intercontinental and longer-haul flights.

Barriers to entry

Within the air cargo market, barriers to entry tend to be very high, with one of the major constraints being access to key locations. Air cargo needs to be transported directly to the area of highest value, as many of the advantages of air freight can be offset when this is not the case, e.g. a long timely connection between point of set down and the final destination. Freight operators are therefore in direct competition with passenger airlines for airport access, as areas of high demand for passenger destinations tend to be the same as areas of high demand for freight. For passenger-only operators, this is not a barrier as passenger and freight services are goods in joint supply. This is the main reason for example why almost half of the air freight in the UK is handled through the busiest passenger airport, London Heathrow. For freight-only operators, however, this is a considerable barrier. The DETR (1998) further highlight that airports may prefer to handle passenger aircraft due to the added overall revenue they bring through passenger tolls and spend within the airport. This lack of access is why some freight-only operations tend to be at night and based around regional airports rather than key (passenger) hubs.

Firm size

The cost structures of air freight operators, with a high proportion of fixed costs, would suggest that there exist considerable economies of scale in air freight operation. This is primarily due to the high level of start-up costs and high proportion of fixed costs involved in the operation of air freight services. However, under the banner of firm size there also exist economies of density, as is also true with passenger operations and which have been broadly exploited by the low-cost carriers. If a company can increase the output produced in terms of revenue-generating traffic by working the existing assets more intensively, then unit costs will be significantly lower. In more basic terms this increases aircraft utilisation in which less time is spent on the ground and more time spent in the air. Whilst economies of density are undoubtedly an important aspect in the operation of line haul operators, it appears at face value to be far less in evidence with the integrated and niche operators. Many of these carriers only fly at night, indicating long periods when the aircraft is on the ground. This would strongly suggest clear market segments and market niches, with large firms dominating the integrated sector and smaller operators competing in the line haul and specialised markets. In many respects such a diversified market structure is very similar to the road haulage sector examined earlier in this chapter.

Price and non price competition

Within all sectors of the air freight sector, price and non price competition play a clear role. Competition for business tends to be very high, thus there is very strong downward pressure on prices. Within the line haul sector, for example, the strong market position of freight forwarders who make up complete consignments tends to drive prices down, whilst the integrated operators market is keenly contested. Price is therefore clearly a factor; however, with a few exceptions prices will tend to vary by very small amounts. How firms compete therefore is not only on price but also on non price factors, particularly the speed and reliability of delivery. For example, slow movers have been quoted as being eaten up by the fast ones in the market (Lobo and Zaira, 1999). Speed of delivery covers a multitude of sins that would also include where it can be sent, when it can be sent and how often it can be sent out, all of which add up to the speed of delivery.

Another form of non price competition clearly in evidence in the air freight industry is firms buying out rival operators in order to enhance their own market position. It is through such business strategies that the major integrated operators, such as FedEx and UPS, have attained their strong market positions. In this respect it follows a similar pattern examined in Chapter 7, where the process of competition tends to be through merger and acquisition which ultimately results in the emergence of large dominant operators.

Yield management

We have already seen in Chapter 9 that airlines practise price discrimination in order to fill the available seat capacity in passenger services. Yield management however is also a key characteristic of the air freight market. Nevertheless, until the recent past it was a topic that had not received a great deal of attention due to the perception of air cargo as an almost 'add-on' and the low marginal costs associated with the activity. Rising competition in the sector, falling yield levels (see above) and increased competition from other transport modes particularly on shorter haul routes, have all considerably changed this perception with a renewed focus on maximising the return on air freight through yield management. There are important differences however between yield management in freight as opposed to passenger air services, and Kasilingam (1997) groups these under the following four broad headings:

- Uncertain capacity
  In the passenger market the total number of seats is known well in advance and hence ticket prices can be controlled in order to fill that available capacity. In the freight market, however, the available capacity is dependent upon a number of other issues, hence cannot be deterministically established before hand
- Three dimensional capacity
  Passenger operations exist in only one dimension, the total number of available seats, and these are filled by standardised units, i.e. one passenger per seat. In air freight, however, the capacity to be filled is in three dimensions, weight, volume and number of container positions. It can thus be very difficult to maximise the load in all three dimensions, and this can lead to under utilisation in one or more of these dimensions. It is mainly this characteristic that airlines seek to overcome through better yield management.
- Itinerary control
  Both passengers and freight forwarders will look to travel or move freight from A to B by the most direct route; the difference with freight however is that within given time constraints, as long as it starts in A and finishes up at point B the route by which it gets there is far less important, although improved tracking has impacted upon this flexibility. Nevertheless, this considerably increases the complexity of the whole operation, as clearly revenues can be maximised by the careful management of priority and non-priority loads and hence the route along which they can be moved. This in some respects adds a fourth dimension to the three stated above.
- Allotments
  Allotments are pre-booked slots that still lie at the heart of the air freight market. These are spaces that are allocated to large regular customers and generally take up a major proportion of the available capacity.

To these four key differences, Becker and Dill (2007) also highlight unequal trade lanes, where passengers tend to go out and back but air freight has imbalances of flows between different locations, and also the customer base – a passenger airline has many hundreds of thousands of individual customers, hence a no show or a problem with one passenger will not have a major impact on the whole business. This however is not the case with air freight, where there is far higher buyer concentration and thus most clients tend to be large and give regular business, hence each single shipment becomes far more critical and no shows or any other problems tend to have a far larger and longer-lasting impact.

Nevertheless, yield management in air freight is a critical aspect and one that is becoming far more important over time as the whole size, structure and development of the industry changes.

The major economic advantages and disadvantages of air freight

Gubbins (2003) highlights four reasons why companies choose to send freight by air. Firstly, the shorter journey times means that the financial outlay in the goods that are being transported is tied up for a shorter period than for other modes. Intercontinental freight by maritime transport can take a considerably longer period of time than air freight, with typical transit times ranging from four to six weeks and in many cases even longer than that. More of the company's finance therefore is tied down in the goods that are being transported and this can have considerable implications on cash flow. A second related advantage is that faster journey times means that goods are at risk from damage, theft or deterioration in quality for a shorter time as compared to other modes of transport. Thirdly, air can be used in an emergency, where speed is of paramount importance and cost is unimportant, e.g. when a sale will enhance goodwill and lead to further business, or to counter a problem such as providing spare parts for machinery that has failed. In addition to this direct benefit a related advantage is that air can be used as a mode of last resort due to the critical nature of J-I-T concepts. It therefore may allow such a system to operate at a critical level in the sure knowledge that a plan 'B' does exist should something go wrong with the normal modes of carriage. Finally, air freight can lower the costs of storage and distribution in the country of sale. This can lead to the centralisation of such activities which may have certain cost advantages.

Against these advantages, the main disadvantages are that firstly the high charges tend to be prohibitive and thus air freight is only used in relatively high-value markets. This considerably lessens and restricts many of the advantages outlined above. Secondly, even in these days of 110 tonne freight capacity, aircraft capacity can be considered as limited. Thirdly, congestion around airports is often cited as a disadvantage of air freight, the argument being that points of access and egress tend to be heavily congested and thus access to and from the airport limited and time consuming. Thus time gained in the air is partly offset by increased transit times on the ground. As highlighted above, the demand for freight destinations, particularly air freight, tend to be in areas of high population, hence road access will inevitably be congested. Whilst in many locations this is undoubtedly true, this disadvantage should not be overstated and viewed in the wider context. For example, in most cases such transfers are only likely to occur over relatively short distances. Fourthly, security is a major issue in air freight, and one heightened by the 9/11 terrorist attacks of 2001. This is because a high percentage of freight is transported in passenger planes, and thus must pass through security checks and controls before being loaded onto the aircraft. This increases lead times and also adds further to the already high cost. Finally, per tonne kilometre transported air freight has the highest detrimental impact on the environment, even higher than road haulage. It may initially be countered that as a high percentage of air freight is transported on passenger aircraft, this represents a very low marginal cost and hence the impact on the environment minimal. Such an argument however is far too naïve and completely ignores the revenue generated from freight carriage. Without this revenue the cost of passenger air tickets would be significantly higher, thus reducing demand which in turn would lead to a contraction in supply.

Air freight summary

Air freight has been the fastest growing mode of freight transport in recent times. Despite economic forecasts of a downturn, these recent trends are predicted to continue well into the future. This is strongly tied with the globalisation of the world economy, where retail outlets have taken a far larger share of sales. Most freight however goes by passenger aircraft with the main economic characteristic being goods in joint supply. Increasing environmental concerns however may limit future growth.

Maritime shipping

This brief outline of maritime shipping is not intended to be a complete overview of the main economics concerning the transport mode. As may be imagined, maritime shipping is a massive area and there are many books that cover the economic characteristics of the shipping industry in some depth, notably Martin Stopford's *Maritime Economics* (Stopford, 2008) and Kevin Cullinane's *Shipping Economics* (Cullinane, 2005). What is outlined here therefore is purely introductory and a general overview of the main economic characteristics of the shipping industry that underline or develop further some of the points raised earlier in the book.

Market segments

In very simple terms, maritime transport can be broken down into roughly four different market segments – inland shipping, coastal shipping, short sea and deep sea shipping. Inland and coastal shipping is based upon navigable rivers such as the Rhine and the Danube, inland lakes and coastal waters. Short sea shipping is difficult to define but consists of relatively short sea crossings, with the main shipping routes in Europe being found in the English Channel, the North Sea, the Baltic, the Black Sea and the Mediterranean. Ferry type operations therefore usually take place in the short sea and coastal shipping sectors. Finally deep sea shipping concerns intercontinental shipping, and this the long distance sector of the mode.

Coastal and short sea shipping are perhaps the great unknowns as regards freight transport. As a common view may be that more freight should be taken off the roads and put on the railways, coastal and short sea have fairly high market shares as it stands. In Britain, for example, as highlighted above 23 per cent of tonne kilometres are carried by boat, compared to only 8 per cent for rail. For the European Union as a whole, shipping's share of freight carriage is considerably higher at around 40 per cent, second behind road (44 per cent) and again considerably higher than rail (8 per cent). Whilst British and European Union figures are not directly comparable, as for example mainland Europe has considerably more navigable rivers and areas of short sea crossings, it does nevertheless show the potential of the mode to take a greater share of the freight transport market.

The international organisation of shipping

Maritime transport, like a number of other services such as the post and telecommunications, has a strong international dimension to it. Over the years, therefore, there have been several attempts to set up an international body to support the needs of the shipping industry. This was eventually achieved at the UN Maritime Conference held in Geneva in 1948, out of which was formed what is now known as the International Maritime Organisation, or IMO for short. The IMO was established to provide the machinery for the co-ordination and co-operation of government regulations in international shipping with the aim of achieving the highest standards possible in terms of safety and efficiency in navigation. It was also established to encourage the removal of discrimination against foreign flags, i.e. foreign registered vessels, engaged in international shipping. The final original three aims of the IMO concerned the monitoring of unfair restrictive practices by shipping concerns, any shipping matters referred to it by UN agencies and finally to provide for the exchange of information between Governments. Two further aims have since been added in the form of maritime pollution, notably liability for oil spillages, and the protection of the marine environment. Today the IMO has 168 member states and 3 associate members.

The IMO is restricted to purely technical matters, and hence does not involve itself in economic or commercial activities, as these remain the preserve of national governments. Its functions can be best summarised by the five standing committees of the organisation. The Maritime Safety Committee is the highest technical body of the IMO. Its remit in simple terms is to examine all technical aspects of safety at sea, both in terms operational aspects that have a safety implication and the construction and instrumentation of sea going vessels. The main activities of the Maritime Environment Protection Committee surround the prevention and control of pollution from ships at sea. The Legal Committee is authorised to deal with any legal issues that arise within the scope of the IMO. The Technical Co-operation Committee is concerned with the implementation of technical co-operation projects. Finally the Facilitation Committee is tasked with enhancing the flow of maritime services through reducing the administrative burden, i.e. red tape, that arise from shipping goods between two different countries. In some ways therefore the IMO performs a regulatory function in the operation of maritime shipping, with all of these aspects relating to qualitative rather than economic regulation. Its role is also as an international forum for international sea shipping services.

Economies of scale

Economies of scale are an essential component in the economics of shipping. In some ways, however, what is commonly known as 'economies of scale' is not what it actually refers to in shipping. The normal view of an economy of scale is where the larger firm has a lower average cost. In shipping, however, as can probably be guessed, economies often refer to ship size rather than firm size, or sometimes a division is made between economies at the firm size level and at the plant (ship) level. In some ways, ship size economies are what would be known in other transport modes as economies of density, as costs fall as more 'output' is spread across the infrastructure. Whilst with roads and railways this makes sense, the infrastructure within shipping is associated with ports, and similar to air transport, there is no infrastructure along which the vessels travel. Hence economies of scale generally relate to ship size.

Economies of scale in shipping are known to be considerable, and hence are central to shipping economics. These arise from two main sources. Firstly, there will be some economies in manufacture, and thus in the associated capital costs of vessels. If for example we were to considerably simplify the problem and assume that the cost of a new ship will rise in direct proportion to its outer surface area, then as size increases the volume will increase by considerably more. A basic mathematical property is that if the size of a box was to increase, the surface area would rise by that number squared but the volume by the number cubed. This was loosely referred previously under road haulage as the 'two thirds rule'. Hence if this was applied to a ship, or indeed a lorry, then the carrying capacity inside would considerably increase. The simple conclusion is that larger ships cost less to build per cubed metre of carrying capacity. Although (over) stressing one of the basic properties, it is nevertheless a considerable oversimplification of the issue. As should be obvious, larger ships require larger engines and more heavy duty materials, but what might not be so obvious is that in the case of container vessels most containers are carried on deck, hence it is the buoyancy that becomes the issue and not the storage capacity. Capital costs in shipping however are fairly significant, with Stopford (2008) illustrating that capital costs in medium-life vessels account for around 40 per cent of the total operating costs, and an even higher 48 per cent in newer vessels. Economies of scale also exist in the operation of vessels, where operating costs do not rise proportionally with the size of the vessel. Unlike say rail freight, where although there are considerable economies in hauling more wagons, there nevertheless comes a point where another locomotive will be required and hence the whole process effectively 'reset', this is far less apparent in shipping. Hence larger ships significantly reduce unit costs. In the past, the whole economies of scale argument, both in terms of ship size and firm size, has led some to investigate if the industry suffered from excessive scale economies and hence certain sectors in danger of becoming natural monopolies. Where a maximum size can be identified however is in port facilities and capacities, where larger vessels will be restricted to only operating between ports that have the capacity to handle ships of such a size.

The shipping business cycle and the shipping 'risk'

One of the main features in the economics of maritime transport is what is known as the 'shipping risk'. This is connected to the shipping business cycle, which tends to go through large highs and very low troughs. When business is good, it is very good, when business is bad, it is very bad. Given such uncertainties about the future, therefore, major question marks arise over the decision of when to invest in new ships and scrap old vessels and when not to. Large tankers, like large passenger aircraft, are large investments. For example in September 2008 a medium-sized ship of around 54500DWT would have cost around €43m from Wright International (Wright International, 2008). If an upturn in trade is expected, then prices would be expected to rise, and these can rise quite considerably, then any owner who does invest in new ships is well positioned to take advantage of this upturn. Not only would they have the new capacity available, but given high prices they could delay scrapping the existing vessels that these ships will ultimately replace. However, if the upturn fails to materialise, then in a period of decline the owner would be burdened with the debt incurred in purchasing the vessel and reduced haulage prices. This in essence is the shipping risk.

Liner conferences

Liner shipping is the scheduled services of general and container cargo between the major ports. Historically, these have been very restricted markets, with Button (1993) highlighting that the major shipping lines used to combine to monopolise these routes and restrict market entry by the setting of a limit price, along the same basis as we saw in Chapter 7 for contestable markets. Liner conferences however provide a very good example of the extent to which the market has been opened up in all aspects of transport services. Most of these conferences existed on the routes between Europe and North America and Europe and the Far East. The reasons behind their formation are largely historical, with their origins in the mid to late 19th century. The industry at that time faced over capacity, hence strong downward pressure on shipping rates, and highly seasonal trade, thus a ship running a regular service would run only half full half of the time. In order to bring stability into what was an unstable market, the main shipping lines at the time agreed to charge similar rates and follow scheduled service patterns, even if the vessels still had spare capacity. The conferences introduced a reduction in rates based upon a rebate system to regular clients, hence the reduction was applied after a period of time had lapsed. It was therefore dependent upon the continued loyalty of the shippers concerned. This tended to tie in shippers into certain conferences, and from these origins developed a system of liner conferences with a fairly intricate system of rates, schedules and ports served. As with many of the major airlines prior to deregulation, freight revenues were generally pooled and shared out between the members of the conference.

Stopford (2008) highlights that liner conferences were generally unpopular with the business community at large, and the system reached its peak in the 1950s. Since then major changes have occurred in the liner sector of the industry. The UN Conference on Trade and Development (UNCTAD) introduced a liner conference code of conduct in 1964 which was eventually formalised in 1974. This attempted to give the national shipping lines of developing countries the right to participate on an equal basis with the shipping lines of developed countries. It thus laid down clearer criteria to regulate entry onto the major shipping routes, in part in much the same way as the Bermuda Agreement did so for the airlines in 1946. The code has been signed by 86 nations, but importantly not the US. The 1980s saw a re-affirmation of some of the liner practices, with the US Merchant Shipping Act restating that liner conferences were excluded from US anti-trust legislation and the EU giving a block exemption (whole sector exemption) from their competition laws in 1986. Over the period, however, the role of the liner conferences had dramatically changed since their high point of the 1950s. They no longer held a stranglehold on the major shipping routes; however, they continued to have a very strong market position – by the mid 1990s, for example, around 60 per cent of the liner capacity on the major routes were part of some conference system. The block exemption in the EU however lasted until 2008, when it was finally withdrawn and the fixing of rates and capacities on the main liner routes out of and into the European Union made illegal. Thus for example on checking one of the liner conference websites (Trans Atlantic Conference Agreement – TACA, 2008), potential clients are given the message that as from 30 June TACA has ceased operations and are referred to individual carrier's tariffs for shipping rates. Liner conference systems in other parts of the world however continue to operate.

Flags of convenience

We have already seen in Chapter 10 the type of regulations that are imposed upon all users of transport systems, from 'simple' pedestrians to the more technical train and plane operators. Shipping, particularly international shipping, is no different. There are a set of rules and standards that apply to both the sea worthiness of the vessel and the competence and hence qualifications of the crew. These are mainly imposed and upheld by the vessel's home state. Thus the ship will be registered in a home country. Deep sea shipping by its very nature however is international, and this raises the question of where exactly is the home nation?

What this has led to is a division in shipping registers and the establishment of 'open' registers. The severity of the regulation tends to vary from country to country, and hence the cost of adhering to these regulations varies considerably. An open register allows foreign national ship owners to register their vessels in a different country and thus be subject to the rules and regulations of that state rather than their 'home' country. This not only applies to shipping regulations, but the labour rules and regulations applying to the crews will come under the jurisdiction of whatever state the ship is registered with. It is one method therefore of bypassing costly labour legislation, which is the main reason why the International Transport Workers Federation are strongly opposed to flags of convenience.

Why countries openly seek to attract shippers to register under their flag is because for many this represents an important inflow of hard currency, i.e. a strong globally traded currency that holds its value, examples of which would include the US Dollar, the Euro, the Pound and the Swiss Franc. Thus the largest maritime fleet is registered in Panama, as it has an open register.

Reasons in favour of flags of convenience are firstly that they allow international shipping lines to register under whatever code will best suit their mode of operation. Thus for example there may be certain advantages to an American ship owner to register the ship elsewhere given the markets that they are in. The other main argument is that many of these companies are multinational concerns, and hence it is no different to many other multinational companies who will move around manufacturing plants into countries that suit them the most. By far the biggest drawback however is that flags of convenience are one of the major issues facing regulation of the deep sea fleet, as companies effectively avoid regulation by registering their fleets overseas; however, the spillover effects can at times literally be spill over effects.

Maritime summary

This is the main mode of transport for long-distance international freight, with the vast bulk going by sea. Improvements in moving cargo by ship have significantly underpinned institutional developments in the process of globalisation. The liner sector of the market has seen considerable reform, with the abolishment in the EU and US of the liner conference system, which has opened up competition in this sector of the market. The international dimension of the mode however remains problematic, and there appears to be far less qualitative control in maritime operations than for example for air services, which is partly related to the sheer scale of the mode (maritime is far larger) and historical development, with maritime mainly being based on private sector companies rather than publicly owned 'flag' carriers.

CHAPTER SUMMARY AND REFLECTION

This chapter has examined the economics of freight transport. On reflection, in many ways this is more of a follow on from Chapter 2 on the relationship between economic development and transport activities. In some ways this is no great surprise, and we have perhaps built on some of these ideas. Two clear points emerged from this chapter. Firstly, that freight transport far more so than passenger transport operates along market principles. What this is very strongly tied to is the derived nature of demand, as unlike passenger transport, without the primary demand there will simply be no rationale for the provision of the service. The other factor that came across very strongly is the diverse nature of freight transport services across the globe. This was most exemplified by rail freight, where very different models of provision exist.

CHAPTER EXERCISES

Exercise 12.1 Freight modal comparison

In each cell of Table 12.4 below, enter on a scale of 1 to 10 your estimate of how each mode of transport is rated for each of the cost and performance attributes (1 = very good; 10 = very bad).

Table 12.4 *Factors in comparison of freight transport modes*

	Lorry	Rail	Combined road/rail	Air	Ship	Pipeline
Economic characteristics						
Terminal costs						
Fuel costs						
Labour costs						
Maintenance costs						
Vehicle/capital costs						
Other characteristics						
Capacity						
Distance						
Speed						
Flexibility						
Frequency						
Reliability						
Weather constraints						
Accessibility						
Environmental impact						
Safety						
Security						

Questions:

a) From carrying out this comparison, what are your overall conclusions regarding the performance of the individual modes of freight transport?

b) To what extent do you consider the 'other characteristics' listed above to be non economic factors?

c) Consider the following freight consignments:

   i) Regular large volume/low value
   ii) Irregular large volume/low value
   iii) High value international merchandise
   iv) High value domestic merchandise
   v) Short-distance low value.

   How would a freight forwarder's choice of mode change with regard to these consignments? You should clearly highlight the main factors from Table 12.4 that lead to these choices.

d) What other factors, apart from those listed in Table 12.4, should a freight shipper consider in their choice of mode of transport, particularly with regard to international freight movements?

Exercise 12.2 Policy options for freight transport

One issue not highlighted in this chapter is that outside of qualitative regulation, policy options for freight transport, particularly road haulage, tend to be very limited at the national level with most policy initiatives arising at the European Union level. In this exercise, you are asked to consider proactive (economic) measures in the freight transport industries. In Chapter 8 a number of policy options were outlined to address the problem of transport's impact on the natural environment. To recap, these were:

- Pigouvian taxes (and subsidies)
- Negotiation and bargaining (Coase Theorem)
- Auctioning pollution rights
- Direct regulation.

a) In this exercise you are asked to consider the practical implementation of these measures to freight transport, by outlining the extent to which each of the measures indicated could be implemented to the freight transport industry in an attempt to control the air emissions of vehicles. You should consider the actual mechanism through which these measures would actually be realised and also consider the extent to which you would seek 'equality' between different modes of transport. Although most of your cases will probably be based upon implementation to the road haulage industry, you should also ensure that you consider what measures you would take with regard to the other modes of freight transport.

b) You should then weigh up the advantages and disadvantages of each of the tools outlined and come to some conclusion regarding which would be your 'preferred' approach. You should highlight the reasons why you favour that particular method giving particular emphasis to the concept of sustainable development.

307

   c) Once you have considered how to implement these measures, you should then identify any potential institutional barriers that may exist concerning the implementation of the policies that you have identified in part (a).

Exercise 12.3 Some thoughts for discussion

1   While we saw in Chapter 10 strong arguments for the co-ordination of public transport services by public sector agencies, do you consider that there are any arguments for similar arrangements to be made for freight transport? As possibly a toned down version of this thought, you may wish to consider more general arguments in favour of greater public intervention in freight transport markets.

2   Why do you consider that little action with regard to addressing the problems facing the freight transport industries occurs at a national level and more at the international level, such as through the European Union? What factors do you believe have to change in order to change thinking on this issue?

3   Are the problems facing the freight transport industry the same as the problems facing passenger transport markets?

4   Why do you consider that freight transport tends to be far lower on the political agenda than passenger transport issues? Do you believe that reading this book has put you in a position that you are now more able to answer this question than you were before?

Chapter 13

Forecasting the demand for transport

Contributed by Geoff Riddington

Learning Outcomes:

On reading this chapter, you will learn about:

- Alternative approaches to generating a forecast of demand for existing, new or improved services
- Issues surrounding asking people how they or the public would react to new or improved transport services and the problems that will occur
- Methods for identifying trends and projecting demand for existing services when no major changes are expected
- Methods for identifying and projecting seasonal change
- Methods for forecasting demand when significant change is expected in the economic and social environment
- Methods for forecasting the impact of new or improved services in a competitive environment.

INTRODUCTION

In order to assess if the provision of a new or improved transport service makes economic sense we need to have some idea of how the public will respond, both immediately and, because transport investment has a very long life, in the far distant future. In Chapter 3 the theory underlying the demand for transport services was discussed. In Chapter 14 you will learn how we take our demand forecasts and assess if they represent a good use of our money. In this chapter we examine the practical issue of generating a forecast.

It should be emphasised from the outset that forecasting is not about applying a mathematical formula to a set of data but rather it is about collecting information from all relevant sources and analysing it in a consistent structured fashion. Remembering that transport is a derived demand, it is only when nothing significant is happening or expected in the external environment that the estimation of a mathematical trend or a pure data relationship is sensible. Thus, for example, when climate change and oil prices are having an impact throughout the world, projecting demand for air transport based only on air traffic data from 1970 to 2000 is not sensible. Huge and environmentally damaging investment in airports based on such trends would appear to be equally debatable.

Integrating information and data about the external environment mathematically can be extremely complex and, indeed, may be impossible. In some cases a set of human brains will produce better forecasts. However, the information in the brain has to be structured and organised or we can be guaranteed biased and inaccurate forecasts. Trend Analysis and unstructured groups vie with each other to produce the very worst outcomes. The cost of transport developments means that poor forecasts will generate significant reductions in the welfare of the public. However because of the regulated monopoly position of many/most transport suppliers, this will not be reflected in lower profits, only higher overall costs. Thus we, the general public, have a vested interest in ensuring that demand forecasting is taken seriously and the effort expended is proportionate to the costs to us all of getting it wrong.

Finally it should be noted that there has been extensive research on how best to forecast, much of which is, unfortunately, regularly ignored. Those wanting to carry out forecasting are recommended to consult *Principles of Forecasting: A Handbook for Forecasters and Practitioners* (ed: J. Scott Armstrong, 2001) which summarises much of the research and offers practical guidance. For the more general reader *Long-Range Forecasting: From Crystal Ball to Computer* by J. Scott Armstrong (1985) is strongly recommended for both entertainment and enlightenment.

GENERAL APPROACHES

There are, broadly speaking, three approaches to forecasting demand:

1 Qualitative: Surveys and Sampling
2 Time Series Analysis
3 Econometric Techniques.

Figure 13.1 provides a decision chart for this first choice of which method may be the most appropriate to use for a given situation.

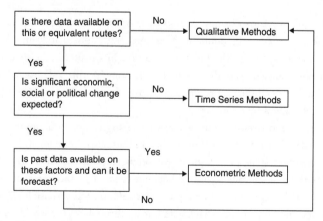

Figure 13.1   Choosing between methods

From this choice diagram there are some methods that will normally be associated with specific types of problems. Time series methods will normally only be relevant in the short term (when little externally will have changed). They are particularly strong at identifying and forecasting seasonal effects.

Econometric methods need a lot of good quality data that can only come from public sources. Some information will not be available for reasons of commercial confidentiality. There will also be some difficulty in forecasting some of the key factors, e.g. the price of oil in 25 years' time. Often we need to develop a range of possible futures for these determining factors (termed scenarios) and generate a separate forecast for each scenario.

Where there is no equivalent to the proposal, e.g. demand for travel to the moon, and no past data, then the intentions of potential customers or the opinions of a range of experts have to be sought. Intention Surveys will, in general, only be appropriate in the very short term. Expert opinions will be required for new products and the very long term that involves significant technological development. We now look at these Qualitative Methods and their potential problems.

QUALITATIVE METHODS

Qualitative Forecasting Methods are based on surveys of either potential customers or 'experts', such as key suppliers. Intentions information can provide the basis of excellent forecasts. As an example forward orders and commitments, such as deposits on holidays or numbers already booked on a service, provide an excellent basis for making forecasts up to one year ahead. Similarly asking existing customers of their intention to repeat the experience can provide excellent results.

The major problem with intentions is identifying who to ask. In some cases the target group may be relatively small and contained. A new bus route to a commercial estate for example will predominantly attract those who work or visit the estate and this group will define what is known as the sample frame. For an accurate representation of what people say we only need ask some of the group, what is known as a *representative sample*. It is important to ensure that no groups are over-sampled and none under-sampled, so it is necessary to ensure that questioning take place throughout the area and throughout the day. If we know the numbers in the various groups that make up the sample frame, e.g. the percentage of females over 60, then we can ensure that each group is properly weighted. Note that the numbers in each stratum do not have to be in proportion (although it can make calculations easier if they are) but there does have to be a significant number in the group sampled.

With new facilities and services, in the short term estimates tend to be too high. This is primarily because people over-estimate their capacity to change and always believe extending their options beneficial. A new bus service or cycle track may seem a wonderful idea when it is suggested but when the car is standing in the drive and the rain is pouring down, a commitment to use the bus or cycle to work will often be ignored. In the long term estimates may be too low because the population itself changes. Individuals without cars will find the estate more attractive as a place to work or shop and workers on the estate will choose accommodation along the bus route. Forecasts from intentions thus need to be adjusted up or down to account for known biases.

In some cases the population concerned is almost impossible to identify or is simply too large to sample properly. For example suppose we are interested in forecasting the number of people who might want to use a weekly service from a local airport to an airport in southern Italy. Potentially anyone in either local area, which will inevitably run into millions, might use the service and will need to be sampled. Suppose the number in both catchment areas is 6 million and we need over 6,000 customers (0.1 per cent) to make the service viable. Even if in fact 9,000 are interested we need a sample of 2,500 people to confirm that we exceed 6,000. If the actual is 20 per cent over the minimum the sample size needed is 12,000. This sampling has to be undertaken in both Italy and the UK adding further to the cost. Given the potential biases already identified and the relatively small cost of short-term transfers of buses, planes and even ferry boats, most firms prefer to simply try out possible routes for a limited period particularly if they can obtain local financial support from the origin and destination areas and they have some indication from 'gravity' models (outlined later in the chapter) that they might be viable.

Forecasting by opinions happens in every organisation at least once a year in the development of budgets. Politically every manager seeks to maximise the income to their divisions without exposing them to unrealistic sales targets. The sales targets will normally be based on the opinions of those 'on the ground' on the likely demand, particularly relative to existing demand. In practice the political imperative of meeting targets leads to diversion of marketing effort often involving price reductions. The outstanding record of low-cost airlines in flying close to capacity is not an indication of excellent forecasting by managers but of a pricing system that combines bookings data and pricing to ensure the plane is filled.

Forecasting using only expert opinion should normally be restricted to novel situations where the alternatives of asking potential customers or using a quantitative model based on similar situations are not available. Even then it is essential that experts from outside transport are involved, indeed it has been said that the only expert that should be used is an expert in forecasting. There are three major problems in seeking expert opinions, anchoring bias, group think and status deferral. Because 'experts' tend to be elderly they give weight to early experiences which may not be appropriate in times of rapid change. Thus anchoring bias often results in underestimates of the rate of change possible. Group think tends to have the opposite effect. In a group, individuals do not have responsibility for the outcome and are tempted towards more risky projects and higher forecasts than warranted. This is particularly apparent if the senior manager in the group is 'entrepreneurial' and a risk taker. In these circumstances ambitious individuals will invariably defer to the higher status individual since opposing, even if perfectly correct, tends to have negative career effects.

To overcome these problems four rules should be adhered to:

1 The group should be facilitated (chaired) by an external
2 Experts from a variety of disciplines should be used
3 All opinions should be given equal weight
4 Reviews of previous forecasts should always be undertaken.

One popular approach known as the Delphi technique (named from the ancient Greek forecaster The Oracle of Delphi) involves a group of individuals from different disciplines (and locations) who are physically separated. The experts individually present their forecasts and the arguments for them to all the others. They then revise their forecasts in the light of the forecasts of others and present them again. This carries out round after round until consensus is reached. The job of the facilitator is to identify, for the participants, the major points of dispute and, if necessary, force agreement on these as a pre-requisite to agreement on the forecast. In the early years the individuals were in separate rooms at the same site but current information technology provides a perfect platform for the technique.

Although expert opinion has a limited role as the sole forecasting method it is important in reviewing and modifying forecasts from the data-based approaches that are now discussed. It should again be emphasised that forecasting is about combining information from all sources in a structured fashion; experts will have knowledge that is not contained within the data.

TIME SERIES ANALYSIS

Introduction

On occasions we want to forecast demand for a transport service that has a long recorded history. Riddington (1999) for example was interested in forecasting the numbers using charter flights to skiing resorts in Europe, data which has been recorded by the Civil Aviation Authority since 1981. The Department for Transport records and forecasts the numbers using the various modes, road, rail, air and sea. Over time certain patterns emerge. The most obvious and important is fluctuations over the seasons.

A further example would be on short sea crossings, where we may expect higher demand in the summer than during the winter. Figure 13.2 shows the total number of passengers travelling on ferries to and from the UK each year and Figure 13.3 shows the number each quarter.

As expected, there is a marked seasonal pattern with passenger numbers rising steeply in the second and third quarters. There is also however a clear downward trend.

In time series analysis, from such cyclical patterns we seek to identify the three elements:

1 The Trend
2 Seasonal or Cyclical factors
3 The unusual (sometimes termed the stochastic factor or noise).

We then assume that these will continue into the future. As discussed earlier this may be reasonable, particularly in the short term. However, in this example, given changes in air fares, holdups

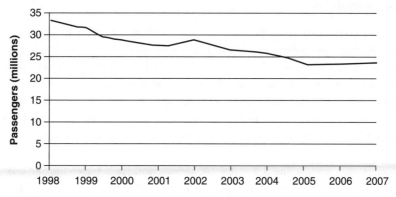

Figure 13.2 *Annual and quarterly short sea passengers, inward and outwards, 1998 to Q2 2008*

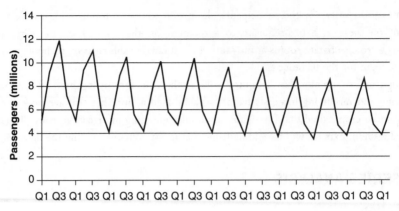

Figure 13.3   *Annual and quarterly short sea passengers, inward and outwards, 1998 to Q2 2008*

and delays at airports and faster ferries, it would be a very brave forecaster who would assume the downward trend illustrated will continue. A very well-known verse attributed to the famous economist Roy Harrod runs:

A trend is a trend is a trend,
the question is will it bend?
Will it change course
through some unforeseen force
and come to a premature end?

If the forecaster is interested in forecasting on a daily or weekly basis then a number of sophisti-cated methods such as ARIMA, ARARMA, Trigg-Leach and Brown's Double Smoothing have been developed. These involve weighted moving averages of the data to obtain an estimate of the underlying level and weighted moving averages of variations from that level. After a number of competitions between them, which method is 'the best' is still subject to much debate. Interested readers are referred to Makridakis and Hibon (2000) for further information.

Trend curve analysis

Most transport economists are primarily concerned with the medium to long term and one advocated approach is trend curve analysis. This approach involves trying to fit a line as closely as possible to the annual (or deseasonalised) series. The procedure of 'fitting' is known as Regression. Those unfamiliar with regression are referred to any introductory book on statistics or web sources such as Wikipedia, which gives a reasonable introductory overview. In essence regression replaces fitting lines by eye with fitting a line that minimises the square of the distance from the line to the point. Figure 13.4 shows the line of best straight line fit associated with the annual sea passenger series.

The formula for a straight line is $Y = \alpha + \beta X$ and the distance between the line and the actual number is known as the stochastic term, the error or the residual term and is symbolised by ε. Thus the formula for the actual number is $Y = \alpha + \beta X + \varepsilon$, where, in this case, Y is the sea

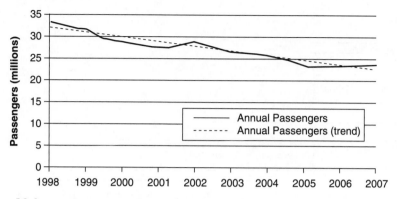

Figure 13.4 *Annual sea passengers, underlying trend*

Table 13.1 *Sea passengers per year*

Y (PAX)	X (YEAR)
33225861	1998
31381282	1999
28516814	2000
27753461	2001
28726426	2002
26523377	2003
25798730	2004
23693468	2005
23465161	2006
23667651	2007

Source: DfT Statistics

passengers and X is the year. To obtain values for α, β and ϵ we employ statistical software such as the Data Analysis Add-In in Excel. Table 13.1 shows the data and Figure 13.5 the output that is generated.

The coefficients give the values of α (2134399282) and β (−1052246.72). To obtain a forecast of passengers in 2020 we simply substitute 2020 for X in the formula $Y = \alpha + \beta X$, which gives 2134399282 − 1052246.72*2020 = 8,860,905. This is considerably (and implausibly) lower than the current level of 23,667,651.

The straight line implies that a fixed number of passengers (1,052,247) will be lost every year. In reality growth and decline is normally a fixed percentage rather than a fixed quantity. This is represented by an exponential curve $Y = \alpha * e^{\beta X}$ rather than a straight line. The exponential term e is rather like π in geometry, and has a fixed value of 2.718282. It is important because the equation results in a fixed growth rate given by β. Depending upon assumptions made about the stochastic term, the values of α and β can be estimated either by linear regression of $\log_e(Y)$ against X or by iteration. In this case the growth rate was found to be −3.8 per cent and the 2020 forecast 13,871,777 considerably higher than the linear forecast.

The question arises which forecast is 'better'. Remembering that forecasting is about

SUMMARY
OUTPUT

Regression Statistics	
Multiple R	0.9593
R Square	0.9203
Adjusted R Square	0.9104
Standard Error	994080.8077
Observations	10

ANOVA

	df	SS	MS	F	Significance F
Regression	1	91345910889887	91345910889887	92.43698	0.0000
Residual	8	7905573217590	988196652199		
Total	9	99251484107477			

	Coefficients	Standard Error	t Stat	P-value	Lower 95%	Upper 95%	Lower 95.0%	Upper 95.0%
Intercept	2134399282	219163227	9.7389	0.0000	1629007975	2.64E+09	1.63E+09	2.64E+09
X (YEAR)	-1052247	109445	-9.6144	0.0000	1304626.64	-799867	-1304627	-799867

RESIDUAL OUTPUT

Observation	Predicted Y (PAX)	Residuals
1	32010333.35	1215528
2	30958086.62	423195.4
3	29905839.9	-1389026
4	28853593.18	-1100132
5	27801346.46	925079.5
6	26749099.74	-225723
7	25696853.02	101877
8	24644606.3	-951138
9	23592359.58	-127199
10	22540112.85	1127538

Figure 13.5   *Excel regression output*

combining knowledge then if there are strong reasons to assume fixed growth (bending trends) and/or that the results are more plausible, then that is the appropriate forecast. However, there are also some indications from the statistics that the 'fit' of the growth rate model is better. A measure of the fit is known as the Adjusted RSquared which for the linear is shown (on the third line of the output table) as 0.910391568. This suggests that we can explain 91 per cent of the variation in the data series by the model with 9 per cent being due to the stochastic noise, i.e. remains unexplained by the model. The adjusted RSquared for the growth rate model is 0.92326468, i.e. the exponential model explains more. It should be emphasised however that a good fit is not the same as a good forecast. Great care should be taken when selecting models using fit statistics because they are dependent upon a number of assumptions about the stochastic term that may well not be true. It should also be noted that, in theory, test statistics from linearised models are not directly comparable with those from simple linear models. That said it is a helpful additional factor in deciding whether a linear or exponential model is better.

Because fit and forecast performance can be radically different, if the data set is long enough, it is good practice to exclude the last few data points when estimating the model. Forecasts from the estimated model are then compared with the actuals (technically known as *ex post* analysis). There is some debate in the relevant literature as to the appropriate measure of the forecast. The most common is the Root Mean Square Error of the one step ahead forecast.

Estimating seasonal fluctuation by seasonal dummies

When planning capacity, if there is marked seasonal fluctuation, then a seasonal forecast is required. Again there are a large number of methods involving weighted averages of the seasonal differences (or ratios) some of which are quite complex. A simple approach utilising regression involves the use of dummy variables. A dummy variable is a variable that takes a value of 1 when the phenomenon is present and zero otherwise. It was originally developed to take account of periods of war in economic models but is equally applicable to the season. In the seasonal case a dummy variable for Q1 has a value of 1 when it is Q1 and zero otherwise. We can thus extend our example in order to incorporate not only the effect of time (the trend) but also seasonal effects into our forecasts. Table 13.2. shows the first two and a half years of the data set up in Excel and Figure 13.6 the results of the linear multiple regression of sales against the year and the seasonal dummies.

It is important to note that when you have four quarterly dummies you cannot also have a constant, as effectively the quarterly dummies are the constants for each season. The coefficient of X indicates the decline per quarter and the coefficients of the dummies are equivalent to the constant term for that quarter. Figure 13.7 shows how closely the model fits the data; some 97 per cent of the variation is explained.

To forecast we take the coefficient of the relevant quarter and add the coefficient of X * the time (i.e. 2020.25 for the second quarter in 2020).

The linear model estimated above implies a constant addition/subtraction to the mean for each quarter. However, most of the time, the seasonal effect is most likely to be a proportion of the underlying mean. As with the growth model a ratio seasonal factor can be estimated by regressing the log of the sales on to the time and the dummies. In fact this log-linear regression produced a remarkable fit and an adjusted R Squared just slightly higher of 97.3 per cent compared to 96.9 per cent for the linear model. Incorporating seasonal effects into our model therefore has improved the overall fit, and hence may be expected to produce better forecasts.

Table 13.2   *Quarterly sea passengers with seasonal dummies – first two and a half years*

Y (PAX)	X (YEAR)	Q1	Q2	Q3	Q4	LogY
5151807	1998.00	1	0	0	0	15.45486
9304349	1998.25	0	1	0	0	16.04599
11801764	1998.50	0	0	1	0	16.28376
6967941	1998.75	0	0	0	1	15.75683
5036822	1999.00	1	0	0	0	15.43229
9452280	1999.25	0	1	0	0	16.06177
10996127	1999.50	0	0	1	0	16.21305
5896053	1999.75	0	0	0	1	15.58979
4179625	2000.00	1	0	0	0	15.24573
8464104	2000.25	0	1	0	0	15.95134
..	..	..	..	..	..	..
..	..	..	..	..	..	..
..	..	..	..	..	..	..
..	..	..	..	..	..	..

SUMMARY OUTPUT

Regression Statistics	
Multiple R	0.9985
R Square	0.9970
Adjusted R Square	0.9696
Standard Error	416052.4587
Observations	42

ANOVA

	df	SS	MS	F	Significance F
Regression	5	2.12E+15	4.24E+14	2447.337	0.0000
Residual	37	6.4E+12	1.73E+11		
Total	42	2.12E+15			

	Coefficients	Standard Error	t Stat	P-value	Lower 95%	Upper 95%	Lower 95.0%	Upper 95.0%
Intercept	0	#N/A	#N/A	#N/A	#N/A	#N/A	#N/A	#N/A
X (YEAR)	-252670	21204	-11.9162	0.0000	-295633	-209707	-295633	-209707
Q1	510286258	42471791	12.0147	0.0000	424230237	5.96E+08	4.24E+08	5.96E+08
Q2	513756509	42477092	12.0949	0.0000	427689746	6E+08	4.28E+08	6E+08
Q3	515932721	42471809	12.1477	0.0000	429876662	6.02E+08	4.3E+08	6.02E+08
Q4	511627864	42477110	12.0448	0.0000	425561064	5.98E+08	4.26E+08	5.98E+08

Figure 13.6   *Output from regression of sea passengers on time and seasonal dummies*

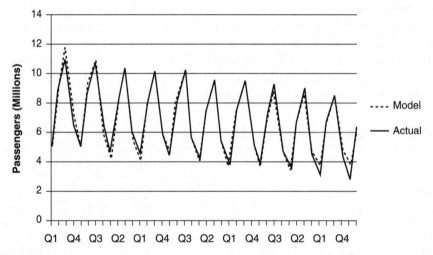

Figure 13.7   *Actual and estimated sea passengers by quarter*

Unlike the trend, the factors that determine different levels throughout a season do not change; Christmas always occurs on December 25th, the summer holidays in July and August etc. Problems do occur when dealing with monthly data due to situations when there are 5 weekends or when Easter occurs in March rather than April but, certainly at quarterly level, estimates of seasonality are accurate and robust. This is, however, not the case with trends. Whatever has caused the decline in sea passengers may quite conceivably reverse or become more important. Investigating what has determined change and using that information to forecast the future is the role of econometrics, which we cover next.

ECONOMETRIC METHODS

Introduction

In Chapter 3 we looked at the factors that broadly determine the demand for transport; income, price, quality of service, price and quality of alternatives, journey time and population size. The object of econometric methods is to try and identify the precise importance of each of these (the usual measure being the elasticity) in order that we can determine the effect on demand of changing these in the future. Unfortunately, as we shall see, this is not necessarily a straightforward task.

The modelling process involves 6 stages

1   *Understanding the Problem*: Identifying all the key factors and making preliminary estimates of the size and direction of the effect. This is covered in Chapter 2.
2   *Obtaining the Data*: Data on ALL the factors has to be acquired. It is no use having price data for your company but not for your competitors. Data is of three broad types:

   a)   Time Series, where the data, going back a significant number of years, relates to a single location
   b)   Cross Section, where the data has been obtained from a series of locations (or individuals) at a specific point in time
   c)   Panel Data, where data has been obtained from the same series of locations over a period of years.

Each type of data has strengths and problems specific to it which we will discuss in the next sections but, generally speaking, the major problem is acquiring good quality data at all. Statistics issued by the government or its agencies are invariably the first place to look, e.g. Transport Statistics, National Statistics, The Census and the National Travel Survey. The Civil Aviation Authority also produces some superb data series. All these are now available on the Web.

It is extremely difficult however to obtain good data on two key factors, Price and Quality. Consider trying to ascertain the impact of a more expensive but faster train from Scotland to England. This needs information on the changing quality of the experience, journey times, frequencies, changes in airport check-in time, queues at security, over-crowding, traffic jams etc.

Equally critical is the actual price paid both on the train and the competitive air, coach and road services. Because the average price paid is a commercial secret we are forced back to published 'normal' prices which may be substantially higher than actual price. In addition, in the case of some airlines, the published price varies from hour to hour depending upon the current loading. The 'cost' in both journey time and ticket price, of getting to the final destination, must also be acquired.

A fundamental problem is that the omission of a key variable totally distorts estimation of the impact of the other factors. Poor or substitute (proxy) data is better than no data but inevitably decreases confidence in the outcomes.

3 *Specifying the Model:* It is tempting to assume that the factors are independent of each other, that the factors are additive in their effects and the effect happens immediately and that all the assumptions relating to the stochastic term are applicable. Unfortunately that is rarely the case. The specification stage involves:

   a) Selecting the functional form (linear, log-log, logistic etc)
   b) Selecting the variables and in time series any lagged effects (e.g. with advertising)
   c) Making reasonable assumptions about the stochastic term (e.g. that the bigger the demand the bigger the stochastic term).

4 *Estimating the specified model*: Identifying values for the parameter estimates for each factor to be used in the forecast α, $\beta 1$, $\beta 2$, $\beta 3$, . . . that makes the predicted values lie as close as possible to the actual values. This normally involves minimising the sum of squares of the residuals.

5 *Validating the Model*: This involves examining the outcomes to ensure:

   a) The values of the coefficients (the elasticities) have the right signs (income positive, price negative and so on) and are of the expected size
   b) The fit is statistically significant (The RSquared and F values in the output table)
   c) The individual variables are statistically significant (the t value in the output table)
   d) The residuals have no pattern over time or location.

   If the model fails these tests then we need to return to the specification stage (or even the understanding).

6 *Simulation/Forecasting:* Once we have the final model then it is a question of inserting expected future values of the factors into the equations. Sometimes we can use forecasts from other organisations but often we need to use suggested values obtained from expert groups. Sometimes different sets of predictions are bundled up to form scenarios. Sometimes we simply use trend extrapolation of the external factors.

This last section illustrates a theme of this chapter. The purpose of econometric modelling is both to obtain information on the effects of the demand factors but also to integrate information from a variety of sources into the forecast. We now look at some important specifications and problems associated with them before illustrating how these come together in assessing demand for a new route.

The gravity model

It would be extremely surprising if the demand for services (which includes the demand for road space for cars and lorries) between two large cities such as London and Manchester was not much, much larger than between two small towns such as Cirencester and Lincoln. It would also be very surprising if the numbers travelling between two adjacent towns say Cambridge and Norwich was not much larger than between Cambridge and a town of a similar size to Norwich in Scotland, say Dundee. Hence the level of transport between two locations will be dependent upon their respective population sizes and the distance between them. In more formal terms, our understanding suggests that the flow of people between two points i and j, F_{ij}, is a function of the size of the origin O_i, the size of the destination D_j and the cost of travelling between them C_{ij}. At this stage it is important to note that the cost is directly related to the distance between i and j and the time taken; a direct motorway will reduce the time and hence decrease what we term the generalised cost.

To estimate our model in order to predict the numbers flowing down a particular route we need data on flows between a number of towns and the generalised cost of travelling a route. This is a typical example of cross sectional data.

The normal specification of the model is of the form:

$$F_{ij} = a O_i^{\beta} D_j^{\gamma} C_{ij}^{\delta} \varepsilon_{ij}$$

where α, β, γ and δ are parameters to be estimated and ε is the stochastic term. In simple terms, what these show is the relative impact each factor will have on the numbers travelling between these two locations taking into account the differing units these may be measured in. Thus for example the β is the impact of the size of the origin on total traffic flow. In a similar fashion, γ is the impact of the size of the destination and so on. The gravity model gets its name from the models of gravitational pull developed by Newton where the size of the bodies is multiplied together with the distance between them.

It is also very easy to estimate the model by taking logs to give:

$$\log F_{ij} = A + \beta \log O_i + \gamma \log D_j + \delta \log C_{ij} + E_{ij}$$

where A is log α and E is log ε. If we assume that E is normally distributed then the normal method of minimising the sum of the squares of the stochastic term (known as Ordinary Least Squares) can be applied.

Riddington (2002) used a gravity specification to forecast the numbers of people who might travel to a new supermarket in town H. The numbers of people in each of the 12 surrounding towns and villages was known. The complication was the existence of 3 other supermarkets in town D which currently attracted custom from the same towns and villages. The two key determinants of the proportion of each settlement that would go to H rather than D was the relative distance to H and the relative size of the shops; the more floor space/goods on offer, the more attractive the destination. It was assumed that a fixed proportion of each settlement would shop in either H or D in any week. A possible range of values for the impact of supermarket size and distance were obtained from other gravity model studies. The mean of these values generated a central forecast, the range of values and the possible range of outcomes. This work showed conclusively that the estimates of diversion from D to H made by the proposers was exaggerated and that, even at the most favourable range of values, the new supermarket would lead to serious problems and small shop closures in the existing town centre.

The gravity model is central to large network planning transport models, particularly the four stage Transport Planning Model, where stage one and two are to estimate the total number of trips within a given area, and then the number of specific flows between two locations, before subsequent stages then apportion these flows to modes and then routes. Gravity models are also extensively applied in models of economic trade and thus used to predict trade flows. Nevertheless, the focus is on populations and generalised costs and the specification is totally unable to describe the massive growth in car and air journeys. For this we turn to traditional demand models formulated over time.

Econometric demand models

Whilst population change is of critical concern in a local context and in developing countries, in the developed world it has been relatively static and is not an explanation for the growth in transport that has been a characteristic of the last century. As seen in Chapter 2, we have tended to associate this growth with the growth of the economy and the associated growth in real personal incomes.

Our understanding based on the theory of Chapter 3 suggests that, at the national/regional level, the demand for a particular mode (road, rail, air, sea) will be determined by National Income, comparative price, comparative journey times, frequency and comparative quality. Data for income over a number of years can be obtained easily. Journey time information for the same years needs to be identified with allowances for travel to public transport and times to enter and exit the terminal (including the time to wait for the service). As discussed earlier, obtaining good quality price data for a number of years is problematic and normally ad hoc series based on what can be obtained over the years has to suffice. Finally there is the issue of comfort. The modern car is significantly more comfortable and reliable than its real price (i.e. net of inflation) equivalent of twenty years ago whilst the low-cost airline is not as luxurious as its historical forebears. We normally either:

1 Simply assume quality changes are part of the stochastic term (not normally appropriate)
2 Allow for these changes by introducing proxy variables that are linked to quality
3 Develop what are known as hedonic price indices.

Broadly speaking econometric demand models have two functional specifications: linear and multiplicative (log-log). There is some evidence that consumer responses to economic changes are constant, e.g. that a 10 per cent rise in incomes will lead to a 7 per cent increase in demand, whatever the current level of income. This is a situation of constant elasticity and is characteristic only of a multiplicative model. Thus, on these grounds alone (there are others), the following specification might be used:

$$Log\ Q_t = a + \beta_1 \log Y_t + \beta_2 Log\ P_t + \beta_3 Log\ J_t + \beta_4 Log\ F_t + \varepsilon_t$$

Where Q_t is number of passengers, Y_t is income, P_t is relative price, J_t relative journey time and F_t is relative frequency. Once again in simple terms the parameter estimates (β terms) are the relative impacts on demand of each of the factors included, taking into account the units in which each is measured.

Because of the difficulty with national data on Price, Journey time and Frequency, a truncated form $Log\ Q_t = a + \beta_1 \log Y_t + \varepsilon_t$ is often found (e.g. DfT traffic forecasts). The relationship between demand and income is very strong and found throughout the developed world. It is also very easy to make forecasts. For example if β_1 (the income elasticity) in a model of car journeys has a value of 1.4 then growth in GDP of 2 per cent will lead to a growth of 2.8 per cent in car journeys. Of course forecasts of GDP for 20 years ahead are required in order to forecast transport demand 20 years ahead. In practice we normally present a range of possible growth rates for the economy and consequently a range of possible forecasts.

It is undoubtedly true that this procedure simply replaces a trend curve projection for passengers with a trend curve projection for the economy as a whole. However, other information about economic factors may be available and one of the most important strengths of this approach is the structured combination of information about the future. Unlike the time series approach outlined earlier, we are not only reliant on a single past trend within the transport system, but also the impacts of external factors upon that trend. Hence if a trend was to bend, there would be a far higher possibility that our forecast will pick it up.

The use of only GDP in the specification rather than all the variables is much more critical (as is the omission of lagged values in short period models). Suppose that over the same period the relative price of motoring has been falling. If it had a price elasticity of −1 and prices fell at 1.5 per cent per annum then the growth rate due to price change is 1.5 per cent. If the total growth is 2.8 per cent then only 1.3 per cent of that growth is attributable to economic income, not the full 2.8 per cent. If the decline in relative price was reversed then growth due to price change would be negative and the growth rate correspondingly lower. Thus it is absolutely essential that we include all relevant variables or the results concerning individual elasticities can be totally misleading. Failure to include the correct variables or the correct functional form is known as misspecification.

Misspecification and the demand for ferry services

Earlier in this chapter we observed the number of ferry passengers in decline. Since foreign travel is a luxury, our economics suggests it is likely to grow with income, hence it will have a positive price elasticity. We might also suspect that cheaper more available air services and the advent of the Channel Tunnel might have an effect on demand for ferries. Table 13.3 shows data collected on passenger numbers by different modes from the Social Trends database.

Our first task is to see how well our basic understanding fits to the data. Graphing the data is always a good start but in this case Figure 13.8 does not tell us much that we did not already know.

Another useful tool is the correlation matrix. This shows how closely any two series are aligned. A figure close to +1 shows a strong positive (complementary) relationship, close to −1 a strong inverse (competitive) relationship. For example we would expect number of cars and sales of petrol to have a high (>0.8) correlation but number of cars and bus passenger numbers to have a strong negative correlation. (<−0.8). Tables 13.4 and 13.5 show the correlation matrices between the numbers by mode and real GDP for data from 1981 and from 1995.

A significant difference between the two is the strong negative correlation between Sea Travel and Income in recent years (−0.93). It may be that this reflects the idea that sea travel on holiday is

Table 13.3 UK international passengers by mode (million)

YEAR	AIR	SEA	TUNNEL	TOTAL	REAL GDP
1981	11.4	7.7	0.0	19.0	56.2
1991	20.4	10.4	0.0	30.8	73.0
1995	28.1	10.0	3.2	41.3	79.5
1996	27.9	10.7	3.5	42.1	81.7
1997	30.3	11.5	4.1	46.0	84.3
1998	34.3	10.5	6.1	50.9	87.1
1999	37.5	10.4	5.9	53.9	89.7
2000	41.4	9.6	5.8	56.8	93.1
2001	43.0	9.7	5.6	58.3	95.3
2002	44.0	10.0	5.3	59.4	97.3
2003	47.1	9.2	5.1	61.4	100.0
2004	50.4	9.0	4.8	64.2	103.3
2005	53.6	8.1	4.7	66.4	105.2
2006	56.5	8.4	4.7	69.5	108.2

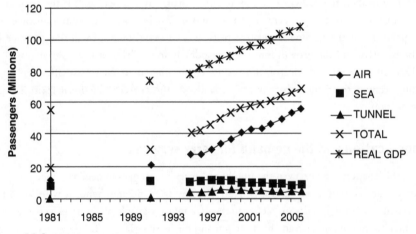

Figure 13.8 UK international passengers by mode

Table 13.4 Correlation matrix. Passengers by mode from 1981

	AIR	SEA	TUNNEL	TOTAL	REAL GDP
AIR	1.0000				
SEA	−0.2784	1.0000			
TUNNEL	0.7433	0.1755	1.0000		
TOTAL	0.9886	−0.1499	0.8270	1.0000	
REAL GDP	0.9900	−0.1485	0.7698	0.9933	1.0000

Table 13.5 *Correlation matrix. Passengers by mode from 1996*

	AIR	SEA	TUNNEL	TOTAL	REAL GDP
AIR	1.0000				
SEA	−0.9471	1.0000			
TUNNEL	0.1440	−0.0812	1.0000		
TOTAL	0.9939	−0.9226	0.2437	1.0000	
REAL GDP	0.9975	−0.9354	0.1044	0.9890	1.0000

an inferior product with a large negative income elasticity, i.e. as we get richer we are ceteris paribus less likely to take our cars on to a ferry to Europe. Conversely we may well believe that this is a short-term effect brought on by rapidly declining air fares in recent years and that the longer series with a very much weaker correlation (−0.148) is a better indication of what to expect in the future. It is important to recognise that our understanding from economic theory of what underlies change is crucial to modelling and forecasting.

To forecast demand for sea ferries we really require the price of ferry services, price of air services and the price of tunnel services. As discussed earlier obtaining a 'price' for a single route is extremely difficult, for a combination virtually impossible. Since we expect price and demand to be quite strongly inversely related we can sometimes use 'numbers' as proxies for prices. In addition the number of air passengers also reflects speculative increases in capacity. Thus it seems quite reasonable to try to explain the number of sea passengers by numbers on the other modes and income.

Figure 13.9 gives the Excel Output of the multiple regression of Number of Sea Passengers on passengers using air services, passengers using the tunnel and GDP.

The overall fit of the model is very good (95 per cent variance explained) but, more importantly, the model coefficients seem to have the right sign. The income elasticity of demand was defined in Chapter 2 as the rate of change in Quantity divided by the rate of change in Income, i.e in symbols $(\Delta Q/Q)/(\Delta Y/Y)$ or $(\Delta Q/\Delta Y)/(Q/Y)$. In a linear model $\Delta Q/\Delta Y$ is given by the slope of the line, i.e. the coefficient (in this case 0.429856). The elasticity will, however, vary over different values of Q and Y so, by convention, it is usually calculated at the mean values of Q and Y. The income elasticity of sea travel calculated at the means in this example is very high at just under 4. Surprisingly the truncated data gives almost identical results.

This modelling exercise is important because it highlights the way that increases in air passengers, rather than the channel tunnel, has been the most important factor in slowing down demand for ferry services. If airline growth is checked because of higher fuel prices and carbon pricing then we would confidently expect significant growth in the ferry market well in excess of the growth of GDP.

It is important to note that if data on prices were available it would be far better than using the proxy variables of passenger numbers. In addition a better modelling strategy, which is illuminated in the case study at the end of this chapter, might well be to model the total market and relate that to GDP and model mode choice separately based on factors such as price and journey time.

The use of ordinary least squares is in theory limited to situations where the stochastic term:

SUMMARY OUTPUT

Regression statisitics	
Multiple R	0.978422
R Square	0.957309
Adjusted R Square	0.944501
Standard Error	0.253175
Observations	14

ANOVA

	df	SS	MS	F	Significance F
Regression	3	14.37331	4.791102	74.74673	3.77E-07
Residual	10	0.640978	0.064098		
Total	13	15.01429			

	Coefficients	Standard Error	t Stat	P-value	Lower 95%	Upper 95%
Intercept	−10.5864	1.869482	−5.66274	0.000209	−14.7519	−6.42093
AIR	−0.51199	0.039174	−13.0696	1.3E-07	−0.59927	−0.4247
REAL GDP	0.429856	0.037769	11.38123	4.8E-07	0.345701	0.51401
TUNNEL	0.232451	0.05696	4.080982	0.002211	0.105537	0.359365

Figure 13.9   *Regression output from Excel*

1   Has Zero mean
2   Is normally distributed
3   Has constant variance
4   Is independent over time and space
5   Is uncorrelated with the independent variables.

As discussed earlier, there are also problems if the factors are not independent of each other. Econometric packages offer a number of estimation methods to deal with these problems and these are important if the main objective is to identify precisely the effect of one factor on another and the data quality is good. However, when we come to forecasting, low-quality data and the problem of obtaining good forecasts of the independents normally means the accuracy will always be limited. In these circumstances research suggests that theoretical sophistication is not as important as structured thought about the future.

MODELLING CHOICE

Background

It is often the case that we are more concerned with forecasting the share of existing traffic than the growth of that traffic. Consider, for example, investing in a new toll motorway that runs almost parallel to an overcrowded existing motorway. The key question is how many vehicles we might expect at various levels of toll. The first task is to generate a gravity type model that incorporates tolls and reduced journey times within the generalised cost function. This will then give us a first estimate at the total traffic on the route. The next task is to share the traffic between the toll and the free motorway. This is not however the end of the game because if the tolls are set too high, traffic will stick to the free motorway, journey times overall will increase and traffic will drop on both. In these type of situations we undertake what is known as *iteration*, i.e. we put the new forecast of traffic and journey time/average price into the model, generate a new share, recalculate total demands and generalised costs, re-estimate shares, re-estimate costs and totals, and so on. Modelling choices and shares is not, however, straightforward.

Based on our economic theory we assume that we will not undertake a journey unless we achieve some Utility (satisfaction). Against that we have to place the Cost, in terms of journey time (J), price (P) and lack of quality (L). We represent the importance of, for example, each minute or of an inch of leg-room by β_1 and β_2. We call the sum of the values generated from the factors the systematic value which for a choice Q is given by $V_q = \alpha - \beta_1 * J_q + \beta_2 * L_q - P_q + \varepsilon$.

Thus say service Q is chosen over service R, or service Q is chosen over service S, and so on, then we assume that it is likely that the systematic value of Q is greater than the systematic value of R, S, ... i.e. the difference between V_q and V_r, V_s, . . . is likely to be greater than 0 (or the ratio >1).

Data and specification

Choice modelling data comes in two forms:

1   Individual Data gathered within one time period
2   Market Share data which can be cross section, time series or panel.

Increasingly, when contemplating quality changes, a survey is undertaken where customers are presented with a number of alternatives and asked to choose between them. For example we might be interested in the best mix of speed, comfort and price on a train route. Customers are presented with a set of combinations of the three at different levels and asked to select their choice. They will then be presented with another set of combinations, and their choice recorded and then a third set and so on. This generates a mass of individual data and is known as a Choice Experiment.

For market share data Pr(Q) symbolises the proportion making a choice (e.g. going by mode Q). For individual data Pr(Q) symbolises the probability that the individual will make a choice (e.g. go by mode Q). Note that we cannot measure this probability, only the result. We assume that the choice with the highest chance of being selected will in practice be selected.

Assume for the moment there is only one alternative to mode Q, mode R. The larger the utility of mode Q relative to R, the higher the value of Pr(Q). It would be possible to simply regress Pr(Q) against the difference in the systematic values of Q and R, e.g. $Pr(Q) = \beta(V_q - V_r) + \varepsilon$. This is illustrated by the straight line SS in Figure 13.10

Note that when the utilities of R and Q are equal, the predicted market share (probability) must be 50 per cent. Note also that $Pr(R) = 1 - Pr(Q)$. Thus ever larger negative values of $V_q - V_r$

increase the probability that an individual will use mode R, whilst ever larger positive values increase the probability that an individual will use mode Q.

There are two major problems with this linear specification:

1 It suggests that it is possible to have more than 100 per cent of the market
2 It contradicts the law of diminishing marginal utility.

In this context the law simply tells us that, even if mode Q is vastly superior to mode R, a few people will still opt for R. Thus we would expect the line of best fit to look more like Figure 13.11

One mathematical function that gives a line of that shape is known as the Logistic and has the form

$$Pr(Q) = \frac{e^{\beta(V_q - V_r)}}{1 + e^{\beta(V_q - V_r)}}$$

where e is the exponential operator (a constant).

With this function when:

$V_q = V_r$, $Pr(Q) = 0.5$,
$V_q - V_r$ is very large, $Pr(Q)$ tends to one,
$V_q - V_r$ is large and negative, $Pr(Q)$ tends to zero.

At first sight this looks very difficult to deal with, but some simple algebra produces:

$$Log_e\left(\frac{Pr(Q)}{1 - Pr(Q)}\right) = \beta(V_q - V_r) + \varepsilon$$

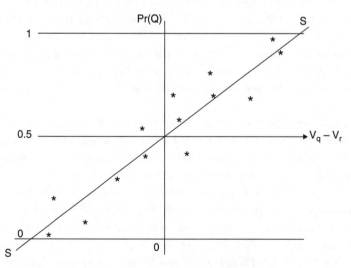

Figure 13.10   *Change in market share versus difference in systematic values*

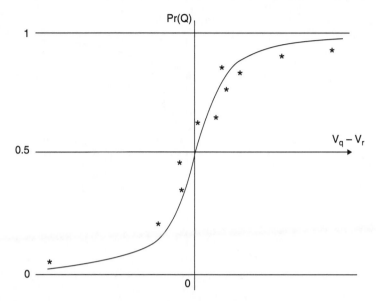

Figure 13.11   *The Logistic curve with market share data*

In order to clarify this 'simple' algebra, if we let $\beta(V_q - V_r) = x$ and $Pr(Q) = y$ then $y = e^x/(1 + e^x)$. Since $(1 + e^x)y = e^x$, $y = e_x(1 - y)$ and $y/(1 - y) = e^x$. Taking logs gives $Log_e(y/(1 - y)) = x$.

The first term is known as the LogOdds and is simple to calculate. For example if mode Q has 60 per cent of the market then R has 40 per cent and the logOdds is $log_e(0.6/0.4) = log_e$ $(1.5) = 0.405$. To estimate β where we have proportions data, we simply carry out the normal regression of the LogOdds against the differences in the systematic values.

The problem with individual data is that we can only observe the choice made, i.e. it is either 100 per cent mode Q or 100 per cent mode R. This is illustrated in Figure 13.12.

Where the difference is very large we would expect the choice to be obvious. However, where our model predicts that for example there is a 53 per cent chance that the individual will choose Q then we will not be very surprised if they choose R. We use this idea to choose the parameters β to ensure that the situations when the predicted likelihood is high, then that is the appropriate choice and are less worried at values close to 0.5. This approach is known as Maximum Likelihood Estimation and is available in large statistical packages such as SPSS, LIMDEP or STATA. It is important to note that, because there is not much information conveyed by each individual about the 'norm', very large amounts of individual data (typically in excess of 1,000 individuals) are needed for reliable forecasts.

Forecasting shares

To summarise, the economic understanding suggests that choices are made on the basis of differences between factors such as journey time and price. Data can be either from individuals on their choices or from the market on the shares. The specified model has to take into account the logical limits of proportions and the law of diminishing marginal utility. One common form is the

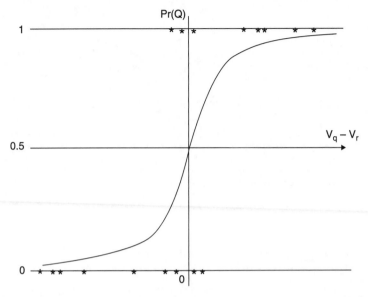

Figure 13.12 *Logistic curve and individual data*

Logistic although other forms such as the cumulative normal, known as the probit, can be used. Estimates of the parameter coefficients are found by regression of the LogOdds on the difference in the factor levels. In the case of proportions data we can use Ordinary Least Squares (OLS) regression (the usual approach) but for individual data we require specialist Maximum Likelihood techniques. Once we have the model estimated then forecasting is simply, as before, a case of substituting new values into the model.

Table 13.6 gives some of the data of mode shares between metropolitan areas (some of which are on islands).

This data generated a model of the form:

$\text{Log}_e(\text{Pr(Land)}/\text{Pr(Air)}) = -0.04 * (\text{Difference in Journey Times}) - 0.03 * (\text{Difference in Price})$

Table 13.6 *Sample data on market shares and differences in systematic values*

| Location | Complete Journey Time (Mins) | | | Price (£) | | | Share | |
	Land	Air	Difference	Train	Air	Difference	Train	Air
1	350	120	230	56	98	−42	0.0%	100.0%
2	280	280	0	98	98	0	50.0%	50.0%
3	35	120	−85	56	98	−42	99.1%	0.9%
4	90	80	10	88	78	10	33.2%	66.8%
5	620	134	486	25	231	−206	0.0%	100.0%
6	324	212	112	45	123	−78	10.5%	89.5%
7	350	220	130	56	98	−42	1.9%	98.1%

Or

Pr(Land) = exp(−0.04 *(Difference in Journey Times) − 0.03* (Difference in Price))/
(1 + exp(−0.04 *(Difference in Journey Times) − 0.03 *(Difference in Price))

Suppose current differences are 60 minutes faster by air and £100 more expensive but increased security increases air journey times by 50 mins. The model forecasts that the current land market share will increase from 64.6 per cent to 93.1 per cent.

Developments in choice modelling

The importance of the topic, coupled with major advances in computer power, have led to very significant and important developments in choice modelling. The most obvious has been extension to models with more than two choices. The simplest of these, the multinomial logistic, has a significant limitation (known as the independence of irrelevant alternatives) and a model that nests choices is often preferred. In the nested case a first choice might be public v private followed by a choice between bus and train after public has been chosen. Estimates can vary significantly depending upon the way the nests are constructed. Figure 13.13 shows two possible structures for a comparison of road, rail, car and coach. Once again our understanding of the way people make decisions is critical to the parameter estimates and ultimately the forecasts.

More recently developments in optimising algorithms have opened the possibility of multi-nomial probits with and without subjective priors (e.g. estimates of the degree of independence between the choices which are made by the modeller on the basis of their experience and understanding). It must be emphasised that these developments are dependent upon many thousands of observations of the choices made, and are most usefully found with choice experiment data. Readers that want to find out more are recommended to read Ben-Akiva and Lerman (1985).

Before concluding this chapter we look at a real case where most of the topics discussed come together.

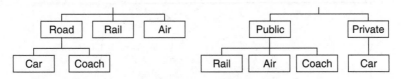

Figure 13.13 *Possible nesting structures for a four mode choice*

Case study 13.1 Forecasting demand for a new ferry service

– This case is based on Riddington (1996).

Background

Islay and Jura are two large adjacent island off the South West of Scotland. Although similar in size (253 and 147 sq miles respectively) they are remarkably different in character. Islay is relatively flat and fertile and sustains a substantial population of 6,500. Jura is a much wilder island with a backbone of mountains known as the Paps. Despite its closeness to the mainland the population is only 461, giving it one of the lowest population densities in the UK. There is only one minor road running up the lower two thirds of the island.

Transport to Islay is based around 3 return services per day from Kennacraig on the mainland to Port Askaig or Port Ellen on Islay, the crossing taking some 2 hours. A short ferry from Port Askaig provides the link to Jura.

On Wednesdays the basic service is modified with the morning boat continuing on via Colonsay to Oban and returning in the afternoon. This service aims to provide the possibility of a day shopping trip to the mainland but clearly demonstrates the relative isolation of the islands, 7 hours on some of the roughest water in Scotland for four hours ashore. Not surprisingly alternative routes and services have been suggested and this case is concerned with one of these, a short sea crossing to Jura.

As can be seen from the map (Figure 13.14) the crossing from Keills to Lagg is only 5.8 miles and would take just over 20 minutes. An hourly service is thus feasible with just one vessel. The vast majority of passengers would then proceed south through Jura to the second 15 minute crossing to Islay. Total journey time to Islay, using the short sea crossing, would be roughly halved.

In 1988 the government commissioned consultants to examine the economics of the pro-posed service. The consultants used *Trend Curve Analysis* to project demand overall and an *Intention Survey* of current customers to identify the proportion of passengers who would transfer to the new service. *Time Series Analysis* was used to identify seasonal fluctuation to identify the capacity that would be required.

This research forecast considerable demand for the new service. However, it was also clear that the road system both on the mainland and on Jura would need to be significantly improved at major cost. In addition it was claimed that the new link would be unsuitable for the heavy lorry traffic from the distilleries and a direct service from Islay would still be required. To the dismay of many local groups, the proposal was not continued because of the substantial road investment required.

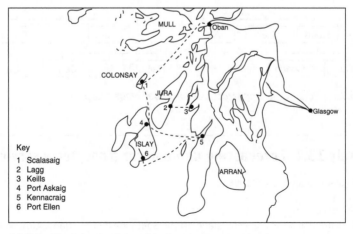

Figure 13.14 The Islands of Argyll in South West Scotland

The forecasts developed used by the consultants were the subject of some criticism and in 1996 were re-examined. In the 1996 case an *Econometric Demand* model was developed and then a *Choice Model* to identify likely market shares.

The model of overall demand

Caledonian MacBrayne, the ferry operator, have published detailed statistics on passenger and vehicle numbers on each of their services for many years which provided an extremely useful dataset to establish the effect of factors such as population, and distance from Central Scotland (the main elements of the *Gravity Model*). In addition prices were obtained from past brochures and incomes from national statistics. The final model specified was

$$Q_{it} = a P_{it}^{\beta 1} \ Y_t^{\beta 2} \ N_i^{\beta 3} \ J_{it}^{\beta 4} \ \varepsilon_{it}$$

Where:

Q_{it} represents the passenger or vehicle numbers going to island i in year t
P_{it} represents the charge for passenger or vehicles going to island i in year t
Y_t represents the income of passengers in year t
N_i represents the resident population of island i
J_{it} represents the total journey time from the central belt to island i in year t

α is a constant, $\beta 1$, $\beta 2$, $\beta 3$, $\beta 4$ are demand elasticities and ε_t represents factors specific to island i in year t.

The separate models for passengers and vehicles were estimated using ordinary least squares and gave the following elasticities:

Table 13.7 *Passenger and vehicle elasticities*

	Price	Income	Population	Journey Time
Passengers	−0.58	1.30	0.68	−0.86
Vehicles	−0.87	1.91	0.78	−0.41

Tourism is an important element in demand for ferries to the islands and demand for those where it was most important (Arran, Mull and Skye) was underestimated. Conversely in Islay/Jura passenger numbers were substantially underestimated, in part because the more spectacular areas of Jura are currently difficult to access, whilst vehicle numbers were over-estimated. This peculiarity is the result of competition in earlier years with a private operator which has resulted in lower vehicle rates than usual for this length of journey. In policy terms the model suggests higher prices will generate higher revenue.

Assuming real prices and populations are relatively constant, a forecast of demand for Islay/Jura was generated assuming 3 different growth rates and a reduction in journey time of an hour. This gave an increase of 29.5 per cent over estimate (fit), 50.4 per cent over actual for passengers and 95 per cent over estimate, 54 per cent over actual for vehicles. These high impacts correspond surprisingly well with the initial report where demands were forecast to rise between 33 per cent and 66 per cent.

333

The choice model

On four islands Arran, Bute, Mull and Skye there were two ferry services, the first a lengthy direct service to the mainland and the second a much shorter, more frequent ferry service but with a much longer drive to and from the central belt. The proportion using the short service to each island over time was available in the data set as was the difference in prices, journey times and frequencies between short and long.

Because of the limitations of public transport, passengers not in vehicles had to travel on the long routes. There was, in effect, no choice for these passengers and hence the choice model was inappropriate.

The basic specification for the vehicles was:

$$Log_e\left(\frac{Pr(Q_{Sit})}{Pr(Q_{Lit})}\right) = \beta_1\,(P_{Sit} - P_{Lit}) + \beta_2\,(F_{Sit} - F_{Lit}) + \beta_3\,(J_{Sit} - J_{Lit}) + \varepsilon_{it}$$

Where, for each island i in year t

$Pr(Q_{Sit})$ is the proportion of vehicles using the Short Sea route
$Pr(Q_{Lit})$ is the proportion of vehicles using the Long Sea route
P_{Sit} is the Price of using the Short Sea route
P_{Lit} is the Price of using the Long Sea route
F_{Sit} is the frequency of the Short Sea route
F_{Lit} is the frequency of the Long Sea route
J_{Sit} is the total journey time using the Short Sea route
J_{Lit} is the total journey time using the Long Sea route
$\beta_1, \beta_2, \beta_3$ are coefficients to be estimated and ε_{it} is the stochastic term

Over 97 per cent of the variance was explained by the model with all coefficients highly significant.

It was thought that the through price to Islay using the short crossing and the Port Askaig ferry would only be slightly cheaper than the long route but would be substantially faster and more frequent. Applying the new journey times and frequencies suggested that just over 80 per cent of vehicles would switch to the short crossing; identical to the Intentions Survey result of 80 per cent.

Conclusion

The econometric model suggests that the numbers travelling to Islay/Jura would increase substantially and that the vast majority of both old and new clients would switch to the new route even if the existing route carried on as now. Of course losing 80 per cent of the business would put the long route into crisis and, one imagines, inevitable closure. The implications of closure on distillery traffic and on the road system in general resulted, as stated previously, in no action. Undoubtedly however with forecasts such as these it will be reconsidered again in the next decade.

CHAPTER SUMMARY AND REFLECTION

This chapter has shown how to set about getting demand forecasts for new and existing services, be they roads, airports, trains or boats. The methods range from simply 'asking customers' to sophisticated 'choice experiments'. There are limitations in the methods described in this chapter and a large number of more complex versions of the methods are available. However, just as fit does not necessarily equate to forecast quality, complexity does not necessarily equate to accuracy. Simple methods applied consistently and intelligently are likely, in the long run, to be more accurate.

CHAPTER EXERCISES

This chapter could end with several number-crunching exercises on forecasting; however, that is all they would be, exercises in number crunching. The basic theme of this chapter has been that we need to THINK when forecasting future transport trends and future demand, because it is through such thoughts that better forecasts are produced. Exercise 13.1 thus concerns a fictional case and asks you to consider the use of different forecasting approaches and the various data requirements necessary to produce an accurate forecast.

Exercise 13.1

A local transport authority is interested in developing Park and Ride facilities. In the short term this could be a dedicated bus service from an out-of-town shopping estate to the city centre. In the longer term there is the possibility of a new 'parkway' station, funded by the local authority. The station would provide both access to main-line services from the city and a park and ride facility to the city centre. The rail operator is worried about rush hour overcrowding and wants to institute a peak hour supplement for travellers. The local authority has extensive road and bus data on a peak/off peak basis and can access more data from outside the region. It has some data from other parkway rail schemes.

1   For the bus service an intentions survey has been suggested

    a)   Suggest an appropriate sample frame
    b)   Discuss the strata that might be used in a stratified random sample

2   Identify how we might forecast in five years time

    a)   Vehicle flows at 8.30am on a Tuesday morning in October
    b)   Vehicle flows at 3pm on a Saturday
    c)   Why the month might be an important factor

3   Explain why a gravity model would be of little use in this problem
4   You are interested in building a model of the number of people who might switch to the bus

a) Identify the factors that you would want to include in your model

b) Discuss the associated data requirement and where such data might be found (or obtained)

c) Explain how a choice experiment might be used to assess the comparative impact of the price of the bus service and of bus priority lanes

5 Discuss in general how you might set about forecasting usage of the new station

a) By those going 'out' from the city on mainline inter-city services

b) By those using it as a park and ride facility going into the city

c) The impact of peak price supplements

Transport appraisal

Contributed by Tom Rye

INTRODUCTION

The topic of this chapter is appraisal – the way in which decisions on when and where to undertake public investment in transport are made. The chapter in some ways builds upon Chapter 2 and first explains the theory underlying appraisal by making direct links to the economic theory outlined elsewhere in the book, before comparing different types of appraisal. It then goes into some detail about the use and drawbacks of one of the most common appraisal techniques, social cost-benefit analysis, and illustrates these points by reference to a case study of one of the first uses of SCBA in UK transport appraisal, the Victoria tube line in London (Foster and Beesley, 1963). Finally, it briefly compares appraisal techniques used in the UK with those from other European countries.

WHAT IS TRANSPORT APPRAISAL AND WHY DO WE DO IT?

Transport involves the expenditure of resources on a combination of investment in capital items (e.g. stations, track, roads) and/or in operations (e.g. subsidy). As we saw at the very beginning of this book, society in general and private investors in particular have limited amounts of resources. Both therefore seek to maximise the return that they obtain from the investment of those resources. The best way to do this is to ensure that they choose to spend their resources on those projects that maximise their return. As we saw in Chapter 3 on the market for transport services, this is called maximising utility.

To briefly recap, utility is the usefulness or enjoyment that individuals get from expending a resource. For example, for many people who like to drink, then the first drink of the day is particularly useful or enjoyable. The next drink is perhaps a little more or a little less so; the next drink, probably less so again. At some point the enjoyment or usefulness that the person gets out of their next drink is worth less to them than the money that they are using to buy it; at this point, the rational person would stop drinking: it is the point at which they have maximised their utility from that particular resource. The basis of economic rationality is therefore that individuals will adjust the amount of money that they spend on different items such that they could not derive any more utility from that expenditure. An identical argument can also be applied to organisations, and indeed that public authorities should act in a similar manner to maximise the utility from the perspective of the whole of society.

Looking at the same issue in a more informal way, you can imagine that you yourself may go through a similar process when trying to decide on large purchases. Think about the following, for example:

- When considering whether to invest in (i.e. purchase) a new vehicle, what are the advantages and disadvantages of different models of car? This information is an appraisal which will guide your purchase decision.
- With a limited budget (and your own house or flat), you may not be able to immediately afford all the home improvements you would like. You may think about those which provide the maximum return on your investment. However, this can become quite complicated as you start to think about long-term versus short-term benefits, and things which add value to the house but also have benefits or costs which you cannot put a money value on.

Appraisal, therefore, is a way of predicting how much utility we as a society will derive from the expenditure of resources on one thing compared to another, by predicting the utility that will arise from each – how much utility would we get from spending £20 million on a new motorway compared to a new railway, for example? In theory we are aiming to expend our societal resources in such a way as to maximise our utility right across the whole society. Why this arises is because of externalities in transport markets, which is an issue first introduced in Chapter 6. It therefore falls upon public authorities to invest in transport facilities as they are the only body in a position to base decisions on maximising the benefit to society as a whole.

It is fundamental to realise that, inherent in appraisal, there is some kind of prediction or forecasting required. Because we have not built a project yet but are only considering whether or not it will be worthwhile, we have to try to forecast the future – sometimes quite far into the future. As we have seen in the previous chapter, this is a very uncertain process, yet one that is crucial to the results of the appraisal. In transport, two main techniques can be used to forecast the effects of future projects:

- Looking at the performance of similar, existing projects
- Using predictive models.

Both options have major drawbacks – principally, the uncertainty that surrounds their results. Predictive models can also be very costly to construct and so are only really justified for the appraisal of larger projects – over £1 million or so. In spite of these uncertainties, appraisal is even more problematic if we do not try to predict the future in some way, and so these methods are used. It is wise always to be circumspect about the results of future predictions, whatever the method used, and consequently circumspect about the results of appraisals; it is the case however that modelling can be a very useful tool to give an indication of which of two or more options performs better compared to the other(s).

It is also important to realise that, in transport investment in Britain, resources have traditionally come from government; government and society are virtually synonymous in this context. Increasingly, however, investment in transport projects involves the private sector as well. This can complicate matters, as utility is perceived differently by society and by private sector companies. The former are driven largely by a need to maximise profits: that is their utility. Society's utility is more widely defined; it may wish to maximise revenue, or environmental benefits, or the number of people who are employed, or increase road safety, or any combination of these and many other factors. This focus on factors other than profit may lead to difficulties when public and private sectors try to use the results of appraisals.

Appraisal therefore is a way of thinking about all the costs and benefits of different spending projects in a systematic manner so that, in theory at least, different projects can be compared and investments made in those which are going to provide the maximum possible return on the investment. This process is illustrated in Figure 14.1.

TRANSPORT APPRAISAL THEORY AND PRACTICE

The theory underlying appraisal has been outlined above – you can read more about it in any number of books on appraisal, including the Treasury Green Book (HM Treasury, 2007; available online at www.hm-treasury.gov.uk/d/green_book_complete.pdf). However, there are reasons that you have probably already started to realise why the theory of appraisal is slightly different from the reality. Firstly, the theory of maximising society's utility is one that would be very hard to put into practice since we do not have complete ('perfect') knowledge of all the benefits or costs that could accrue as a result of every single possible project. Secondly, in the public sector, at least, money to invest in projects is not allocated in a theoretically perfect manner. Rather than all projects – from a new hospital to a new jet fighter – being compared together, money tends to be controlled by different government departments. Appraisal is carried out within departments, but much less between them (although in the UK large projects are reviewed at a governmental level

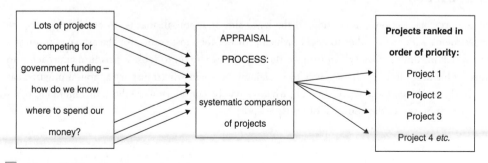

Figure 14.1   The appraisal process

by the Treasury). Thus, from the point of view of theoretical economics, utility may be maximised within departments, but not between them.

Thirdly, it is extremely difficult to find a common unit in which to measure and express all costs and benefits. Thus each appraisal will have uncertainties and imperfections within it, making it more difficult to compare with the results of appraisals of other projects. Finally, and perhaps most importantly, appraisal is not the only basis on which projects are selected for funding: politics often play a major role. Politicians may have 'non-rational' reasons for wanting or not wanting projects, and these may have little to do with the results of appraisals. A good example is the Jubilee Line Extension on the London Underground, which opened in 2000 at a final cost of £3.5 billion. Even on initial cost estimates, the ratio of benefits to costs was very small, and other schemes were judged to have greater potential to deliver benefits. Nonetheless, the scheme went ahead because the then Minister of the Environment, Michael Heseltine, wanted it to open up the London Docklands. The EU research project EVATREN (2008) looked at 9 transport case studies mainly from Western Europe and found that appraisal had been carried out in all bar one case, but frequently after the decision to build the project had been taken – it was not an ex ante investigation of whether the project fulfilled its objectives, but rather an ex post justification of a political decision already taken. Appraisal provides, therefore, only advice on whether a project is worthy of funding, and this advice may often be ignored by politicians. As we have seen before in this text, whilst economists can advise on projects through, for example, appraisal methods, it is politicians who take the ultimate decision as to which transport projects to support and which ones to not. Nevertheless, where funding for a project is sought from a higher level of government or an international body, such as the World Bank, appraisal may be critical to successfully obtaining the money.

Conclusion to this section

This section has reviewed the basis of appraisal in transport. It has summarised why we carry out appraisal in theory and in practice, and hinted at some of the problems that appraisal of projects can encounter. Now we go on to consider different forms of appraisal in a little more detail.

THE EVOLUTION OF APPRAISAL FROM BENEFIT COST APPRAISAL (BCA) THROUGH TO MULTI-CRITERIA ANALYSIS

Introduction

In the previous section, we considered the basic aim of appraisal: that is, to be able to compare investments with one another to decide which provides the most return for the available resources (or which maximises society's utility). In this section, we go on to look at practical approaches to this problem in more detail, as a way of explaining how and why transport appraisal practice has evolved over the past few years. As such, what we will be considering are the actual methodologies that are employed in the appraisal of transport projects.

Cost-benefit analysis appraisal methodology

Cost-Benefit Analysis (CBA) estimates and totals up the equivalent money value of the benefits and costs to the community of projects to establish whether they are worthwhile. These projects may be dams and highways or can be training programmes and health care systems, in other words basically any public project. The result of a cost-benefit analysis is a number: this shows the ratio of benefits to costs for the scheme. If it is less than 1 (i.e. costs exceed benefits) then the rational government or organisation would be expected to be unlikely to fund the scheme. On the other hand, values above 1 would indicate that the scheme will be of overall benefit to society and the higher the ratio the higher the net benefit, thus the more likely that the scheme would be funded in preference to other proposed projects.

The basis of cost-benefit analysis therefore is that a monetary value needs to be allocated to all benefits and costs associated with a given project. This then allows these to be added together and the total costs subtracted from the total benefits in order to obtain a net value upon which to advise on the final decision as to whether to invest or not. In reality however the monetisation of these costs and benefits will fall into a number of categories. Some costs and benefits can easily be expressed in money terms, such as the price of tickets, the cost of building roads or operating trains; some that can probably be expressed in some kind of money terms (e.g. accidents); some that can be quantified but are more difficult to monetise (e.g. noise); and finally some that are extremely difficult to quantify at all (e.g. change in the quality of the landscape). This is a fundamental difficulty with cost-benefit analysis approaches with which economists have grappled since the approach was first developed in the late 1950s.

For the private sector organisation that is conducting a cost-benefit analysis, the problem is relatively straightforward: these organisations are interested mainly in the costs and benefits that can be bought and sold in a market – for example, fare revenue, maintenance or construction costs. Since they can be bought and sold, they have a direct monetary value and are therefore easily added up to derive the overall ratio of benefit to cost for a project. This is called financial cost-benefit analysis.

In the public sector, however, cost-benefit analysis considers a wider range of costs and benefits. Ideally, it should include them all – since all are of importance to society. In practice, it does not, due to the difficulty and uncertainty of expressing some costs and benefits in monetary terms. The challenge for the appraiser is therefore to decide which costs and benefits to include and which to exclude.

In UK transport practice, public sector cost-benefit analysis in transport typically includes:

- Costs: capital and operating costs (e.g. maintenance, electricity for trams, bus drivers' wages).
- Benefits: time savings, accident reductions, revenues and reductions in operating costs (e.g. decreased petrol costs for drivers who switch to a new tram). There is an increasing tendency also to monetise reductions in noise and certain air pollutants, health benefits, and greenhouse gas emissions (GHGs).

You will note from this list that there are some factors – particularly time and accident savings – that you cannot buy on the open market. You cannot go into a shop and ask to buy an hour's worth of time, nor can you pay directly for a reduction in accident (risk). Nonetheless, public sector cost-benefit analysis normally includes time (indeed, as we will see for many transport projects the largest benefit is often the time saving). Because this type of cost-benefit analysis includes factors without a direct market value but with a social value, it is often known as social cost-benefit analysis (SCBA) and this is the term that will be used here.

There is no fixed rule as to which factors should be monetised and included in SCBA and which should not. In the UK, until recently, changes in air quality or noise were not included in SCBA, whereas in many other northern European countries these factors are included. It is a reasonable assumption that, whichever factors are included in a monetised cost-benefit analysis, there will always be some that are left out. Yet there are strong arguments for including them all, somehow, in the appraisal of your project(s). The main question is: how to do this? There is a subsidiary issue, which is that those factors that are left out of the cost-benefit analysis may well be viewed as being less important than those that are included. As the EU EVATREN project (2008) noted in its review of case studies of transport SCBA from across the EU, most environmental factors were not incorporated and therefore there was no consideration given to the possibility of funda-mentally changing the schemes evaluated, or abandoning them, even if environmental costs were seen to be large. This is because somehow they sat 'outside' the SCBA, which was seen as the main arbiter of whether or not to proceed with the scheme.

These difficulties could be solved, at least in theory, by monetising all impacts and incorpor-ating them all into a SCBA. Even if this were possible, however, a more fundamental issue would still remain: that the result of the SCBA shows only how the scheme performs in terms of the factors included in the analysis – but not necessarily how it performs in relation to the objectives set for the scheme.

The lack of a direct clear relationship in SCBA between outputs and objectives is perhaps the key reason why transport appraisal in the UK has changed recently, from one dominated by SCBA to one that considers transport schemes in relation to transport policy objectives. This is called objectives-based appraisal although it is very similar to another technique called multi-criteria analysis. This change is summarised in Figure 14.2.

Good objectives-based appraisal needs clear objectives. These should be specific, measurable, agreed, realistic and time-dependent, otherwise known as SMART objectives. It is sometimes useful to classify objectives according to their level. For example, the Treasury Green Book distinguishes between ultimate, intermediate and immediate objectives, but it is particularly useful to distinguish between ultimate and immediate ones.

Ultimate objectives are usually framed in terms of strategic or higher-level variables, such as the level of economic growth, social cohesion or sustainable development. These objectives may be stated in White Papers, or in Departmental or Agency plans or in annual reports.

Immediate objectives are those which can be directly linked with the outputs of a particular policy, programme, or project. Consideration of a proposed option needs to concentrate on those criteria which contribute to the immediate, and hence to the ultimate, objectives.

In the UK, central Governments have chosen five key objectives against which to assess transport projects. These are:

- Economy
- Environment

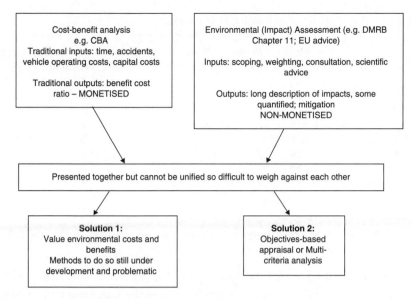

Figure 14.2 *Comparison of appraisal methodologies: a summary*

- Safety
- Integration
- Accessibility and social inclusion.

This choice of objectives is not necessarily ideal and there exists some overlap in definitions between them. This leads to a loss of clarity in the appraisal process and increases the risk of double counting of benefits and costs as they are assessed against various objectives. This risk may be compounded by the addition of local transport objectives as additional elements of the appraisal process. It is also worth remembering that one person's top priority transport policy objective may be at the bottom of someone else's list. For example if you were to spend 5 minutes to come up with your own list of objectives for transport policy and appraisal, who do you think might not be in support of your objectives? What this clearly shows is the level of divergence that can and does exist in the setting of objectives for transport projects. This element of political controversy in objectives-based appraisal can be reduced by consulting carefully on possible objectives before using them; however, SCBA approaches avoid this altogether – it is very difficult to argue against a project that appears to be good value for money, whereas it is quite easy to argue against a project that performs well against an objective with which you do not agree.

Quantification or not?

The difference between objectives-based appraisal and multi-criteria analysis is that the latter will normally attach numerical weightings to the achievement of objectives, allowing a score for each scheme to be derived and compared with other schemes. Objectives-based appraisal does not: the achievement of each objective may be assessed in money terms, quantitative terms or qualitatively, making it impossible to 'score' the scheme or investment overall.

Table 14.1 *Objectives-based appraisal matrix – toasters*

Options	Price	Reheat setting	Warming rack	Adjustable slot width	Evenness of toasting	Number of drawbacks
Boots 2-slice	£18				☆	3
Kenwood TT350	£27	✓	✓	✓	☆	3
Marks & Spencer 2235	£25	✓	✓		★	3
Morphy Richards Coolstyle	£22				☆	2
Philips HD4807	£22	✓			★	2
Kenwood TT825	£30				☆	2
Tefal Thick'n'Thin 8780	£20	✓		✓	★	5

A tick indicates the presence of a feature.

Source: Which?, November 1995, cited in Dodgson, Spackman, Pearman and Phillips (1999), p 14.

The example below is taken from Dodgson, Spackman, Pearman and Phillips' (1999) *Multi-Criteria Analysis: A Manual* (full citation given in references section), although they based it on an article in *Which?* magazine. As you will see, it has nothing to do with transport! Nonetheless, the matrix conforms to the basic principles of objectives-based appraisal: the objectives are listed across the top and the 'schemes' or options listed down the left hand side.

To try and gain some appreciation of the problems surrounding the use of objectives-based criteria in transport investment appraisal, consider the matrix in Table 14.1 and, on the basis of the information presented, try to decide which toaster you would buy. Does this cause any difficulties? Would it be more difficult if there were more objectives and they were more different from one another? What we are actually working with here is a very crude form of objectives-based appraisal, and hence the problems encountered will only be multiplied in a more complex example, such as any typical transport project appraisal.

That however is not the only problem with objectives-based appraisal, as these 'objectives' need to be combined to derive an overall view to allow us to rank each toaster accordingly from 'worst' to 'best'. Therefore, we need to try to develop a methodology that will allow us to derive an overall score for each toaster. To do this, obviously we will need to score each toaster's performance against each objective, and then add the scores together. But you may think that certain features – or objectives – are less important than others (after all, what is a warming rack? And just how vital is 'adjustable slot width'?). How would we take that into account in our appraisal? What we would have to eventually develop is what is called a multi-criteria analysis, hence you should consider the relevant weight to attach to each attribute and the score to give each of the ratings.

The final element to consider in this example is the further objectives that maybe should be included in the matrix. How would we go about determining this or has *Which?* got it right?

Whilst obviously quite subjective in the assignment of scores to each option, the form of multi-criteria analysis (MCA) that we developed in this example – weights for each attribute and scores for each toaster's performance in relation to that attribute – has the advantage of making both scoring and weighting of objectives transparent, and so is of greater use to the decision maker than the simple presentation of results such as those for the toasters, shown in Table 14.1. One drawback of MCA comes if the comparison of very different scales or types of projects is attempted – for example, if a new railway line is compared with a regional cycle network, it is very difficult to capture the relative contribution of each scheme to the achievement of objectives within the confines of an MCA score. This is akin to attempting to compare apples with oranges. If you are interested in reading more about MCA then you should read the UK Government publication *Multi-criteria Analysis* by Dodgson, Pearson, Spackman and Phillips (1999).

Currently in the UK transport appraisal uses a form of objectives-based appraisal with five overall objectives (see www.webtag.org.uk), although SCBA is used to calculate a project's performance against the economy objective. This objective is also weighted more highly than the others; all the rest should, according to guidance, receive the same weighting. The rationale for the higher weight applied to the economy objective is justified by the Treasury (UK Finance Ministry) on the basis that this shows whether a project gives 'true' value for money. The objectives-based appraisal is summarised for presentation in something known as an appraisal summary table (AST), an example of which, for a road improvement, can be found at www.highways.gov.uk/ roads/projects/15950.aspx, or simply type 'appraisal summary table' into any web search engine.

In this section we have looked at the differences between a SCBA-centred approach to appraisal, and objectives-based appraisal. Now the chapter goes on to consider the operation of SCBA in much more detail, as it remains a key input to objectives-based appraisal in transport across the world.

The principles upon which cost-benefit analysis is based

It is very important to understand the principles on which cost-benefit analysis is based. This is because, even though many countries have adopted a multi-criteria-based approach to the appraisal of transport projects, SCBA still forms a fundamental part of such appraisals – it remains one of the key criteria on which transport projects are assessed. For example all professionals that work in the transport planning field will undoubtedly have had to deal with some form of SCBA, hence it is very important to understand how it works.

Origins of cost-benefit analysis

Cost-benefit analysis originated in the USA in work immediately before and after WW2. Initially it was applied to flood-prevention schemes and to military investment and was concerned with injecting some intellectual rigour into the informal objective of 'getting most bang for a buck'.

The first use of SCBA in the UK was in its application to the assessment of the M1 motorway in 1960 and, as we shall see later, to the Victoria Line on London's underground in 1967. At this time, SCBA also became more widely accepted – or required – in Government, initially in the nationalised industries, where it became possible to appraise projects not only against the financial income that they generated, but also in relation to the non-market benefits that they might also realise. Since 1967, SCBA has become a key aspect of UK appraisal techniques.

How does CBA work?

The purpose of cost-benefit analysis (CBA) is to weigh up the costs and benefits of a project to see whether the benefits are greater than the costs and, if so, by how much. For example in Gothenburg, Sweden, the local traffic authority recently built a bypass. This is a rather unusual bypass, because it is for trams: the tram network has become congested in the city centre, so a bypass is being built around it in order to provide faster journey times across town and to provide new journey opportunities.

In order to assess whether or not this scheme was worth building, the traffic authority is likely to have gone through some of the following steps:

- Choose one or more alternative options against which to assess the tram bypass scheme. The base option (let's call it Option B) would have been to build nothing, or make only minor improvements to the existing network. We can call the tram bypass Option A.
- Choose a length of time – probably several decades – over which to assess the costs and benefits of the scheme.
- Use a predictive model to calculate the likely ridership during the whole evaluation period on the tram network in Options A, B and any other possible options that were subject to evaluation. From this, calculate likely revenue.
- Use the same predictive model to calculate total journey times on the different options over the whole evaluation period.
- For Option A, calculate the journey time savings likely to result from the project by taking away the total journey time for all passengers on Option A from the total journey time for all passengers on Option B (or possibly restricting this part of the analysis to total journey time to those passengers who would use Option A *or* Option B, and not to include the passengers who are attracted to the tram because the network is improved).
- In a similar way, calculate journey time savings on the road network resulting from the tram bypass, if people are predicted to transfer from car and/or bus to tram.
- Calculate construction, maintenance and operating costs of the different options.
- Take away the benefits (revenue plus journey time savings) from the costs for Option A to find out whether benefits exceed costs and, if so, by how much.

This is all summarised in Figure 14.3.

It follows from the discussion above that there are some key elements to any SCBA. These include:

- Project appraisal period
  A transport project such as a new road produces benefits in the year that it is built and over the years into the future. The CBA must decide how many of these future years will be taken into account; conventionally, in the UK, projects were until recently assessed over a 30 year period but this is quite an arbitrary number, related to accounting conventions, the discount rate and to the accuracy of predictive modelling. In 2006 the Department for Transport in the UK increased the appraisal period to 60 years. As we will see later, however, the length of time chosen for the CBA can have a critical impact on the end result.

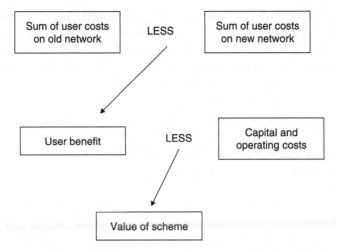

Figure 14.3 *Principles of SCBA*

- The benefits that are assessed

  These normally include changes in the costs to users of the transport network as a result of a new project. For example, a new road or rail line can often be expected to relieve congestion on existing routes. This is a change in user costs – the journey time (a user cost) would normally be expected to fall, at least in the short to medium term.

  The user costs that are most typically included in SCBA are:

  - travel time (and variants of it, e.g. parking search time)
  - revenues (e.g. fares, parking charges, road user charges)
  - vehicle operating costs (e.g. fuel)
  - accident costs
  - (increasingly), noise and air pollution.

  All these costs are expressed in monetary values, e.g. £, Euros, $. The presumption of a SCBA is that user costs on the transport network as a whole will fall as a result of the investment. Thus the user costs on the new network (e.g. the network that includes the new investment) must be compared to those on the old network (that without the new investment). This reduction in user costs on the new network compared to the old is the benefit measured by the SCBA. The capital (e.g. construction) and revenue (e.g. operating, maintenance) costs must be weighed against the measured benefit.

- Forecasting and modelling

  It is clear that a pre-requisite for a SCBA is a model that will predict travel on the transport network – and hence user costs – for the life of the scheme. As discussed in the first section of this chapter, modelling outputs should be treated as indicative only.

  The most significant example of forecasting assumptions affecting the outcome of appraisals is that which existed in UK trunk road assessment up until 1994. Prior to this time, it was assumed that the amount of traffic that would use do-something road network would be the same as that which would use the do-minimum network; that is, no account was taken of what is known as induced traffic. It is possible that an appraisal that does not take account of induced traffic may overestimate the benefits of a new road – since the induced traffic can increase congestion, thus increasing network travel time and total user costs to a greater degree than was predicted by the modelling. On the other hand, if the amount of induced traffic is less than that which would cause congestion, but more than that which would be predicted by a fixed trip matrix approach, the benefits of the road will be underestimated by the latter approach. Unfortunately, the prediction of the amount of induced traffic remains an extremely difficult science, and one that lies outwith the scope of this chapter, but if you are particularly interested in it you should read the SACTRA report (Department for Transport, 1994).

■ Present value

If the project is assessed over a number of years, then the predictive model used will normally calculate the benefits and costs for each year of the project. However, consider the following situation: your model gives a predicted benefit for the year 2010 of £25,000 and for 2015, also £25,000. Disregarding any inflation that might exist, can you simply add these values together along with the other benefits for all the other years of the appraisal in order to derive the total benefit? The answer is an unequivocal no. This is because even if you could buy the same amount of goods with £25,000 in 2015 as in 2010, the two sums would be worth different amounts from the point of view of the present. This is because you would have to wait longer before you would enjoy the benefit arising from the investment in 2015, consequently there is a cost involved of having to wait that additional time before deriving the benefit. Don't worry if you do not entirely grasp this idea now, as we will return to it later in this chapter, but take it as read for now that before costs and benefits that are predicted to arise in different years are added together, they must be subject to a process that converts them to a common unit known in SCBA as their (Net) Present Value (NPV). Benefits will sometimes be expressed as Net Present Benefit (NPB) and costs as Net Present Cost (NPC).

■ Values of time

Time savings are normally the most significant benefit in SCBA of transport schemes (with the possible exception of safety improvements), and so the value of time used is absolutely critical to the final outcome of the evaluation. The normal procedure used is to take the total time saving predicted for each group of users (e.g. car drivers travelling on works' business; pedestrians going shopping) for each year of the evaluation. This is then multiplied by the relevant value of time for that user group to derive an overall value of time for the scheme.

You should be aware that, often, the total time saving for the scheme is the result of multiplying very small individual journey time savings by a very large number of users over a long period. Think, for example, of a 5 km bypass of a small town; the average time saving per vehicle may be of the order of only two or three minutes, but with much traffic on the road, these small time savings multiplied many times aggregate to one large – and valuable – time saving.

The values of time that are used in SCBA are standard for the UK – but different from those in many other parts of Europe. These values are derived from stated preference surveys, which ask people about hypothetical travel choices from which these monetary values are then calculated. They can also sometimes be more reliably derived from observing people's actual behaviour where they can choose between paying for a shorter journey or taking a longer route to avoid paying a toll. For example, before 2008 the Kincardine Bridge across the west end of the Forth estuary in Scotland had no toll, whereas there was a toll on the Forth Bridge. Studying driver route choice in such cases can help us to understand how drivers trade off cost against time, and hence to derive values of time. Similar studies have been undertaken of crossings of the Severn from Bristol to Wales, and the opening of the M6 Toll motorway around Birmingham in 2005 also presents similar opportunities.

Different values of time apply to those people deemed to be travelling in working time and in non-working time. Examples of trips that are made in working time include lorry drivers at work; bus drivers at work; and people who are travelling to meetings, or sales representatives, who are travelling in time during which they are being paid by their employer. All other trips, including trips made to and from work where the traveller is not being paid by their employer, are deemed to be made in non-work time. However, in UK transport appraisal practice, a recent innovation made in 2006 was to separate non-working time into two categories: time for commuting trips, and time spent travelling for all other types of trip. As shown in the EU research project EVATREN (2008), there are wide variations across the EU in the way that time is valued in SCBA (categories into which it is divided such as work and non-work, as well as the actual values that are applied).

The value of trips made in non-work time is less than those made in work time. This is because there is no market for work time – it cannot be bought and sold. Values of non-work time represent the opportunity cost of the time involved, meaning the value that people attach to time because of what they could do with it instead of travelling. (This of course is related, indirectly, to wage rates and to the proportion of people who are employed.) In contrast, there is a market for working time – employers buy it and employees sell it all the time – and so the values used for people travelling in working time approximate to average wage rates paid to these groups of people. Within the UK, data from the on-going National Travel Survey (see for example DfT (2007) in the references section for further details) are used to derive the average pay rates of the average person making the average trip on works business by car, bus and other modes. You can see the effect of this in Table 2/1 of the DfT's *Transport Economics Note* (see below). If you are particularly interested in this topic, you should read Mackie *et al.* (2001).

A number of assumptions normally support the use of standard values of working time in SCBA of transport schemes. Without these assumptions it becomes more difficult to justify the use of averaged wage rates as proxies for the value of working time for appraisal purposes. These assumptions are:

- That time spent travelling cannot be used for working, therefore the time saved thanks to any investment in a transport scheme increases the amount of productive work that a person can do. As a consequence this increases output per employee and/or saves the employer money. With the advent of laptop computers and mobile phones this assumption is increasingly open to challenge but for the moment it remains in place.

- That time saved due to the investment in a transport scheme is used by an employee to do more productive work – not to, for example, have a longer lunch break or to get home earlier because you can fit in all your business meetings in a shorter time!

Given that there is a relationship, either direct or indirect, between values of time and wage rates, you may be asking yourself why UK transport appraisal practice currently uses standard values of time right across the country, when wage rates differ markedly on a regional basis. From the point of view of economic theory, it is actually nonsensical to use averaged values of time: theory dictates that the value of time savings is greater in those areas where values of time are higher, and therefore investment in a scheme with similar time savings would be of greater value in an area of high wage rates than lower wage rates.

Other countries have less standardised values of time than used in the UK – in Sweden, for example, different values of time are used for rail passengers travelling first class and standard class (Bristow and Nellthorp, 2000).

- Accident valuation

The costs of an accident are several:

- The costs of policing the accident and clearing up the mess
- The loss of economic production from the victims who are injured or killed
- The costs of medical treatment
- The pain and suffering inflicted on the victim and those close to them
- The general feeling of a less safe travel environment for all those who travel by the mode of transport in general (and therefore people's willingness to pay for safety improvements).

In the UK, all these various factors are taken into account in deriving values of a standard life used for calculating the cost of road accidents. This means that the UK has one of the highest values for accident savings used in Europe. Portugal and Greece have very low rates, reflecting in part their lower rates of pay and hence lower willingness to pay for safety improvements, but mostly because their accident valuations are based largely on insurance costs. These countries also have some of the highest rates of traffic accidents in the European Union, perhaps partly because the low value of accident savings makes it less attractive to invest in safety improvement schemes than in countries with higher valuations for accidents.

In the UK, different valuations are used for accidents on railways and the underground. This is justified on the basis of willingness to pay studies, which have discovered that, because people feel less in control while travelling on these modes of transport compared to driving, they are willing to pay more for safety improvements. Furthermore, any accidents on these systems also tend to have far wider impacts on the general society, as for example evidenced by the Southall and Ladbroke Grove rail accidents in 1997 and 1999 respectively. Recent research however has cast doubt on the higher accident values used on the railways but, up to now, they have been used to justify greater spending on safety measures per passenger km than on the roads.

As part of a SCBA it is necessary to predict the number of accidents that will occur on the new network. On road schemes, this is largely a function of traffic speed, road type and junction layout. There is a massive amount of historic data about actual accidents that has been collected in the UK over the years. Using regression techniques, engineers are able to fairly confidently predict the number of accidents that will take place on new roads into the future, and to input this to SCBA appraisal. For other modes, predictions of future accidents must be made on a more ad-hoc basis and are far more problematic due to the unpredictable nature of the extent of the accident, as these can range from relatively minor derailments to major catastrophes, such as Ladbroke Grove, which involve heavy loss of life.

■ Operating costs

Operating cost savings are likely to accrue from investment in a transport scheme. For example, if a bus lane increases average bus speeds then the bus company will be able to operate more services with a given number of buses and drivers, or the same service with fewer, and hence save money. By raising average speeds and reducing congestion, a new road is likely to reduce operating costs for all road users.

On the other hand, many transport schemes may also lead to an increase in operating costs. For example, running additional buses or new trams will have an operating cost associated with it. A new road will have operating (i.e. maintenance) costs. Remember that at all times the operating costs that are included in the appraisal must be net – for example, a new tram scheme will lead to an increase in operating costs, but these may in part be offset by a reduction in bus operating costs if the tram substitutes for some bus services.

■ Revenue

Viewed simply, the net effect of revenue in a SCBA is neutral, since it is a cost to users (fares or parking charges) but it reduces the operating costs of the scheme; it is thus a simple transfer of funds from one group to another. However, it is increasingly useful to set out this flow of money in a SCBA because it may be from one sector of society – normally consumers – to another, perhaps government, or private companies, as these groups may have differing marginal utility rates of money, i.e. £1 or one Euro is effectively worth more to one group than the other.

There is a more complex but also more accurate way of viewing revenue in a scheme. A new tram, for example, will (if it is properly designed) reduce journey times for travellers compared to a previous bus service. Let us imagine that the previous bus service carried 2,000 passengers a day, each paying £1. The tram carries 2,500, each paying £1. Let us consider only the 500 'new' passengers. If all of them are rational economic actors, then the value of the travel time saving brought about by the tram to the 500th passenger (the marginal passenger) is exactly £1. However, if we assume that the demand curve for the tram is a normal shape, then many of the other new passengers would have been willing to pay more, or enjoy less of a time saving compared to the bus, and who will still travel on the new tram. Effectively the benefit to them of using the tram is *more* than £1, so this means that the revenue gathered is not equal to the benefit that the tram delivers. You should recall from Chapters 7 and 8 that this is known as the area of consumer surplus, and what is being considered here is the change in the area of consumer surplus as a result of an improved quality of service. In simple terms, if the additional revenue raised is used as a measure of the value that 'new' consumers attach to the improvement, this will considerably underestimate the actual benefit being accrued. This is because what is actually required is the change in the area of consumer surplus, not the change in revenue, as it is that which will measure the

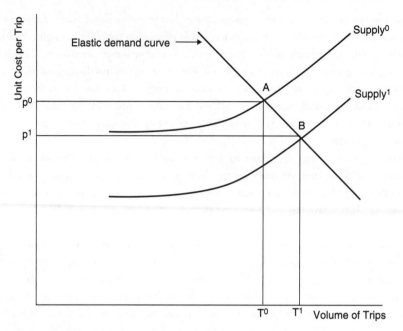

Figure 14.4 *Change in consumer surplus and the rule of a half*

total benefit being derived. In order to estimate this change, the 'rule of half' is employed. This is a set formula that allows this to be calculated, and found by multiplying the change in demand by half of the maximum benefit enjoyed. This can be seen in Figure 14.4. The change in consumer surplus is represented by the area P^0P^1AB; it is halved to derive the additional benefit to consumers resulting from the scheme.

- Discounting

An SCBA calculates benefits and costs for each year of the life of the scheme. As argued earlier, however, these cannot simply be added up to give the total costs and benefits of the scheme, since a benefit of £1 is worth less to us if we have to wait ten years before we receive it. Put another way, if you took £10 now and invested it in a fixed-rate savings account at 6 per cent interest, in 10 years it would be worth £17.90 (i.e. £10 × 1.06^{10}). This could therefore be used as an approximation for the 'cost' of having to wait ten years for that £10. Therefore, if you had £10 to invest in a project that realised benefits in year 10, you would want to know that the predicted benefit in year 10 would be more than £17.90, i.e. was 'worth' waiting for, otherwise there would be no point in you putting the money into the project and having to wait ten years to realise the benefit. Furthermore, there is an associated risk that it might not actually realise even that 'minimum' value.

In SCBA, therefore, a process called discounting is used to transform all costs and benefits to a common value – that is, their value in a common year, known as the price base year. A standard discount rate is also used, and is related to the general rate of return on money invested in banks and government bonds. At the current time in the UK the discount rate is 3.5 per cent and the price base year is 2002. As you will understand when you do the exercise at the end of the chapter, it is important that all projects are appraised using a common discount rate and price base year, as well as a common length of time over which they are appraised.

The formula for discounting a benefit received in year n (Bn) to its value in the price base year 2002 (B_{2002}) is as follows:

$$B_{2002} = Bn/(1 + r)^n$$

In using this equation you should remember that for 2002 $n = 0$ and $r = 0.035$.

To calculate the total benefits from a project, the predicted benefit for each year is discounted and then added together. Costs are also not always incurred in year one of a project – indeed, operating costs occur throughout a project's life – and so these too must be discounted.

The total summed discounted costs and benefits are called Net Present Cost (NPC) and Net Present Benefit (NPB) because they give the current value of the total costs and benefits from the project. Subtracting the NPC from the NPB gives the Net Present Value (NPV) of the scheme, which will normally be positive. NPC, NPB and NPV are the key terms in SCBA.

The price base year currently changes approximately once every 4–5 years. The previous price base year used in UK transport appraisal was 1998. The Treasury sets the discount rate for public sector SCBA project appraisal, and they have recently lowered it from 6 per cent to 3.5 per cent, in order to encourage investment in projects that realise benefits over a long timescale. Their argument is also that the 'risk' element of the discount rate should be dealt with much more systematically by sensitivity testing and other techniques and so they have removed this element from the discount rate – the 3.5 per cent is supposed only to reflect the fact that future benefits are lower because we have to wait for them.

It is important not to confuse inflation with discounting. The streams of costs and benefits in appraisal are measured in real pounds sterling, that is, £s with the same buying power regardless of the year that the cost or benefit occurs. However, after the NPB, NPC and NPV are calculated for the price base year, it is possible to adjust these figures for the effects of inflation – that is, to express them in today's money – by carrying out a simple multiplication. Thus for example a project evaluated using 1998 as the base year can be given a current net present value by:

$$\text{NPV (or NPB or NPC)}_{\text{Present Day}} = \text{NPV}_{1998} \times (\text{Retail price index at present day}/ \text{Retail price index 1998})$$

The Retail price index (RPI) is readily available in Government statistical publications.

Criticisms of and problems with SCBA

There are several criticisms that can be levelled at SCBA and it is these that have in part led to the UK Government nominally reducing its overall importance in transport project appraisal – although it still retains a key role.

Valuing time savings

We have already discussed the theoretical problems with using average values of time right across the country when in fact values of time vary. However, there are other difficulties with the assumptions that underlie the valuation of time savings in SCBA.

The first is that very small time savings are valued proportionally the same as large time savings: the value of an hour in standard SCBA is simply 120 times the value of 30 seconds. You may wish to test the validity of this assumption yourself. Think about the way that you normally get to work or to go shopping: how large a time saving would have to be delivered by a new project before you would notice the time saving as part of that regular journey? Fifteen seconds? Thirty seconds? Probably not. For most of us, a saving of at least three to five minutes would be needed before we would even start to register it. Yet for SCBA, there is, proportionally, no difference, and as long as the total of all the fifteen second time savings is enough to outweigh the costs of the project over the life of the appraisal, then the project is deemed worthwhile. Thus for example a project with a large number of very small time savings may be valued far higher than a project with a much smaller number of very large time savings. As a consequence, the first, a project that in reality makes very little difference to a lot of people, would be preferred over the second, one that makes a very large difference to a small number of people. There are, however, immense difficulties in trying to decide on a 'cut-off' time saving, less than which would not be included in a SCBA.

The second key difficulty with the valuation of time savings in SCBA in transport appraisal is what we actually do with the time saved. Since there has been a lot of money invested in transport projects in the UK over the past 30 years, and given that the justification for many of these projects is that they reduced journey times, one might expect that people would now be spending less time travelling than they did 30 years ago. In fact, the opposite is the case: we spend about 25 per cent more time travelling, and we travel twice as far per person per year (again see the National Travel Survey, available on the web). Thus the effect of reducing travel times appears to be that, in the medium to long term at least, we change our behaviour and re-invest travel time saved from new transport schemes into travelling longer distances.

A typical example of this might be an improved road from Edinburgh to Dunbar, which lies approximately 30 miles to the east of Edinburgh. Initially, for all those people who used to travel on the old slow road, the new road provides a time saving. But because it is now quicker to travel from Edinburgh to Dunbar and vice-versa, some of those people may make the journey more often than they used to. Some other people, who spend half an hour travelling to and from work by bus within Edinburgh, may realise that the new road would allow them to live in Dunbar and spend 35 minutes travelling by car to and from work every day. In the longer term therefore, the road leads to people travelling further and perhaps spending a little more time travelling than they did before. This is not to say that there is no benefit to the person who decides to move to Dunbar, nor to the person who can travel more often between Dunbar and Edinburgh; but rather the validity of the measurement of this benefit in terms of the net journey time saving may be highly questionable. Some other measure, such as the change in property values, might be a more appropriate proxy but this is not yet accepted practice in SCBA.

What to value?

Many costs and benefits of transport investment are currently left out of SCBA, largely because it is methodologically too difficult to derive monetary values for many impacts of a scheme. Theoretical economists advocate further work on valuation in order to get round this problem; pragmatists prefer multi-criteria analysis. Therefore what purports to be an 'objective' valuation of a scheme's net benefit or cost can become a subjective assessment based upon the costs and benefits that are included and those that are not.

Discount rate and length of time of project appraisal

From the Exercise 14.2 on discounting, you should hopefully work out that a lower discount rate makes a project seem more attractive, because future benefits have a higher present value than if a higher discount rate is used. Thus choice of discount rate can be critical to a project's feasibility when assessed using SCBA. Similarly, a longer appraisal period will generally make a project appear more attractive, especially where the bulk of the costs are expended early in the project's life time. This is one reason why, as explained earlier, the UK increased its project appraisal period from 30 to 60 years.

The choice of discount rate and appraisal period is to an extent arbitrary, yet can spell the difference between negative and positive NPV. The critical aspects in appraising different transport projects is to ensure that discount rates and appraisal periods are the same for all the projects being considered to ensure that they are being assessed on a 'level playing field'.

What does NPV show us?

This point was discussed in the previous section, but is one that is worth reiterating here. Simply because a project or scheme has a high NPV when assessed using SCBA, this does not necessarily mean that it will help us to achieve transport objectives. For example, one of our objectives may be to enhance road safety, so we may decide to have a blanket 20 mph speed limit. Another might be to bring about mode shift from car to bus for congestion reduction and environmental reasons. If assessed using a SCBA, such schemes would be likely to have a poor NPV because they involve increasing some people's travel time. This would remain a problem for SCBA even if it included all possible costs and benefits.

Equity and distributional effects

From the point of view of economic theory, aggregate increases in utility represent a benefit, regardless of how many people, or to whom, they accrue. Consider the following examples: each pair would be considered to have equal value in a SCBA:

- Sixty people each saving one minute's travel time, or one person saving 60 minutes' travel time.
- Vehicle operating cost savings arising from a new road scheme built in a wealthy area, or equal vehicle operating cost savings arising from a road scheme built in a poor area.

■ A scheme that increased total travel car drivers' journey costs by £900 but reduced bus users' journey costs by £1,000 would have equal benefit to one which increased bus users' costs by £900 and reduced car drivers' costs by £1,000.

It is obvious, however, that some of these options would be more politically acceptable than others, or might accord more with policy objectives than others. At the present time, for example, nominal government policy is to assist bus users, particularly those from poor ('socially excluded') areas. Also, few nominally democratic governments would often choose the scheme that benefited one person rather than sixty, unless there were other important reasons for choosing that scheme. For example, in Scotland or Norway, transport schemes in small island communities are funded because there is a general presumption that to support such communities is a desirable societal objective – even though very few people will benefit directly from the investment. But the SCBA would have provided the decision maker with no guidance on any of these choices; it would classify all pairs as equal. This can be summarised by saying that SCBA does not take into account equity or distributional effects. Out of all of the criticisms cited here, given what SCBA purports to do, i.e. estimate the benefit of a particular scheme to society, this is probably its greatest shortcoming.

Project pricing – optimism and inaccuracy

For many large transport projects, forecast NPV is not high, and the ratio of benefits to costs is normally in the range 1.2:1 to 3:1 for large schemes. Thus the appraisal is highly sensitive to increases in project construction and operating costs.

It has become increasingly obvious to the HM Treasury that there is what is known as 'optimism pricing bias' in transport scheme appraisal – that is, construction and operating cost estimates are priced optimistically in order to make the scheme look more appealing than it is. This deliberate under-pricing is compounded by a simple lack of knowledge about the true costs, due to engineering uncertainties and because modern transport investment involves many different parties, each of whom has their own pricing structure and need to make profit. Thus costs escalate massively; research by the UK Treasury (Mott MacDonald, 2002; HM Treasury, 2003) indicates that for transport projects, actual outturn costs are on average 44 per cent greater than the costs included in appraisals, and sometimes much higher. This is confirmed by work in the EU EVATREN (2008) and HEATCO (2005) projects.

Case study 14.1 The Victoria Line in London

The Victoria underground line in London was opened in 1969 and 1970, and was one of the first transport projects in the UK to which SCBA was applied as a technique for making the case for the line (Foster and Beesley, 1963). It forms a useful illustration of many of the points made earlier in this chapter, particularly since it was studied in detail by Mann *et al.* (1996), who compared the SCBA techniques used in 1963 to those in use by London Transport three decades later.

Foster and Beesley were pioneers in the field and thus had few precedents on which to base their methodology. In addition, they did not have powerful computer models at their disposal to predict the likely use of the proposed line, and so had to make many assumptions. They put a monetary value on the following factors:

- Travel time savings for all modes (but, with regard to road traffic, these were modelled only in the corridor paralleling the Victoria Line)
- Improvements in comfort and convenience for passengers
- Operating cost savings for buses and underground
- Operating cost savings for motorists
- Fares savings for travellers who switched to the new line, travelled less far and consequently (at that time, due to distance-based fares) paid less
- A 'catch-all' benefit of half the other user benefits again, to capture benefits that could not be modelled.

In addition, they used a 6 per cent discount rate and a 50 year appraisal period, and assumed that wages were a benefit (by reducing unemployment). This resulted in a benefit-cost ratio (BCR) of 1.03:1. It is notable that this BCR is so marginal that today it would be unlikely to have been accepted – particularly because it was based on a cost that ultimately proved to be a massive underestimate of the final out-turn.

Mann *et al.* (1996) then re-ran the appraisal using mid-1990s modelling and assumptions – notably an 8 per cent discount rate and 30 year appraisal period, but also much improved modelling techniques and better knowledge about actual patronage on the line, which Foster and Beesley under-predicted. These factors changed the BCR to 1.07:1. Finally, by changing the appraisal period and discount rate to 50 years and 6 per cent respectively, the authors secured a BCR of 1.77:1; and by including a key Foster and Beesley assumption on the operating cost savings to buses and underground, they managed to achieve 1.94:1. This very clearly demonstrates how sensitive the results of an SCBA are to the inputs but particularly to the assumptions used; and that we owe the Victoria Line's existence largely to decisions made about discount rates and appraisal periods.

APPRAISAL TECHNIQUES COMPARED: THE APPROACHES OF DIFFERENT COUNTRIES

It is instructive to end the chapter with a brief comparison of transport appraisal techniques across Europe, if only to demonstrate that there is no single correct way to carry out appraisals. The European research project EVATREN (2008) sought to develop a common appraisal methodology for transport projects (although, without European Union competence in the area and legislation to back it up, it would be very difficult to ensure that it was used across the EU for anything except projects receiving some or all of their funding from the EU). The starting point for this work was to consider the methods currently in use by member states. This work found that there was a pattern of appraisal common to most of the member states considered, which was SCBA alongside some form of MCA and/or Environmental Impact Assessment. However, within this, significant variations were found in the following parameters:

- The factors included in the SCBA. Whilst the UK is typical in its selection of criteria to monetise and include in the SCBA, other countries often include other factors, such as greenhouse gases, local air pollution, noise and also (in Germany in particular) local economic development. In Spain, employment is still included as a benefit rather than a cost, because it is assumed that the labour force needed will reduce the cost to society of unemployment (as per Foster and Beesley's 1963 appraisal of the Victoria Line).
- Values of time. These varied from as low as 1 Euro per hour in Spain to 65 Euros per hour in Denmark, related to the nature of the traveller and the type of trip being taken.
- The ways in which values of time are disaggregated. For example, there is no distinction in Spain between working and non-working time. In other countries, such as Sweden, different values of time are used for different classes of train passenger.
- The length of project appraisal period. Some countries used a value as low as 20 years (Czech Republic), but others as long as 75 years (Spain), or infinity (Switzerland). The review found a tendency in many countries to use different appraisal periods depending on the nature of the project in question, and related to its likely lifetime. Thus rail vehicles would be assessed over a shorter period than rail infrastructure.
- The discount rate. In north western Europe this appeared, in 2005 (HEATCO), to be around 4 per cent, but averaged 6 per cent in southern and eastern Europe, reaching as high as 12 per cent in Cyprus.

EVATREN also looked at 9 transport case studies mainly from Western Europe and found that in all cases there were cost over-runs and revenue forecasts were over-optimistic. Nonetheless, only a minority of countries include either sensitivity analysis, or optimism bias, in their project appraisals. From the case studies examined in HEATCO, where alternatives to the reference project were considered, they tended very much to be route variations rather than totally different modes or fundamentally different ways of addressing project objectives. This is possibly also because project objectives were often confused, changed during the project, and/or were not agreed between the different stakeholders concerned; and/or because, as noted above, the decision to build the project had already been taken.

CHAPTER SUMMARY AND REFLECTION

This chapter has given an overview of appraisal techniques and how they are currently used in Europe, with a particular focus on social cost-benefit analysis. It has demonstrated the links between appraisal and the wider field of transport economics, and has tried to highlight the methodological problems with appraisal as it is used today. In spite of these problems, there is no doubt that appraisal will remain an important element of transport planning in the future, particularly for projects for which external funding is sought, and thus how it works and the key drawbacks of the methodology remain critical elements in transport appraisal.

CHAPTER 14 EXERCISES

Exercise 14.1 The value of time

Read Section 1.2 of the Department for Transport publication WebTAG Chapter 3.5.6 on values of time and operating costs, available at http://www.webtag.org.uk/webdocuments/3_Expert/ 5_Economy_Objective/3.5.6.htm. Decide which values of time you should use for a person who is travelling by underground train on works' business; and for a person who is travelling to work by bus. Why do you think that values of time when travelling in working time are highest for travellers on the underground and lowest for those on the bus?

Exercise 14.2 The effect of the discounting rate and project time period

First, discount the following stream of benefits from a project and derive a total NPB for price base year 2002. Use a discount rate of 3.5 per cent.

■ *Table 14.2*

Year	Benefit (undiscounted) (£)
2003	35,000
2006	60,000
2008	100,000
2010	25,000
2014	40,000
2017	70,000

Secondly, do the exercise again but use a discount rate of 2 per cent. What effect does this have on the NPB?

Thirdly, if the majority of a project's costs were incurred in its first few years, but benefits continued to accrue for many years afterwards, over how many years would you wish to appraise the project if you were trying to get it approved for funding? Can you think of any reasons why in the UK the appraisal period changed in 2006, along with the discount rate, from 30 years to 60 years and from 6 per cent to 3.5 per cent, respectively?

Exercise 14.3 Using an appraisal summary table (AST)

Using a search engine, find a current AST summarising the appraisal of a project. The Highways Agency website www.highways.gov.uk is a good place to look. Consider how easy you think it would be for a decision maker to decide, from the information in the AST, whether to recommend construction of the scheme or not.

Chapter 15

Final thoughts and reflections

This last brief chapter pulls together the ideas outlined in the book in an attempt to come to some overall conclusions concerning the economics of transport. We began with an introduction into economic issues and finished with Tom Rye's chapter on transport appraisal. The intervening chapters covered considerable ground. This began with an examination of the relationship between transport and economic development and society at large. This chapter largely focused on the fact that transport is important to economic well being and modern society. The other early chapters surrounded the workings of the market and attempted to explain the market actions and inter-actions of individual consumers and transport suppliers. This also revealed a number of different approaches, in the form of economic systems, to solving the basic economic problem of scarcity. These ranged from little government intervention in the form of the free market, through to one of complete government intervention in the form of the command economy. What was also shown was that all societies in the world today employ some hybrid of these two approaches, the mixed market economy, and that this was no more so in evidence than in the provision of transport services and facilities. As a consequence of this mixed approach, economic questions surrounding transport issues are resolved as a result of the combined actions of individual buyers and sellers in the market place and transport planning authorities' actions impacting upon that market place. This mix was found to be true even in markets which are considered as 'deregulated' or 'privatised', and hence often mistakenly believed to operate along purely free market principles. The difference in the mix therefore was not in the type of transport market – deregulated, regulated or publicly owned – but rather on the role played by public authorities within that market. In deregulated transport markets, the levels of transport provided are as a result of the actions of individuals, with transport authorities historically acting in the role of an enabler rather than as an active participant. A number of examples of such markets were shown in Chapter 12 on freight, where for example road haulage and shipping lines broadly operate along market principles within the overall framework. Historically, however, transport has tended to see a far higher level of state intervention than other industries, with railways throughout Europe all nationalised by 1948 and most urban-based public transport modes run by local authorities. Other sectors, notably aviation and road haulage, have either been publicly owned or tightly controlled through market regulation. Why this was the case was specifically illustrated in Chapter 6 with the introduction of the concept of 'market failure', which is anything present in the market which is inconsistent with the assumptions of the economist's model of perfect competition. Most of these breaches arise from two particular characteristics, externalities that cause the negative impacts of transport activities to spill over into other areas of society and the natural environment, and other aspects that lead to imperfectly competitive markets in the provision of public, freight and private transport services. As a consequence this results in transport markets that in most cases cannot be left entirely to market forces. Most however still operate along the line of economic principles, thus for example services in many areas are subsidised or regulated in order to take into account external market effects.

As seen in Chapter 10, however, there has been a marked shift away from the public ownership model of delivery for public transport services, with the onus moving to a combination of private/public or full private provision through regulation. Nevertheless, whilst past paradigms have assumed that public transport can pay for itself, a view no better encompassed than by Beeching in the 1960s and his search for the profitable railway, today there is a far more general overview taken of public transport and the role it plays in the wider economy and society in general. In its most extreme form this standpoint would be that rising patronage requires more subsidy not less. This is something that in part we saw in Chapter 2 in the case of London, which had experienced this apparent contradiction of rising patronage and rising subsidy levels.

Most of the issues within public transport markets surround the issue of the payment of subsidy and reforms that attempt to bring in further aspects of private sector involvement. Reformation of public transport services however based on more market-focused principles has not been a smooth process. In many cases these difficulties are related to the basic problems identified with private sector involvement in the first place and eulogised in the views of Herbert Morrison of public transport provided by a single public corporation on the basis of the public interest and not on the basis of profit. What we have also seen in the course of the text, although never specifically highlighted, is a development of the knowledge of transport economics itself over the last 20 years or so. Over that period, the understanding of bus economics has been enhanced considerably, and a lot more is known and understood today about such issues than was known at the time of bus industry reform in Britain in 1985. Thus whilst bus operations may appear not to meet the exact conditions of perfect competition, they certainly do appear to meet them close enough to suggest that competition in the market is both achievable and sustainable. Nevertheless, experience has improved understanding and more is known about the process of reform and the impact that has on the supply side of the market, particularly the tendency for industry consolidation and thus eradication of competition. As a consequence, no other urban bus reforms have followed the British deregulated model.

Railway economics is also developing, with Professor Chris Nash once announcing his thanks to the British government in providing him with a lifetime's worth of study into railway economics due to their privatisation of the British rail network! Whilst intended as a light hearted comment, there nevertheless was and still remains much truth in Professor Nash's statement. This is because what was termed in Chapter 7 as the 'traditional' view of railway economics of a single integrated state-owned railway was previously the only view that prevailed. As a consequence, the understanding of railway economics was restricted to a comparison of different systems that in nature and ethos were basically very similar. Railway reform across Europe and many other parts of the world has introduced a range of different forms of railway organisation and delivery, and has thus presented the opportunity to study and develop the field of railway economics through a comparison of systems that are very different in nature. Thus the impacts of vertical and horizontal separation can be considered, tendering and open access services, the potential roles of the public and private sectors in railway delivery and so on can all be better understood. Nonetheless, there still appears to be a long way to go until the full consequences of reform are identified, as the restructuring of rail services towards more market-driven approaches continue to be problematic. Attempts at major change in Britain and other countries, notably Germany, have been labelled by some as complete disasters, and the problems refuse to go away. We saw in Chapter 10 that the reasons why this has proved so problematic are unclear; however, one potential contributory factor put forward was the difficulty in replacing 'poor' performers, and hence the market for rail services would appear to be far more imperfect than the market for bus operations due to monopoly effects. As a consequence, private sector involvement becomes more problematic.

The economics surrounding the use of the private car also remains problematic and is becoming increasingly acute, as the car remains central to modern-day living for most individuals. Over the last few years there has been a significant rise in out of town shopping and ever more dispersed and decentralised patterns of employment, hence making it difficult for public transport to serve. Some balance however needs to be struck between the two, and the economic solution, i.e. make users pay the full cost, is just not viable.

No one is anti-car, the question is finding a balance, thus the issue is over the use of the car, not over a total embargo on car use. There was once the example given of a hypothetical world in which there is only one form of transport, the bus. All individuals in this world therefore have no alternative but to use the bus. Average bus times take 20 minutes and everyone lives rather naively using the bus to get to work, which enables them to play and generally 'live' hard! All are therefore happy and as a result industrial productivity rises. With increased productivity comes increased incomes. One person therefore goes out and buys a car. Average bus journey time is still 20 minutes, but by car the journey time is only ten minutes. Passengers using the bus every morning see their old friend, the ex-bus user, fly by in their car and soon realise that they too could cut their journey times if they purchased a car. Note also that as incomes are rising, the opportunity cost of that time is increasing and hence the motivation to reduce journey times, i.e. purchase a private vehicle, grows. Therefore others go out and also purchase a car. To cut a long process short, there will come a situation when congestion becomes an issue, hence all road traffic slows down considerably. Thus the car journey that was ten minutes eventually becomes a tiresome 35 minutes, and the bus at 50 minutes takes even longer. In such a situation if given the choice all would want to return to the original position of the 20 minute bus journey, but no one is going to do it, and in fact more passengers will continue to leave the bus and switch to the car. That however is not an inevitable everlasting cycle, as in some parts of the world there has been a reverse of this general pattern, London being the prime case in point. In that instance, however, the transport system had reached a point that could be considered to be far beyond anything that could be remotely termed as optimum before such a change took place. It also required the action of a third party, namely Transport for London, in order to help enable that change to come about.

Most transport economics texts tend to treat transport like any other normal economic good or service and this one whilst also guilty is hopefully less so than others. Much space and attention therefore is devoted to outlining the forces of supply and demand, the factors behind them in the form of demand elasticities and cost structures, and finally market structures in terms of the theory of the firm. In other words, this is public and freight transport, both of which conform far more to the idea of a normal economic good or service. Even here, however, some fail to move on from there and only briefly consider market externalities and the potential solutions in the form of market regulation and the payment of subsidy. The major omission however is that over 80 per cent of passenger transport is in the form of the private car. What about the economics of the private car, therefore, and has any of that previous analysis taught us anything at all? The one thing that we learned is about market failure, and private transport suffers from a whole range of market failures. This ranges from a high degree of externalities, in the form of pollution and time constraints, to the problems with perfect information and the fact that most decisions on the use of the private car are based upon incomplete or downright false information. As a consequence, the economics surrounding the use of the private car remain problematic. Nevertheless, the perceived problems facing the road industry are not new – problems of congestion were identified in Britain as long ago as 1962 in the Buchanan Report; however, little notice appears to have been taken of that. Even when the problems of congestion and the negative environmental impact of the private car became far more acute during the 1980s, still not much appeared to change. Whilst in some cases the introduction of congestion charging has alleviated some of the problems, the level of charge that would have to be imposed to completely eradicate it would be unacceptable to most. This is not so much market failure as almost market meltdown. Over time, the price has come to mean increasingly less when it comes to decisions based on the use of the private car. In simple terms, whilst the study of economics allows us to come to a far better understanding of the underlying issues involved, it does not provide any viable answers. This is market failure in its purest form, i.e. one for which there is no economic solution. Solutions of course are available, such as severely tax the car, but the implementation of such measures would probably be economically inefficient, as the impact this would have upon the economy and wider society would far outweigh any benefits that would result as a consequence of such actions. Addressing these problems will have to be done over a long period of time and is a political, not an economic, issue, but one that nevertheless still requires economic measures. As noted above early examples of such action are already present in Northern Europe, with the imposition of congestion charging in London and several other major cities such as Stockholm and Oslo. One major change is that whilst these may now be considered as physical realities, such measures in the 1980s and 1990s were associated with political suicide and simply incomprehensible.

This in turn will impact upon public transport markets; however, due to social change these will have to be very different public transport markets to those of the pre-1990s. In many respects the changing economics of transport have in part been brought about by major social change, where as we saw in Chapter 10 choice is a greater part of society in general and the social profile of your 'average' commuter very different from that of thirty years ago. Whilst in the past therefore your 'typical' user would have simply put up with any bus service that was provided, no matter how bad, today they will not. The net result in many cases is that while buses could be operated for a profit, people will simply not pay for the standard of service they expect or that is offered by alternative forms of transport.

Choice, quality and consumer focus are what are required; however, the overall perspective will have to be very different. David Hensher (2006) perhaps puts this most succinctly, when he states that focus needs to shift from operator performance to institutional performance. In other words, less significance should be attached to how well or badly a particular operator is performing to a specified contract and far more onus attached to how well the whole mechanism and all of its constituent parts (public and private) are in delivering strategic transport goals.

A basic understanding of the economics of transport will go a long way to understanding the continual evolution of transport services in the very long term. Whilst private transport may have been described above as suffering from 'market meltdown' and a case of 'market failure in its purest form', this is only because realistic economic solutions are unviable and potentially regressive in the short term. Over the longer run however they will undoubtedly play an increasingly important role in the shaping of future transport patterns and the provision of private, public and freight transport services. We hope that in reading this book you have gained that basic understanding and in the process found it to be an interesting and enjoyable experience.

Notes

Chapter 1

1 This is not strictly true as some bus services are specified by the local authority on the grounds of a social necessity. These however tend to be a small proportion of all bus services, with UK figures indicating that such services account for around 12 per cent of all bus kilometres in the major conurbations.

2 A real piece of history can be found by simply typing in 'Glasgow Transport 1980' into the search box of Youtube. This gives the full '1980' experience, including bad fashions, a groovy 1980s soundtrack and 'sensible' looking men with excessive facial hair talking about very important things! Be warned, however, there are three parts to this epic that total 30 minutes and mainly involve large segments of men working in dark tunnels! The first part of part 1 and most of part 3 are probably best for operational issues, although the film very much shows its origins as a promotional tool for SPT.

Chapter 2

1 The CBO is an American federal agency responsible for government budget calculations and analysis. It is a body therefore that has a strong interest in the impact of government expenditure in all areas of public provision, including obviously transport provision.

Chapter 4

1 This is a considerably simplified example in order to illustrate the underlying principles. Outlined in this chapter have been elasticities that are commonly known as 'arc' elasticities, which are elasticity values calculated across a particular range of the demand curve. There are however also 'point' elasticities, which are values that relate to a particular point on the demand curve, i.e. the rate of change in demand in relation to the rate of change of price. In the example illustrated, Goodwin's values are average values taken from studies that will almost certainly be point elasticities; however, in order to illustrate the underlying principles these have been substituted into the basic arc elasticity formula. The principles however are exactly the same, hence a 10 per cent rise in price will cause a 2.8 per cent fall in demand, but this will occur at a specific point on the demand curve and not across a range. There is also a second example of this simplification in Case study 4.2 relating to cross price elasticity between waterway and rail, where Oum *et al.*'s (1990) elasticity values were subjective qualitative assessments based on studies that again would almost certainly have calculated point elasticities. The issue is slightly complicated further however by the fact that the calculation of Goodwin's average value and the estimation of Oum *et al.*'s subjective value based on a range means that in neither case could these be termed as either 'arc' or 'point' elasticities as neither is calculated from source data, i.e. primary data. In order to avoid any confusion however you should nevertheless be aware of the differences in these types of elasticities and the simplifications made in this chapter in order to illustrate the underlying concepts.

Chapter 5

1 The explanations given in Figure 5.2 relate to industry-wide concepts with regard to technical and cost efficiency. Those with some prior knowledge of economic analysis however may recognise that this is

very similar to the idea of an isoquant curve and an isocost line. These however refer to production by the individual firm rather than the whole industry. The two however are related. The industry-wide efficiency frontier will be outlined by a combination of individual points on the most technically efficient firms' isoquant curves at different levels of the two inputs.

2 Just to make this clear it may be worthwhile to consider a non-economic example. If three people were in a room, aged 20, 30 and 40, then the average age in the room would be 30. If a fourth person who was 22 was to walk in, however, the marginal age would be 22 (simply the age of the last person to walk in the room). The average age of the four however would now be 28. This is because the last person's age was less than the average, hence they brought down the average age. Alternatively, if this person had been 38, then because this is above the average age it would pull the average up to 32.

Chapter 6

1 Giordano's figures were quoted in terms of tonne kilometres, specifically the MES point was quoted as 2 million tonne kilometres. In order to put this into a more understandable context, an estimate was made of how many lorries would be required to haul this cargo per year. Figures were taken from McKinnon (2006) and Zaniewski and Butler (1983) and then calibrated against DfT Statistics (DfT, 2006) to allow an estimation to be made of tonne kilometres per year per lorry from which this could then be derived.

2 All figures based on British bus transport statistics (DfT, 2007).

Chapter 7

1 Baumol's original work on contestable markets used the production of mineral water as an example, where production costs and entry costs into the market would be minimal. Such prevailing market conditions however are very rarely found in practice, and certainly not within the transport industries.

Chapter 8

1 The section on price fixing is based on Ison, S. (2007), BA Price Fixing, *British Economy Survey*, 38(1), pp. 55–8.

Chapter 9

1 Revised European emissions standards were first introduced in 1993 with Euro I. These relate to emissions from new vehicles that are sold within the European Union and do not apply to vehicles already on the road. Ever increasingly stringent standards were introduced with Euro II in 1996, Euro III in 2000 and Euro IV in 2005. Further measures were introduced for light passenger and commercial vehicles with Euro V in 2008/9, with further standards to follow with Euro VI in 2014. These regulate nitrogen oxides, carbon monoxides and hydrocarbon emissions, but not carbon dioxide. The latter category has been subject to voluntary agreed targets; however, the failure to meet these targets means that regulatory measures will almost certainly be introduced to cover this group of vehicle emissions.

Chapter 10

1 The Monopoly and Mergers Commission was the predecessor of the Competition Commission, which took over its functions in 1999.

Chapter 11

1 If you don't quite follow this argument have a look at Chapter 3 again, particularly the impact of changing costs on the position of the supply curve.

References

Adams, W. and J. Hendry (1957). *Trucking mergers, consolidation and small business: an analysis of Interstate Commission Competition Policy.* Washington DC: US Government Printing Office.

Adnett, N. (1998). The Acquired Rights Directive and Compulsory Competitive Tendering in the UK: An Economic Perspective. *European Journal of Law and Economics,* Vol. 6, pp. 69–81.

Alexandersson, G. and S. Hultén (2006). Competitive tendering of regional and interregional rail services in Sweden. Paper presented at the ECMT Workshop on Competitive Tendering of Rail Passenger Services: Experience to Date, Paris, January 06.

Alexandersson, G and S. Hultén (2006). Theory and practice of competitive tenders in passenger railway services. Paper presented at the 4th Conference on Railway Industry Structure, Competition and Investment, Madrid, 19th–21st October (available on the web at www.eco.uc3m.es/temp/agenda/mad2006/papers/04.%20Hulten,%20Staffan.pdf, accessed on 11th September 2008).

Alternative Fuels Contact Group (2003). *Development of Alternative Fuels.* NGV Holland.

Armstrong, J. Scott (1985). *Long-range Forecasting: From Crystal Ball to Computer.* Wiley, 1985.

Armstrong, J. Scott (2001) (Editor). *Principles of Forecasting: A Handbook for Researchers and Practitioners.* Springer, 2001.

Aschauer, D. (1989). Is public expenditure productive? *Journal of Monetary Economics,* 23 (2), 177–200.

ATOC (2002). *Passenger Demand Forecasting Handbook, 4th Edition.* ATOC, London.

Bain, J. S. (1956). *Barriers to New Competition.* New York: Harvard University Press.

Bannister, D. (2002). *Transport Planning (Transport, Development and Sustainability).* London: Spon Press.

Barns, S. (2002). Fuel price and consumption in New Zealand: would a fuel tax reduce consumption? Paper presented at the 8th New Zealand Agricultural and Resource Economics Society Annual Conference, 2002.

Barr, N. (2004). *The Economics of the Welfare State.* Oxford: Oxford University Press.

Baumol, W. (1959). *Business Behavior, Value and Growth.* New York: Macmillan.

Baumol, W. (1982). Contestable markets: an uprising in the theory of industry structure. *American Economic Review,* 72(1), pp. 1–15.

BBC (2008). 'UK House Prices, City of Edinburgh', Found at: http://news.bbc.co.uk/1/shared/spl/hi/in_depth/uk_house_prices/html/qp.stm, accessed on 22nd October 2008.

Becker, B. and N. Dill (2007). Managing the complexity of air cargo revenue management. *Journal of Revenue and Pricing Management,* 6 (3), pp. 175–87.

Befahy, F. (1992). Transport growth in question: environmental, global and local effects. Paper presented at the 12th International Symposium on Theory and Practice in Transport Economics, ECMT, Paris.

Ben-Akiva, M.E. and S. R. Lerman (1985). *Discrete Choice Analysis: Theory and Application to Travel Demand.* Massachusetts: MIT Press.

Boeing (1998). *World air cargo forecast, 1997–8.* Chicago: The Boeing Company.

Boeing (2007). *World air cargo forecast 2006–7*. Only available on the web at: www.boeing.com/commercial/cargo/index.html, accessed on 29th August 2008.

Booz, Allen and Hamilton (1999). *Railtrack's Expenditure Needs 2001–2006: A Report to the Office of the Rail Regulator*. BAH, London.

BRB (1965). *The Development of the Major Trunk Routes*. British Railways Board, London. Available on line from the Railway Archive at http://www.railwaysarchive.co.uk/docSummary.php?docID=14, accessed on 15th June 2008.

Bristow, A. and Nellthorp, J. (2000). Transport project appraisal in the European Union. *Transport Policy*, 7 (1), pp. 51–60.

British Railways Board (1988). *Annual Report and Accounts, 1987/88*. London: British Railways Board.

Button, K. (1993). *Transport Economics*. Cheltenham, UK: Edward Elgar.

Button, K. (2006). Is the debate over the contestability of airline markets really dead? In Jourquin, B., P. Rietveld and K. Westin (eds) *Towards Better Performing Transport Networks*, Volume 1, Part 3, March 2006, pages 111–35, London: Routledge.

Cambridge City Council (2008). Parking, http://www.cambridge.gov.uk/ccm/navigation/transport-and-streets/parking/ Last Accessed 15th November 2008.

Chapman, L. (2006). Transport and climate change: a review. *Journal of Transport Geography*, 15, 354–67.

Cole, S. (2004). *Applied Transport Economics*. London: Kogan Page.

Competition Commission (2004). *National Express Group plc and the Greater Anglia franchise: A report on the acquisition by National Express Group plc of the Greater Anglia franchise*. London: Competition Commission.

Congressional Budget Office (CBO) (1991). *How Federal Spending for Infrastructure and Other Public Investments Affects the Economy*. Washington, DC: CBO.

Cowie, J. (1995). The structure and efficiency of European railways. PhD Thesis, Glasgow Caledonian University.

Cowie, J. (1999). The Technical Efficiency of Public and Private Ownership in the Rail Industry – The case of Swiss private railways. *Journal of Transport Economics and Policy*, 33 (3), pp. 241–52.

Cowie, J. (2002). Acquisition, efficiency and scale economies: an analysis of the British bus industry. *Transport Reviews*, 22(2), pp. 147–57.

Cowie, J. (2002). Subsidy and Productivity in the Privatised British Passenger Railway. *Economic Issues*, 7 (1), 25–38.

Cowie, J. (2008). Bus efficiency and changing market conditions; the long run outcome of the deregulated bus market. SEBE Seminar Series, 2008/9.

Cowie, J. (2008). Costs and contestability – the impact on operating costs of the unregulated contestable market in the British Bus Market. School of Engineering and the Built Environment Seminar Series 2007/8, Edinburgh Napier University, 23rd May 2008.

Cowie, J. (2009). The British passenger rail privatisation – conclusions on subsidy and efficiency from the first round of franchises. *Journal of Transport Economics and Policy*, 43(1), article in press.

Cullinane, K. (2005). *Shipping Economics: Research in Transportation Economics*, Vol. XII. Amsterdam: Elsevier.

Dargay, J. and M. Hanly (1999). Bus Fare Elasticities. ESRC Transport Studies Working Paper 1999/26, University College London.

Department for Transport (2004). Feasibility study of road pricing in the UK, At: www.dft.gov.uk/pgr/roads/introtoroads/roadcongestion/feasibilitystudy/studyreport/feasibilityfullreport, Last accessed: 1 September 2008.

Department for Transport (2004). *National Travel Survey, 2004 Edition*. London: HMSO.

Department for Transport (2005). *Transport Trends, 2005*. London: Department for Transport.

Department for Transport (2006). *Transport Statistics Great Britain 2006*. London: Department for Transport.

Department for Transport (2007). *Transport Statistics Great Britain, 2007*. London: Department for Transport.

Department for Transport (2007). *Transport Statistics 2007*, London: Department for Transport.

Department for Transport (2007). *Transport Statistics Bulletin: National Travel Survey 2006.* London: Department for Transport, and found on the web at www.dft.gov.uk/162259/162469/221412/221531/223955/322743/NTS2006V3.pdf (last accessed on 5th December 2008).

Department for Transport (2007a). *Achieving Sustainability*. London, Visit: www.dft.gov.uk/about/howthedftworks/sda/secsusdevactplan07/susdevactionplan07 Last Accessed 25 October 2008.

Department for Transport (2007b). *Transport Statistics Great Britain 2007*, London, The Stationery Office.

Department for Transport (2008). *Concessionary travel – reimbursement guidance*. London: Department for Transport.

Department of the Environment, Transport and the Regions (1998). *UK Air Freight Study*. London: Department for Transport.

Directgov (2008). *How to tax your vehicle*. At: http://www.direct.gov.uk/en/Motoring/OwningAVehicle/HowToTaxYourVehicle/DG_10012524, accessed on 19th November 2008.

Dodgson, J., M. Spackman, A. Pearman and L. Phillips (1999). *DTLR multi-criteria analysis manual.* London: DTLR. Available at www.communities.gov.uk/documents/corporate/pdf/146868.pdf, last accessed on 5th December 2008.

Downie, J. (1958). *The Competitive Process*. London: Duckworth.

Erickson, T. (2001). Urban freight economics: a new rail paradigm for large lots. *Transportation Journal*, 40 (3), pp. 5–15.

Eurostat (2007). *Panorama of Transport*. Luxembourg: Office for Official Publications of the European Communities.

EVATREN (2008) *Improved Decision-Aid Methods and Tools to Support Evaluation of Investment for Transport and Energy Networks in Europe*. European Commission funded Framework 6 Research Project 2006–2008. Results available at www.eva-tren.eu/home.htm

Ezcurra, R., C. Gil, P. Pascual and M. Rapún (2005). Inequality, polarization and regional mobility in the European Union. *Urban Studies*, 42, 1057–76.

FHWA (1992). *Assessing the relationship between transportation infrastructure and productivity*, Policy Discussion Series No 4, Washington D. C. Federal Highways Agency.

Filippini, M. and R. Maggio (1992). The cost structure of the Swiss private railways. *International Journal of Transport Economics*, 3, 307–27.

Foster, C.D. and M.E. Beesley (1963). Estimating the social benefit of constructing an underground railway in London. *Journal of the Royal Statistical Society*.

Freight on Rail (2008). DfT Ports Policy consultation – Rail freight's role, Freight on Rail guidelines for responses. Found at hrl:www.freightonrail.org.uk/GuidancePortsStrategy.htm, accessed on 6th November 2008.

FTA (2008). *Freight as an employer and vital business sector.* FTA website found at: http://www.fta.co.uk/about/about-the-industry/employer/, accessed on 21st July 2008.

García-Ferrer, A., M. Bujosa, A. de Juan and P. Poncela (2006). Demand forecast and elasticities estimation of public transport. *Journal of Transport Economics and Policy*, 40 (1), pp. 45–67.

Gardiner, J. and S. Ison (2007). Literature review on air freight growth, Report for the Sustainable Development Commission, March 2007 (and available on line at www.sd-commission.org.uk/publications/downloads/Air%20freight%20growth.pdf, accessed on 24th November 2008).

Gilbert, C. L. and H. Jalilian (1991). The demand for travel and travelcards on London Regional Transport. *Journal of Transport Economics and Policy*, 25 (1), pp. 3–29.

Gillen, D. (1997). Transportation infrastructure and economic development: A review of recent literature. *Logistics and Transportation Review*, 32 (1), 39–62.

Giordano, J. (1997). Returns to scale and market concentration among the largest survivors of deregulation in the US trucking industry. *Applied Economics*, 29, 101–10.

Glaister, S., J. Burnham, H. Stevens and T. Travers (2006). *Transport Policy in Britain (Public policy and politics)*. London: Palgrave Macmillan.

Gómez-Ibáñez, J. (2004). Railroad Reform: an overview of the options. Paper presented at Conference on Railway Reform, Rafael del Pino Foundation, Madrid, September 18–19 (and available on line at www.hks.harvard.edu/taubmancenter/pdfs/working_papers/gomezibanez_04_railway.pdf, accessed on 27th October 2008).

Goodwin, P. (1992). A review of new demand elasticties with special reference to short and long run effects of price charges. *Journal of Transport Economics and Policy*, 26 (2), pp. 155–70.

Graham, D. (2005). *Wider economic benefits of transport improvements – the link between agglomeration and productivity: Stage 1 report*. London: UK Department for Transport.

Grimshaw, F. (1984). Public transport fare elasticities: evidence from West Yorkshire. Seminar paper, Report 246, Oxford University, Transport Studies Unit.

Gubbins, E.J., (2003). *Managing Transport Operations*, 3rd Edition, London: Kogan Page.

Harmatuck, D. (1997). The influence of transportation infrastructure on economic development. *Logistics and Transportation Review*, 32 (1), 63–76.

Harrison, A. (1963). Economies of scale and the structure of the road haulage industry. *Oxford Economic Papers*, 15(3), 287–307.

Hauge, O. (1999). Experimental tendering: An analysis of experiences from the road/ferry sector in Norway. Paper presented at the 6th conference on Competition and Ownership in Land Passenger Transport (Thredbo 6), Cape Town, South Africa (and available on the web at: www.itls.usyd.edu.au/conferences/thredbo/thredbo6/hauge.pdf, accessed on 10th September 2008).

HEATCO (2005). Developing Harmonised European Approaches for Transport Costing and Project Assessment. European Commission funded Framework 6 Research Project 2003–2005. Results available at http://heatco.ier.uni-stuttgart.de/

Henshaw, D. (1995). *The Great Rail Conspiracy: Fall and Rise of Britain's Railways since the 1950s*. Basingstoke: Leading Edge Books.

Hensher, D. (2006). Contracts in the bus industry: a global perspective. Paper presented at the BIC Annual Conference, Canberra, 31 October.

Hensher, D. and I. Wallis (2005). Competitive tendering as a contracting mechanism for subsidising transport. *Journal of Transport Economics and Policy*, 39(3), pp. 295–321.

HM Treasury (2003) *Supplementary Green Book Guidance on Optimism Bias*. London: HM Treasury.

HM Treasury (2007) *The Green Book: Appraisal and Evaluation in Central Government*. London: TSO.

Hotelling, H. (1929). Stability in competition. *Economic Journal*, 39, 41–57.

ICC (1954). *Explanation of the development of motor carrier costs with statements as to their meaning and significance*, pp. 71–99. (Statement No. 1–54).

International Energy Agency (IEA) (2002). *Transportation and Energy*. Visit: www.iea.org. Last accessed 21 October 2008.

Ison, S. (2007). BA Price Fixing. *British Economy Survey*, 38(1), p.55–8.

Jain, P., S. Cullinane and K. Cullinane (2008). The impact of governance development models on urban rail efficiency. *Transportation Research Part A*, article in press.

Johansen, K (1999). Contractual form and performance in the Norwegian bus industry, 1986–96. Paper presented at the 6th conference on Competition and Ownership in Land Passenger Transport (Thredbo 6), Cape Town, South Africa (and available on the web at: www.itls.usyd.edu.au/conferences/thredbo/thredbo6/johansen.pdf, accessed on 10th September 2008).

Karlaftis, M. and P. McCarthy (1998). Operating subsidies and performance in public transit: an empirical study. *Transport Research Part A: Policy and Practice*, 32(5), pp. 359–75.

Kasilingam, R. (1997). Air cargo revenue management: characteristics and complexities. *European Journal of Operational Research*, 96, pp. 36–44.

Keynote (2007). *Distribution Industry Market Review 2007*. Middlesex: Keynote Publications

Khazzoom, J.D. (1991). The impact of a gasoline tax on auto exhaust emissions. *Journal of Policy Analysis and Management*, 10 (3), 434–54.

Lacey, E. (1990). Regulation or competition in road transport, *The OECD Observer*, Dec 1990/Jan 1991, 27–30.

Land Transport Authority, Results of August 2008 Second Open Bidding Exercise for Certificates of

Entitlement, 20 August 2008, www.lta.gov.sg/corp_info/index_corp_press.htm Last Accessed 30 August 2008.

Leibenstein, H. (1966). Allocative efficiency v x-efficiency. *American Economic Review*, 56(3), pp. 392–415.

LEK (2000). *Benchmarking of Railtrack's Freight Charges and Costs*. LEK, London.

Lewis, I., J. Semeijn and D. B. Vellenga (2001). Issues and Initiatives Surrounding Freight Transportation in Europe. *Transportation Journal*, 40 (4), pp. 23–31.

Lloyd Wilson, G. (1950). An Appraisal of Nationalized Transport in Great Britain – Part I. *The American Economic Review*, 40 (2), pp. 234–247

Lobo, I. and M. Zaira (1999). Competitive Benchmarking in the air cargo industry. *Benchmarking: An International Journal*, 6 (2), pp. 164–191.

Lodge, M. (2002). The wrong type of regulation? Regulatory failure and the railways in Britain and Germany. *Journal of Public Policy*, 22(3), pp. 271–97.

Mackie, P. J., S. Jara-Díaz and A. S. Fowkes (2001). The value of travel time savings in evaluation. *Transportation Research Part E: Logistics and Transportation Review*, 37 (2–3), pp. 91–106.

McKinnon, A. (2006). Government plans for lorry road user charging in the UK: a critique and an alternative. *Transport Policy*, 13, 204–216.

McKinnon, A. (2006). Life without trucks: the impact of a temporary disruption of road freight transport on a national economy. *Journal of Business Logistics*, 27(2), pp. 227–50.

Makridakis, S. and M. Hibon (2000). The M3 competition: results, conclusions and implications. *International Journal of Forecasting*, 16(4) pp. 451–76.

Mann, C., G. Bailey, K. Bowler and M. Stucky (1996). *The Victoria Line 30 Years On*. Proceedings of 23rd Annual Summer Meeting of PTRC, Warwick.

Maslow, A. (1943). A theory of human motivation. *Psychological Review*, 50, 370–96.

Mixon, J. and S. Tohamy (2008). Cost curves and how they relate. Found at hrl: http://csob.berry.edu/faculty/economics/CostCurves/CostCurves.htm, accessed on 7th October 2008.

MMC (1995). *The supply of bus services in the north-east of England*, August 1995, London: HMSO.

Moshandreas, M. (1994). *Business Economics*. London: Routledge.

Mott MacDonald (2002), Review of Large Public Procurement in the UK. HM Treasury, London.

Munby, D. (1965), The economics of road haulage licensing. *Oxford Economic Papers*, 17(1), 111–29.

Munnell, A.H. (1992). Infrastructure investment and economic growth. *Journal of Economic Perspectives*, 6 (4), 189–98.

Nash, C. (1982). *Economics of Public Transport*. London: Longman.

Nash, C (1985). European rail comparisons – what can we learn?, in Button, K. and P. Pitfield (eds) *International Railway Economics: studies in management and efficiency*. Aldershot, Hampshire: Avebury.

Nash, C. (1985). International rail comparisons – what can we learn?, in Button K. and D. Pitfield (eds) *International Railway Economics*. London: Heinemann.

Nebesky, W., B. Starr McMullen and M. Lee (1995). Testing for market power in the US motor carrier industry. *Review of Industrial Organisation*, 10, 559–76.

NERA (2000). Review of overseas rail efficiency. A draft final report for the Office of the Rail Regulator. London: NERA.

ONS (2008). *Consumer Trends, Q1 2008, No 48*. London: Office for National Statistics.

ORR (2008). *Office of Rail Regulation Annual Report and Resource Accounts, 07/8*. London: ORR.

Oum, T. and D. Gillen (1983). The structure of intercity travel demands in Canada: theory, tests and empirical results. *Transportation Research Part B (Methodological)*, 17B, pp. 175–91.

Oum, T. (1989). Alternative demand models and their elasticity estimates. *Journal of Transport Economics and Policy*, 23, pp. 163–87.

Oum, T., W. G. Waters II and J. S. Yong (1990). A survey of recent estimates of price elasticities of demand for transport. World Bank Review, Working paper, WPS 359.

Parker, D. (1994). Nationalisation, privatisation, and agency status within government: testing for the

371

importance of ownership, in Jackson, P. and C. Price (eds) *Privatisation and Regulation – a review of the issues*. London and New York: Longman.

Paulley, N., R. Balcombe, R. Mackett, H. Titheridge, J. Preston, M. Wardman, J. Shires and P. White (2006). The demand for public transport: the effects of fares, quality of service, income and car ownership. *Transport Policy*, 13 (4), pp. 295–306.

Peppers, L. and D. Bails (1987). *Managerial Economics. Theory and applications for decision making*. New Jersey: Prentice Hall.

Pollitt, M.G. and Smith, A.S.J. (2002). The restructuring and privatisation of British Rail: was it really that bad? *Fiscal Studies*, 23(4), pp. 463–502.

Potter, S. (2008). Purchase, Circulation and Fuel Taxation, Chapter 2 in *Implementation and Effectiveness of Transport Demand Management Measures: An International Perspective*, Edited by Ison, S. and T. Rye, Ashgate Publishing Limited.

Preston, J. (1994). Does size matter? Paper presented at the 27th Universities Transport Study Group Annual Conference, Leeds, January.

Preston, J. (1998). Public transport elasticities: time for a rethink? Paper presented at 30th UTSG Annual conference, Dublin, January, and published as Working Paper 856, Oxford University Transport Studies Unit.

Preston, J. (2001). Regulation policy in land passenger transportation in Europe. Paper presented at the 7th conference on Competition and Ownership in Land Passenger Transport (Thredbo 7), Molde, Norway (and available on the web at: www.itls.usyd.edu.au/conferences/thredbo/thredbo7/preston.pdf, accessed on 11th September 2008).

Prud'homme, R. and C.W. Lee (1999). Size, sprawl, speed and the efficiency of cities. *Urban Studies*, 36 (11), 1849–58.

Pucher, J., A. Markstedt and I. Hirschman (1983). Impacts of subsidies on the costs of urban public transport. *Journal of Transport Economics and Policy*, 17, 155–76.

Pucher, J. and S. Kurth (1995). Verhehrsverbund: the success of regional public transport in Germany, Austria and Switzerland. *Transport Policy*, 2 (4), pp. 279–91.

Puller, S. and L. Greening (1999). Household adjustment to gasoline price change: An analysis using 9 years of US survey data. *Energy Economics*, 21 (1), pp. 37–52.

Purvis, D. (1985). *Declining Productivity and Economic Growth*, Ontario: John Deutsch Institute, Queen's University.

Railtrack (1999). *May 1999 Cost Submission to the Office of the Rail Regulator*. London: Railtrack plc.

Rice, P. and A. Venables (2004). Spatial developments of productivity: analysis for the regions of Great Britain. CEP Discussion Papers, dp0642, Centre for Economic Performance, LSE. (Available on line at http://cep.lse.ac.uk/pubs/download/dp0642.pdf, last accessed on 2nd July 2008.)

Riddington, G. (1996). How Many for the Ferry Boat? *ORInsight*, 9(2), pp. 26–32.

Riddington, G (1999). A comparison of learning curve and varying coefficient models of ski demand. *Journal of Forecasting*, 18, pp. 205–14.

Riddington, G. (2002). Combating the experts with expertise: the role of community OR in a planning inquiry. *ORInsight* 15(2), pp. 3–10.

Rodda, C. (2001). *Economics for International Students – an on line textbook*. Found on the web at www.cr1.dircon.co.uk/TB/2/monopoly/contestablemarkets.htm, accessed on 14th January 2008.

Rodríguez-Pose, A. and U. Fratesi (2004). Between development and social policies: the impact of European Structural Funds in Objective 1 regions. *Regional Studies*, 38, pp. 97–113.

Rosenthal, S. and W. Strange (2004). Evidence on the Nature and Sources of Agglomeration Economies, in Henderson, J. V. and J. F. Thisse (eds) *Handbook of Urban and Regional Economics*, Volume 4 (1), 2119–71.

Roy, W. and A. Yvrande-Billon (2007). Ownership, Contractual Practices and Technical Efficiency: The Case of Urban Public Transport in France. *Journal of Transport Economics and Policy*, 41(2), pp. 257–82.

Royal Commission on Environmental Pollution (1994). Twentieth Report on Transport and the Environment, London, The Stationery Office, Cm 2674.

Rye, T. and M. Carreno (2008). Concessionary fares and bus operators, reimbursement in Scotland and Wales: no better or no worse off? *Transport Policy*, 15(4), pp. 242–50.

Rye, T. and D. Scotney (2004). The factors influencing future concessionary bus patronage in Scotland and their implications for elsewhere. *Transport Policy*, 11, pp. 133–40.

Sakano, R., K. Obeng and G. Azam (1997). Subsidies and inefficiency: a stochastic frontier approach. *Contemporary Economic Policy*, 15, pp. 113–27.

Schipper, L., L. Scholl and L. Price (1997). Energy use and carbon emissions from freight in 10 industrialized countries: an analysis of trends from 1973 to 1992. *Transportation Research Part D: Transport and Environment*, 2 (1), pp. 57–76.

Schipper, L. and L. Fulton (2005). Carbon dioxide emissions from transportation: trends, driving factors and forces for change, in Hensher, D. and K. Button (eds) *Handbook of Transport and the Environment*. Sydney: Elsevier.

Shires, J. and J. Preston (1999). Getting back on track or going off the rails? An assessment of ownership and organisational reform of railways in Western Europe. Paper presented at the 7th Conference on Competition in Land Passenger Transport (Thredbo 6), Cape Town, South Africa.

Shirley, R. (1969). Analysis of motor carrier cost formula developed by the Interstate Commerce Commission. *Transportation Journal*, pp. 22–4.

Short, J. (1995). Freight transport as an environmental problem. *World Transport Policy and Practice*, 1(2), pp. 7–10.

Smykay, E. (1958). An appraisal of economies of scale in the motor carrier industry. *Land Economics*, 34, pp. 143–8.

Stern Review on the Economics of Climate Change, 2006, HM Treasury.

Stigler, G.J. (1971). The Theory of Economic Regulation. *Bell Journal of Economics and Management Science*, 2(1), pp. 3–21.

Stittle, J. (2002). Regulatory Control of the Track Access Charges of Railtrack plc. *Public Money & Management*, 22(1), pp. 49–54.

Stopford, M. (2008). *Maritime Economics*. London: Routledge.

Swann, D. (1988). *The Retreat of the State: Deregulation and privatisation in the UK and US*. Harvester Wheatsheaf: Hertfordshire.

Sweezy, P (1939). Demand Under Conditions of Oligopoly. *The Journal of Political Economy*, 4, pp. 568–73.

TACA (2008). Transatlantic Conference Agreement Homepage. (www/tacaconf.com, last accessed on 14th August 2008 but now defunct.)

The Eddington Transport Study, The case for action: Sir Rod Eddington's advice to Government, 2006, London: HMSO.

TIE (2007). *Trams for Edinburgh, Post Election briefing note*, Edinburgh: Transport Initiatives Edinburgh.

Times Online, BA's secret talks with Virgin in full, August 1 2007, http://business.timesonline.co.uk/tol/business/industry_sectors/transport/article2178713.ece Last Accessed 5 September 2008.

Townley, J. (2006), A case study in perfect competition: The US bicycle industry. Found at http://www.jaytownley.com/the-bicycle-industry-competition, accessed on 15th July 2008.

Transport for London (TfL) (2007). *London Travel Report 2007*, London: TfL.

TRL (2004). The demand for public transport: a practical guide. TRL Report No 593.

TSSA (2008). Freight on rail – dispelling commonly held myths, TSSA Website: http://www.tssa.org.uk/article-3.php3?id_article=1596, accessed on 19th August 2008.

US Department of Transportation (2006). *Freight in America*. Washington: Department of Transportation, and found on the web at www.bts.gov/publications/freight_in_america/pdf/entire.pdf, accessed on 23rd August 2008.

van de Velde, D. (2003). Regulation and competition in the European land transport industry: some recent evolutions. Paper presented at the 8th Conference on Competition and Ownership in Land

Passenger Transport (Thredbo 8), Rio de Janeiro (Brazil), 14–18 September (and available at www.thredbo.itls.usyd.edu.au/downloads/thredbo8_papers/thredbo8-plenary-van_de_Velde.pdf, accessed on 28th October 2008).

Waverley Rail Partnership (2007), Welcome Page (www.waverleyrailwayproject.co.uk, accessed on 17th August, 2007).

Weber, A. (1909). Uber den standort der industrien, translated by C. J. Friedrich (1929), *Alfred Weber's Theory of the Location of Industries*. Chicago: University of Chicago Press.

White, P. (1981). Recent developments in the pricing of local public transportation services. *Transport Reviews*, 1 (2), pp. 127–50.

White, P. (2008). *Public Transport: Its Planning, Management and Operation*. London: Routledge.

Williamson, O. (1963). Managerial Discretion and Business Behavior. *American Economic Review*, 53, pp. 1032–57.

World Business Council for Sustainable Development, The Sustainable Mobility Project, WBCSD, Switzerland, 2002, Progress Report.

Wright International (2008). Webpage – new build cargo boats for sale. (www.wright-international.com/new-cargo.php, accessed on 22nd September 2008).

Ying, J. (1990). Regulatory reform and technical change: new evidence of scale economies in trucking. *Southern Economic Journal*, 56 (4), 996–1009.

Zaniewski, J. and B. Butler (1983). Vehicle operating costs related to operating mode, road design and pavement condition, in Gillespe, T. and M. Sayers (eds) *Measuring Road Roughness and Its Effects on User Cost and Comfort: A Symposium*. Pennsylvania: Astm International.

Index

Page numbers in *italics* denotes a table/illustration

375

383